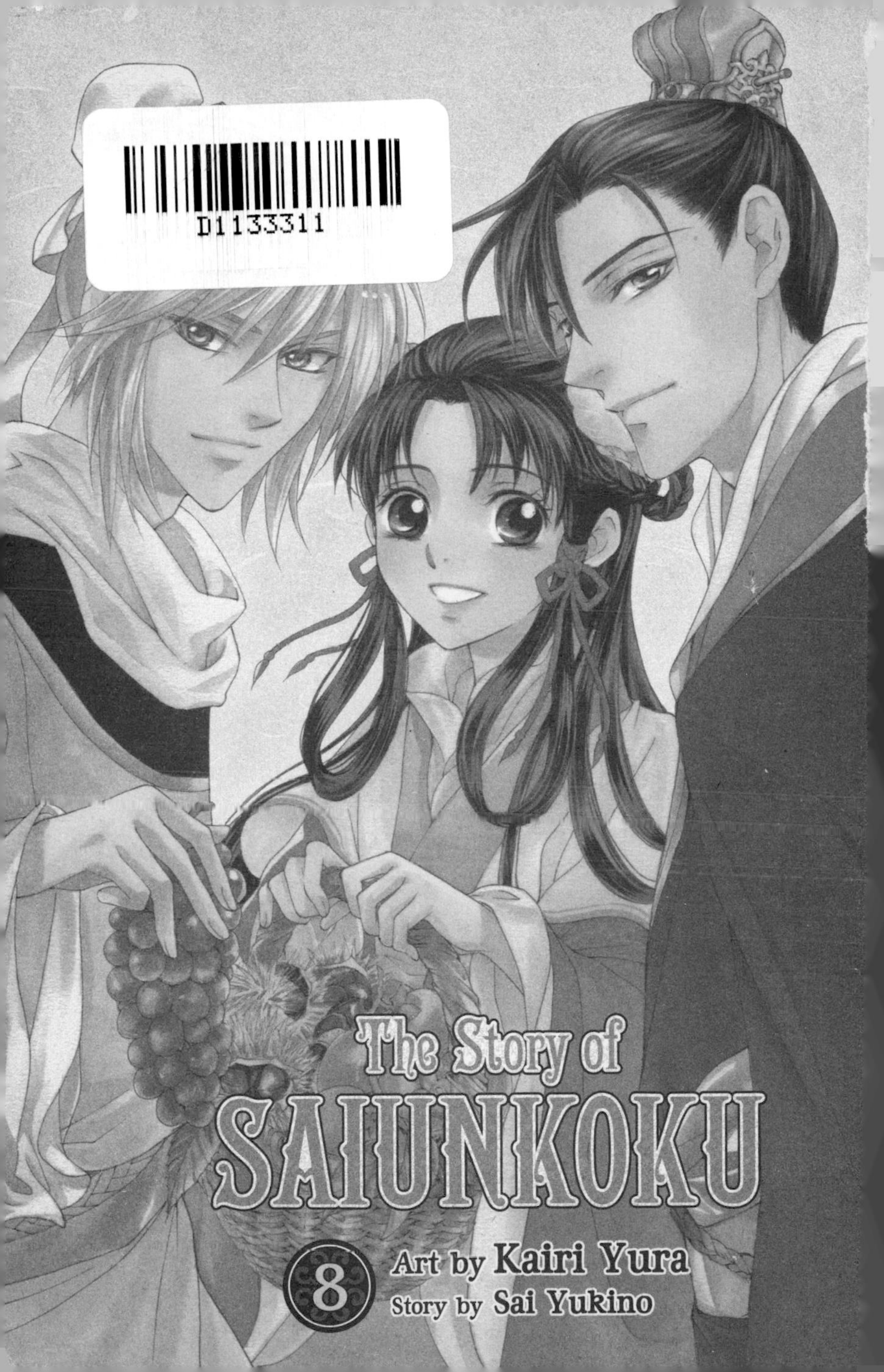
The Story of
SAIUNKOKU
8
Art by Kairi Yura
Story by Sai Yukino

Volume 8
Contents

Story Thus Far

After passing the Imperial Civil Exam with high marks, Shurei Hong becomes the country of Saiunkoku's first female civil servant... But she finds herself shunned by her colleagues in the all-male imperial court. They continue to single her out for unfair treatment because she is female, and even accuse her of falsifying her Imperial Civil Exam results. Now that her sponsor, Reishin, has been placed under house arrest (albeit voluntarily) for his possible involvement, Shurei prepares for a public inquest in which she will be given the chance to prove herself worthy once and for all! Clinging to this final ray of hope, Shurei begins compiling her notes for the inquest. Unfortunately she and Eigetsu are suddenly trapped and held under guard at Kogaro...

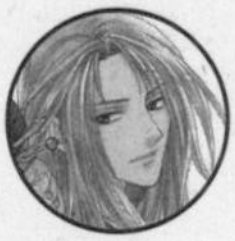

Ryuki Shi
The young emperor of Saiunkoku. He has been pining ceaselessly for Shurei since her departure from the Inner Court.

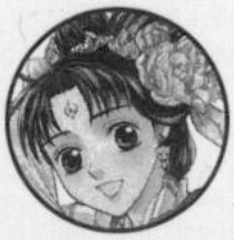

Shurei Hong
A young noblewoman of the prestigious but impoverished Hong Clan. Having passed the Imperial Civil Exam, she is now the country's first female civil servant.

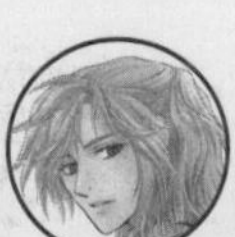

Seiran Shi
After being taken in by Shurei's father, Shoka, Seiran has served the Hong household as its faithful retainer ever since. He is actually Ryuki's older brother.

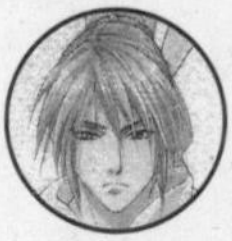

Koyu Ri
A civil servant renowned throughout the court as a genius, currently stuck in a frivolous position (perhaps?) serving Ryuki. He has a hopelessly bad sense of direction.

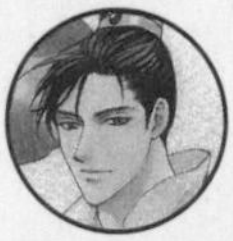

Shuei Ran
A military officer. He is a general of the Yulin Guard, a squad of soldiers charged with protecting the emperor. He is inseparable from Koyu (much to his friend's ire).

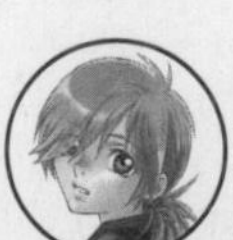

Eigetsu Toh
At 13 years old, he is the youngest person to pass the Imperial Civil Exam with the top score. He has a quiet, low-key personality.

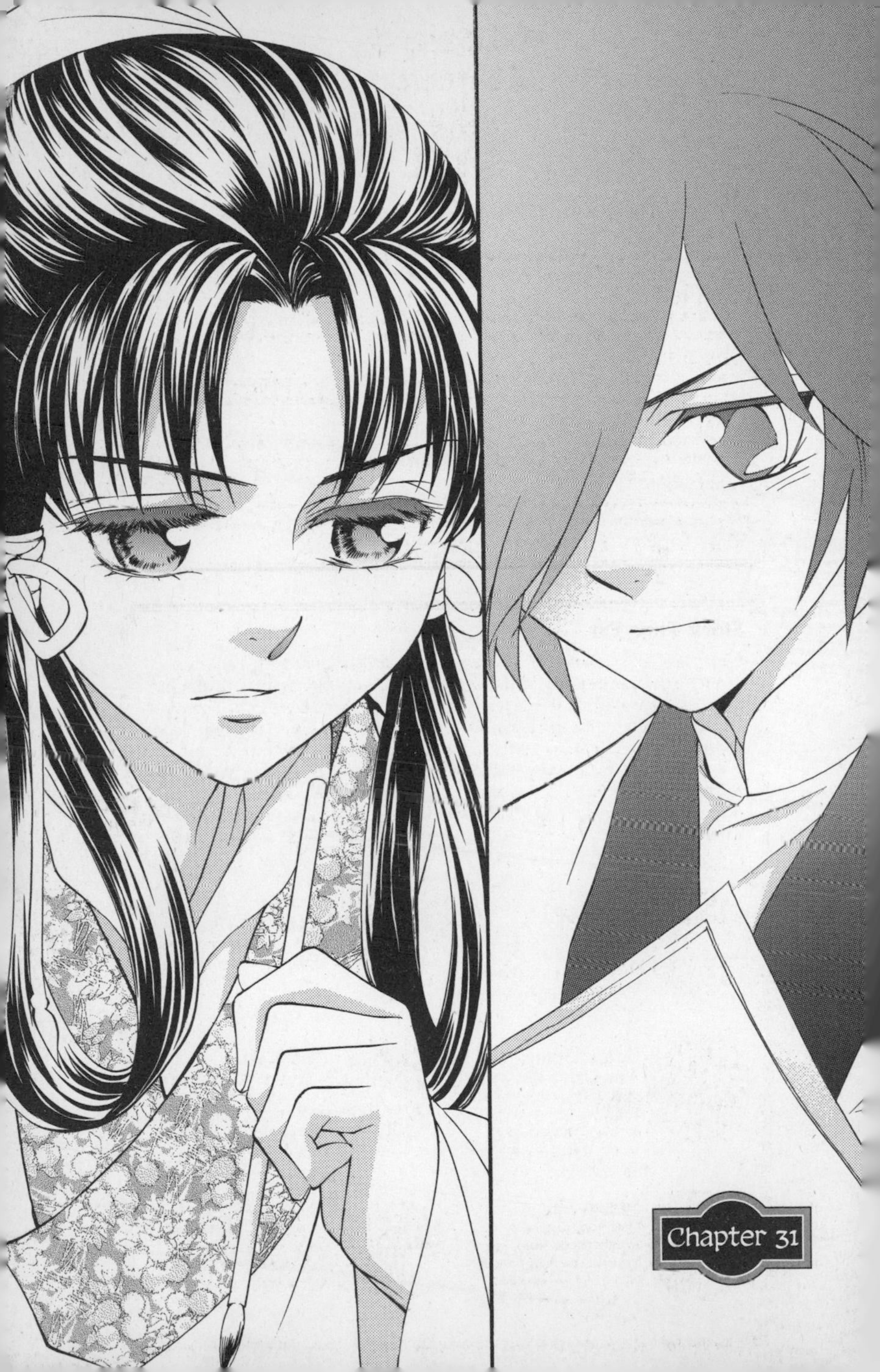
Chapter 31

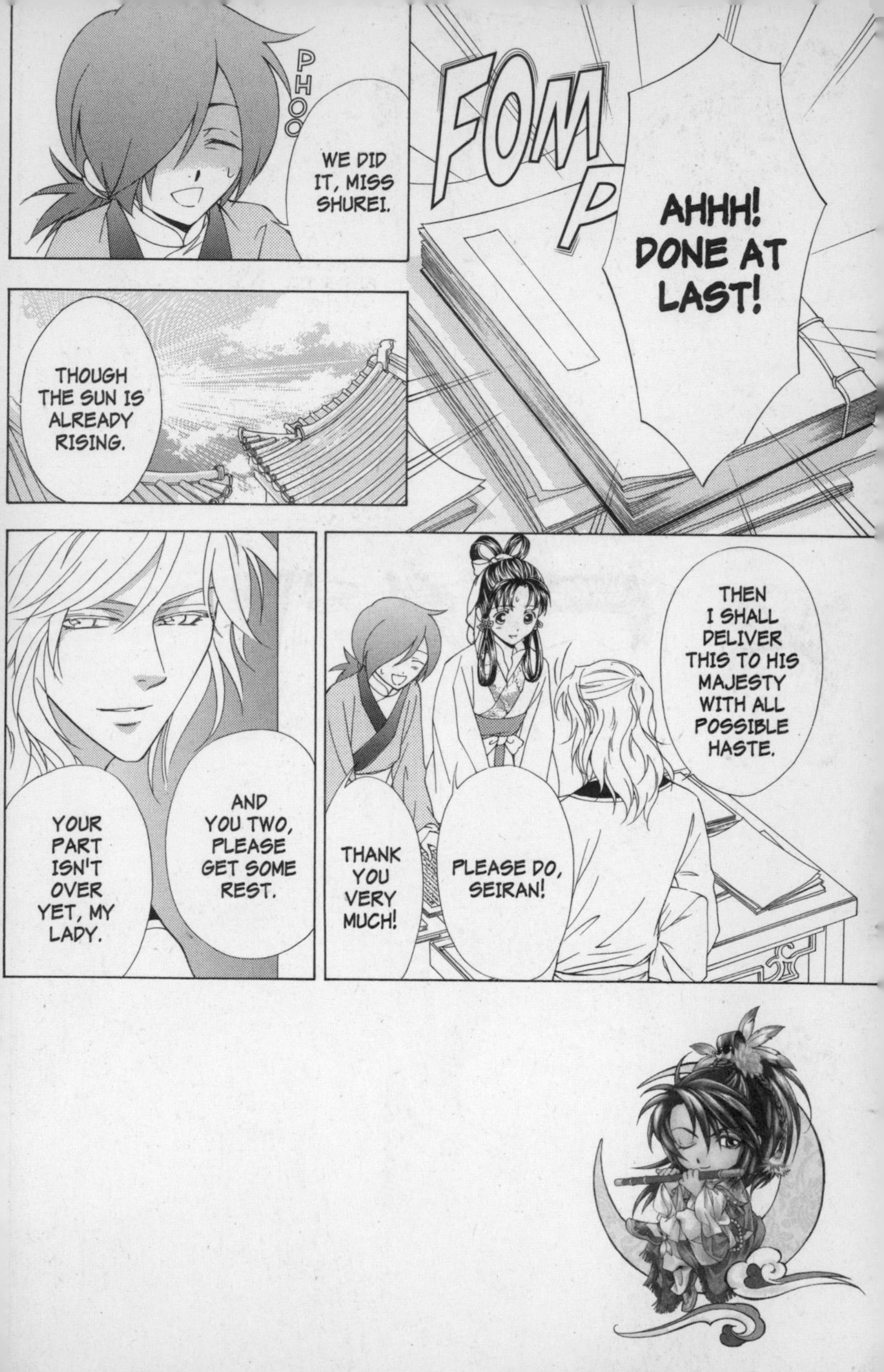
FOMP
AHHH! DONE AT LAST!
PHOO
WE DID IT, MISS SHUREI.
THOUGH THE SUN IS ALREADY RISING.
THEN I SHALL DELIVER THIS TO HIS MAJESTY WITH ALL POSSIBLE HASTE.
PLEASE DO, SEIRAN!
THANK YOU VERY MUCH!
AND YOU TWO, PLEASE GET SOME REST.
YOUR PART ISN'T OVER YET, MY LADY.

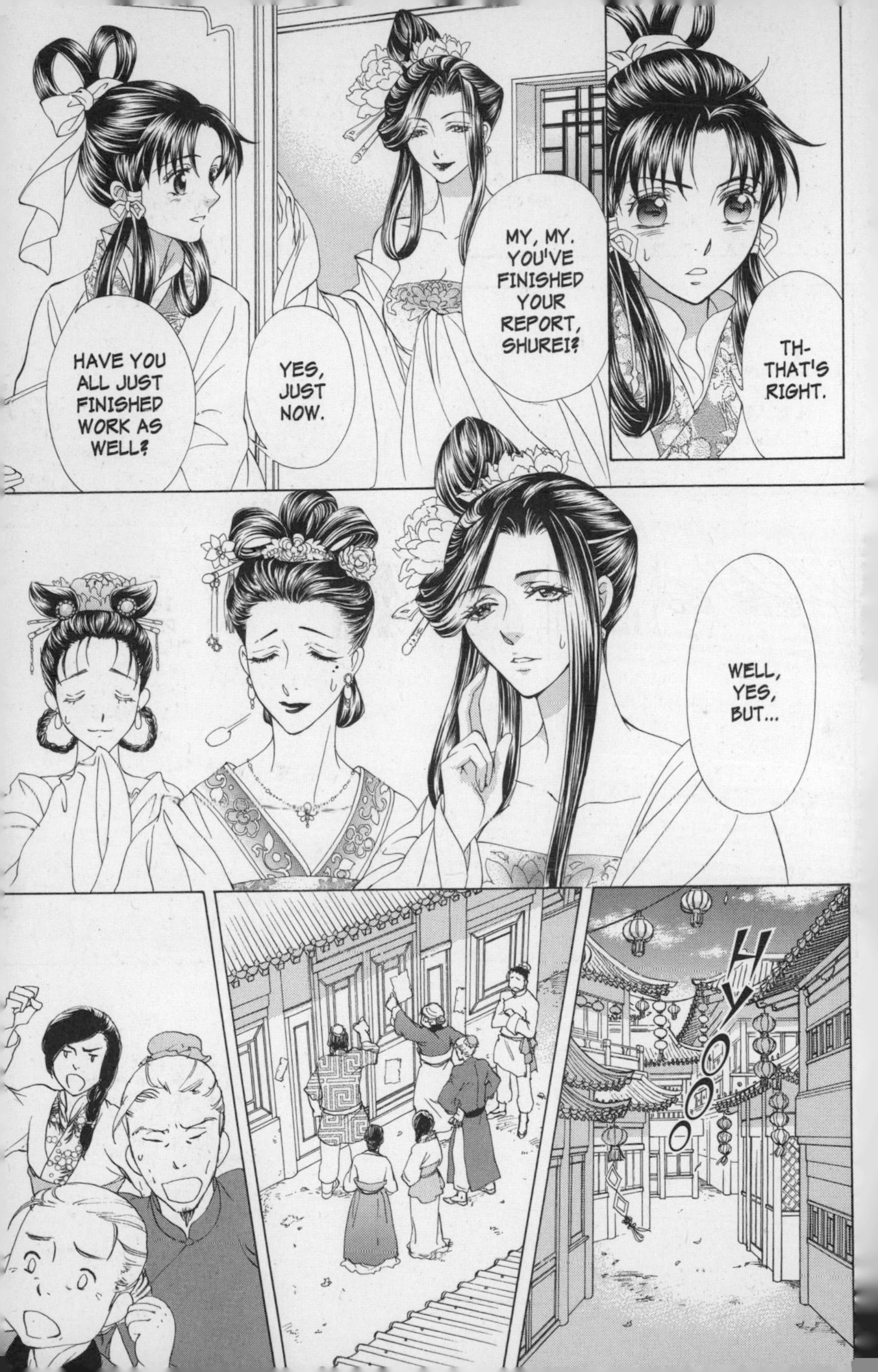
TH-THAT'S RIGHT.
MY, MY. YOU'VE FINISHED YOUR REPORT, SHUREI?
YES, JUST NOW.
HAVE YOU ALL JUST FINISHED WORK AS WELL?
WELL, YES, BUT...
HYOOOO

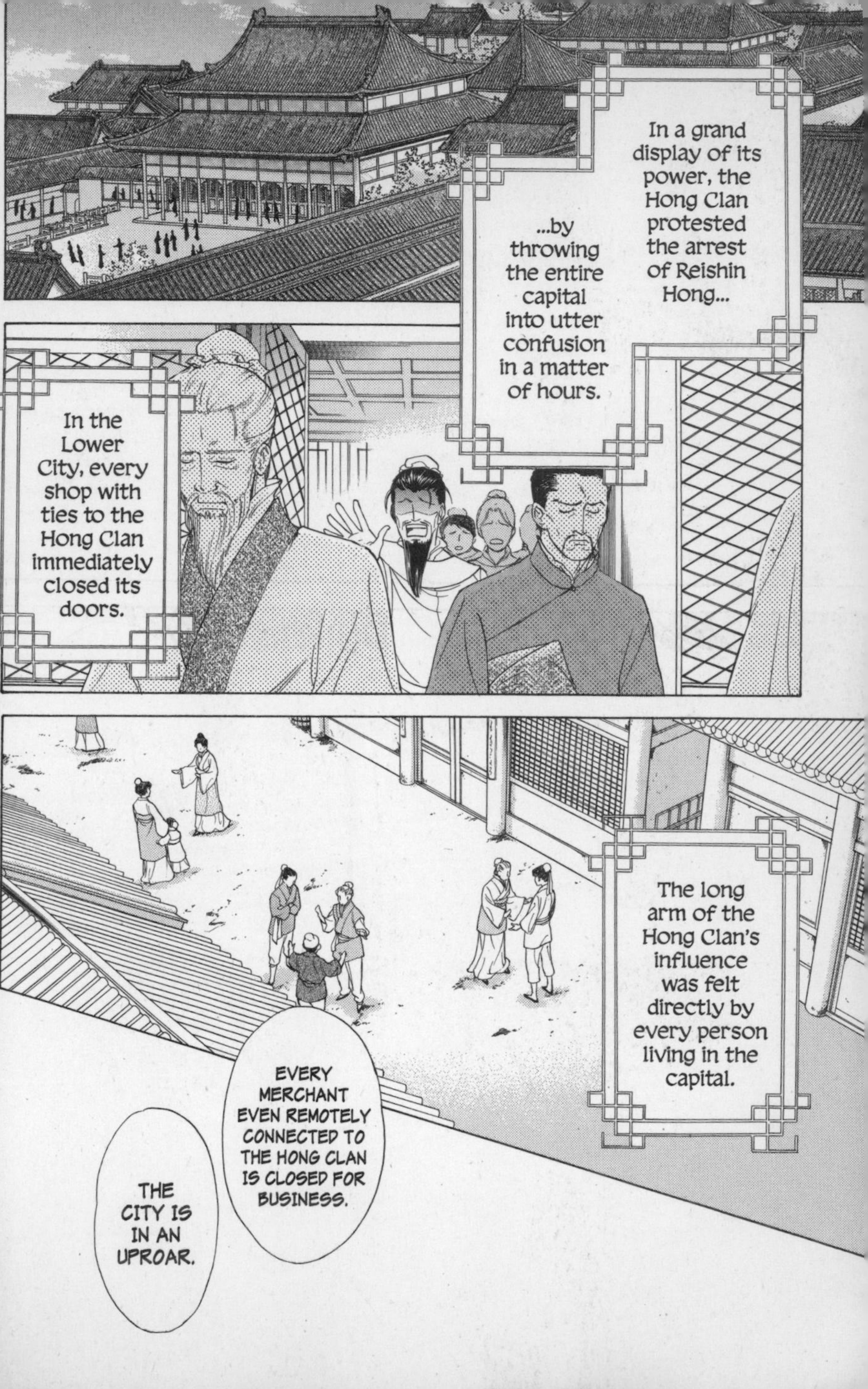
In a grand display of its power, the Hong Clan protested the arrest of Reishin Hong...
...by throwing the entire capital into utter confusion in a matter of hours.
In the Lower City, every shop with ties to the Hong Clan immediately closed its doors.
The long arm of the Hong Clan's influence was felt directly by every person living in the capital.
EVERY MERCHANT EVEN REMOTELY CONNECTED TO THE HONG CLAN IS CLOSED FOR BUSINESS.
THE CITY IS IN AN UPROAR.

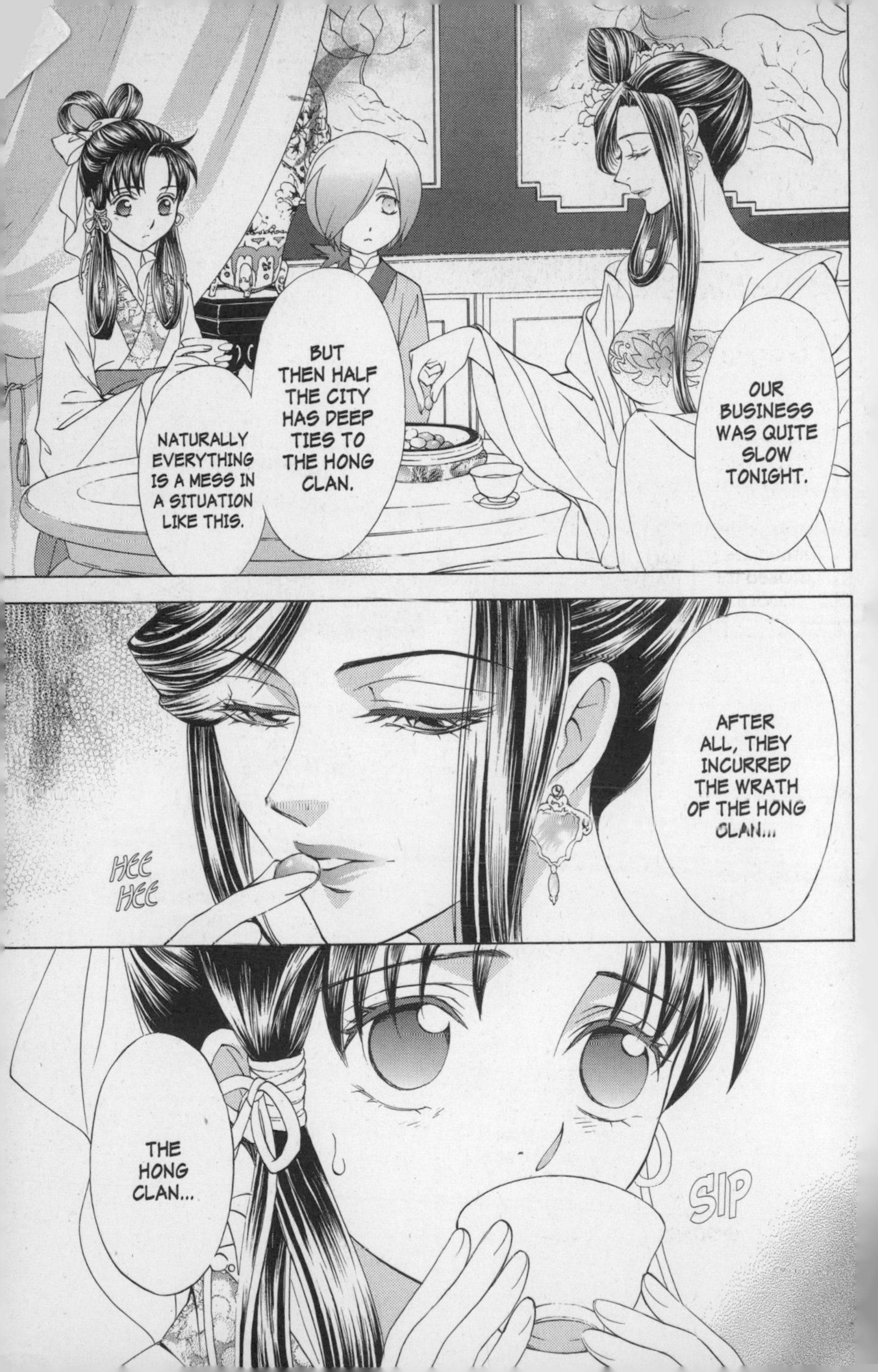
OUR BUSINESS WAS QUITE SLOW TONIGHT.
BUT THEN HALF THE CITY HAS DEEP TIES TO THE HONG CLAN.
NATURALLY EVERYTHING IS A MESS IN A SITUATION LIKE THIS.
AFTER ALL, THEY INCURRED THE WRATH OF THE HONG CLAN...
HEE HEE
SIP
THE HONG CLAN...

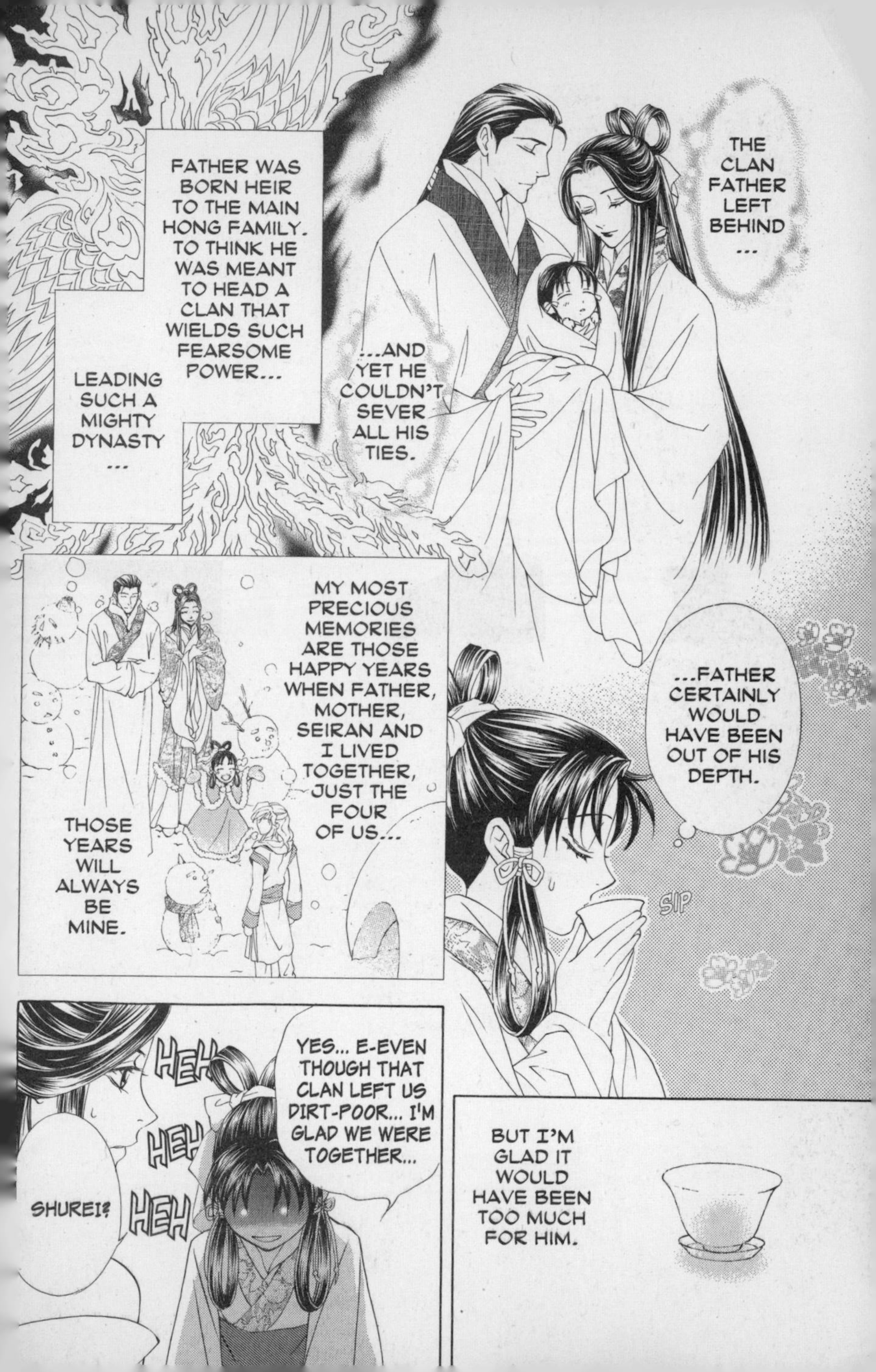
THE CLAN FATHER LEFT BEHIND...
...AND YET HE COULDN'T SEVER ALL HIS TIES.
FATHER WAS BORN HEIR TO THE MAIN HONG FAMILY. TO THINK HE WAS MEANT TO HEAD A CLAN THAT WIELDS SUCH FEARSOME POWER...
LEADING SUCH A MIGHTY DYNASTY...
...FATHER CERTAINLY WOULD HAVE BEEN OUT OF HIS DEPTH.
SIP
MY MOST PRECIOUS MEMORIES ARE THOSE HAPPY YEARS WHEN FATHER, MOTHER, SEIRAN AND I LIVED TOGETHER, JUST THE FOUR OF US...
THOSE YEARS WILL ALWAYS BE MINE.
BUT I'M GLAD IT WOULD HAVE BEEN TOO MUCH FOR HIM.
YES... E-EVEN THOUGH THAT CLAN LEFT US DIRT-POOR... I'M GLAD WE WERE TOGETHER...
HEH
HEH
HEH
SHUREI?

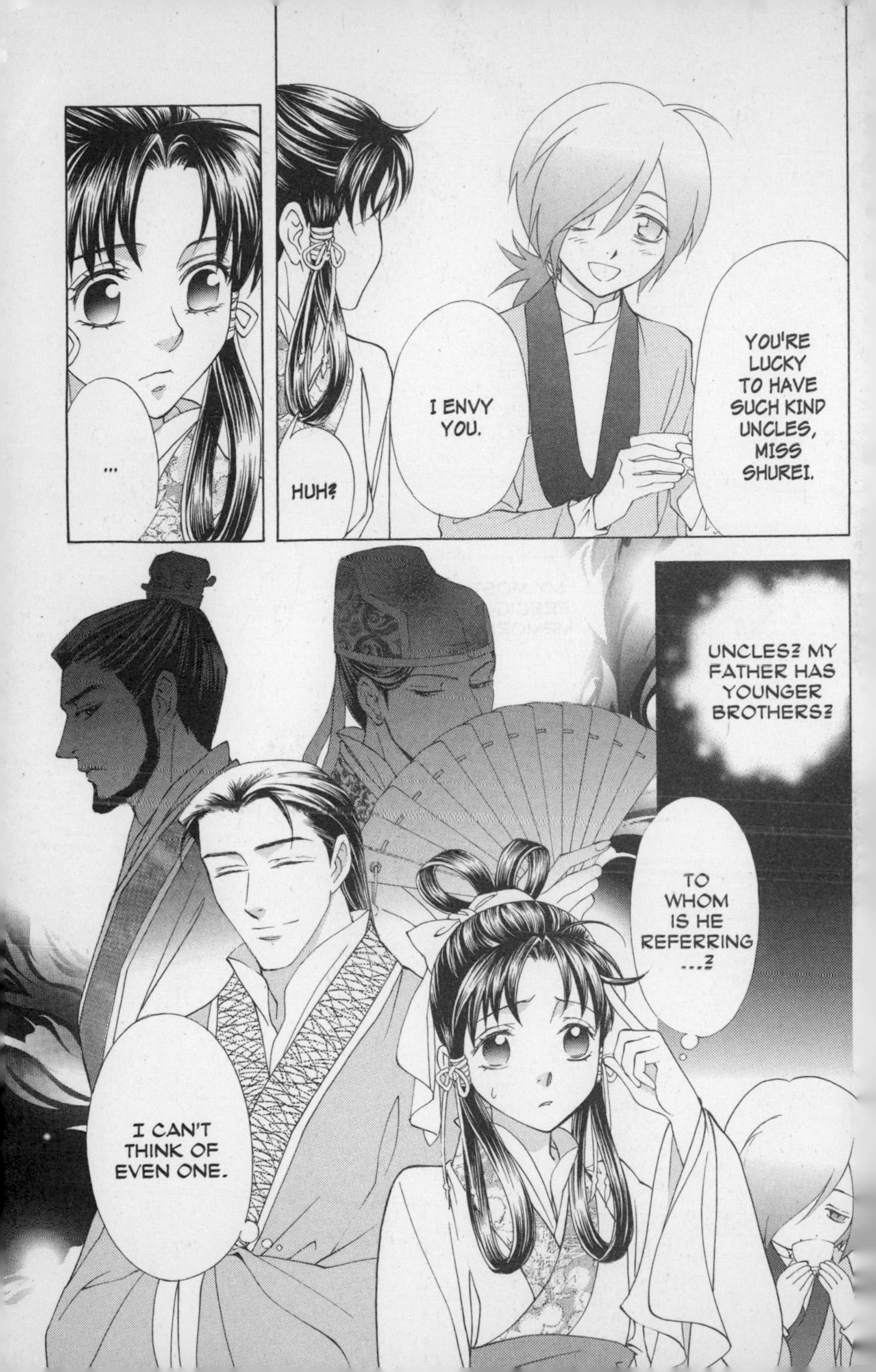
YOU'RE LUCKY TO HAVE SUCH KIND UNCLES, MISS SHUREI.
I ENVY YOU.
HUH?
...
UNCLES? MY FATHER HAS YOUNGER BROTHERS?
TO WHOM IS HE REFERRING ...?
I CAN'T THINK OF EVEN ONE.

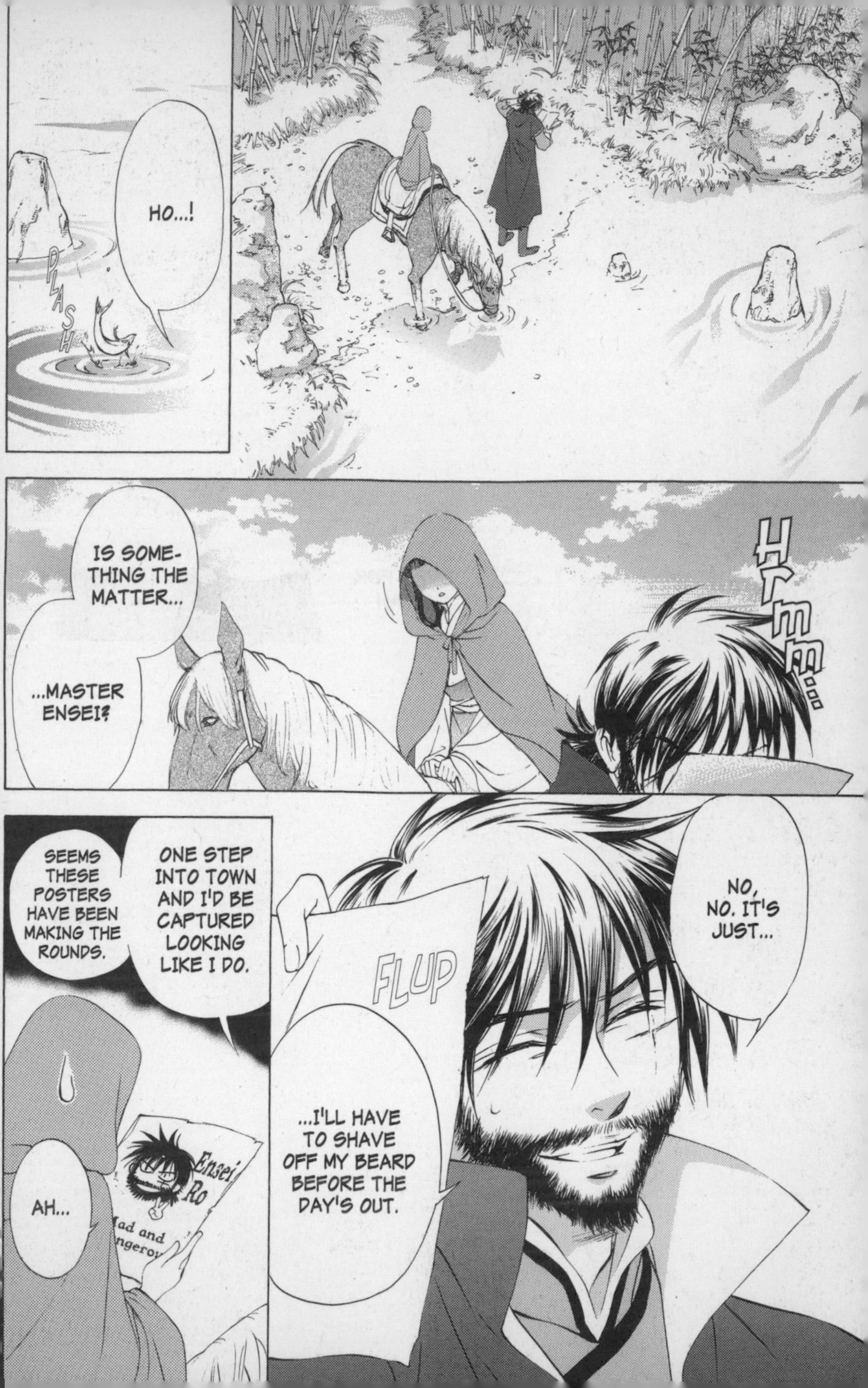
HO...!
PLASH
Hrmm...
IS SOME-THING THE MATTER...
...MASTER ENSEI?
NO, NO. IT'S JUST...
ONE STEP INTO TOWN AND I'D BE CAPTURED LOOKING LIKE I DO.
SEEMS THESE POSTERS HAVE BEEN MAKING THE ROUNDS.
FLUP
...I'LL HAVE TO SHAVE OFF MY BEARD BEFORE THE DAY'S OUT.
Ensei Ro
Mad and
AH...

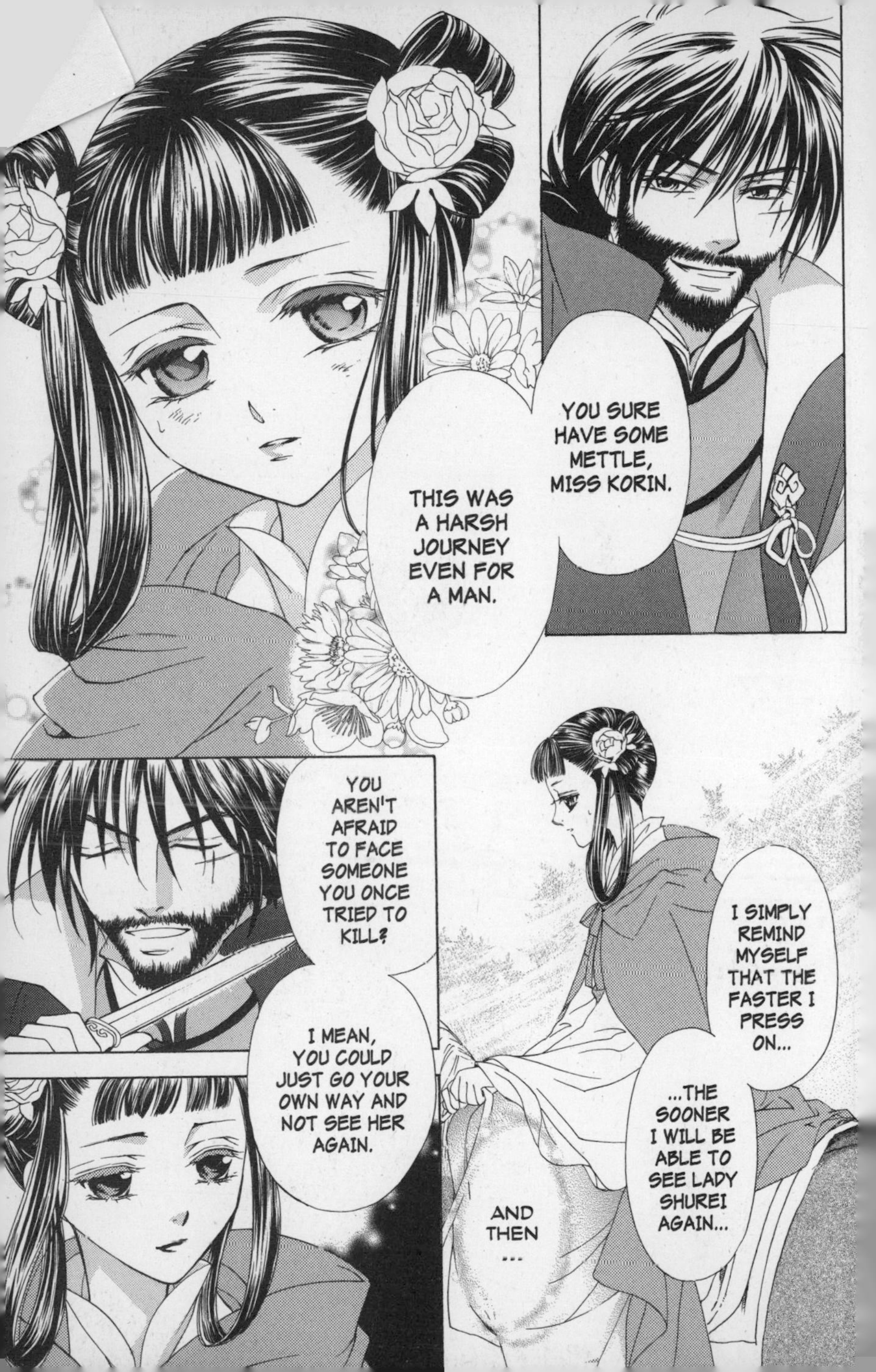
YOU SURE HAVE SOME METTLE, MISS KORIN.
THIS WAS A HARSH JOURNEY EVEN FOR A MAN.
I SIMPLY REMIND MYSELF THAT THE FASTER I PRESS ON...
...THE SOONER I WILL BE ABLE TO SEE LADY SHUREI AGAIN...
AND THEN ...
YOU AREN'T AFRAID TO FACE SOMEONE YOU ONCE TRIED TO KILL?
I MEAN, YOU COULD JUST GO YOUR OWN WAY AND NOT SEE HER AGAIN.

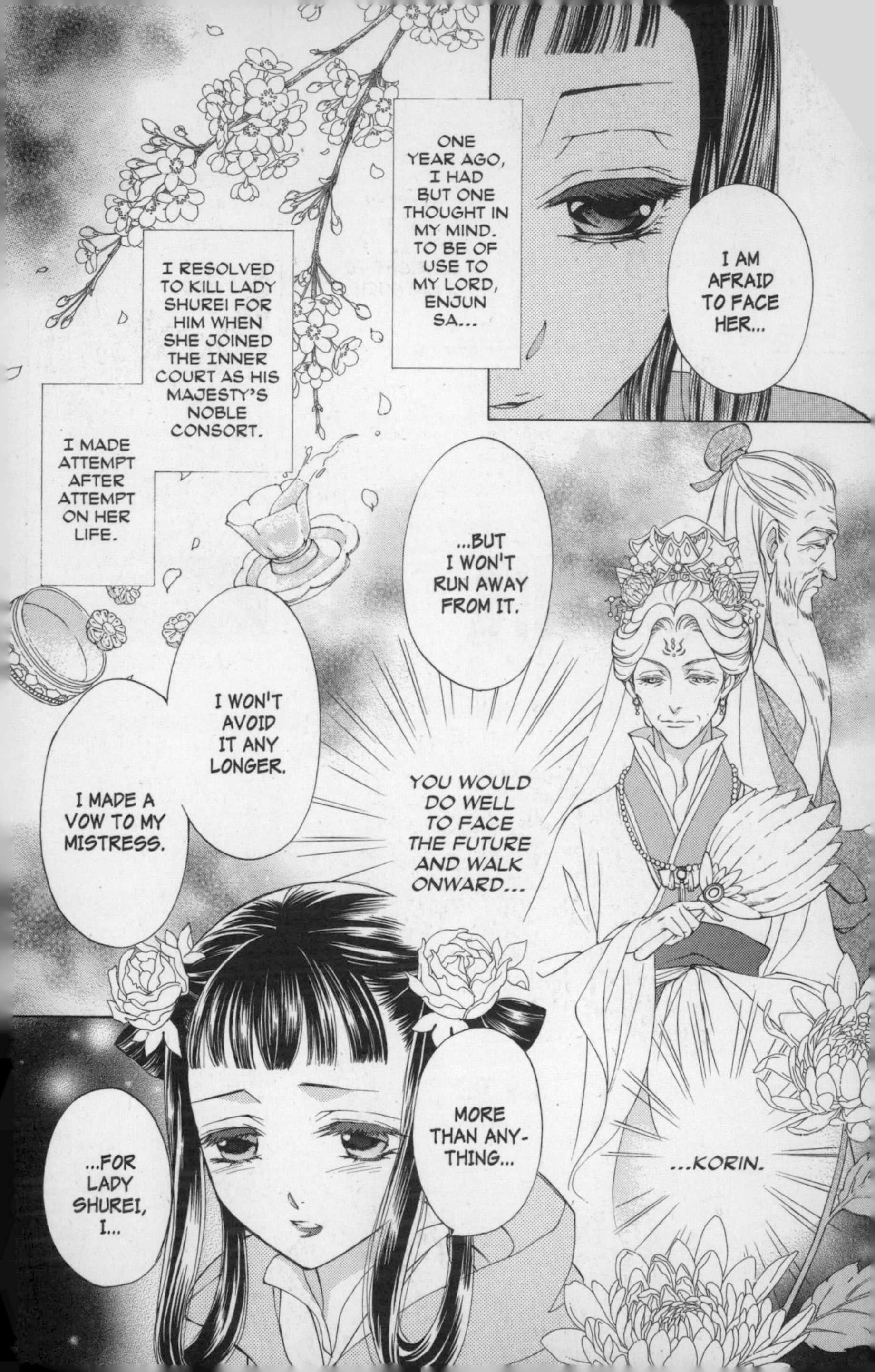
I AM AFRAID TO FACE HER...
ONE YEAR AGO, I HAD BUT ONE THOUGHT IN MY MIND. TO BE OF USE TO MY LORD, ENJUN SA...
I RESOLVED TO KILL LADY SHUREI FOR HIM WHEN SHE JOINED THE INNER COURT AS HIS MAJESTY'S NOBLE CONSORT.
I MADE ATTEMPT AFTER ATTEMPT ON HER LIFE.
...BUT I WON'T RUN AWAY FROM IT.
I WON'T AVOID IT ANY LONGER.
I MADE A VOW TO MY MISTRESS.
YOU WOULD DO WELL TO FACE THE FUTURE AND WALK ONWARD...
...KORIN.
MORE THAN ANY-THING...
...FOR LADY SHUREI, I...

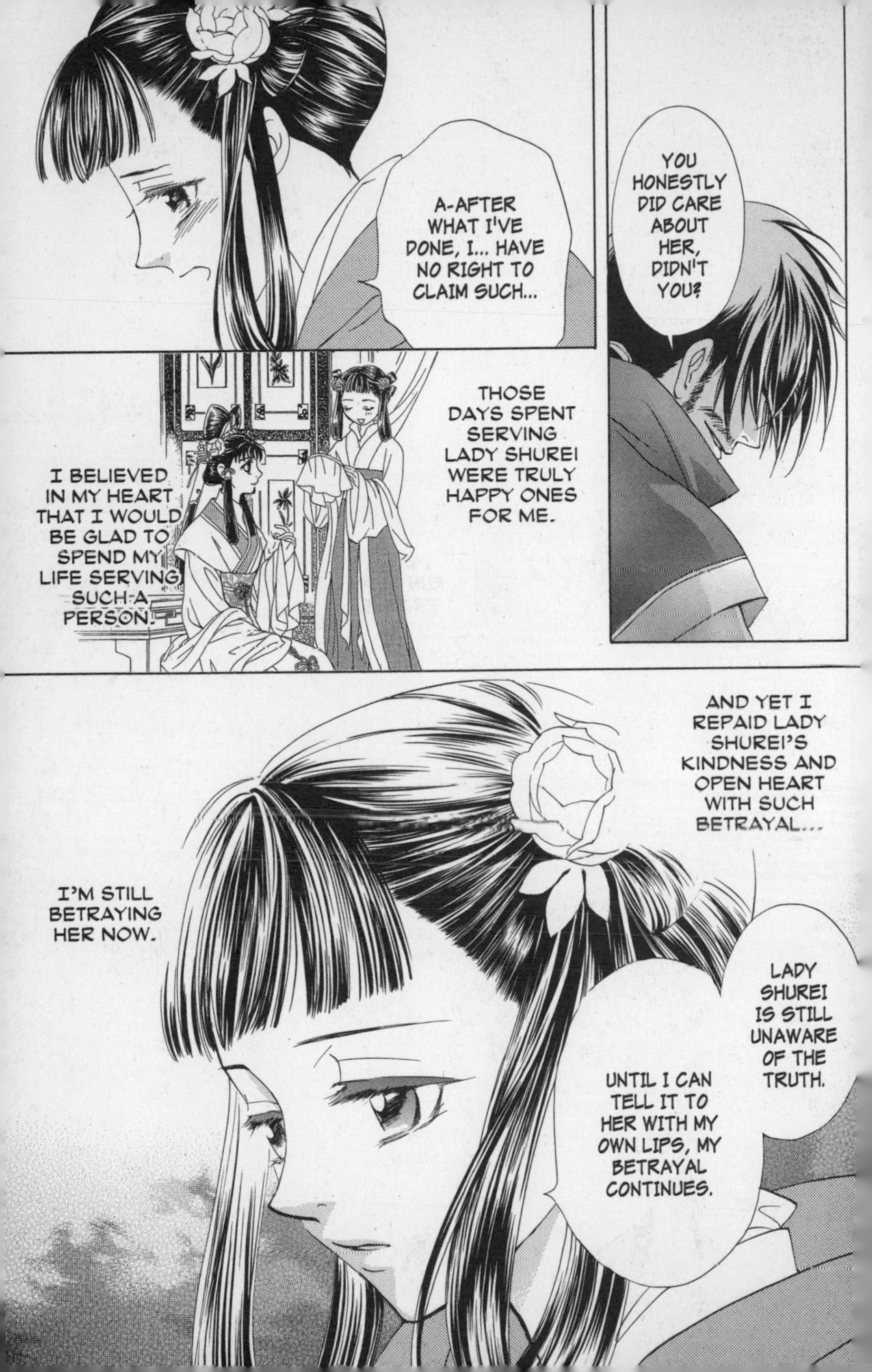
YOU HONESTLY DID CARE ABOUT HER, DIDN'T YOU?
A-AFTER WHAT I'VE DONE, I... HAVE NO RIGHT TO CLAIM SUCH...
THOSE DAYS SPENT SERVING LADY SHUREI WERE TRULY HAPPY ONES FOR ME.
I BELIEVED IN MY HEART THAT I WOULD BE GLAD TO SPEND MY LIFE SERVING SUCH A PERSON.
AND YET I REPAID LADY SHUREI'S KINDNESS AND OPEN HEART WITH SUCH BETRAYAL...
LADY SHUREI IS STILL UNAWARE OF THE TRUTH.
UNTIL I CAN TELL IT TO HER WITH MY OWN LIPS, MY BETRAYAL CONTINUES.
I'M STILL BETRAYING HER NOW.

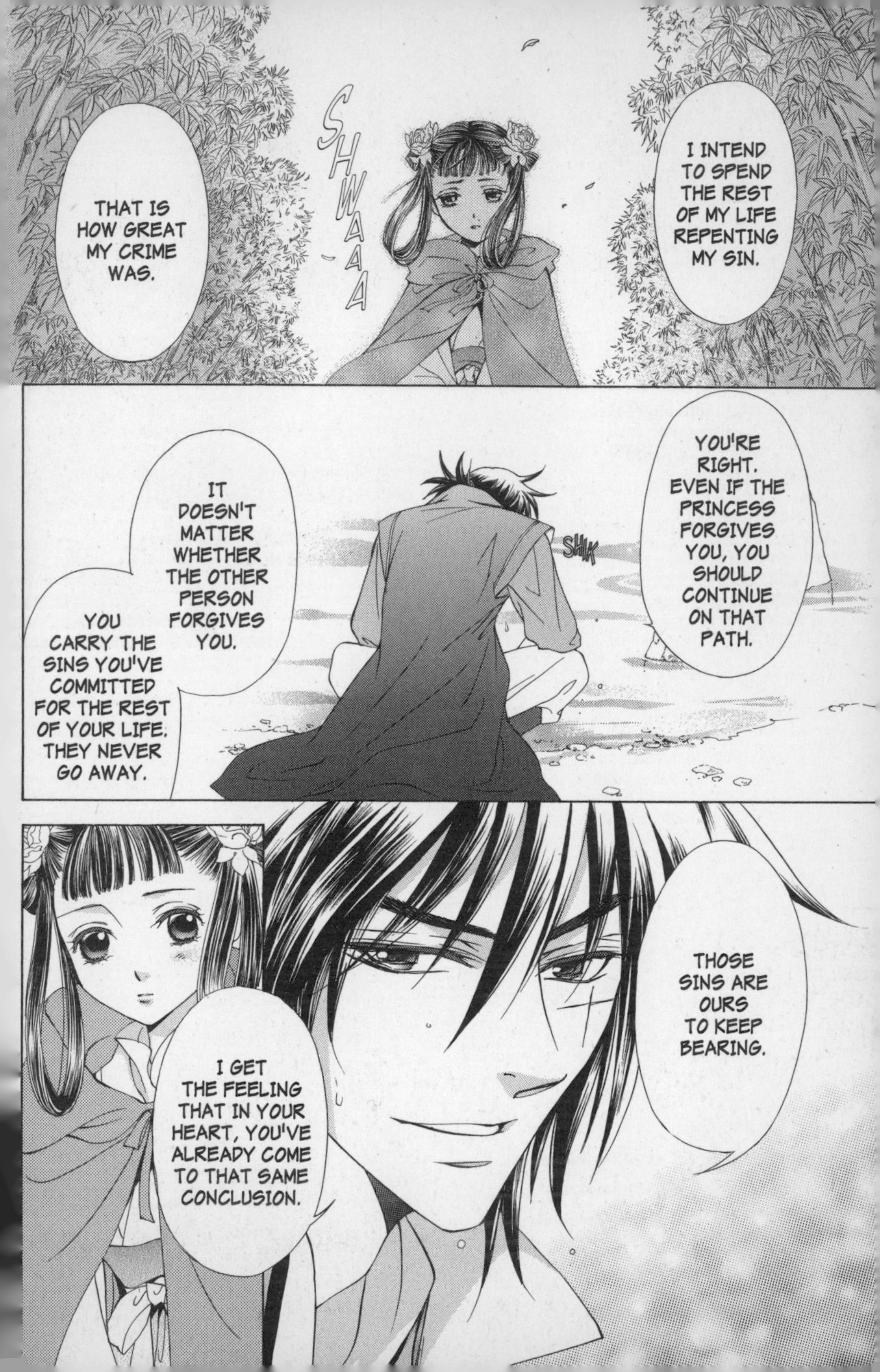
I INTEND TO SPEND THE REST OF MY LIFE REPENTING MY SIN.
SHWAAAA
THAT IS HOW GREAT MY CRIME WAS.
YOU'RE RIGHT. EVEN IF THE PRINCESS FORGIVES YOU, YOU SHOULD CONTINUE ON THAT PATH.
SHIK
IT DOESN'T MATTER WHETHER THE OTHER PERSON FORGIVES YOU.
YOU CARRY THE SINS YOU'VE COMMITTED FOR THE REST OF YOUR LIFE. THEY NEVER GO AWAY.
THOSE SINS ARE OURS TO KEEP BEARING.
I GET THE FEELING THAT IN YOUR HEART, YOU'VE ALREADY COME TO THAT SAME CONCLUSION.

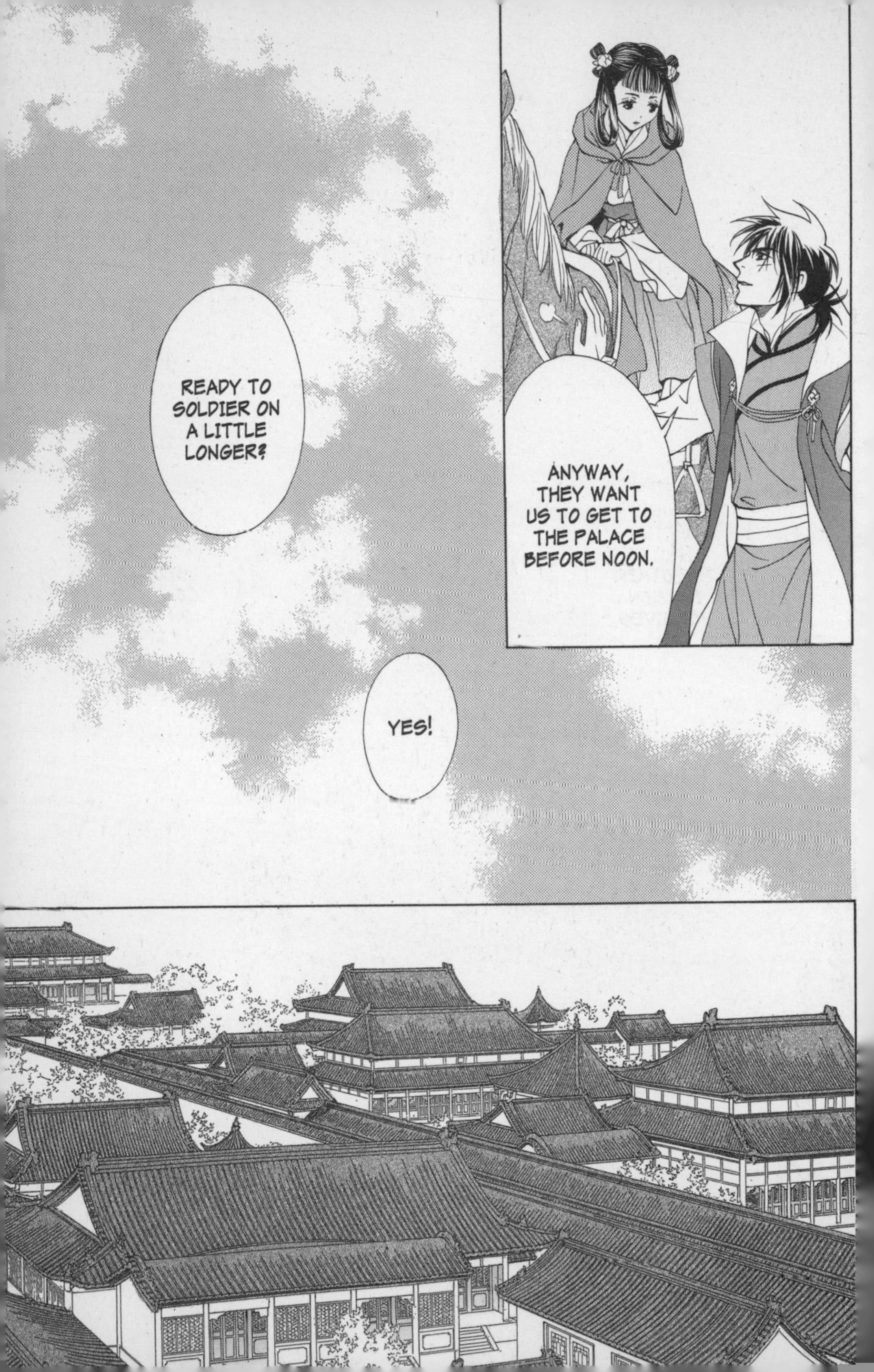
ANYWAY, THEY WANT US TO GET TO THE PALACE BEFORE NOON.
READY TO SOLDIER ON A LITTLE LONGER?
YES!

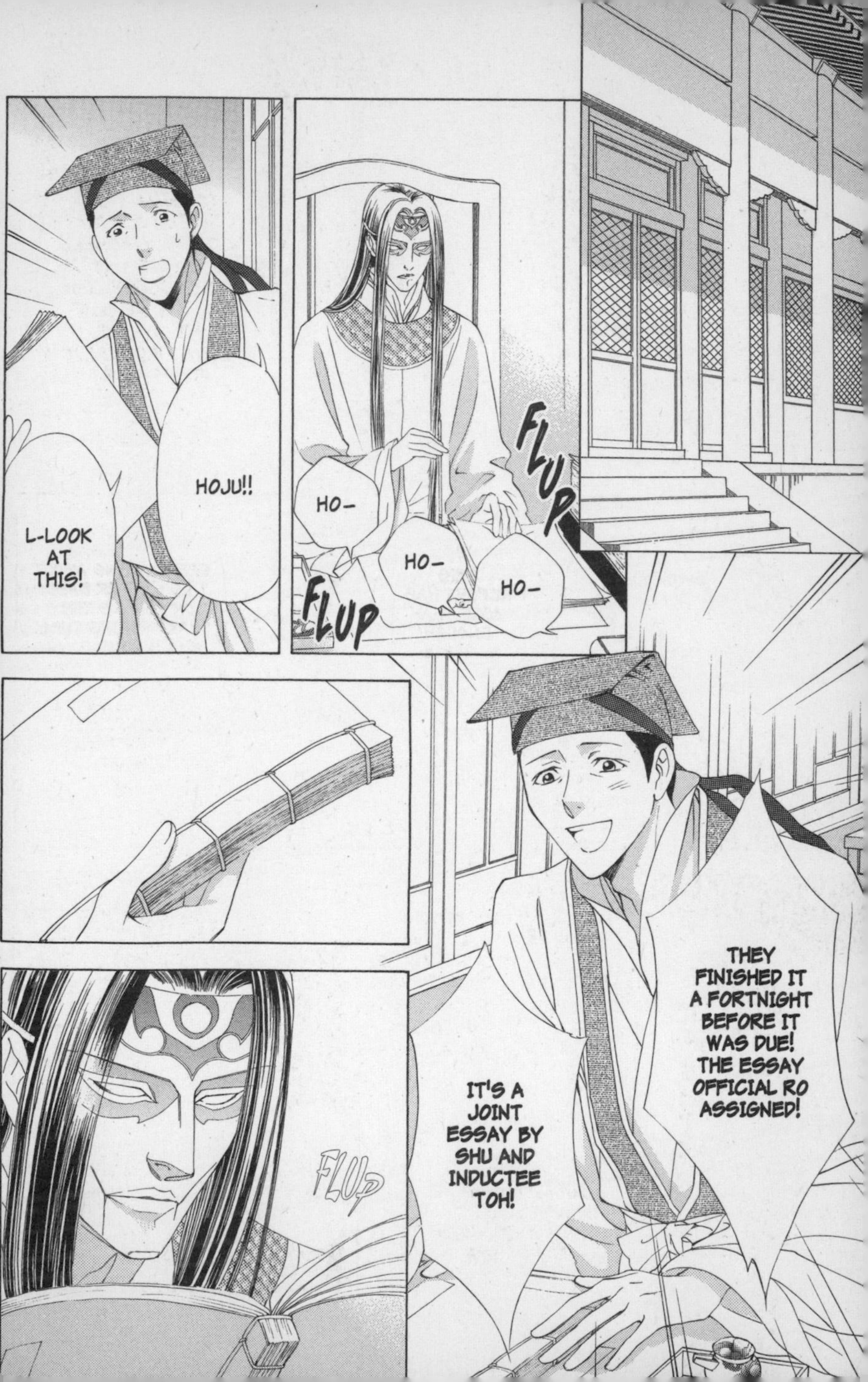
FLUP
HO-
HO-
HO-
FLUP
HOJU!!
L-LOOK AT THIS!
THEY FINISHED IT A FORTNIGHT BEFORE IT WAS DUE! THE ESSAY OFFICIAL RO ASSIGNED!
IT'S A JOINT ESSAY BY SHU AND INDUCTEE TOH!
FLUP

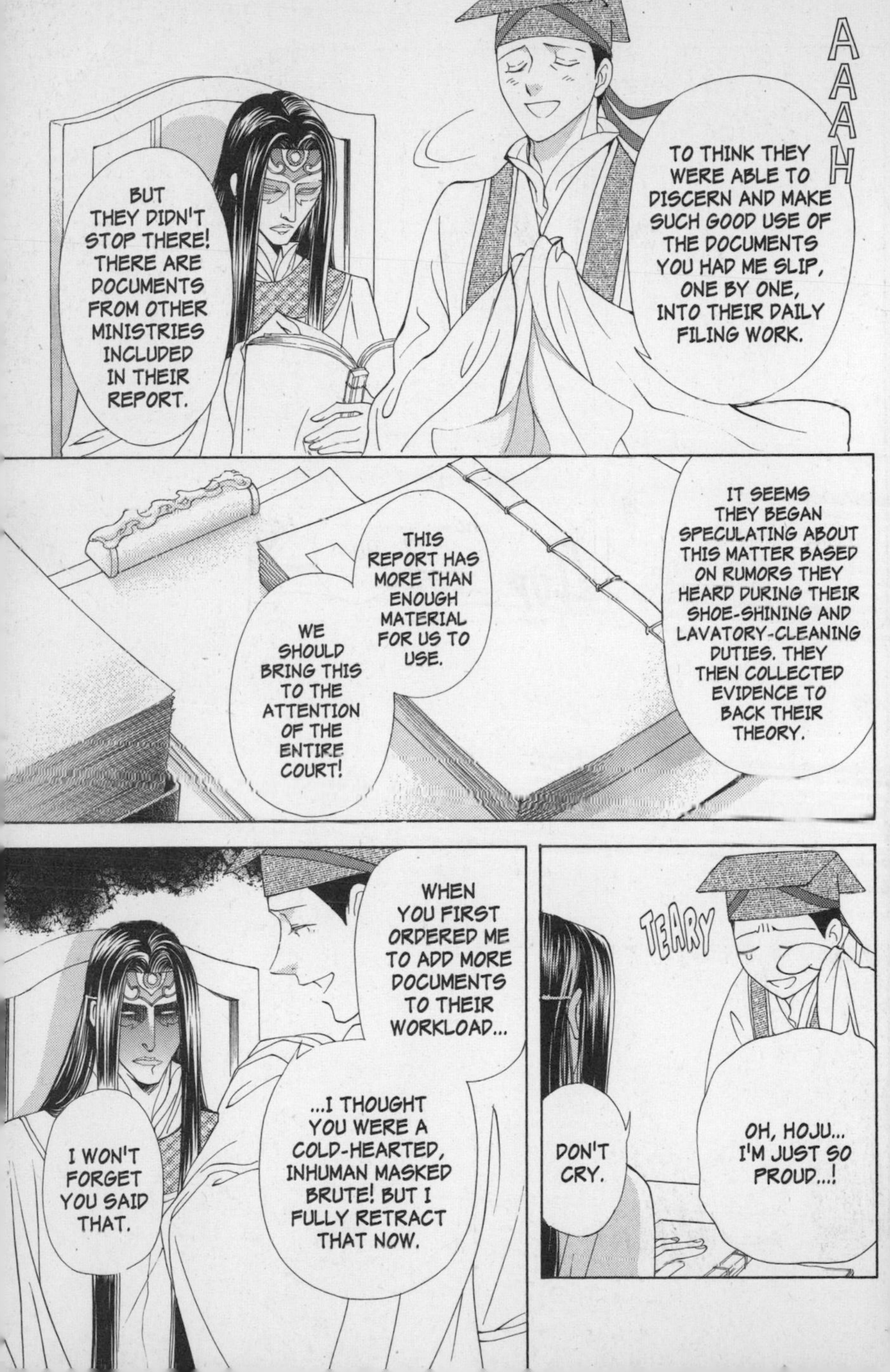
AAAAH
TO THINK THEY WERE ABLE TO DISCERN AND MAKE SUCH GOOD USE OF THE DOCUMENTS YOU HAD ME SLIP, ONE BY ONE, INTO THEIR DAILY FILING WORK.
BUT THEY DIDN'T STOP THERE! THERE ARE DOCUMENTS FROM OTHER MINISTRIES INCLUDED IN THEIR REPORT.
IT SEEMS THEY BEGAN SPECULATING ABOUT THIS MATTER BASED ON RUMORS THEY HEARD DURING THEIR SHOE-SHINING AND LAVATORY-CLEANING DUTIES. THEY THEN COLLECTED EVIDENCE TO BACK THEIR THEORY.
THIS REPORT HAS MORE THAN ENOUGH MATERIAL FOR US TO USE.
WE SHOULD BRING THIS TO THE ATTENTION OF THE ENTIRE COURT!
TEARY
OH, HOJU... I'M JUST SO PROUD...!
DON'T CRY.
WHEN YOU FIRST ORDERED ME TO ADD MORE DOCUMENTS TO THEIR WORKLOAD...
...I THOUGHT YOU WERE A COLD-HEARTED, INHUMAN MASKED BRUTE! BUT I FULLY RETRACT THAT NOW.
I WON'T FORGET YOU SAID THAT.

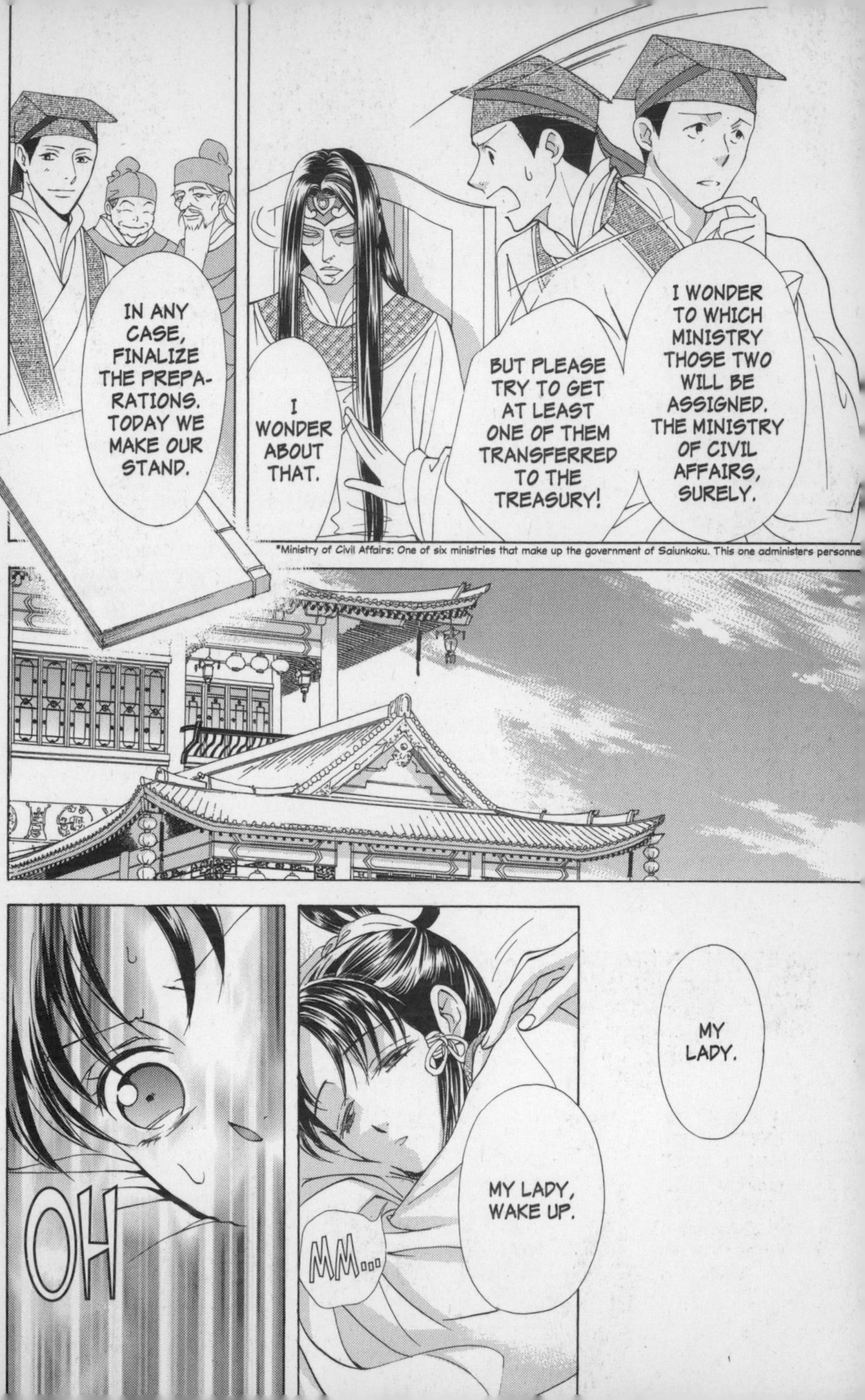
I WONDER TO WHICH MINISTRY THOSE TWO WILL BE ASSIGNED. THE MINISTRY OF CIVIL AFFAIRS, SURELY.
BUT PLEASE TRY TO GET AT LEAST ONE OF THEM TRANSFERRED TO THE TREASURY!
I WONDER ABOUT THAT.
IN ANY CASE, FINALIZE THE PREPARATIONS. TODAY WE MAKE OUR STAND.
MY LADY.
MY LADY, WAKE UP.
MM...
OH

*Ministry of Civil Affairs: One of six ministries that make up the government of Saiunkoku. This one administers personne

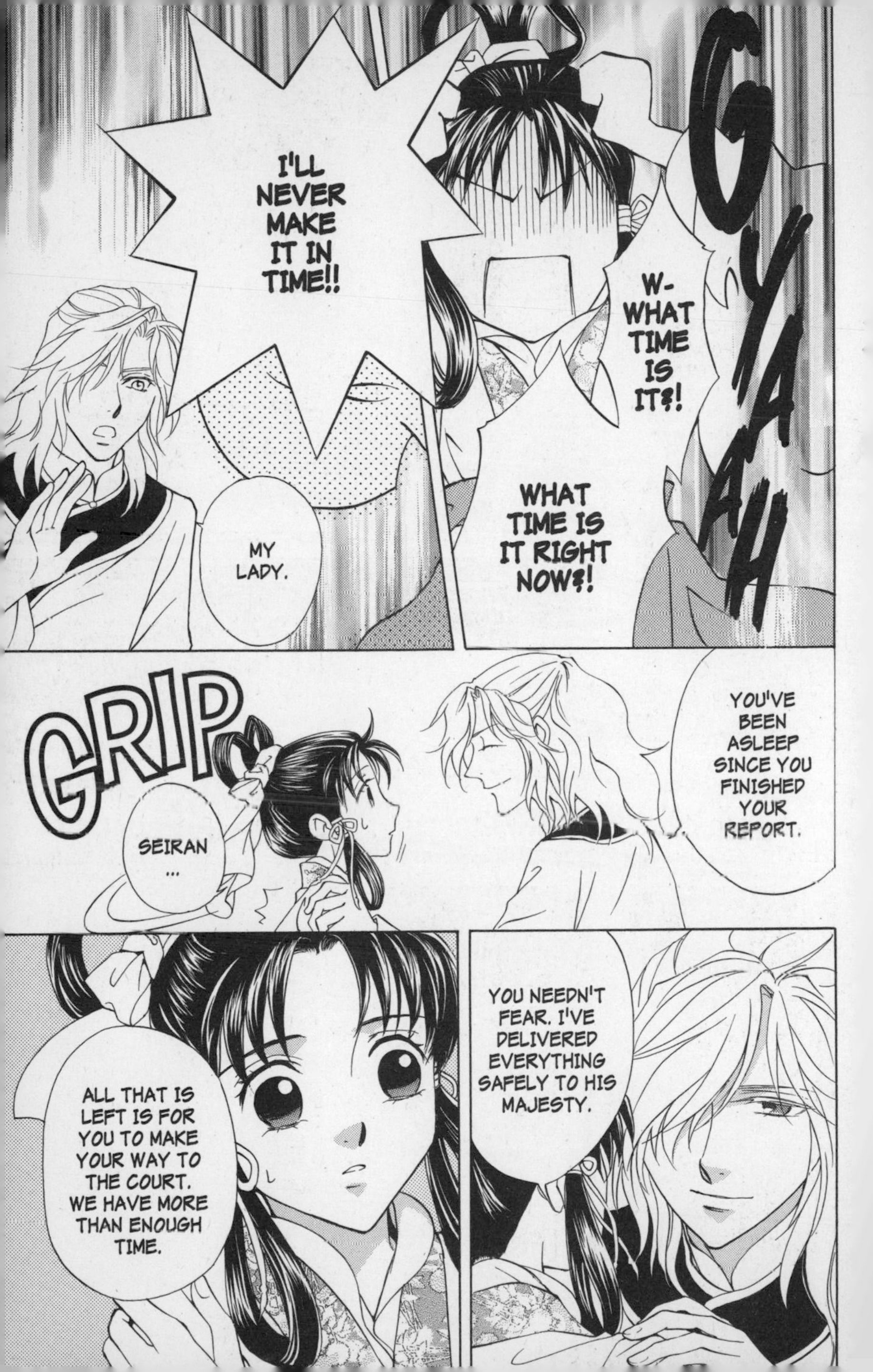
GYAAH
W-WHAT TIME IS IT?!
WHAT TIME IS IT RIGHT NOW?!
I'LL NEVER MAKE IT IN TIME!!
MY LADY.
YOU'VE BEEN ASLEEP SINCE YOU FINISHED YOUR REPORT.
GRIP
SEIRAN ...
YOU NEEDN'T FEAR. I'VE DELIVERED EVERYTHING SAFELY TO HIS MAJESTY.
ALL THAT IS LEFT IS FOR YOU TO MAKE YOUR WAY TO THE COURT. WE HAVE MORE THAN ENOUGH TIME.

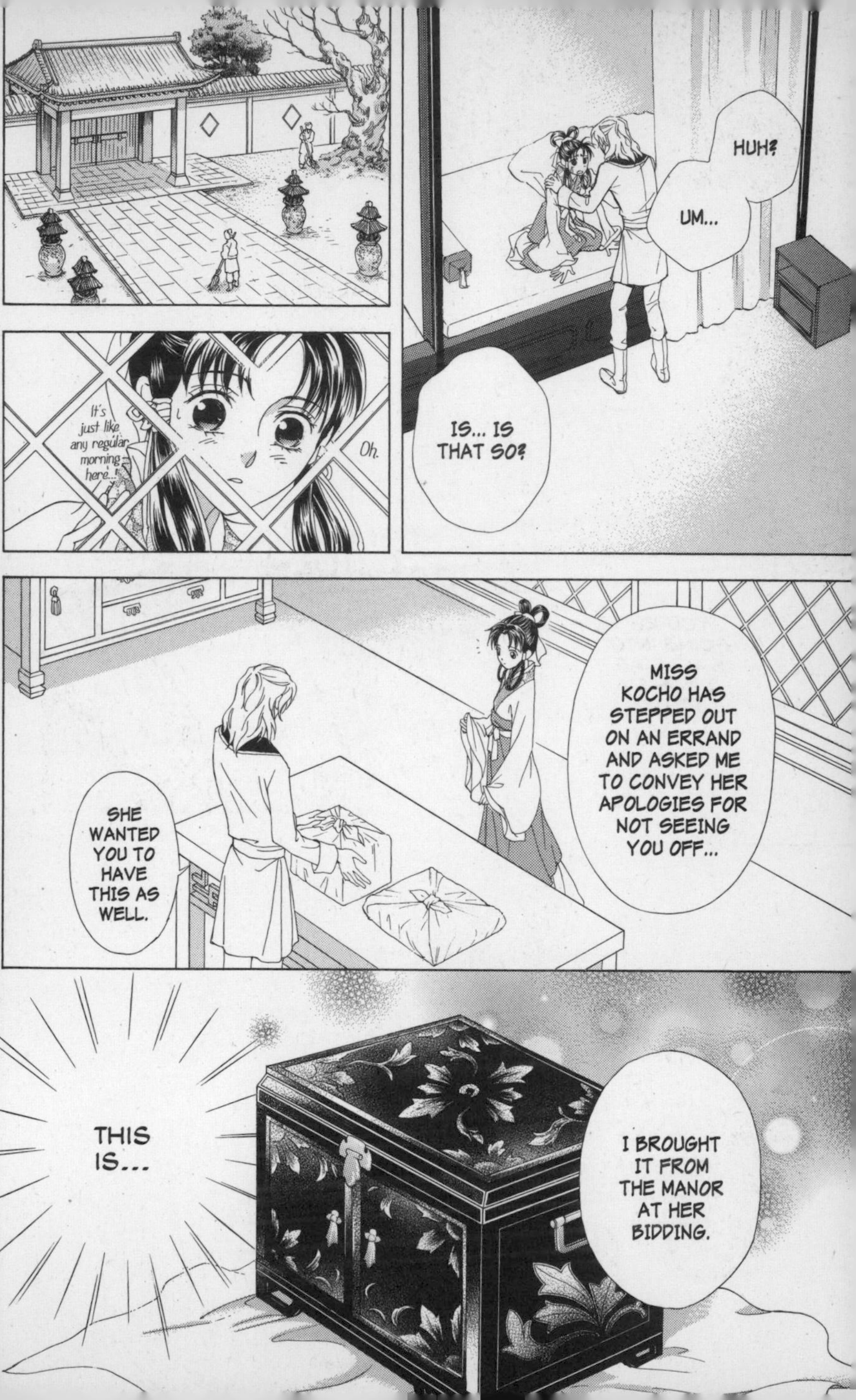
HUH?
UM...
IS... IS THAT SO?
Oh.
It's just like any regular morning here...
MISS KOCHO HAS STEPPED OUT ON AN ERRAND AND ASKED ME TO CONVEY HER APOLOGIES FOR NOT SEEING YOU OFF...
SHE WANTED YOU TO HAVE THIS AS WELL.
I BROUGHT IT FROM THE MANOR AT HER BIDDING.
THIS IS...

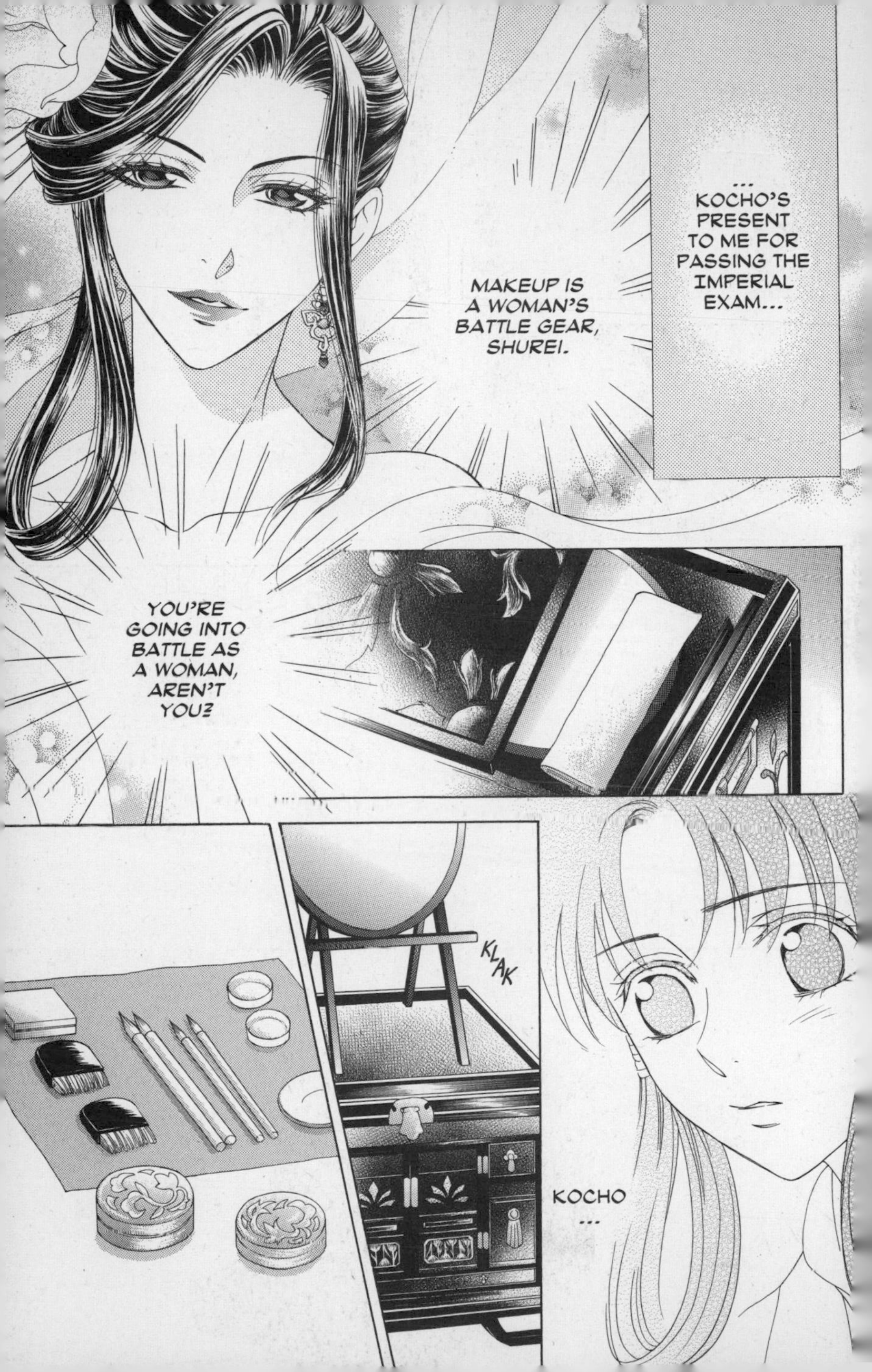
...KOCHO'S PRESENT TO ME FOR PASSING THE IMPERIAL EXAM...
MAKEUP IS A WOMAN'S BATTLE GEAR, SHUREI.
YOU'RE GOING INTO BATTLE AS A WOMAN, AREN'T YOU?
KOCHO ...
KLAK

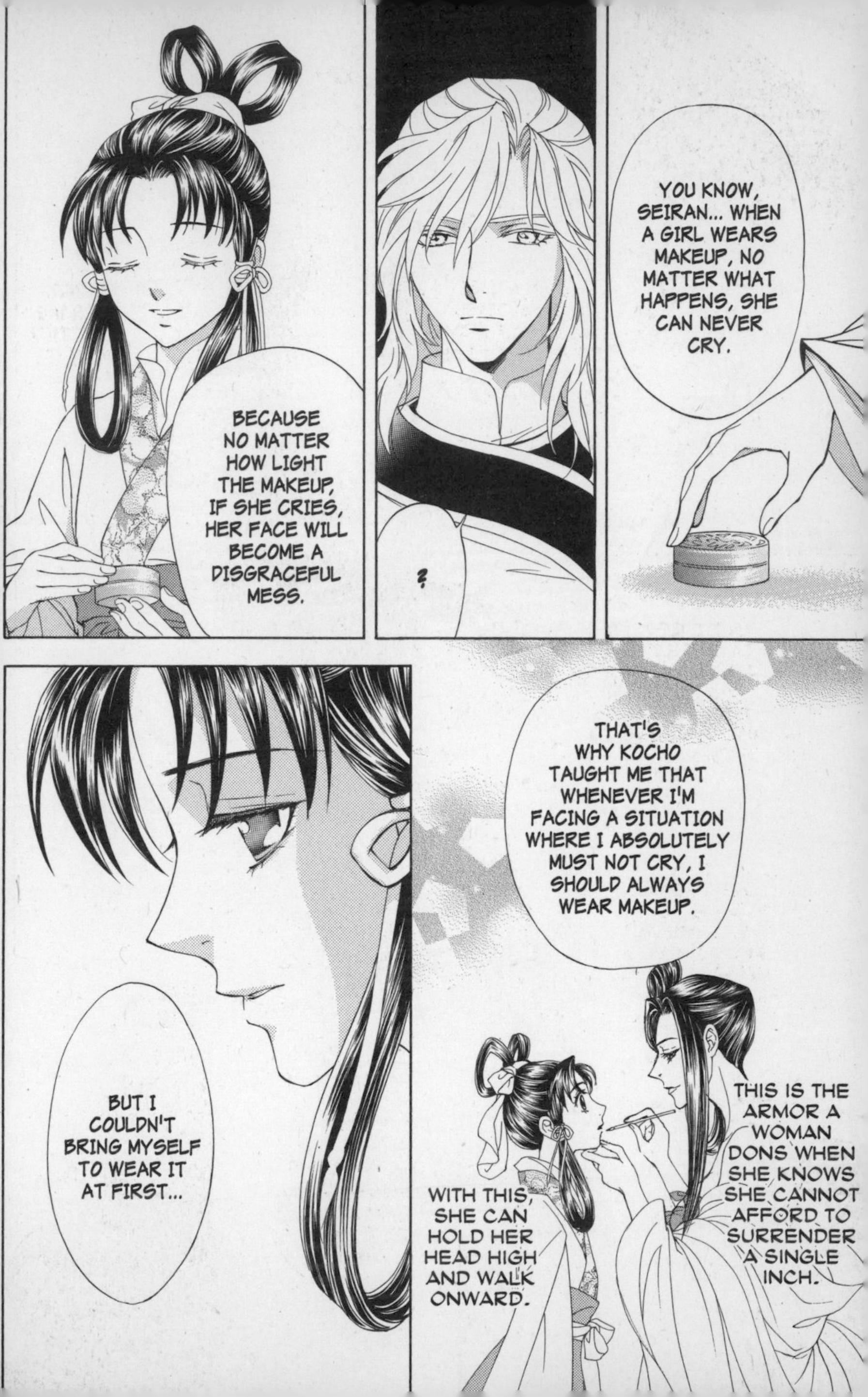
YOU KNOW, SEIRAN... WHEN A GIRL WEARS MAKEUP, NO MATTER WHAT HAPPENS, SHE CAN NEVER CRY.
?
BECAUSE NO MATTER HOW LIGHT THE MAKEUP, IF SHE CRIES, HER FACE WILL BECOME A DISGRACEFUL MESS.
THAT'S WHY KOCHO TAUGHT ME THAT WHENEVER I'M FACING A SITUATION WHERE I ABSOLUTELY MUST NOT CRY, I SHOULD ALWAYS WEAR MAKEUP.
THIS IS THE ARMOR A WOMAN DONS WHEN SHE KNOWS SHE CANNOT AFFORD TO SURRENDER A SINGLE INCH.
WITH THIS, SHE CAN HOLD HER HEAD HIGH AND WALK ONWARD.
BUT I COULDN'T BRING MYSELF TO WEAR IT AT FIRST...

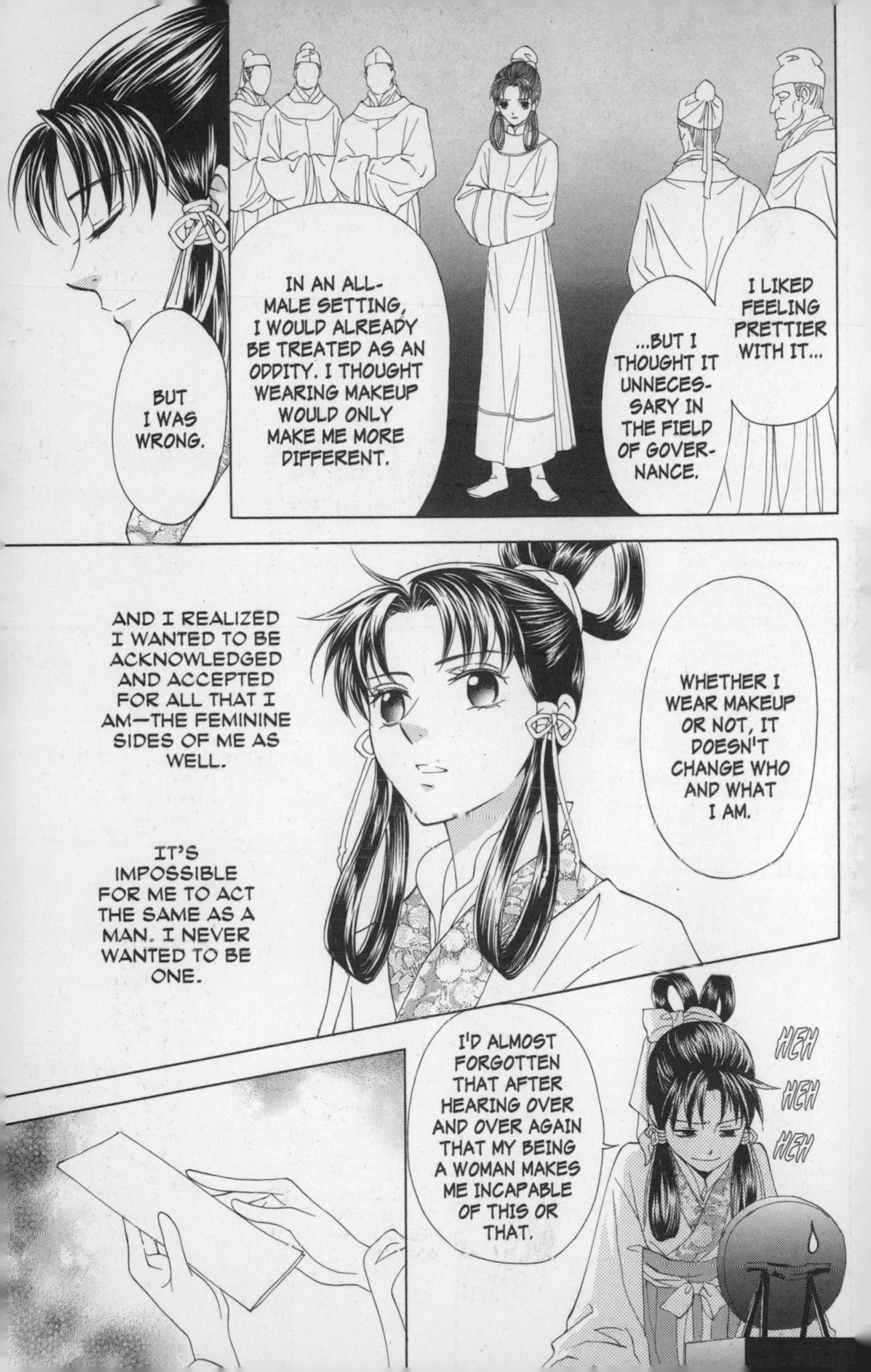
I LIKED FEELING PRETTIER WITH IT...
...BUT I THOUGHT IT UNNECES-SARY IN THE FIELD OF GOVER-NANCE.
IN AN ALL-MALE SETTING, I WOULD ALREADY BE TREATED AS AN ODDITY. I THOUGHT WEARING MAKEUP WOULD ONLY MAKE ME MORE DIFFERENT.
BUT I WAS WRONG.
WHETHER I WEAR MAKEUP OR NOT, IT DOESN'T CHANGE WHO AND WHAT I AM.
AND I REALIZED I WANTED TO BE ACKNOWLEDGED AND ACCEPTED FOR ALL THAT I AM—THE FEMININE SIDES OF ME AS WELL.
IT'S IMPOSSIBLE FOR ME TO ACT THE SAME AS A MAN. I NEVER WANTED TO BE ONE.
HEH
HEH
HEH
I'D ALMOST FORGOTTEN THAT AFTER HEARING OVER AND OVER AGAIN THAT MY BEING A WOMAN MAKES ME INCAPABLE OF THIS OR THAT.

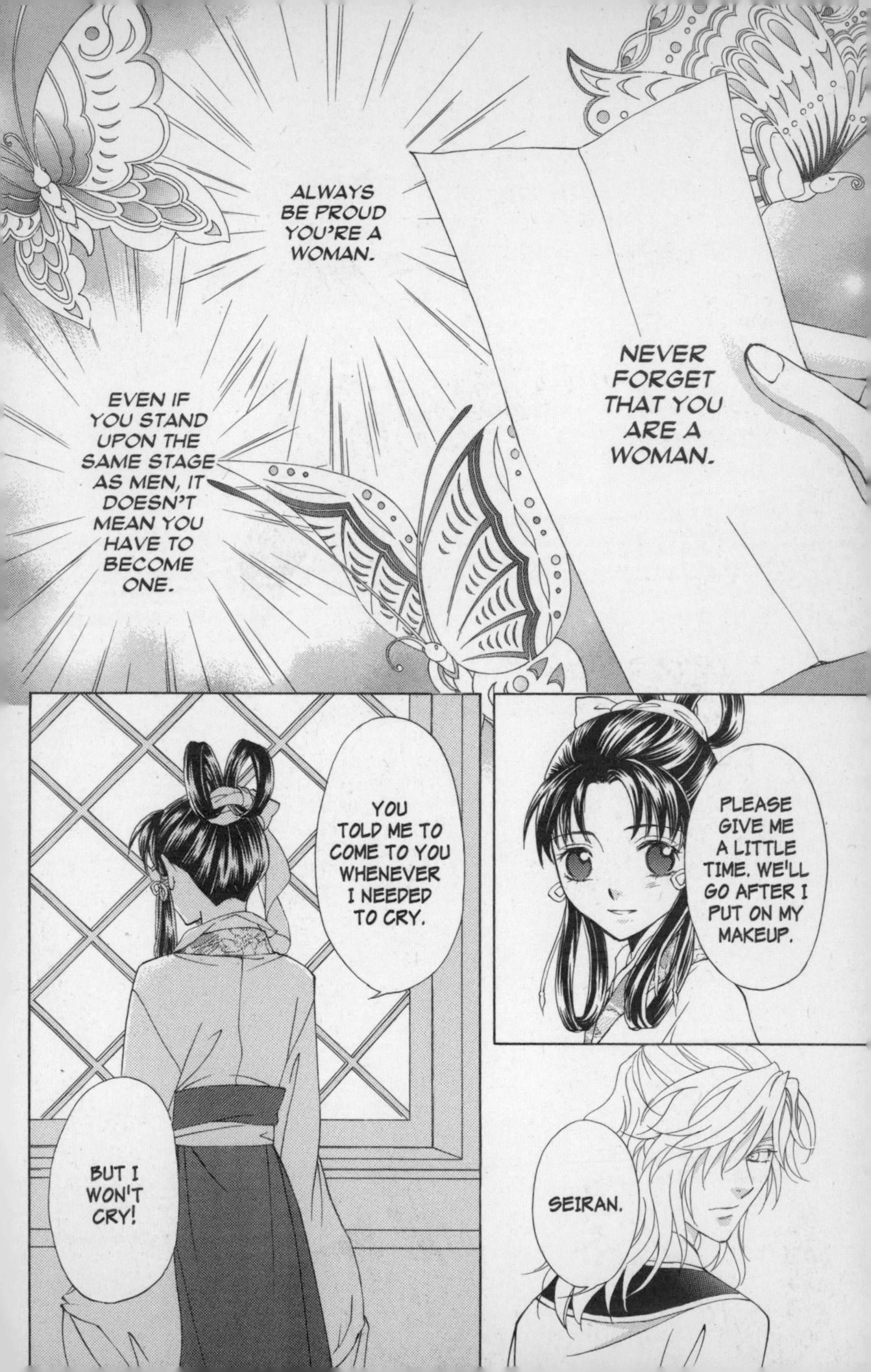
NEVER FORGET THAT YOU ARE A WOMAN.
ALWAYS BE PROUD YOU'RE A WOMAN.
EVEN IF YOU STAND UPON THE SAME STAGE AS MEN, IT DOESN'T MEAN YOU HAVE TO BECOME ONE.
PLEASE GIVE ME A LITTLE TIME. WE'LL GO AFTER I PUT ON MY MAKEUP.
SEIRAN.
YOU TOLD ME TO COME TO YOU WHENEVER I NEEDED TO CRY.
BUT I WON'T CRY!

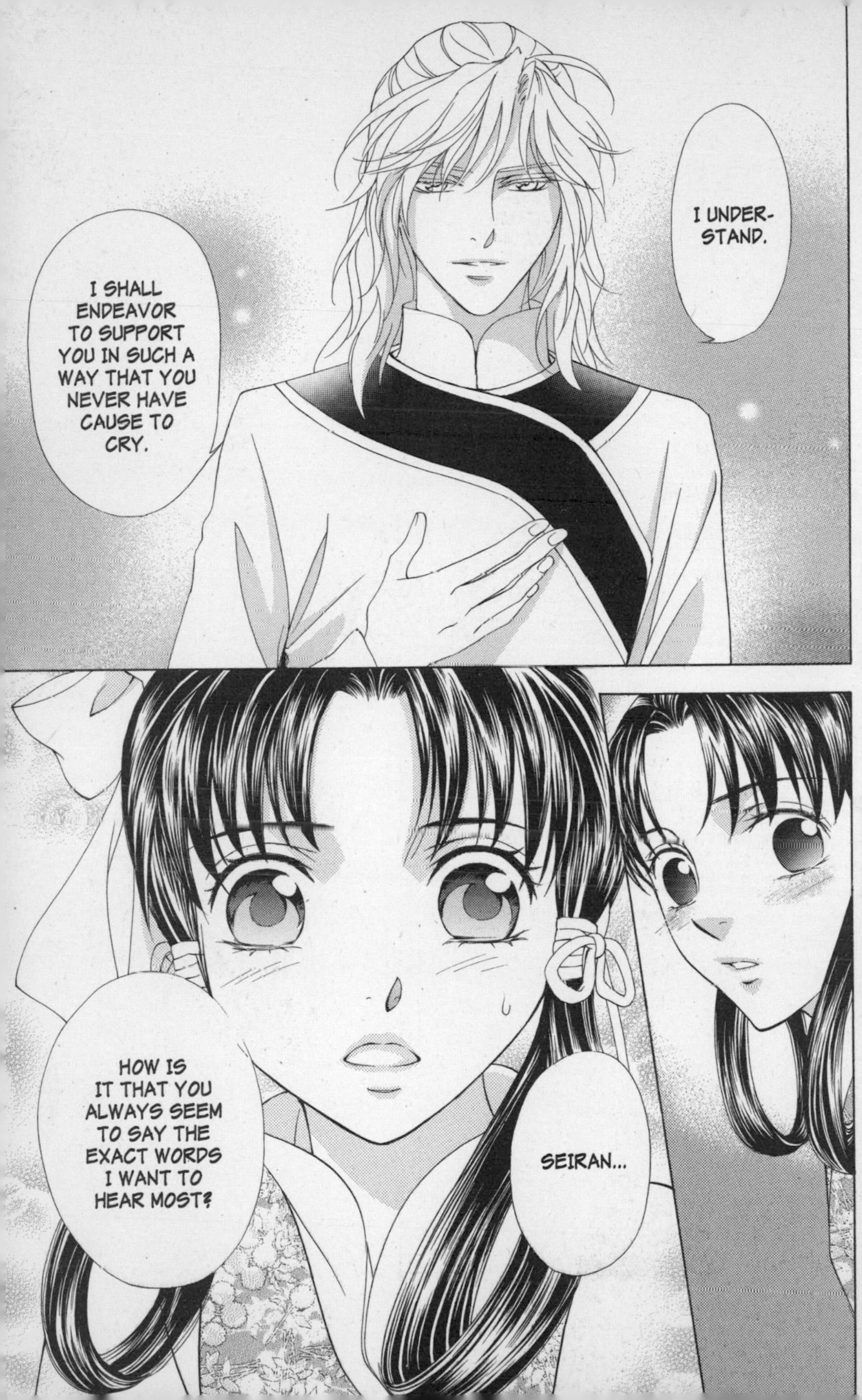
I UNDER-STAND.
I SHALL ENDEAVOR TO SUPPORT YOU IN SUCH A WAY THAT YOU NEVER HAVE CAUSE TO CRY.
SEIRAN...
HOW IS IT THAT YOU ALWAYS SEEM TO SAY THE EXACT WORDS I WANT TO HEAR MOST?

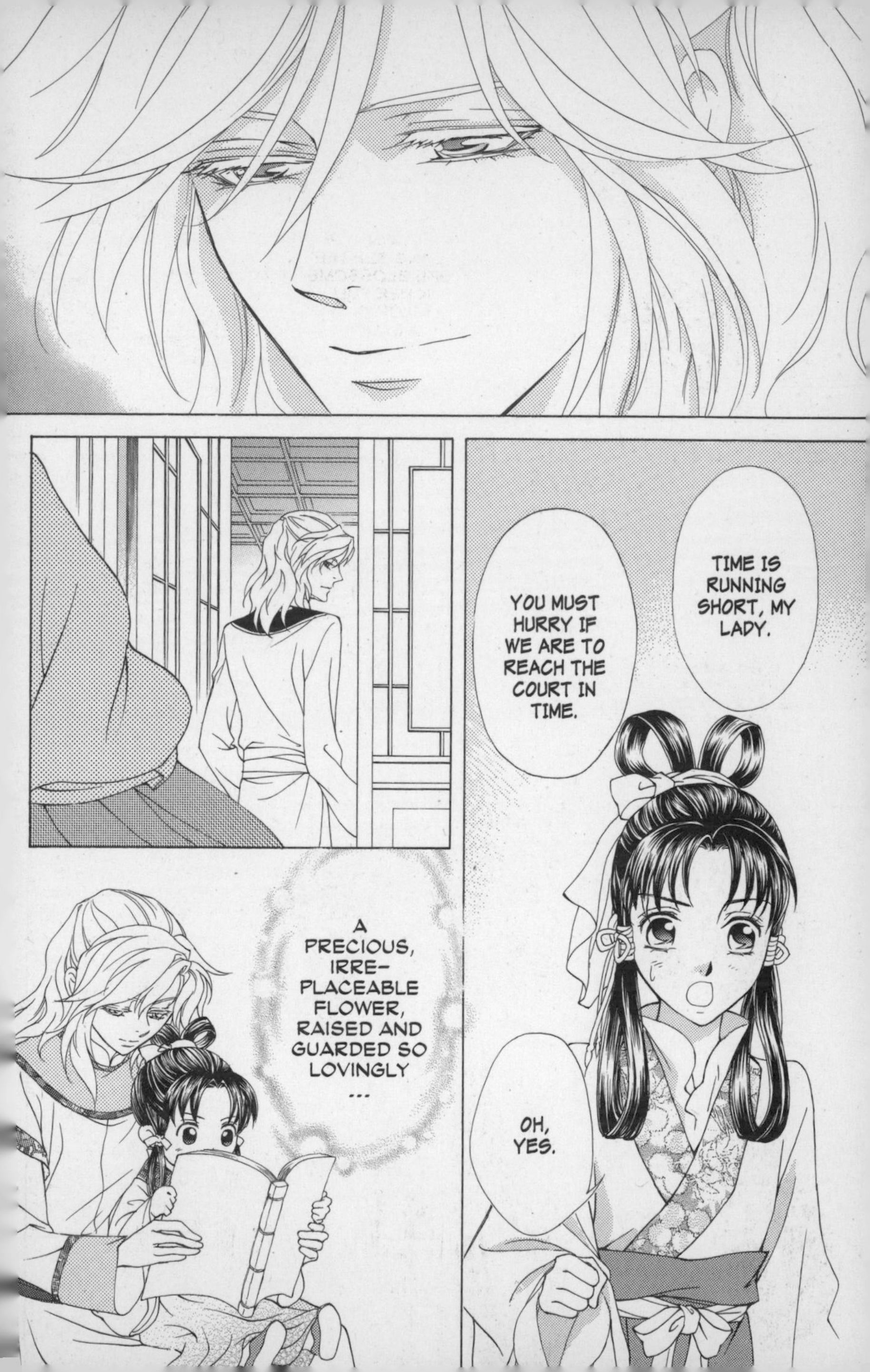
TIME IS RUNNING SHORT, MY LADY.
YOU MUST HURRY IF WE ARE TO REACH THE COURT IN TIME.
OH, YES.
A PRECIOUS, IRRE-PLACEABLE FLOWER, RAISED AND GUARDED SO LOVINGLY ...

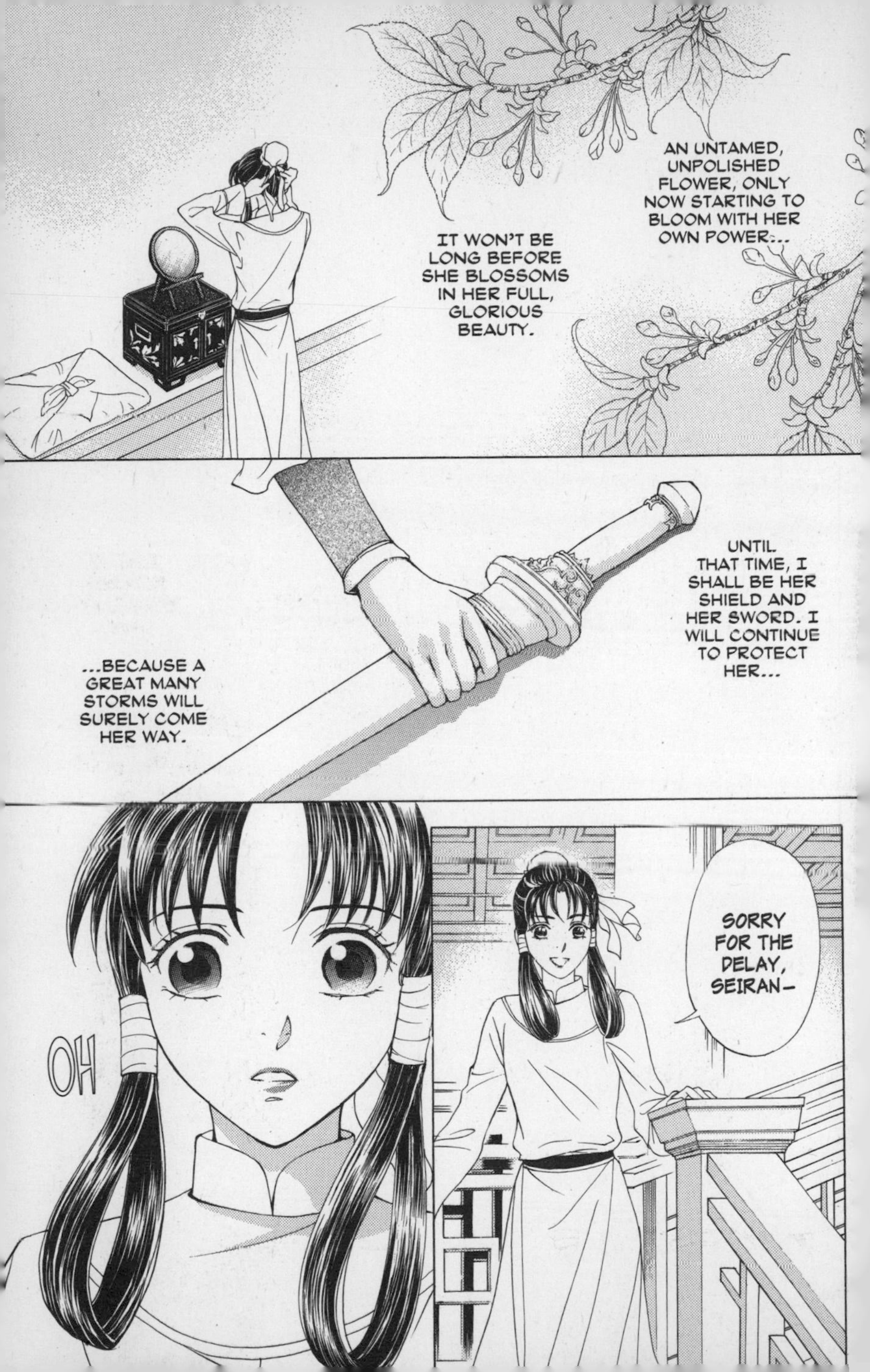
AN UNTAMED, UNPOLISHED FLOWER, ONLY NOW STARTING TO BLOOM WITH HER OWN POWER...
IT WON'T BE LONG BEFORE SHE BLOSSOMS IN HER FULL, GLORIOUS BEAUTY.
UNTIL THAT TIME, I SHALL BE HER SHIELD AND HER SWORD. I WILL CONTINUE TO PROTECT HER...
...BECAUSE A GREAT MANY STORMS WILL SURELY COME HER WAY.
SORRY FOR THE DELAY, SEIRAN—
OH

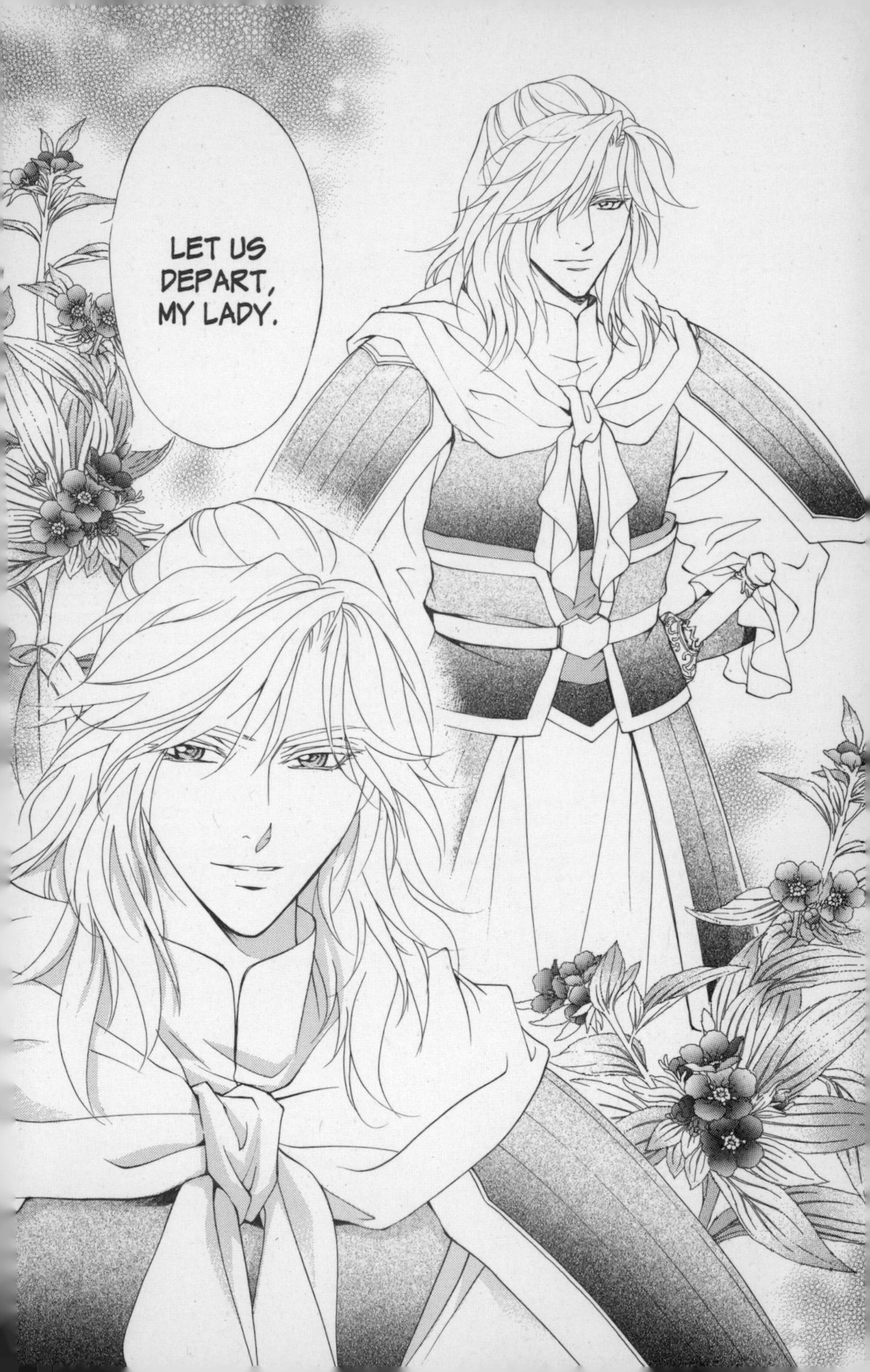
LET US DEPART, MY LADY.

The Story of
SAIUNKOKU

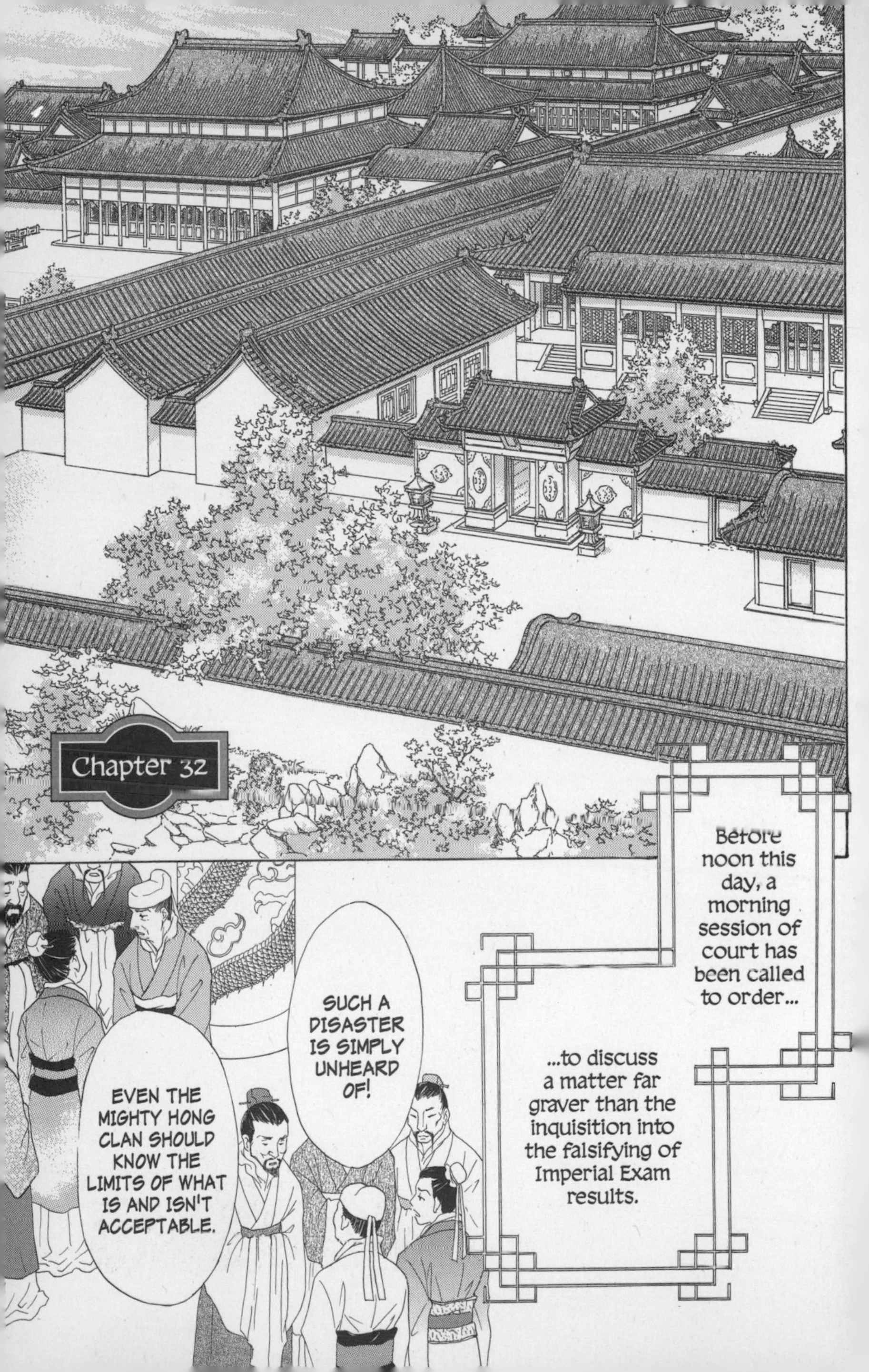
Chapter 32
Before noon this day, a morning session of court has been called to order...
...to discuss a matter far graver than the inquisition into the falsifying of Imperial Exam results.
SUCH A DISASTER IS SIMPLY UNHEARD OF!
EVEN THE MIGHTY HONG CLAN SHOULD KNOW THE LIMITS OF WHAT IS AND ISN'T ACCEPTABLE.

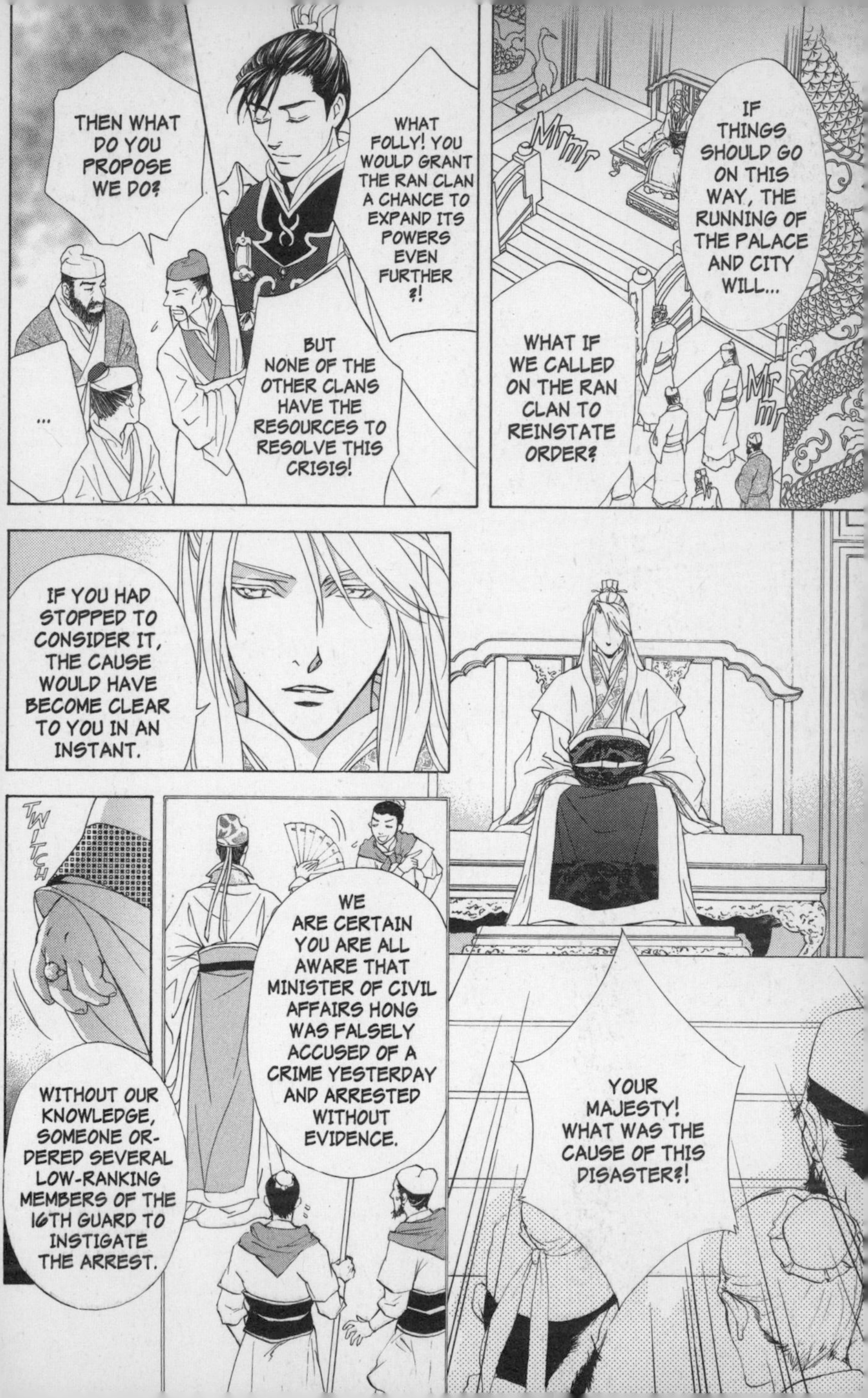
IF THINGS SHOULD GO ON THIS WAY, THE RUNNING OF THE PALACE AND CITY WILL...
Mrmr
WHAT IF WE CALLED ON THE RAN CLAN TO REINSTATE ORDER?
Mr mr
WHAT FOLLY! YOU WOULD GRANT THE RAN CLAN A CHANCE TO EXPAND ITS POWERS EVEN FURTHER?!
BUT NONE OF THE OTHER CLANS HAVE THE RESOURCES TO RESOLVE THIS CRISIS!
THEN WHAT DO YOU PROPOSE WE DO?
...
YOUR MAJESTY! WHAT WAS THE CAUSE OF THIS DISASTER?!
IF YOU HAD STOPPED TO CONSIDER IT, THE CAUSE WOULD HAVE BECOME CLEAR TO YOU IN AN INSTANT.
WE ARE CERTAIN YOU ARE ALL AWARE THAT MINISTER OF CIVIL AFFAIRS HONG WAS FALSELY ACCUSED OF A CRIME YESTERDAY AND ARRESTED WITHOUT EVIDENCE.
TWITCH
WITHOUT OUR KNOWLEDGE, SOMEONE OR-DERED SEVERAL LOW-RANKING MEMBERS OF THE 16TH GUARD TO INSTIGATE THE ARREST.

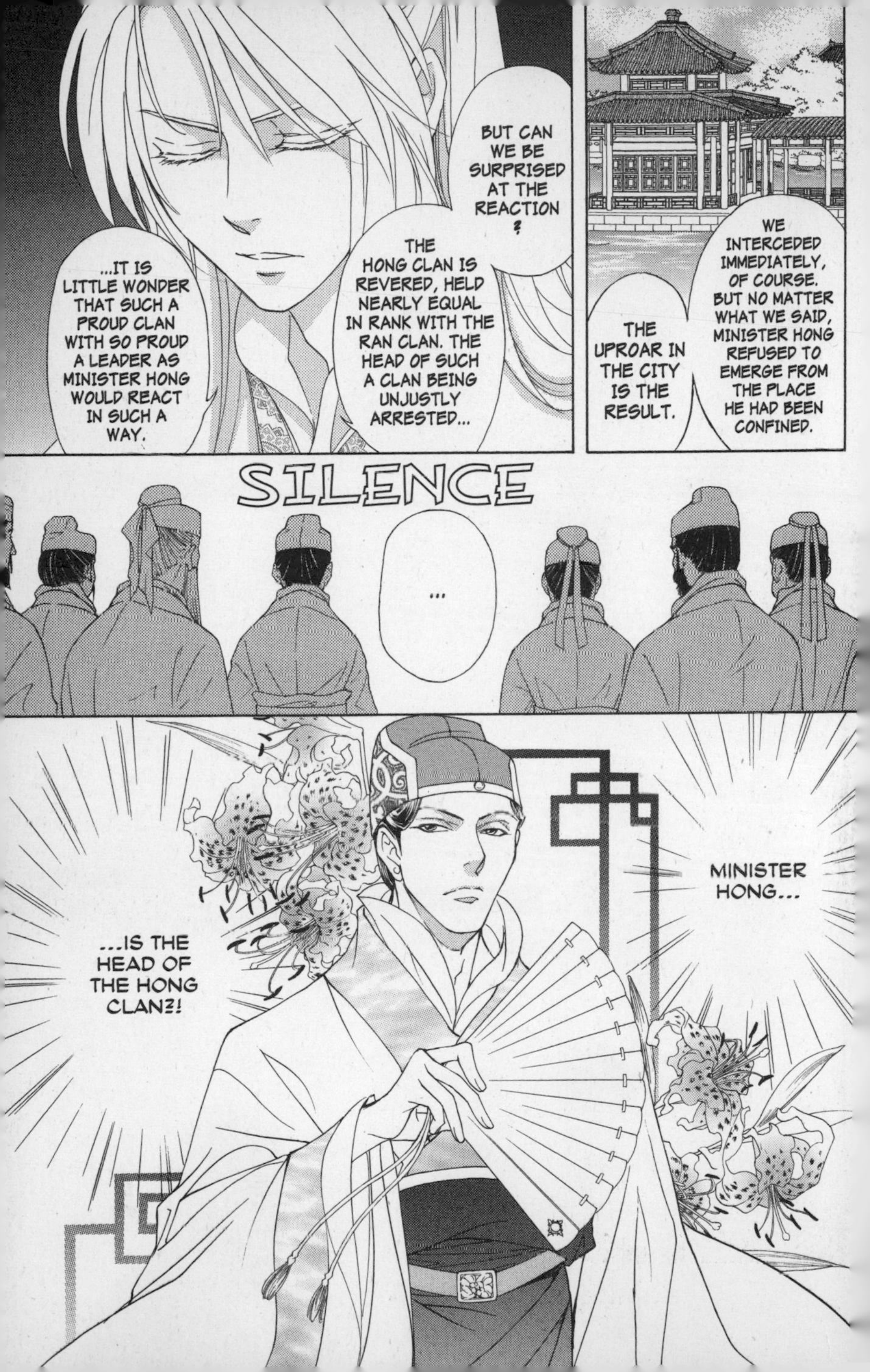
WE INTERCEDED IMMEDIATELY, OF COURSE. BUT NO MATTER WHAT WE SAID, MINISTER HONG REFUSED TO EMERGE FROM THE PLACE HE HAD BEEN CONFINED.
THE UPROAR IN THE CITY IS THE RESULT.
BUT CAN WE BE SURPRISED AT THE REACTION?
THE HONG CLAN IS REVERED, HELD NEARLY EQUAL IN RANK WITH THE RAN CLAN. THE HEAD OF SUCH A CLAN BEING UNJUSTLY ARRESTED...
...IT IS LITTLE WONDER THAT SUCH A PROUD CLAN WITH SO PROUD A LEADER AS MINISTER HONG WOULD REACT IN SUCH A WAY.
SILENCE
...
MINISTER HONG...
...IS THE HEAD OF THE HONG CLAN?!

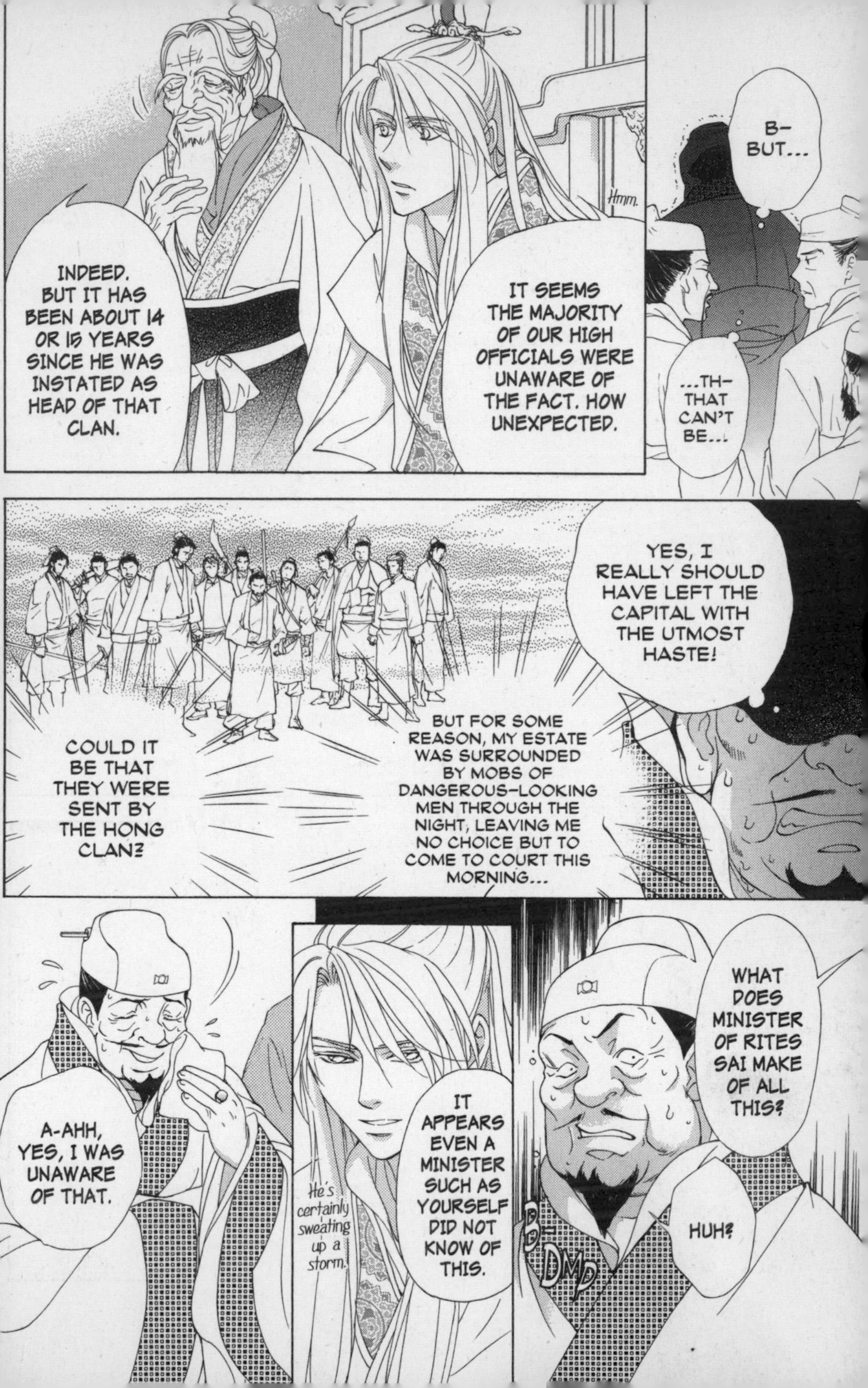
B-BUT...
...TH-THAT CAN'T BE...
Hmm.
IT SEEMS THE MAJORITY OF OUR HIGH OFFICIALS WERE UNAWARE OF THE FACT. HOW UNEXPECTED.
INDEED. BUT IT HAS BEEN ABOUT 14 OR 15 YEARS SINCE HE WAS INSTATED AS HEAD OF THAT CLAN.
YES, I REALLY SHOULD HAVE LEFT THE CAPITAL WITH THE UTMOST HASTE!
BUT FOR SOME REASON, MY ESTATE WAS SURROUNDED BY MOBS OF DANGEROUS-LOOKING MEN THROUGH THE NIGHT, LEAVING ME NO CHOICE BUT TO COME TO COURT THIS MORNING...
COULD IT BE THAT THEY WERE SENT BY THE HONG CLAN?
WHAT DOES MINISTER OF RITES SAI MAKE OF ALL THIS?
HUH?
B-DMP
IT APPEARS EVEN A MINISTER SUCH AS YOURSELF DID NOT KNOW OF THIS.
He's certainly sweating up a storm.
A-AHH, YES, I WAS UNAWARE OF THAT.

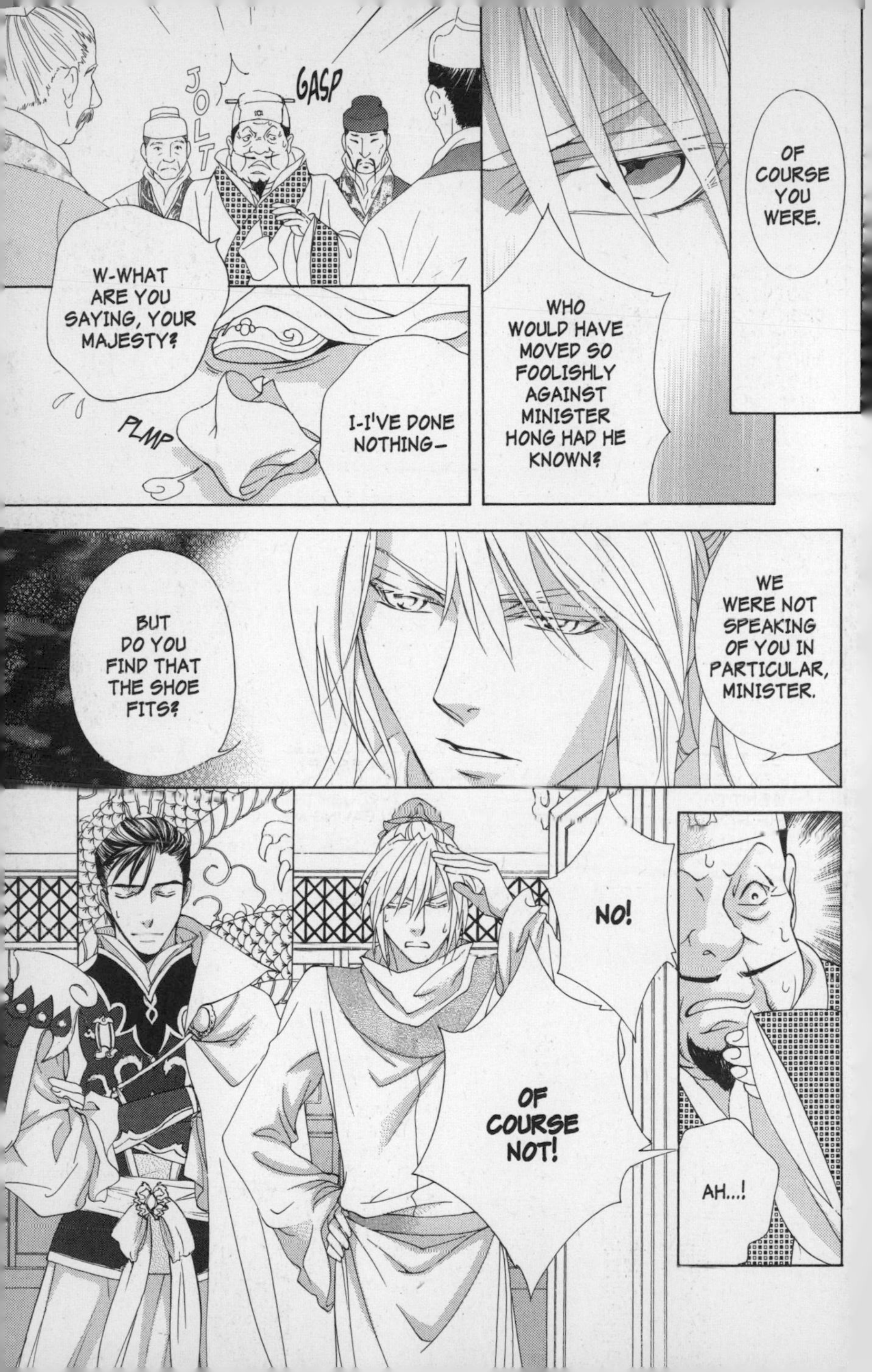
OF COURSE YOU WERE.
WHO WOULD HAVE MOVED SO FOOLISHLY AGAINST MINISTER HONG HAD HE KNOWN?
GASP
JOLT
W-WHAT ARE YOU SAYING, YOUR MAJESTY?
I-I'VE DONE NOTHING—
PLMP
WE WERE NOT SPEAKING OF YOU IN PARTICULAR, MINISTER.
BUT DO YOU FIND THAT THE SHOE FITS?
AH...!
NO!
OF COURSE NOT!

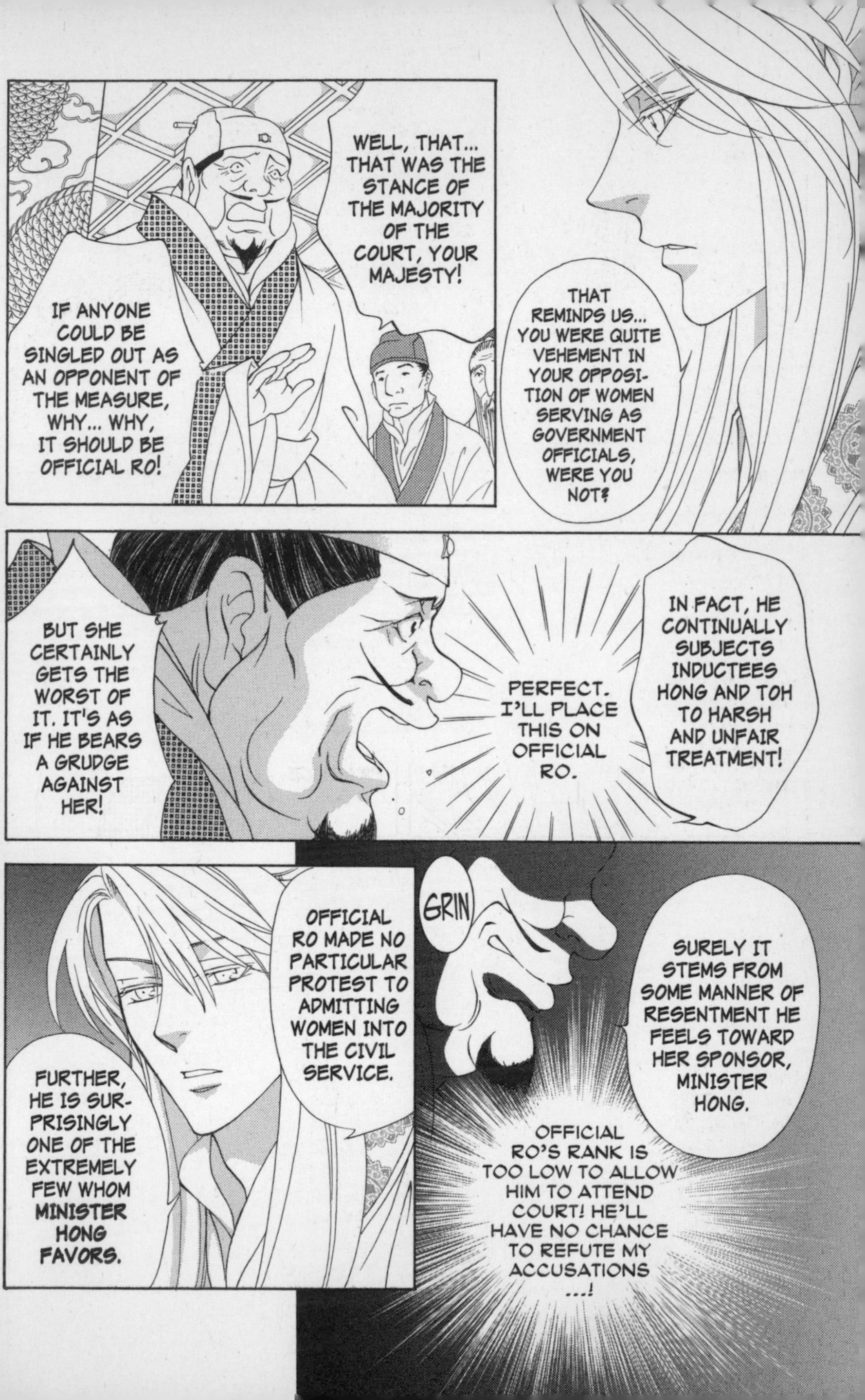
THAT REMINDS US... YOU WERE QUITE VEHEMENT IN YOUR OPPOSITION OF WOMEN SERVING AS GOVERNMENT OFFICIALS, WERE YOU NOT?
WELL, THAT... THAT WAS THE STANCE OF THE MAJORITY OF THE COURT, YOUR MAJESTY!
IF ANYONE COULD BE SINGLED OUT AS AN OPPONENT OF THE MEASURE, WHY... WHY, IT SHOULD BE OFFICIAL RO!
IN FACT, HE CONTINUALLY SUBJECTS INDUCTEES HONG AND TOH TO HARSH AND UNFAIR TREATMENT!
PERFECT. I'LL PLACE THIS ON OFFICIAL RO.
BUT SHE CERTAINLY GETS THE WORST OF IT. IT'S AS IF HE BEARS A GRUDGE AGAINST HER!
GRIN
SURELY IT STEMS FROM SOME MANNER OF RESENTMENT HE FEELS TOWARD HER SPONSOR, MINISTER HONG.
OFFICIAL RO'S RANK IS TOO LOW TO ALLOW HIM TO ATTEND COURT! HE'LL HAVE NO CHANCE TO REFUTE MY ACCUSATIONS ...!
OFFICIAL RO MADE NO PARTICULAR PROTEST TO ADMITTING WOMEN INTO THE CIVIL SERVICE.
FURTHER, HE IS SURPRISINGLY ONE OF THE EXTREMELY FEW WHOM MINISTER HONG FAVORS.

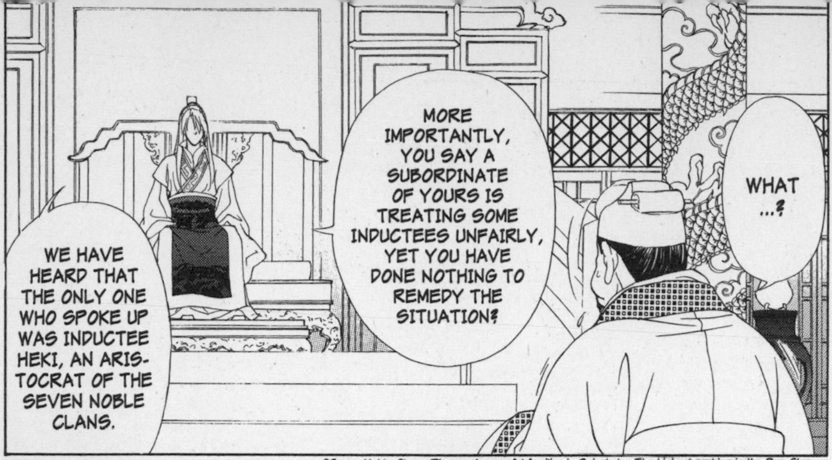
WHAT ...?
MORE IMPORTANTLY, YOU SAY A SUBORDINATE OF YOURS IS TREATING SOME INDUCTEES UNFAIRLY, YET YOU HAVE DONE NOTHING TO REMEDY THE SITUATION?
WE HAVE HEARD THAT THE ONLY ONE WHO SPOKE UP WAS INDUCTEE HEKI, AN ARISTOCRAT OF THE SEVEN NOBLE CLANS.

*Seven Noble Clans: The most powerful families in Saiunkoku. The highest ranking is the Ran Clan, followed by the Hong Clan, Ko Clan, Heki Clan, Haku Clan, Koku Clan and Sa Clan.

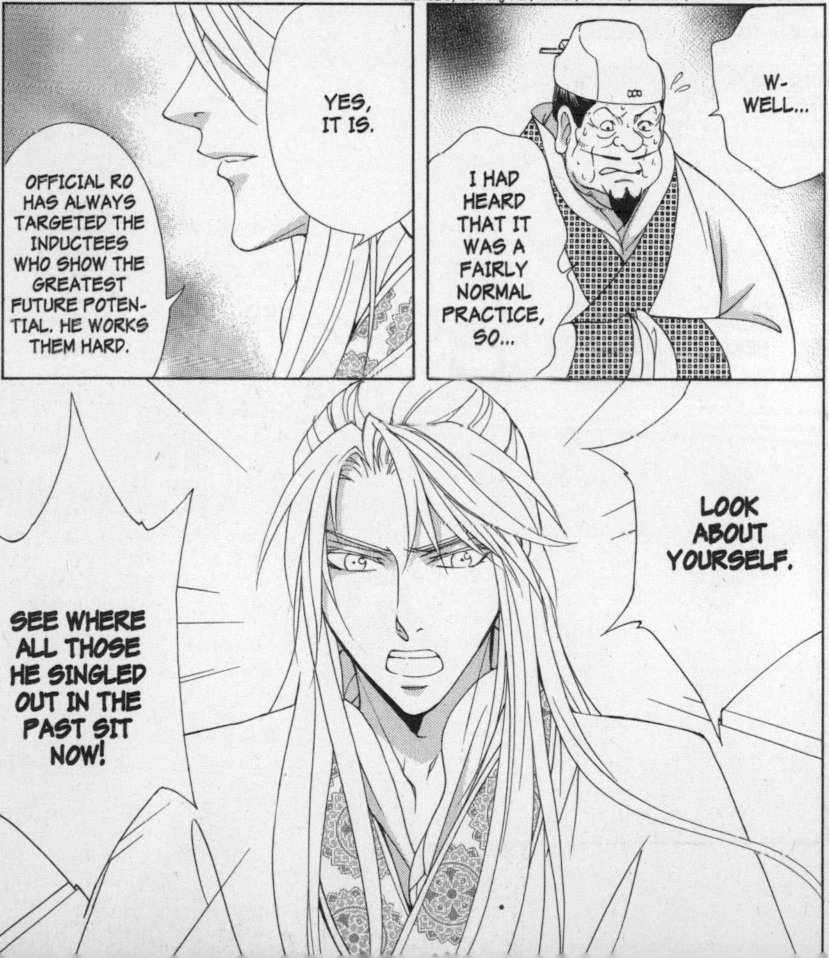
W-WELL...
I HAD HEARD THAT IT WAS A FAIRLY NORMAL PRACTICE, SO...
YES, IT IS.
OFFICIAL RO HAS ALWAYS TARGETED THE INDUCTEES WHO SHOW THE GREATEST FUTURE POTENTIAL. HE WORKS THEM HARD.
LOOK ABOUT YOURSELF.
SEE WHERE ALL THOSE HE SINGLED OUT IN THE PAST SIT NOW!

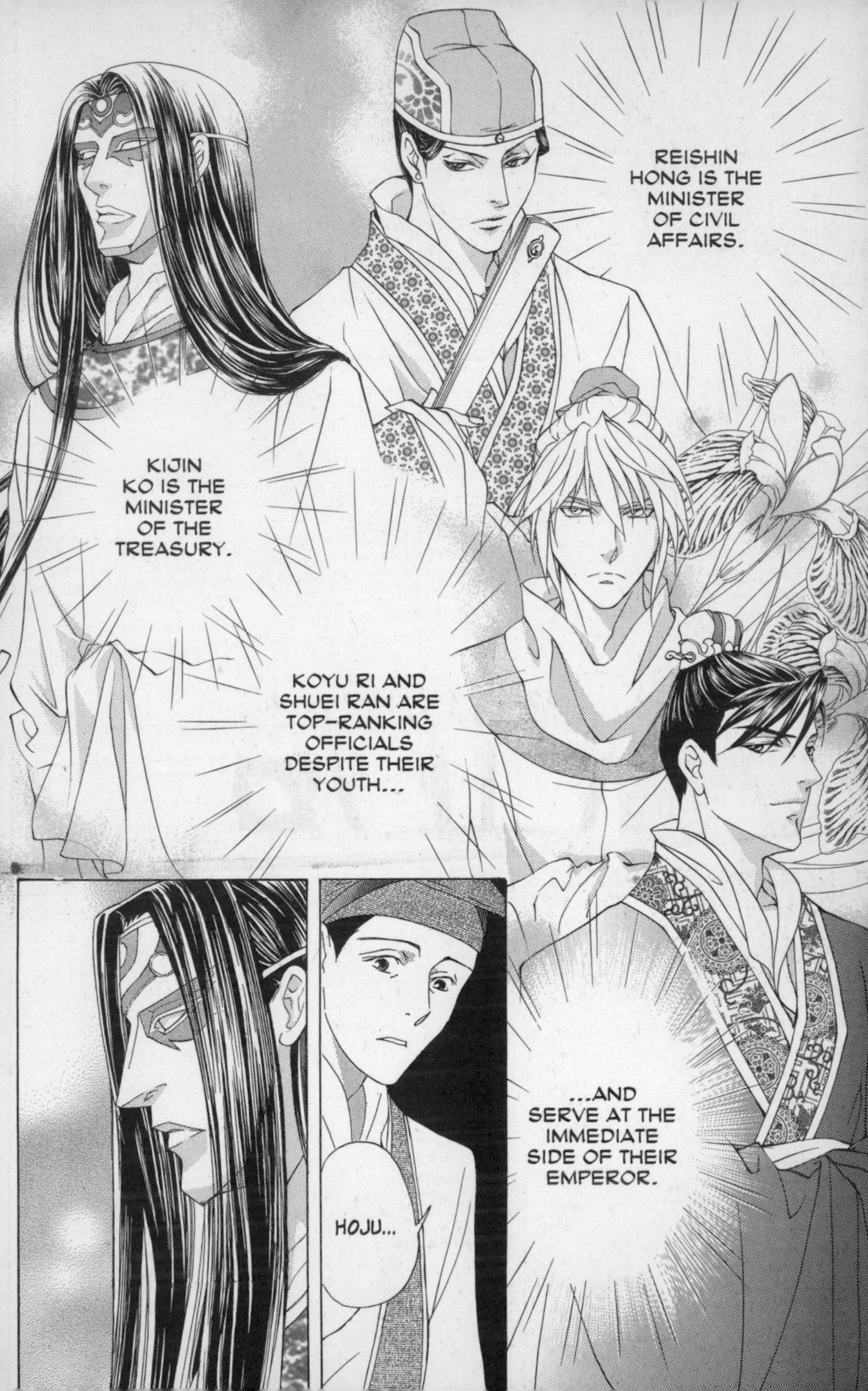
REISHIN HONG IS THE MINISTER OF CIVIL AFFAIRS.
KIJIN KO IS THE MINISTER OF THE TREASURY.
KOYU RI AND SHUEI RAN ARE TOP-RANKING OFFICIALS DESPITE THEIR YOUTH...
...AND SERVE AT THE IMMEDIATE SIDE OF THEIR EMPEROR.
HOJU...

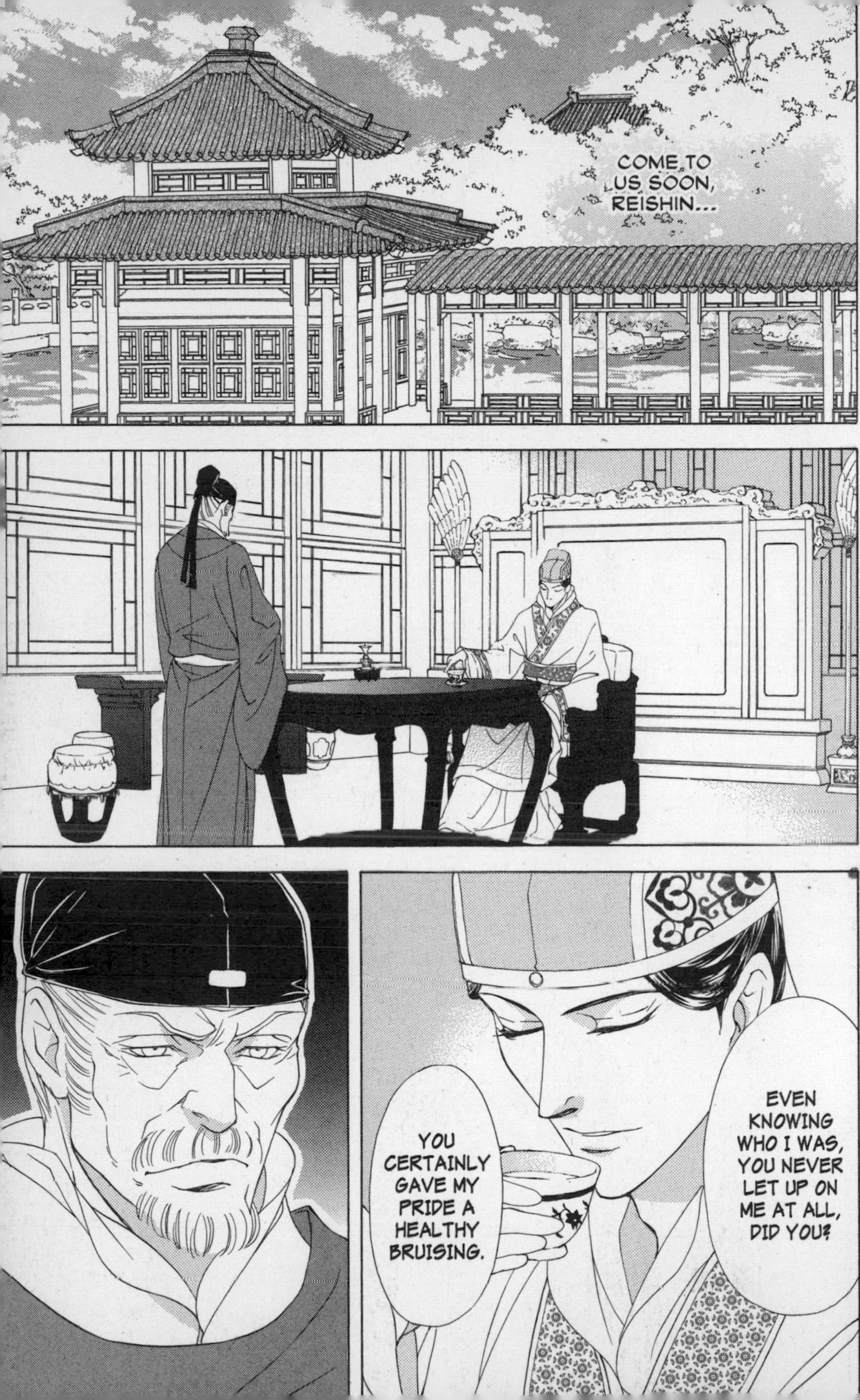
COME TO US SOON, REISHIN...
EVEN KNOWING WHO I WAS, YOU NEVER LET UP ON ME AT ALL, DID YOU?
YOU CERTAINLY GAVE MY PRIDE A HEALTHY BRUISING.

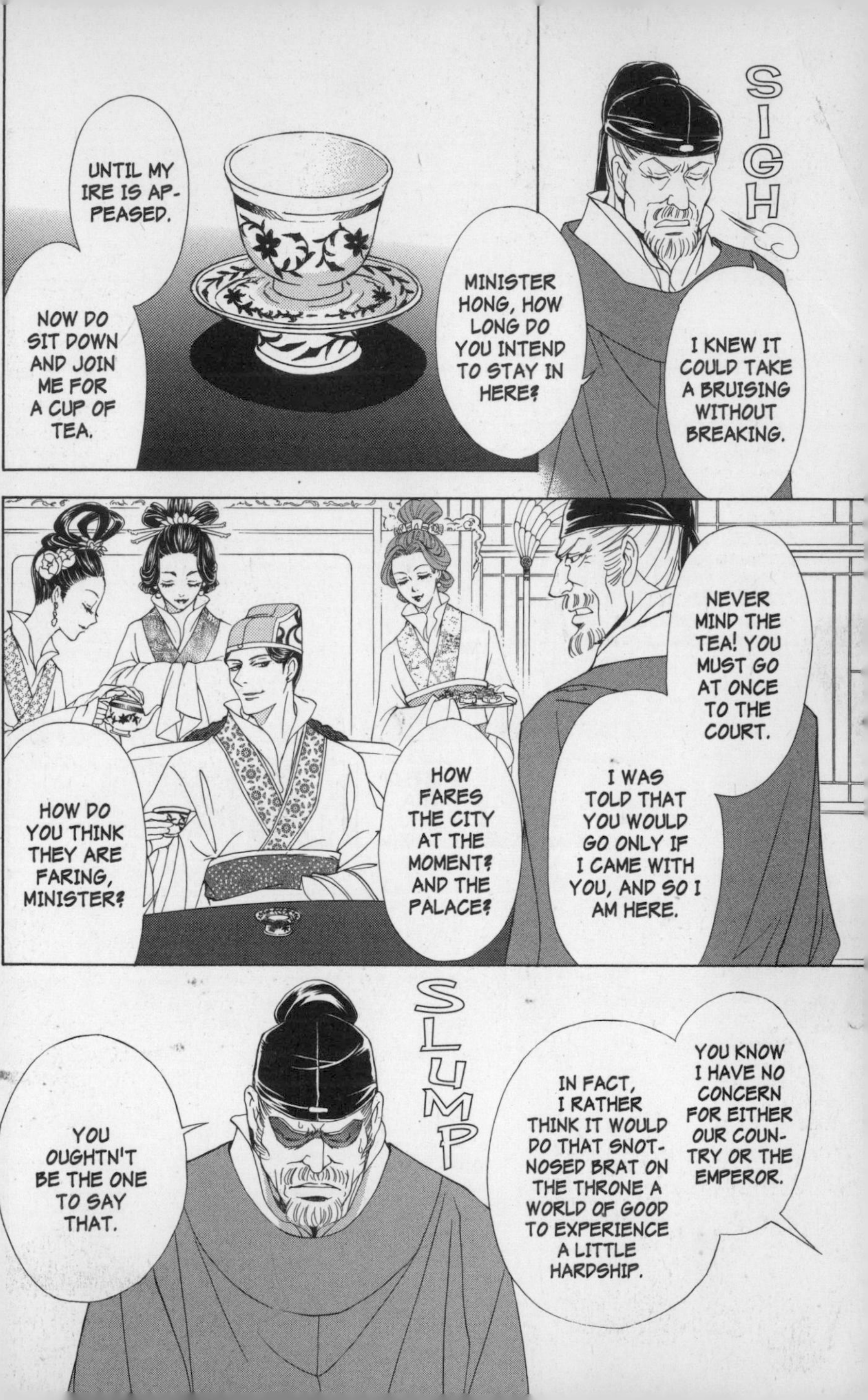
SIGH
I KNEW IT COULD TAKE A BRUISING WITHOUT BREAKING.
MINISTER HONG, HOW LONG DO YOU INTEND TO STAY IN HERE?
UNTIL MY IRE IS AP-PEASED.
NOW DO SIT DOWN AND JOIN ME FOR A CUP OF TEA.
NEVER MIND THE TEA! YOU MUST GO AT ONCE TO THE COURT.
I WAS TOLD THAT YOU WOULD GO ONLY IF I CAME WITH YOU, AND SO I AM HERE.
HOW FARES THE CITY AT THE MOMENT? AND THE PALACE?
HOW DO YOU THINK THEY ARE FARING, MINISTER?
YOU KNOW I HAVE NO CONCERN FOR EITHER OUR COUN-TRY OR THE EMPEROR.
IN FACT, I RATHER THINK IT WOULD DO THAT SNOT-NOSED BRAT ON THE THRONE A WORLD OF GOOD TO EXPERIENCE A LITTLE HARDSHIP.
SLUMP
YOU OUGHTN'T BE THE ONE TO SAY THAT.

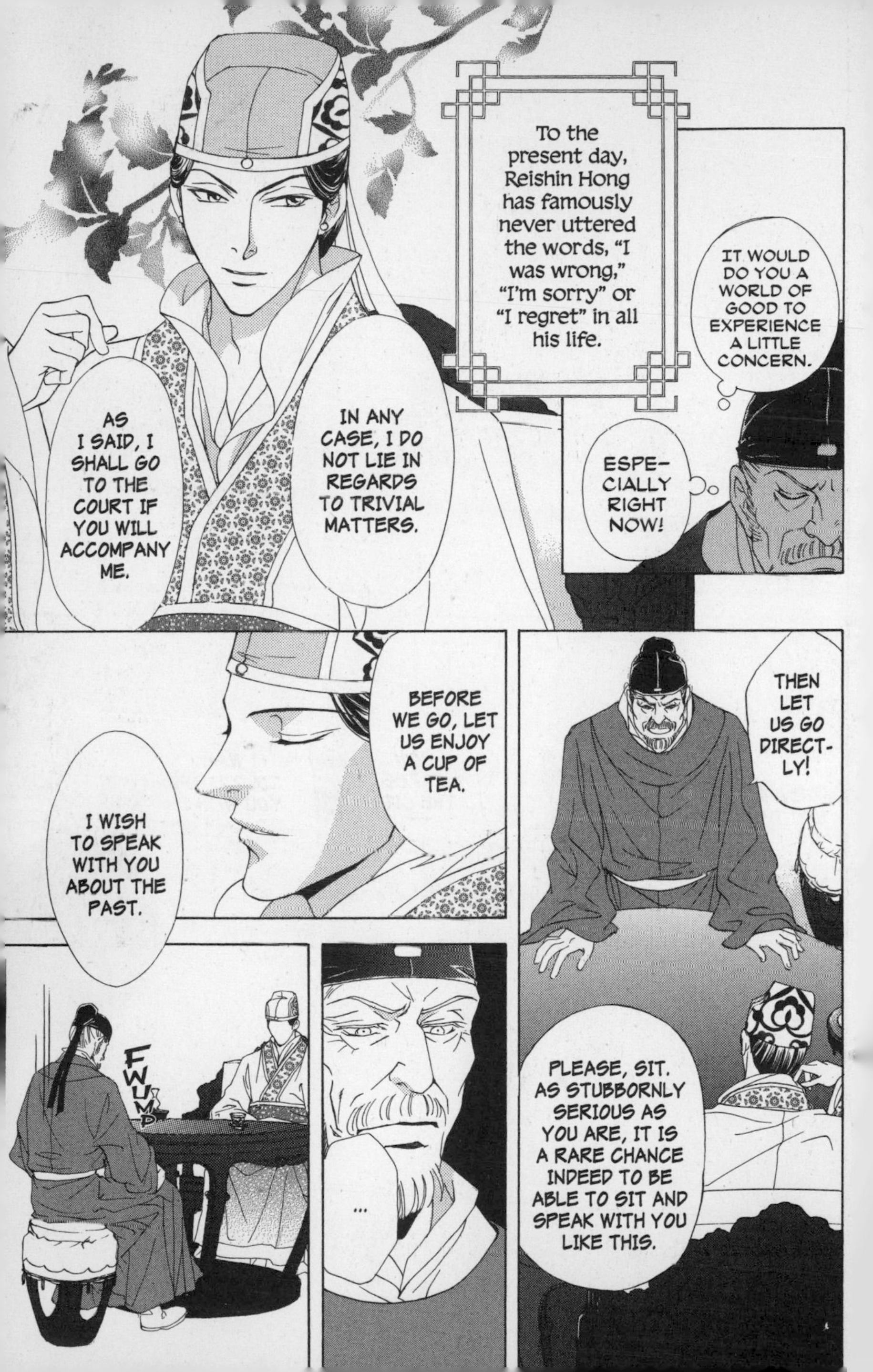
To the present day, Reishin Hong has famously never uttered the words, "I was wrong," "I'm sorry" or "I regret" in all his life.
IT WOULD DO YOU A WORLD OF GOOD TO EXPERIENCE A LITTLE CONCERN.
ESPE- CIALLY RIGHT NOW!
IN ANY CASE, I DO NOT LIE IN REGARDS TO TRIVIAL MATTERS.
AS I SAID, I SHALL GO TO THE COURT IF YOU WILL ACCOMPANY ME.
THEN LET US GO DIRECT- LY!
PLEASE, SIT. AS STUBBORNLY SERIOUS AS YOU ARE, IT IS A RARE CHANCE INDEED TO BE ABLE TO SIT AND SPEAK WITH YOU LIKE THIS.
BEFORE WE GO, LET US ENJOY A CUP OF TEA.
I WISH TO SPEAK WITH YOU ABOUT THE PAST.
...
FWUMP

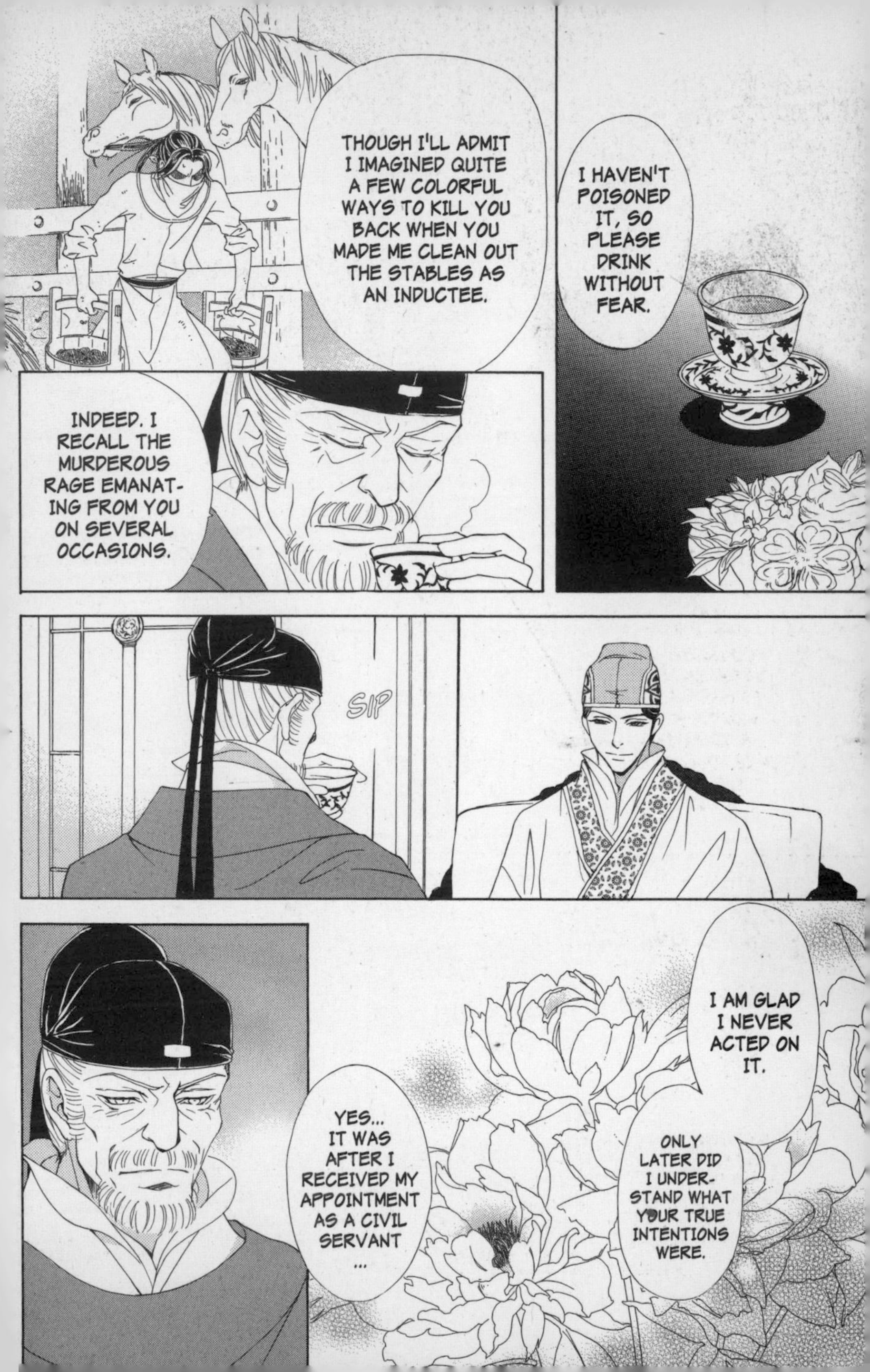
I HAVEN'T POISONED IT, SO PLEASE DRINK WITHOUT FEAR.
THOUGH I'LL ADMIT I IMAGINED QUITE A FEW COLORFUL WAYS TO KILL YOU BACK WHEN YOU MADE ME CLEAN OUT THE STABLES AS AN INDUCTEE.
INDEED. I RECALL THE MURDEROUS RAGE EMANAT-ING FROM YOU ON SEVERAL OCCASIONS.
SIP
I AM GLAD I NEVER ACTED ON IT.
ONLY LATER DID I UNDER-STAND WHAT YOUR TRUE INTENTIONS WERE.
YES... IT WAS AFTER I RECEIVED MY APPOINTMENT AS A CIVIL SERVANT ...

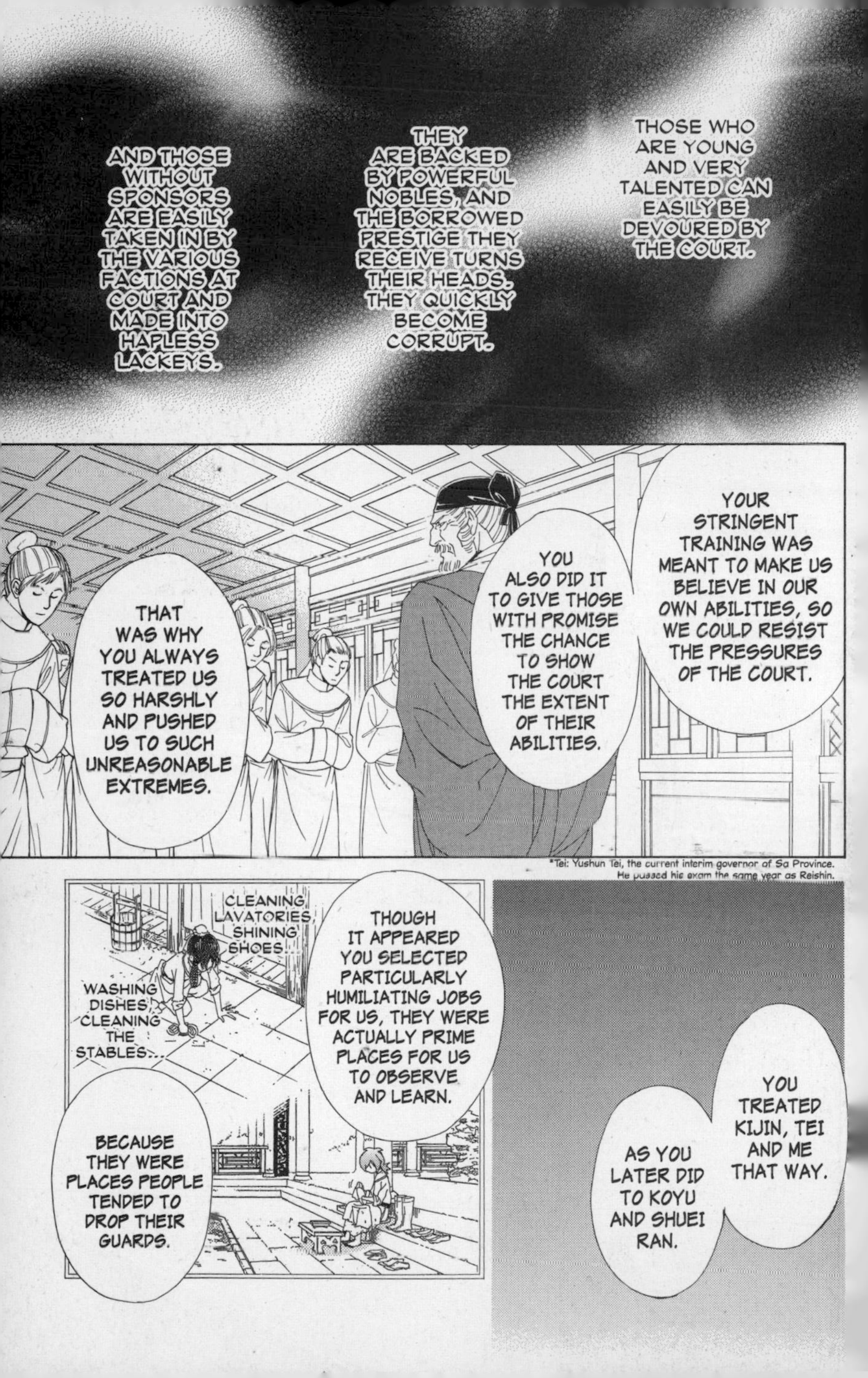
THOSE WHO ARE YOUNG AND VERY TALENTED CAN EASILY BE DEVOURED BY THE COURT.
THEY ARE BACKED BY POWERFUL NOBLES, AND THE BORROWED PRESTIGE THEY RECEIVE TURNS THEIR HEADS. THEY QUICKLY BECOME CORRUPT.
AND THOSE WITHOUT SPONSORS ARE EASILY TAKEN IN BY THE VARIOUS FACTIONS AT COURT AND MADE INTO HAPLESS LACKEYS.
YOUR STRINGENT TRAINING WAS MEANT TO MAKE US BELIEVE IN OUR OWN ABILITIES, SO WE COULD RESIST THE PRESSURES OF THE COURT.
YOU ALSO DID IT TO GIVE THOSE WITH PROMISE THE CHANCE TO SHOW THE COURT THE EXTENT OF THEIR ABILITIES.
THAT WAS WHY YOU ALWAYS TREATED US SO HARSHLY AND PUSHED US TO SUCH UNREASONABLE EXTREMES.
*Tei: Yushun Tei, the current interim governor of Sa Province. He passed his exam the same year as Reishin.
YOU TREATED KIJIN, TEI AND ME THAT WAY.
AS YOU LATER DID TO KOYU AND SHUEI RAN.
THOUGH IT APPEARED YOU SELECTED PARTICULARLY HUMILIATING JOBS FOR US, THEY WERE ACTUALLY PRIME PLACES FOR US TO OBSERVE AND LEARN.
CLEANING LAVATORIES, SHINING SHOES...
WASHING DISHES, CLEANING THE STABLES...
BECAUSE THEY WERE PLACES PEOPLE TENDED TO DROP THEIR GUARDS.

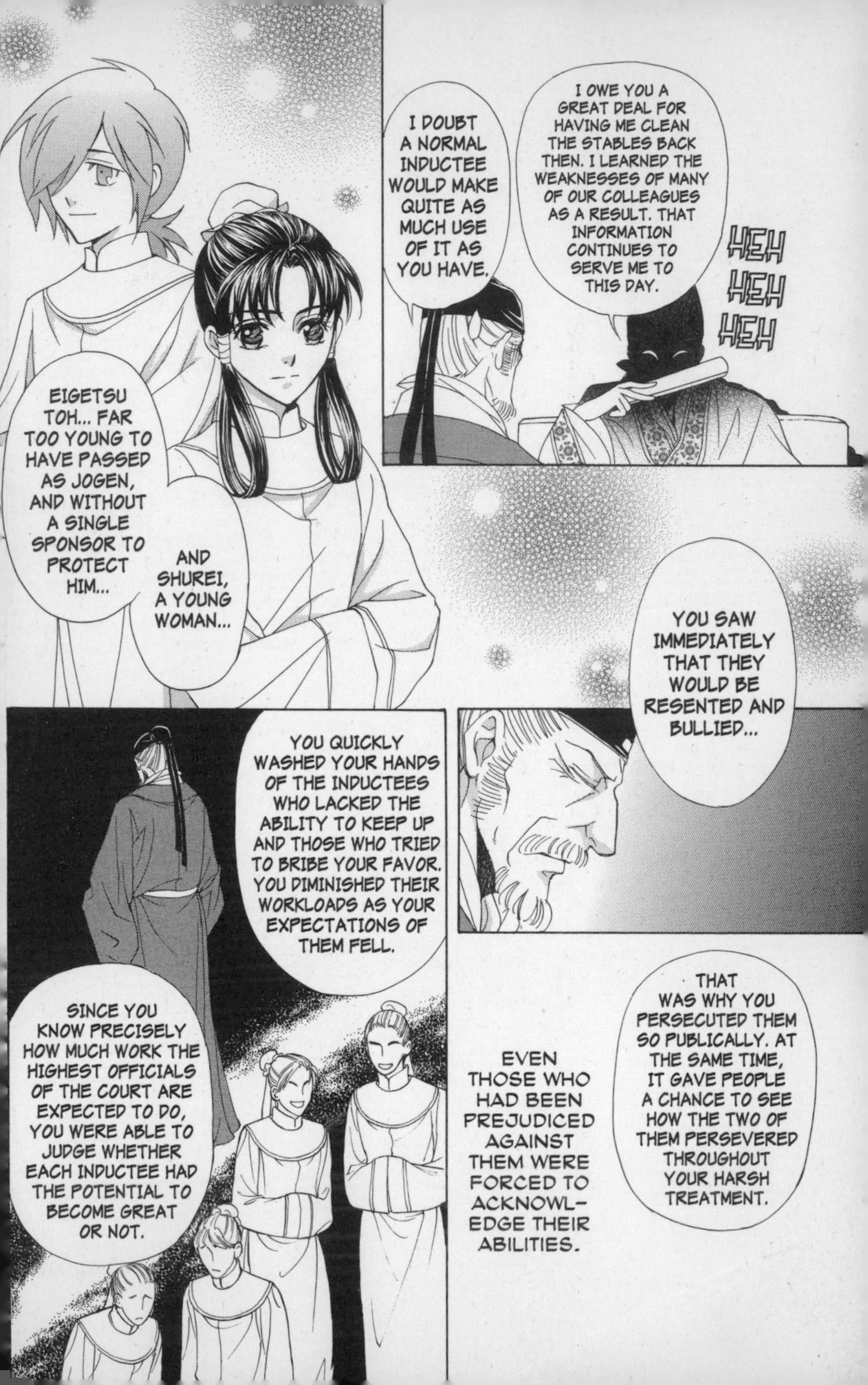
I OWE YOU A GREAT DEAL FOR HAVING ME CLEAN THE STABLES BACK THEN. I LEARNED THE WEAKNESSES OF MANY OF OUR COLLEAGUES AS A RESULT. THAT INFORMATION CONTINUES TO SERVE ME TO THIS DAY.
HEH HEH HEH
I DOUBT A NORMAL INDUCTEE WOULD MAKE QUITE AS MUCH USE OF IT AS YOU HAVE.
EIGETSU TOH... FAR TOO YOUNG TO HAVE PASSED AS JOGEN, AND WITHOUT A SINGLE SPONSOR TO PROTECT HIM...
AND SHUREI, A YOUNG WOMAN...
YOU SAW IMMEDIATELY THAT THEY WOULD BE RESENTED AND BULLIED...
THAT WAS WHY YOU PERSECUTED THEM SO PUBLICALLY. AT THE SAME TIME, IT GAVE PEOPLE A CHANCE TO SEE HOW THE TWO OF THEM PERSEVERED THROUGHOUT YOUR HARSH TREATMENT.
EVEN THOSE WHO HAD BEEN PREJUDICED AGAINST THEM WERE FORCED TO ACKNOWL-EDGE THEIR ABILITIES.
YOU QUICKLY WASHED YOUR HANDS OF THE INDUCTEES WHO LACKED THE ABILITY TO KEEP UP AND THOSE WHO TRIED TO BRIBE YOUR FAVOR. YOU DIMINISHED THEIR WORKLOADS AS YOUR EXPECTATIONS OF THEM FELL.
SINCE YOU KNOW PRECISELY HOW MUCH WORK THE HIGHEST OFFICIALS OF THE COURT ARE EXPECTED TO DO, YOU WERE ABLE TO JUDGE WHETHER EACH INDUCTEE HAD THE POTENTIAL TO BECOME GREAT OR NOT.

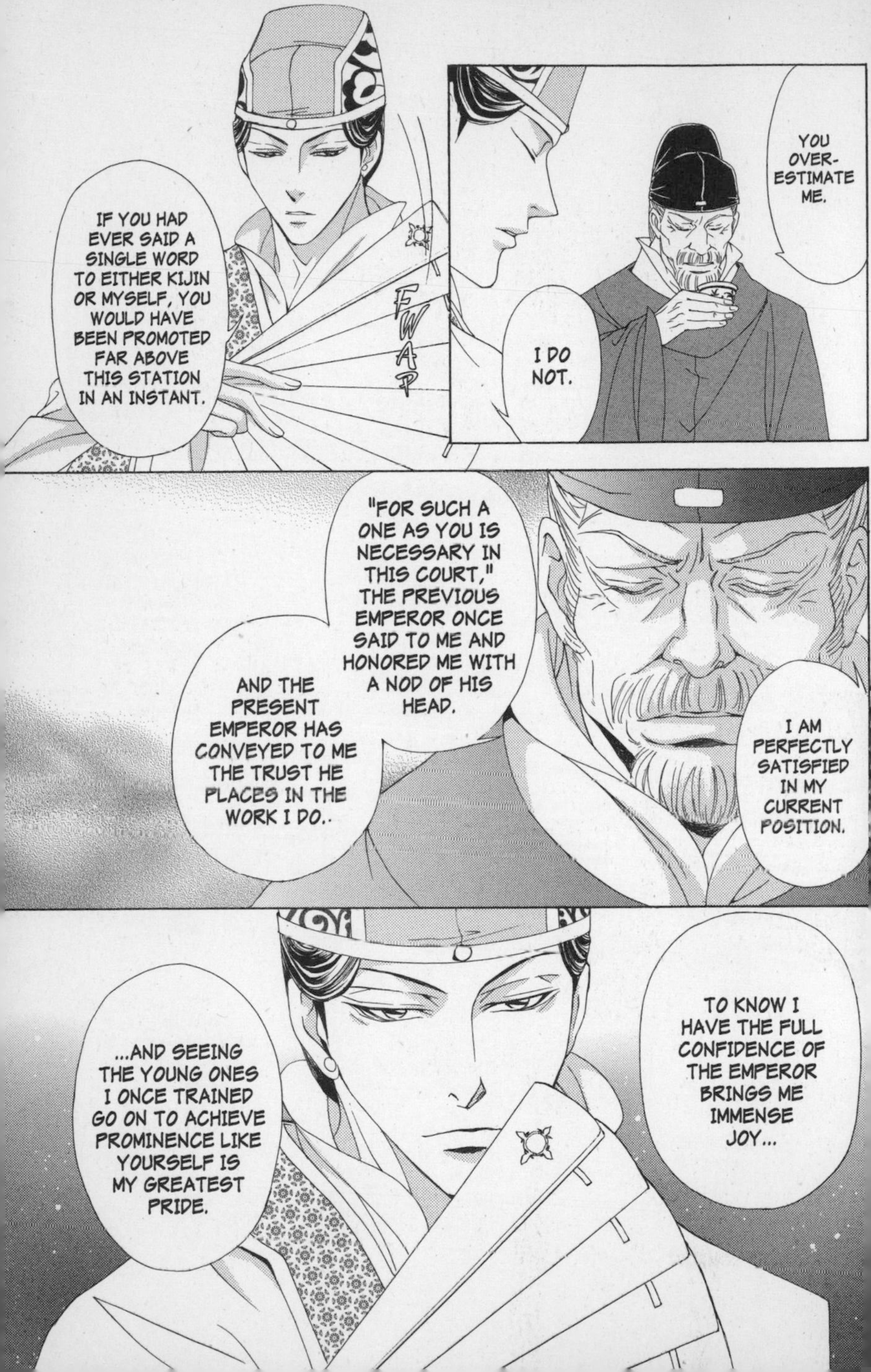
YOU OVER-ESTIMATE ME.
I DO NOT.
FWAP
IF YOU HAD EVER SAID A SINGLE WORD TO EITHER KIJIN OR MYSELF, YOU WOULD HAVE BEEN PROMOTED FAR ABOVE THIS STATION IN AN INSTANT.
I AM PERFECTLY SATISFIED IN MY CURRENT POSITION.
"FOR SUCH A ONE AS YOU IS NECESSARY IN THIS COURT," THE PREVIOUS EMPEROR ONCE SAID TO ME AND HONORED ME WITH A NOD OF HIS HEAD.
AND THE PRESENT EMPEROR HAS CONVEYED TO ME THE TRUST HE PLACES IN THE WORK I DO..
TO KNOW I HAVE THE FULL CONFIDENCE OF THE EMPEROR BRINGS ME IMMENSE JOY...
...AND SEEING THE YOUNG ONES I ONCE TRAINED GO ON TO ACHIEVE PROMINENCE LIKE YOURSELF IS MY GREATEST PRIDE.

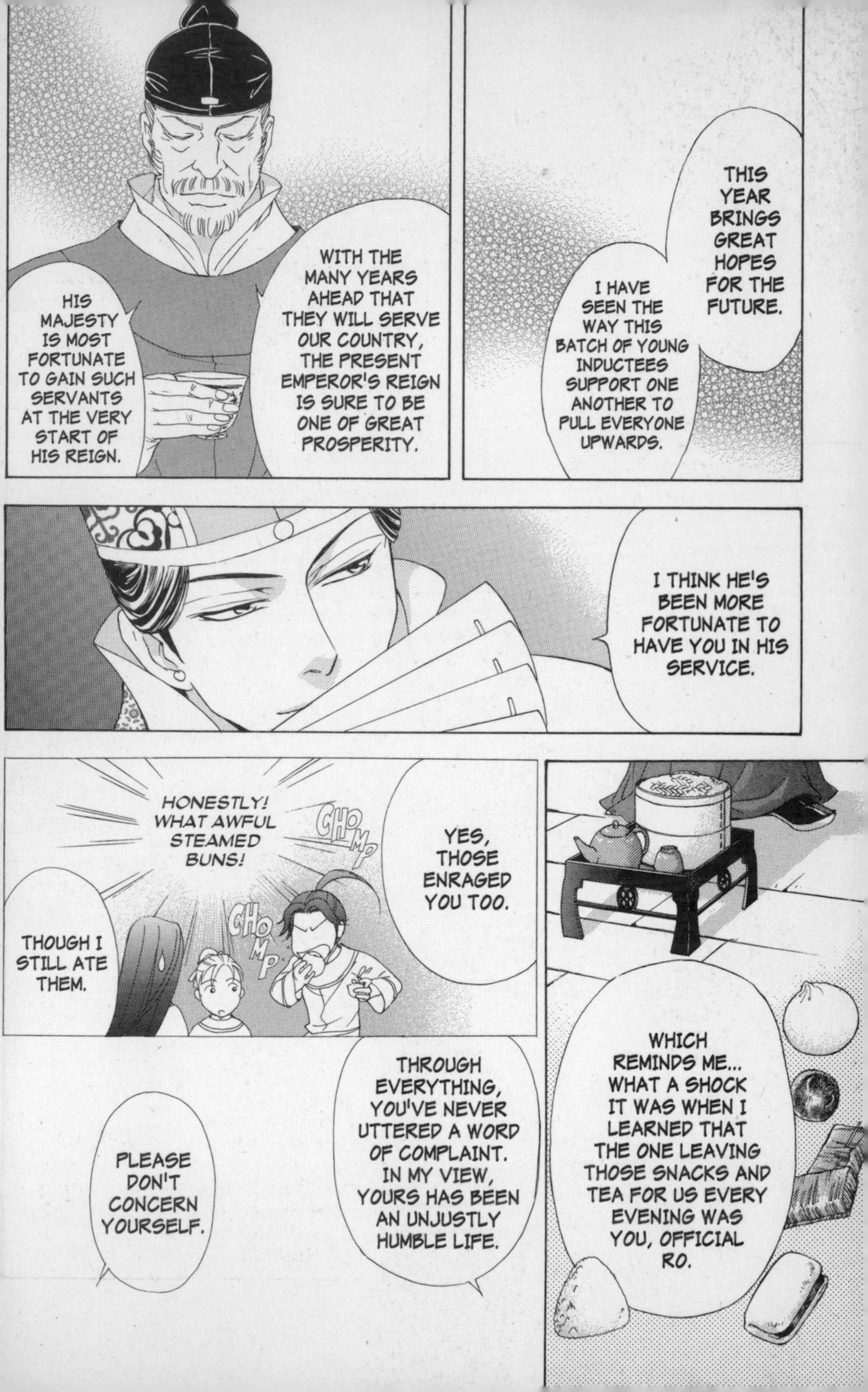
THIS YEAR BRINGS GREAT HOPES FOR THE FUTURE.
I HAVE SEEN THE WAY THIS BATCH OF YOUNG INDUCTEES SUPPORT ONE ANOTHER TO PULL EVERYONE UPWARDS.
WITH THE MANY YEARS AHEAD THAT THEY WILL SERVE OUR COUNTRY, THE PRESENT EMPEROR'S REIGN IS SURE TO BE ONE OF GREAT PROSPERITY.
HIS MAJESTY IS MOST FORTUNATE TO GAIN SUCH SERVANTS AT THE VERY START OF HIS REIGN.
I THINK HE'S BEEN MORE FORTUNATE TO HAVE YOU IN HIS SERVICE.
WHICH REMINDS ME... WHAT A SHOCK IT WAS WHEN I LEARNED THAT THE ONE LEAVING THOSE SNACKS AND TEA FOR US EVERY EVENING WAS YOU, OFFICIAL RO.
YES, THOSE ENRAGED YOU TOO.
CHOMP
HONESTLY! WHAT AWFUL STEAMED BUNS!
CHOMP
THOUGH I STILL ATE THEM.
THROUGH EVERYTHING, YOU'VE NEVER UTTERED A WORD OF COMPLAINT. IN MY VIEW, YOURS HAS BEEN AN UNJUSTLY HUMBLE LIFE.
PLEASE DON'T CONCERN YOURSELF.

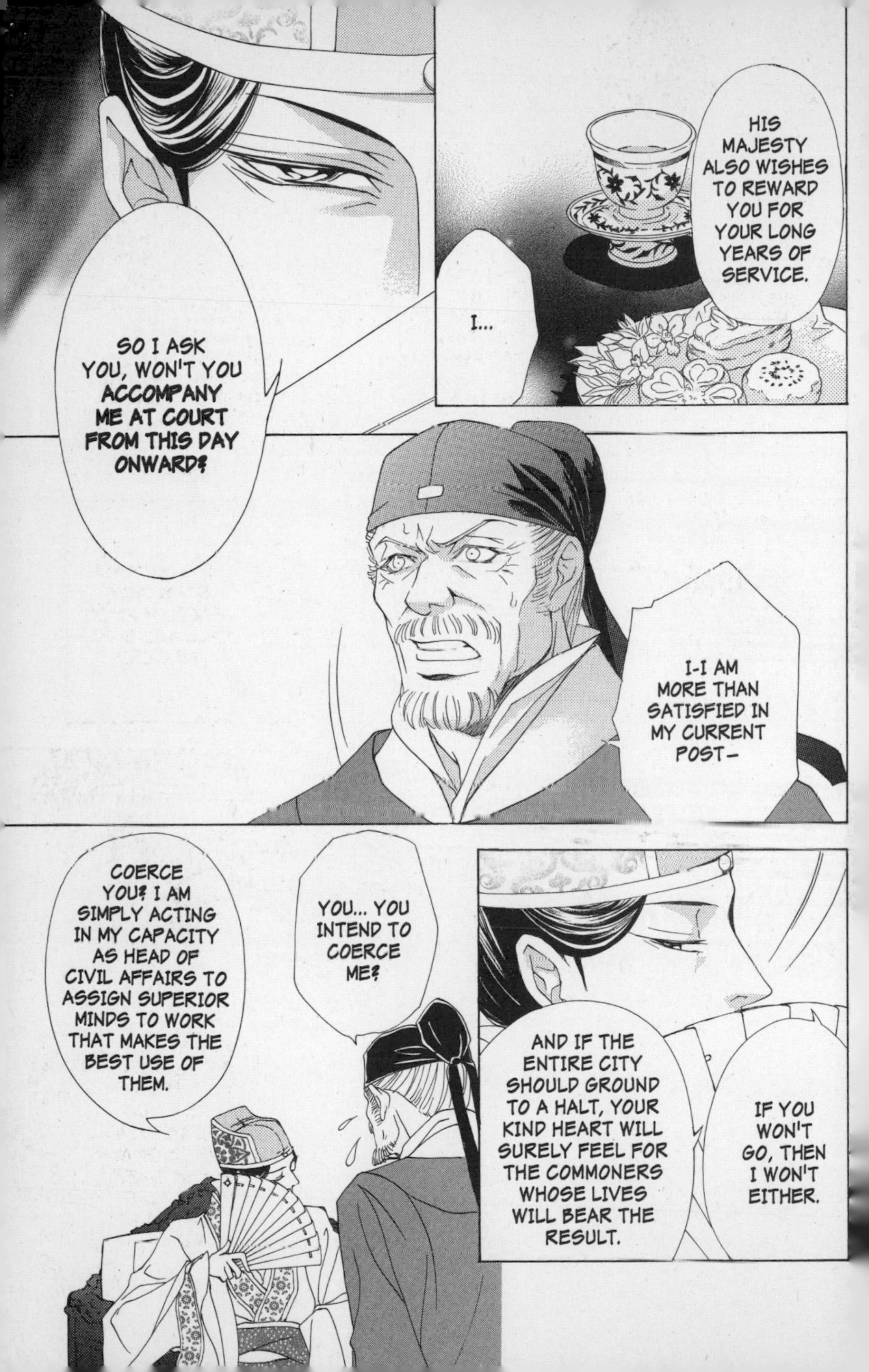
HIS MAJESTY ALSO WISHES TO REWARD YOU FOR YOUR LONG YEARS OF SERVICE.
I...
SO I ASK YOU, WON'T YOU ACCOMPANY ME AT COURT FROM THIS DAY ONWARD?
I-I AM MORE THAN SATISFIED IN MY CURRENT POST—
IF YOU WON'T GO, THEN I WON'T EITHER.
AND IF THE ENTIRE CITY SHOULD GROUND TO A HALT, YOUR KIND HEART WILL SURELY FEEL FOR THE COMMONERS WHOSE LIVES WILL BEAR THE RESULT.
YOU... YOU INTEND TO COERCE ME?
COERCE YOU? I AM SIMPLY ACTING IN MY CAPACITY AS HEAD OF CIVIL AFFAIRS TO ASSIGN SUPERIOR MINDS TO WORK THAT MAKES THE BEST USE OF THEM.

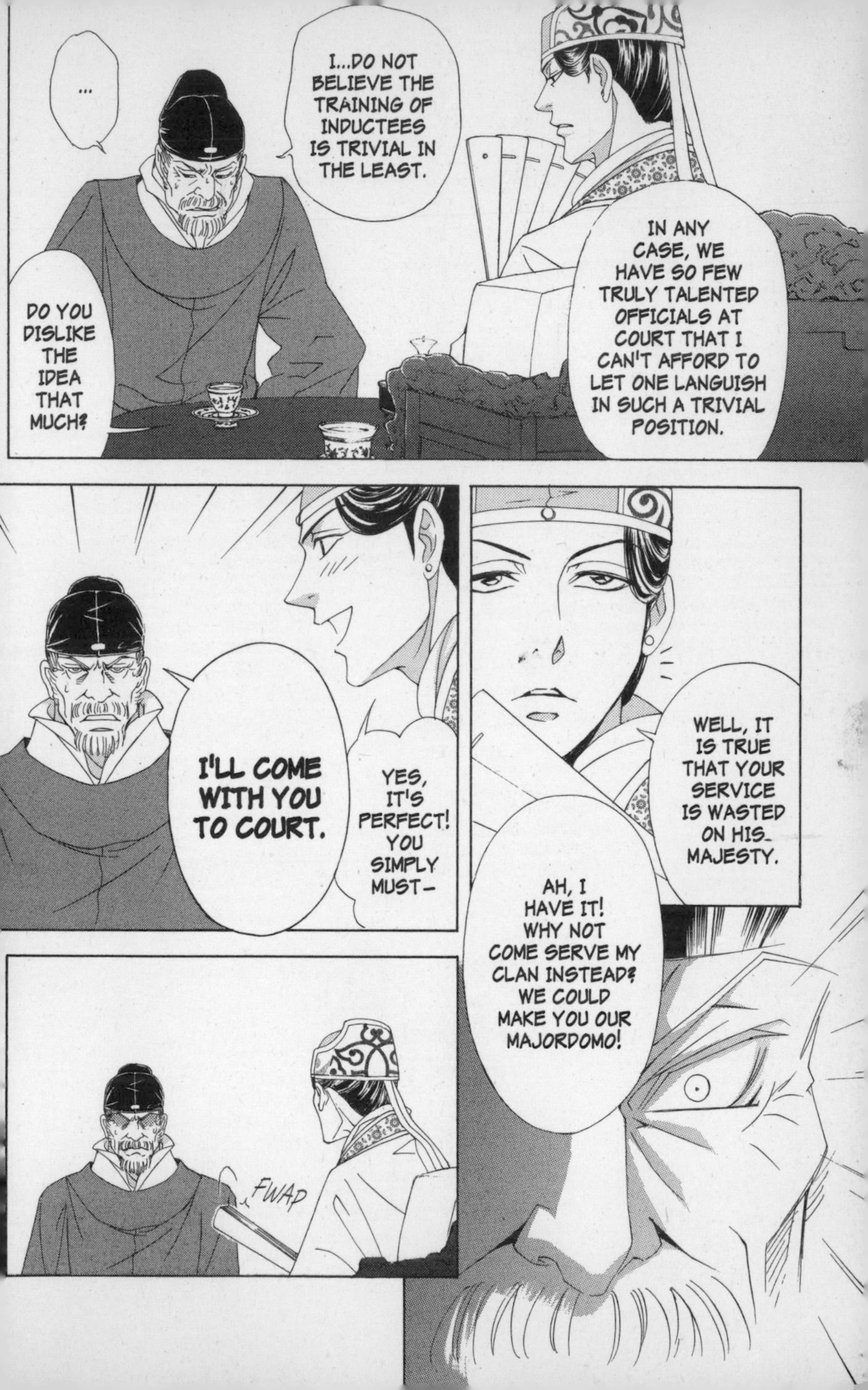
I...DO NOT BELIEVE THE TRAINING OF INDUCTEES IS TRIVIAL IN THE LEAST.
IN ANY CASE, WE HAVE SO FEW TRULY TALENTED OFFICIALS AT COURT THAT I CAN'T AFFORD TO LET ONE LANGUISH IN SUCH A TRIVIAL POSITION.
DO YOU DISLIKE THE IDEA THAT MUCH?
...
WELL, IT IS TRUE THAT YOUR SERVICE IS WASTED ON HIS MAJESTY.
AH, I HAVE IT! WHY NOT COME SERVE MY CLAN INSTEAD? WE COULD MAKE YOU OUR MAJORDOMO!
YES, IT'S PERFECT! YOU SIMPLY MUST—
I'LL COME WITH YOU TO COURT.
FWAP

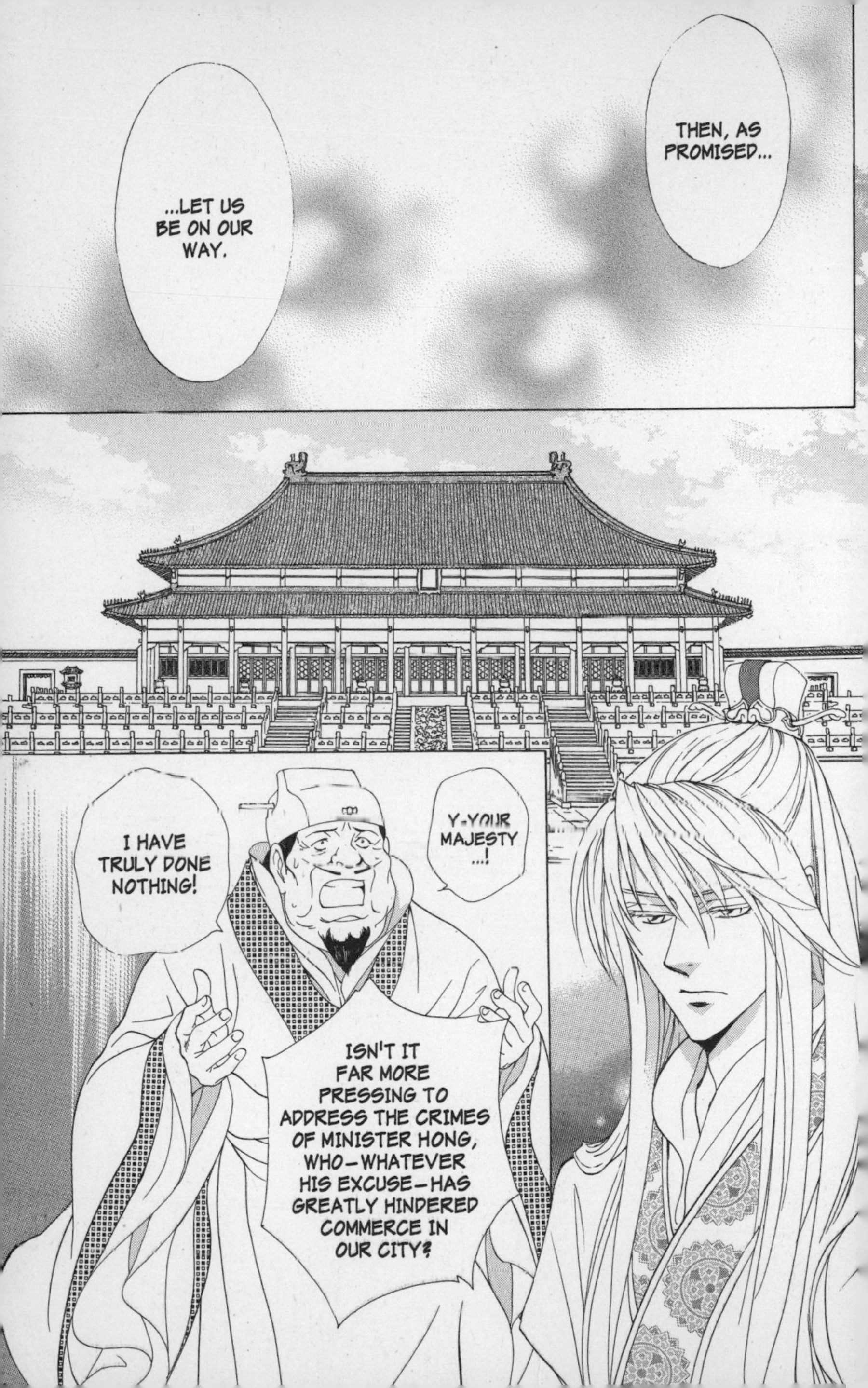
THEN, AS PROMISED...
...LET US BE ON OUR WAY.
Y-YOUR MAJESTY ...!
I HAVE TRULY DONE NOTHING!
ISN'T IT FAR MORE PRESSING TO ADDRESS THE CRIMES OF MINISTER HONG, WHO—WHATEVER HIS EXCUSE—HAS GREATLY HINDERED COMMERCE IN OUR CITY?

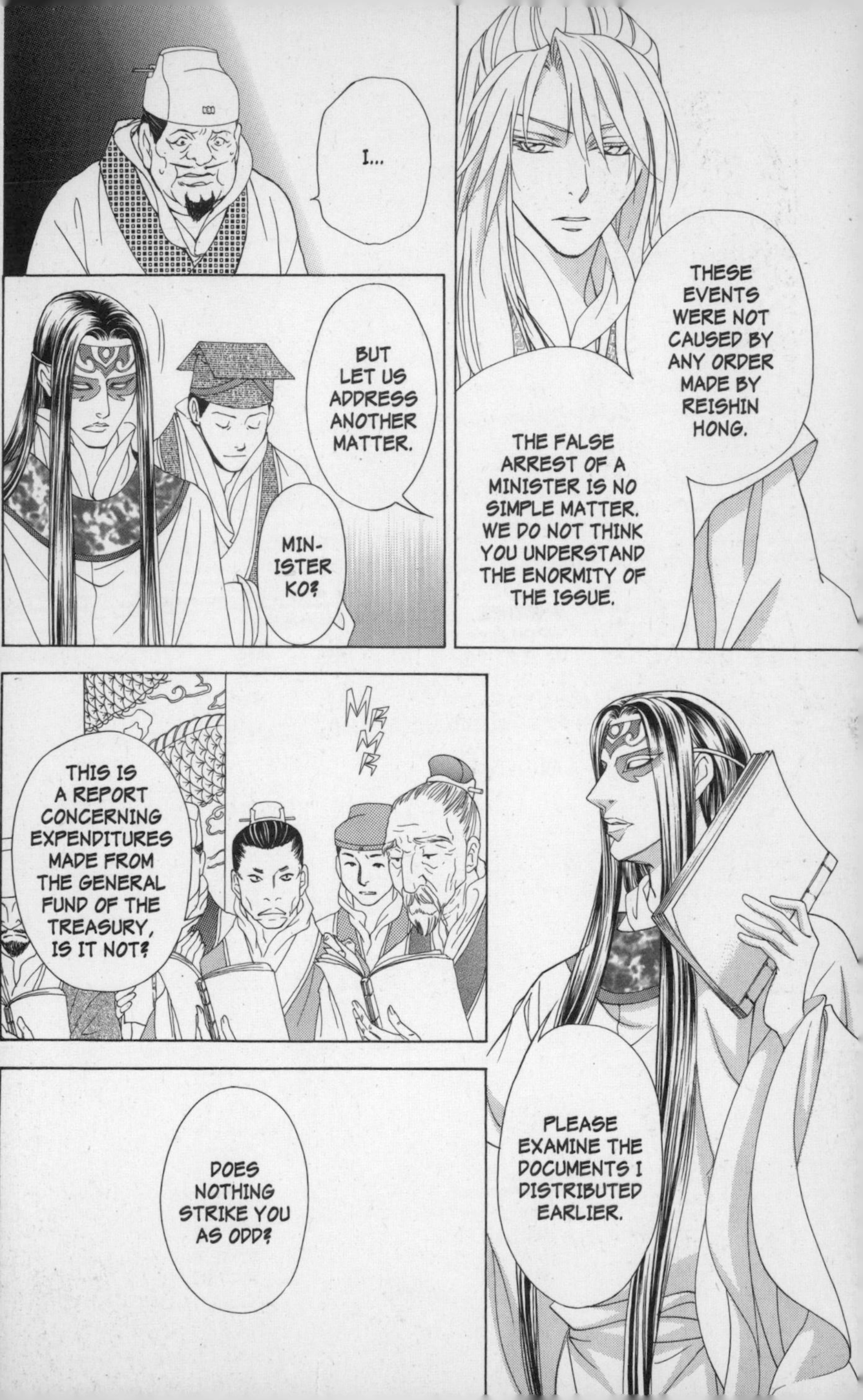
THESE EVENTS WERE NOT CAUSED BY ANY ORDER MADE BY REISHIN HONG.
THE FALSE ARREST OF A MINISTER IS NO SIMPLE MATTER. WE DO NOT THINK YOU UNDERSTAND THE ENORMITY OF THE ISSUE.
I...
BUT LET US ADDRESS ANOTHER MATTER.
MIN-ISTER KO?
PLEASE EXAMINE THE DOCUMENTS I DISTRIBUTED EARLIER.
MRMR
THIS IS A REPORT CONCERNING EXPENDITURES MADE FROM THE GENERAL FUND OF THE TREASURY, IS IT NOT?
DOES NOTHING STRIKE YOU AS ODD?

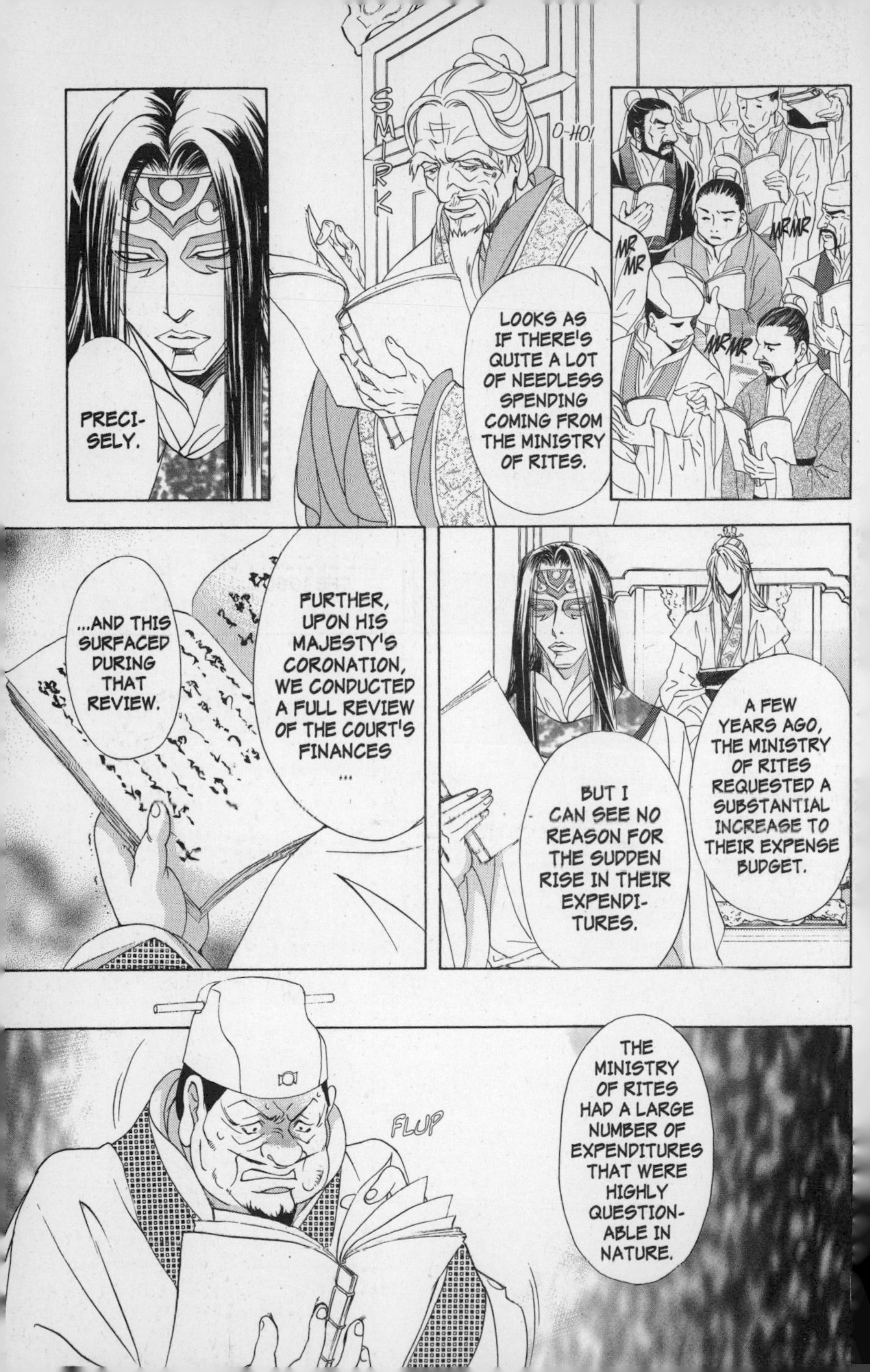
MRMR
MR MR
MRMR
SMIRK
O-HO!
LOOKS AS IF THERE'S QUITE A LOT OF NEEDLESS SPENDING COMING FROM THE MINISTRY OF RITES.
PRECI-SELY.
A FEW YEARS AGO, THE MINISTRY OF RITES REQUESTED A SUBSTANTIAL INCREASE TO THEIR EXPENSE BUDGET.
BUT I CAN SEE NO REASON FOR THE SUDDEN RISE IN THEIR EXPENDI-TURES.
FURTHER, UPON HIS MAJESTY'S CORONATION, WE CONDUCTED A FULL REVIEW OF THE COURT'S FINANCES...
...AND THIS SURFACED DURING THAT REVIEW.
THE MINISTRY OF RITES HAD A LARGE NUMBER OF EXPENDITURES THAT WERE HIGHLY QUESTION-ABLE IN NATURE.
FLUP

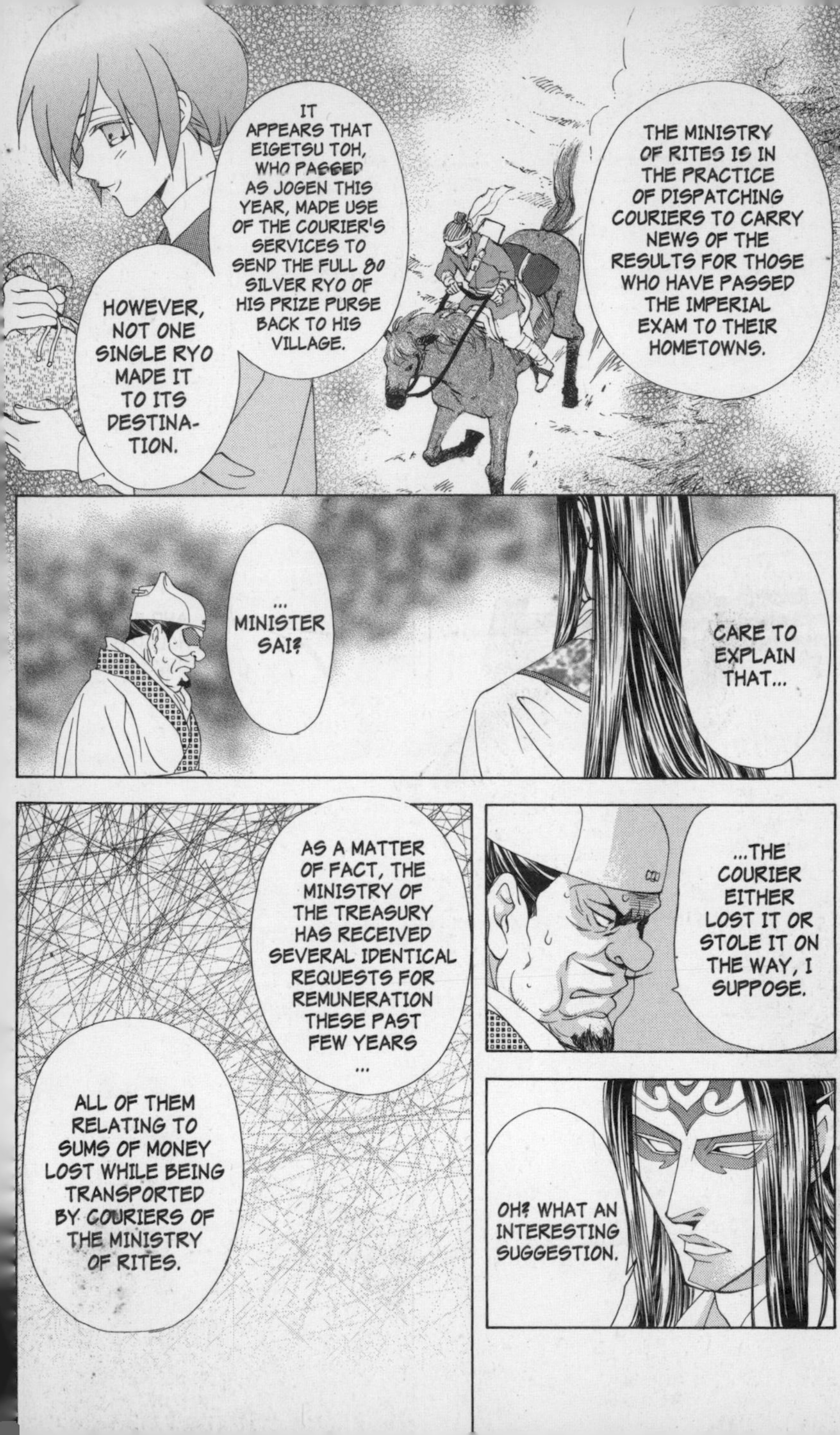
THE MINISTRY OF RITES IS IN THE PRACTICE OF DISPATCHING COURIERS TO CARRY NEWS OF THE RESULTS FOR THOSE WHO HAVE PASSED THE IMPERIAL EXAM TO THEIR HOMETOWNS.
IT APPEARS THAT EIGETSU TOH, WHO PASSED AS JOGEN THIS YEAR, MADE USE OF THE COURIER'S SERVICES TO SEND THE FULL 80 SILVER RYO OF HIS PRIZE PURSE BACK TO HIS VILLAGE.
HOWEVER, NOT ONE SINGLE RYO MADE IT TO ITS DESTINA-TION.
CARE TO EXPLAIN THAT...
... MINISTER SAI?
...THE COURIER EITHER LOST IT OR STOLE IT ON THE WAY, I SUPPOSE.
OH? WHAT AN INTERESTING SUGGESTION.
AS A MATTER OF FACT, THE MINISTRY OF THE TREASURY HAS RECEIVED SEVERAL IDENTICAL REQUESTS FOR REMUNERATION THESE PAST FEW YEARS ...
ALL OF THEM RELATING TO SUMS OF MONEY LOST WHILE BEING TRANSPORTED BY COURIERS OF THE MINISTRY OF RITES.

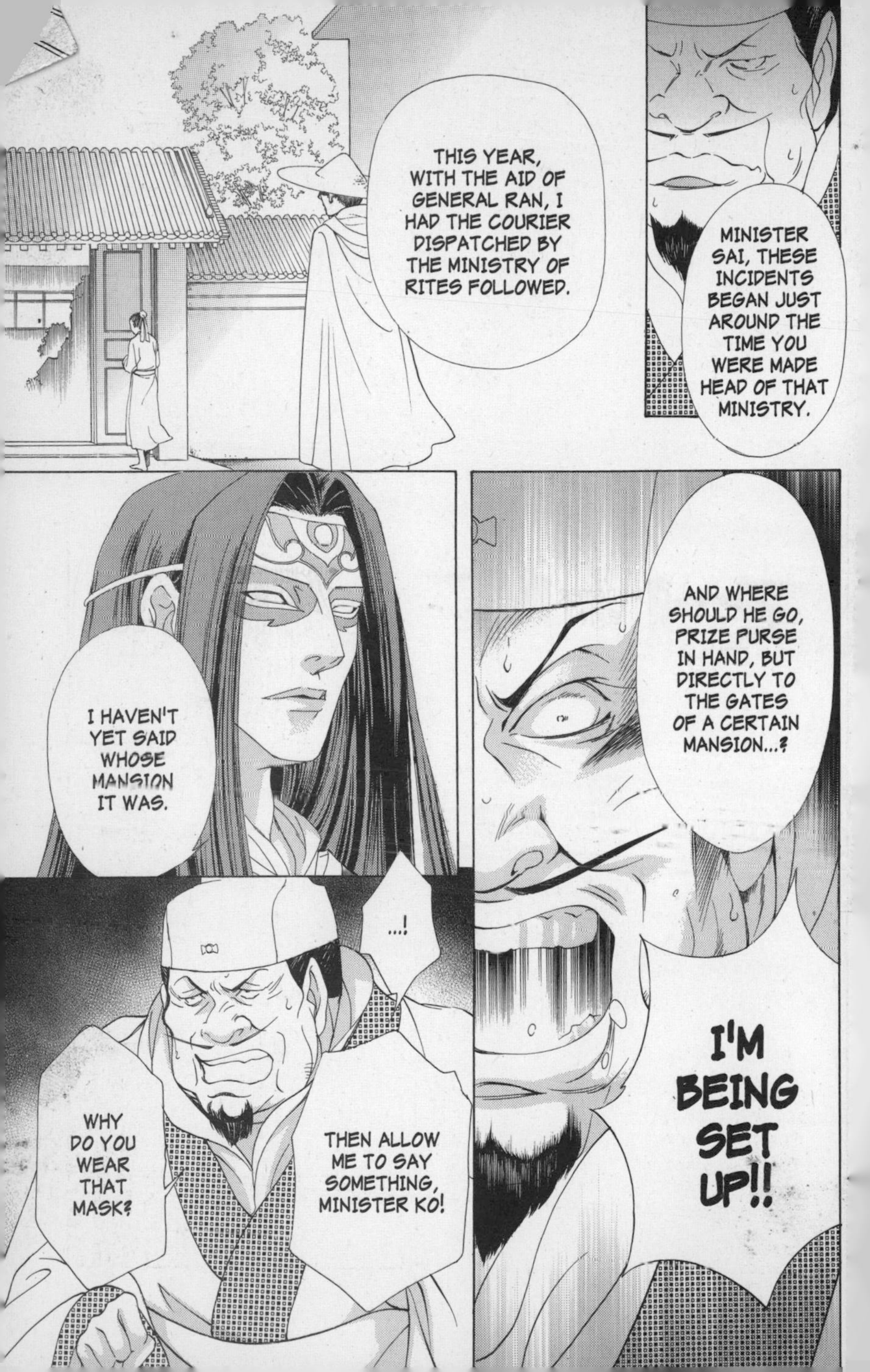
MINISTER SAI, THESE INCIDENTS BEGAN JUST AROUND THE TIME YOU WERE MADE HEAD OF THAT MINISTRY.
THIS YEAR, WITH THE AID OF GENERAL RAN, I HAD THE COURIER DISPATCHED BY THE MINISTRY OF RITES FOLLOWED.
AND WHERE SHOULD HE GO, PRIZE PURSE IN HAND, BUT DIRECTLY TO THE GATES OF A CERTAIN MANSION...?
I'M BEING SET UP!!
I HAVEN'T YET SAID WHOSE MANSION IT WAS.
...!
THEN ALLOW ME TO SAY SOMETHING, MINISTER KO!
WHY DO YOU WEAR THAT MASK?

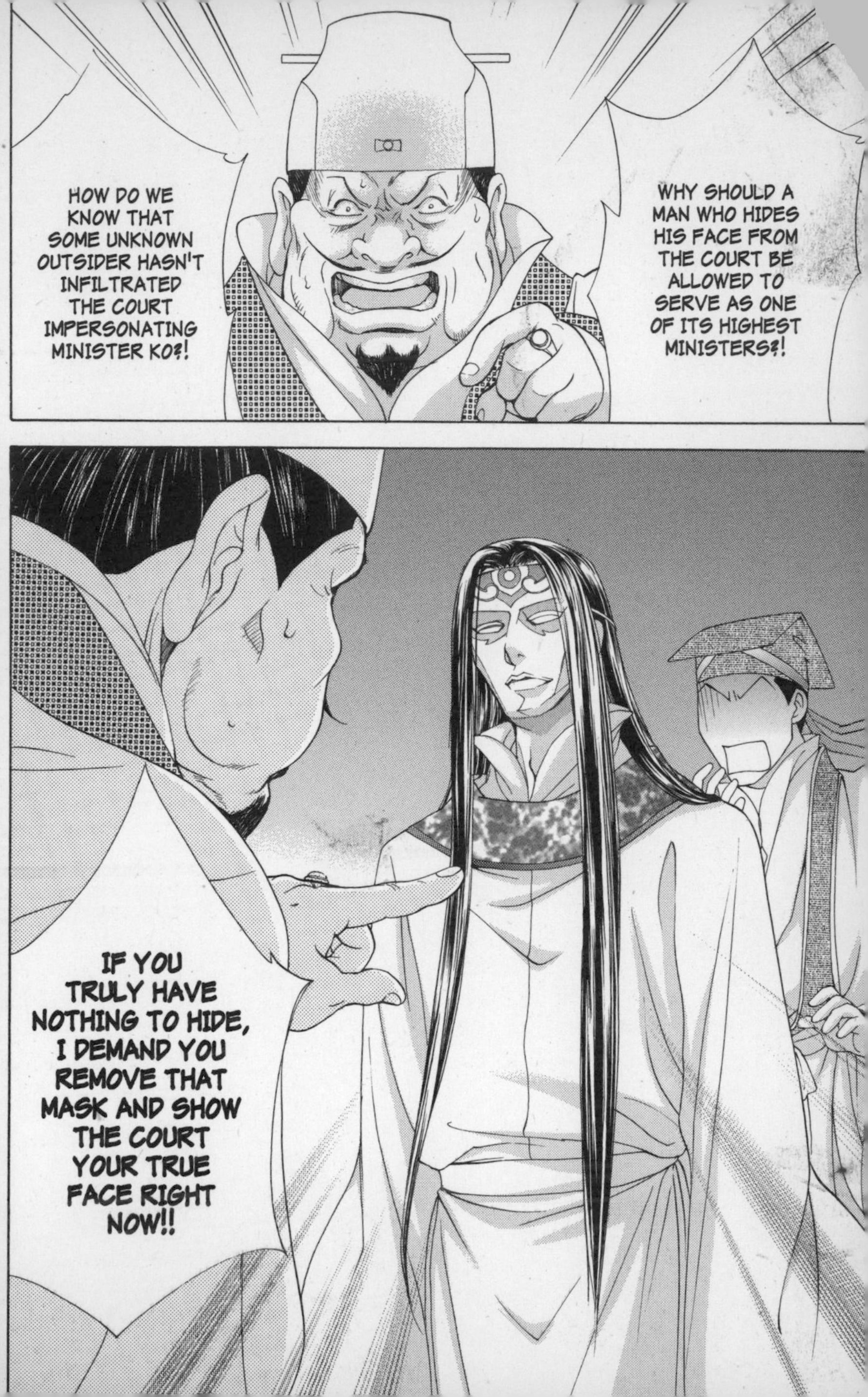
WHY SHOULD A MAN WHO HIDES HIS FACE FROM THE COURT BE ALLOWED TO SERVE AS ONE OF ITS HIGHEST MINISTERS?!
HOW DO WE KNOW THAT SOME UNKNOWN OUTSIDER HASN'T INFILTRATED THE COURT IMPERSONATING MINISTER KO?!
IF YOU TRULY HAVE NOTHING TO HIDE, I DEMAND YOU REMOVE THAT MASK AND SHOW THE COURT YOUR TRUE FACE RIGHT NOW!!

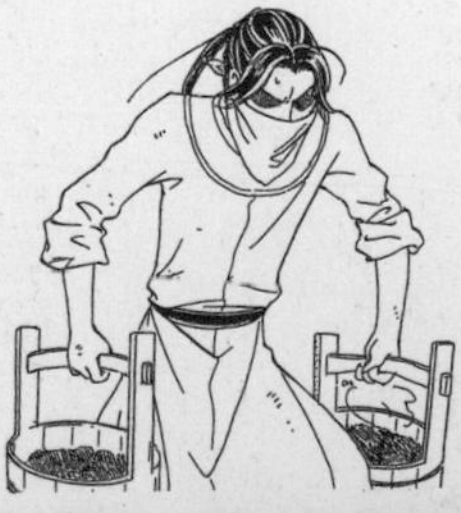

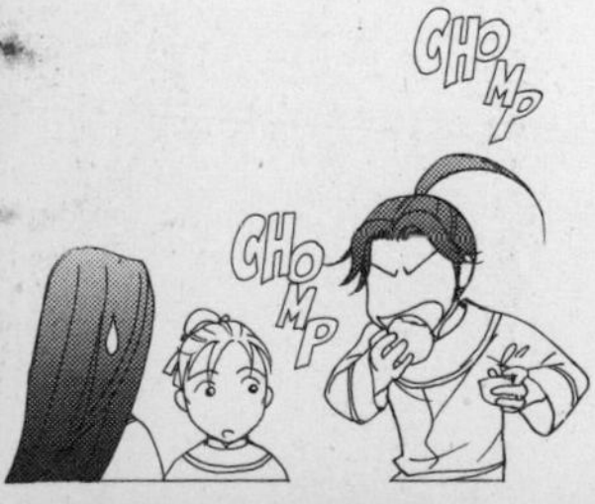
CHOMP
CHOMP

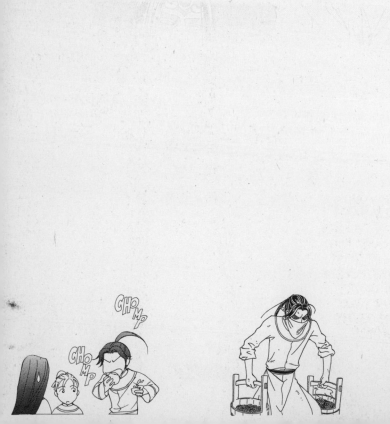

The Story of
SAIUNKOKU

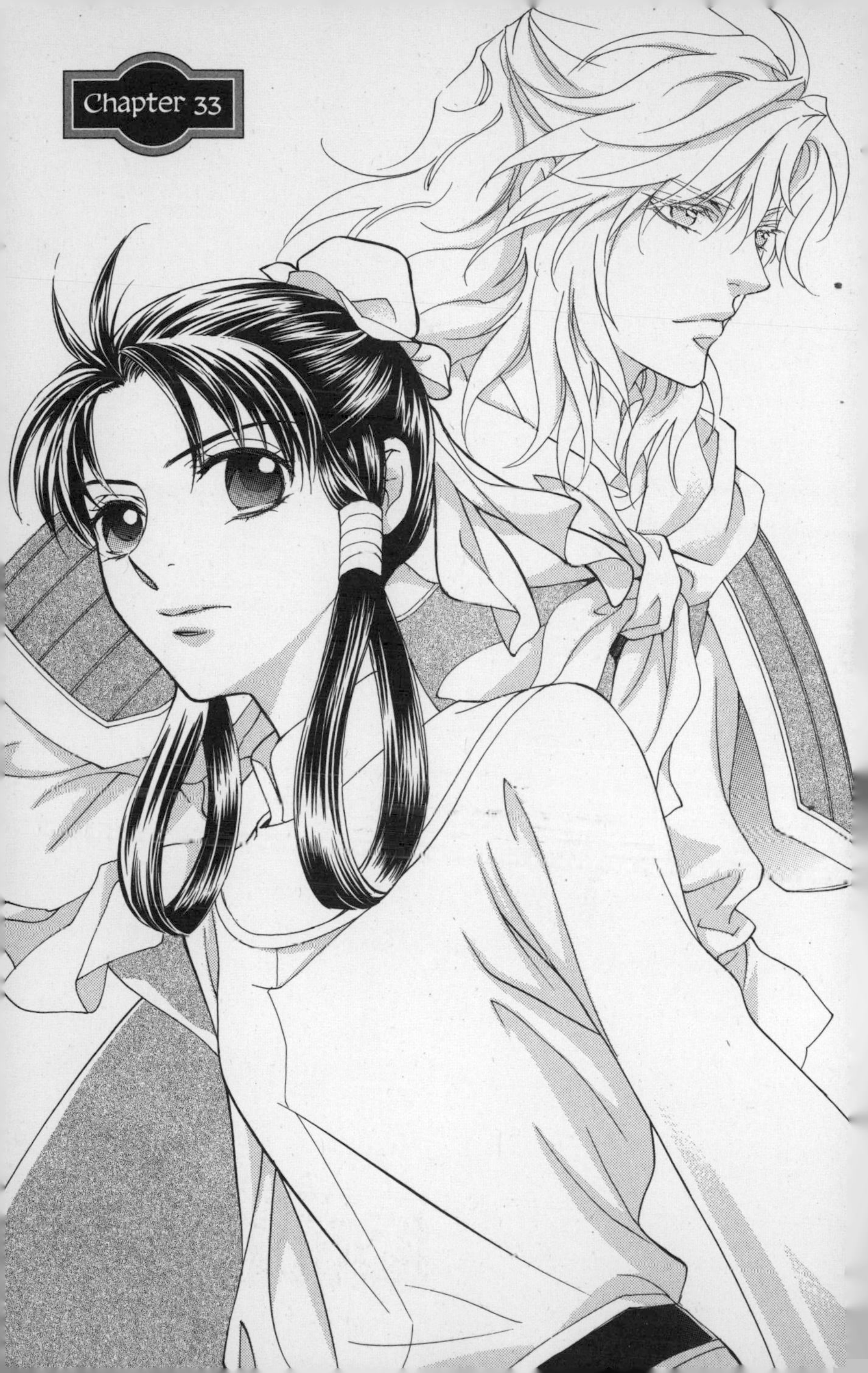
Chapter 33

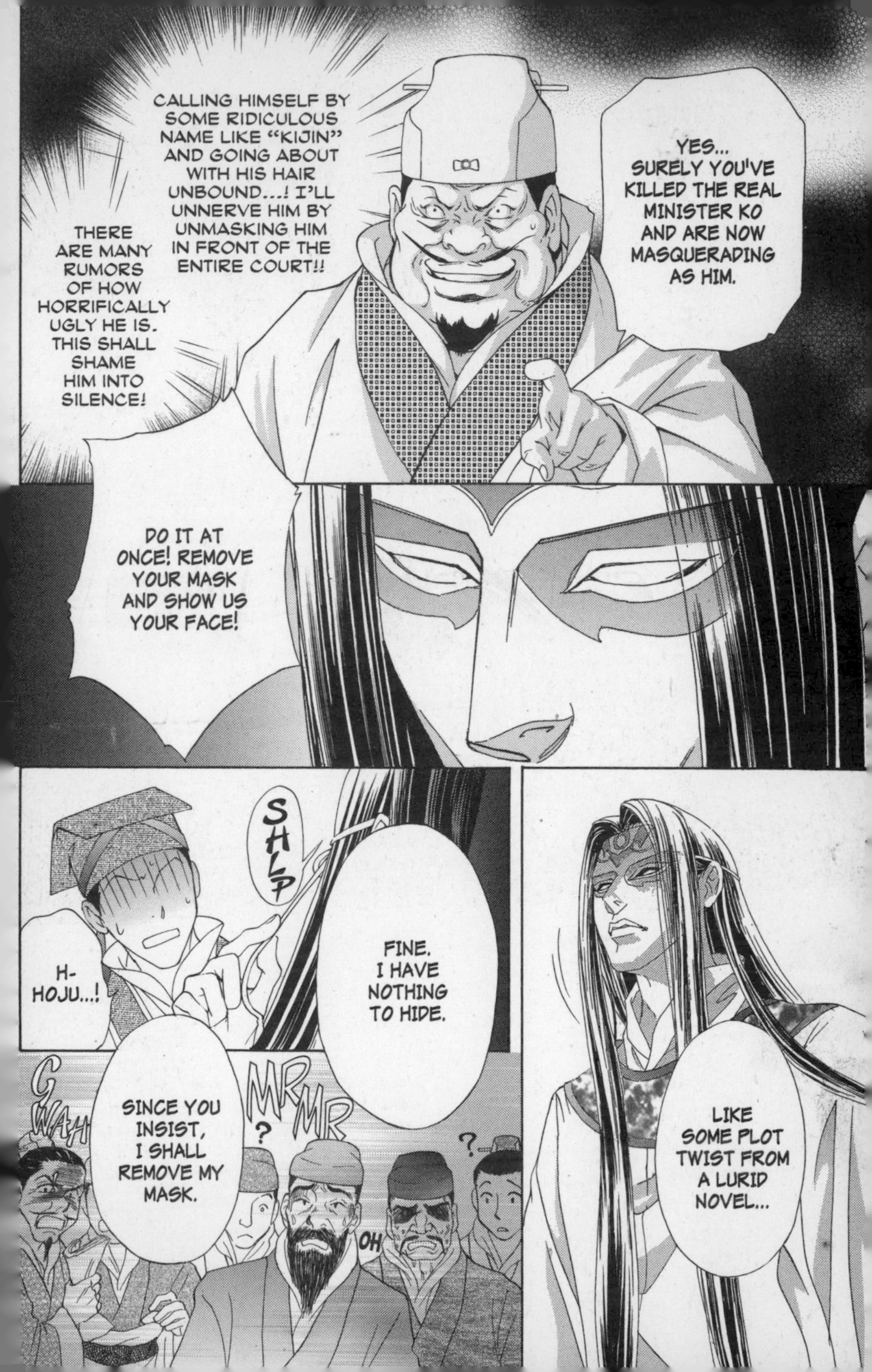
YES... SURELY YOU'VE KILLED THE REAL MINISTER KO AND ARE NOW MASQUERADING AS HIM.
CALLING HIMSELF BY SOME RIDICULOUS NAME LIKE "KIJIN" AND GOING ABOUT WITH HIS HAIR UNBOUND...! I'LL UNNERVE HIM BY UNMASKING HIM IN FRONT OF THE ENTIRE COURT!!
THERE ARE MANY RUMORS OF HOW HORRIFICALLY UGLY HE IS. THIS SHALL SHAME HIM INTO SILENCE!
DO IT AT ONCE! REMOVE YOUR MASK AND SHOW US YOUR FACE!
LIKE SOME PLOT TWIST FROM A LURID NOVEL...
FINE. I HAVE NOTHING TO HIDE.
SHLP
H- HOJU...!
SINCE YOU INSIST, I SHALL REMOVE MY MASK.
MR MR
?
?
GWAH
OH

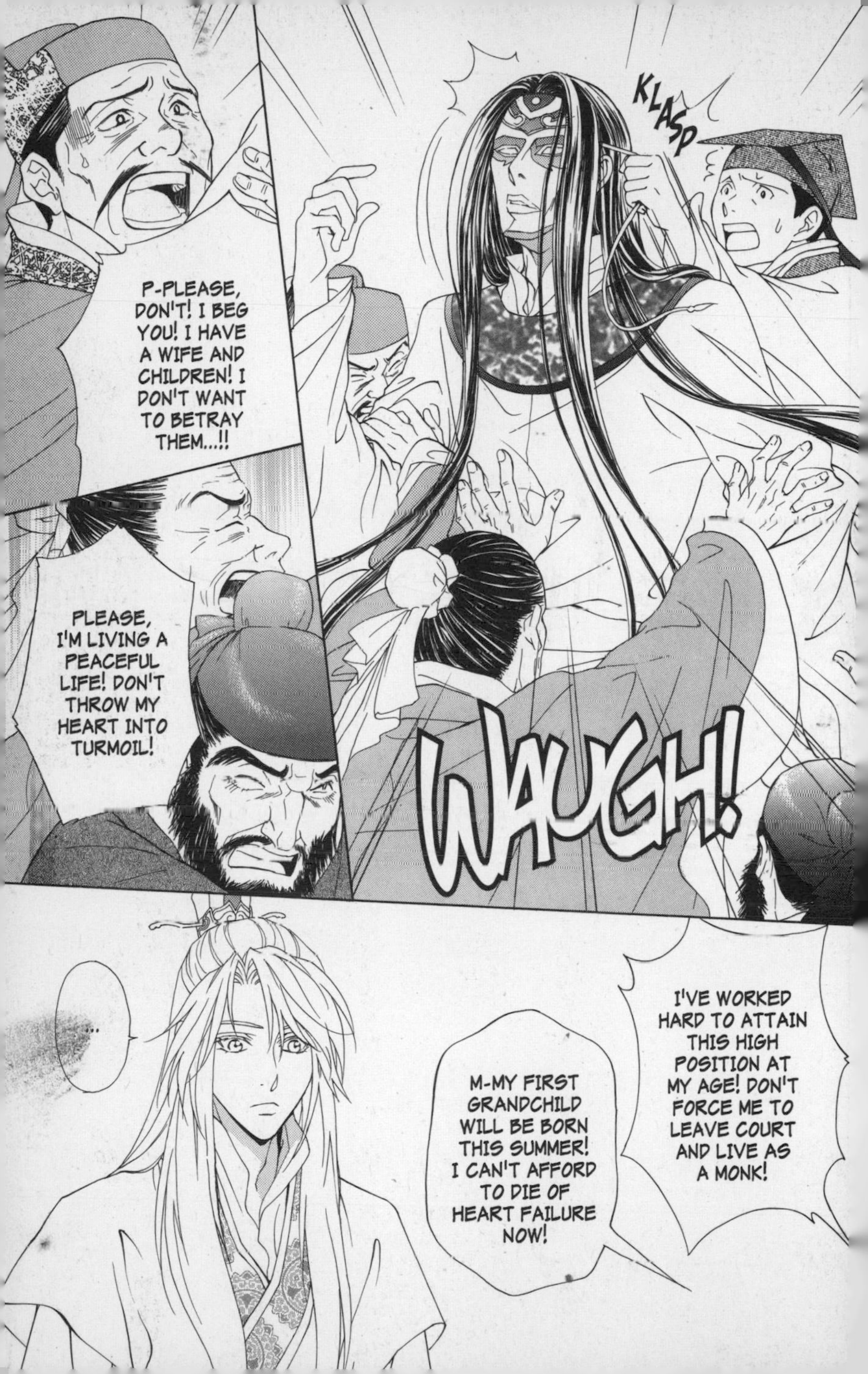
KLASP
WAUGH!
P-PLEASE, DON'T! I BEG YOU! I HAVE A WIFE AND CHILDREN! I DON'T WANT TO BETRAY THEM...!!
PLEASE, I'M LIVING A PEACEFUL LIFE! DON'T THROW MY HEART INTO TURMOIL!
I'VE WORKED HARD TO ATTAIN THIS HIGH POSITION AT MY AGE! DON'T FORCE ME TO LEAVE COURT AND LIVE AS A MONK!
M-MY FIRST GRANDCHILD WILL BE BORN THIS SUMMER! I CAN'T AFFORD TO DIE OF HEART FAILURE NOW!
...

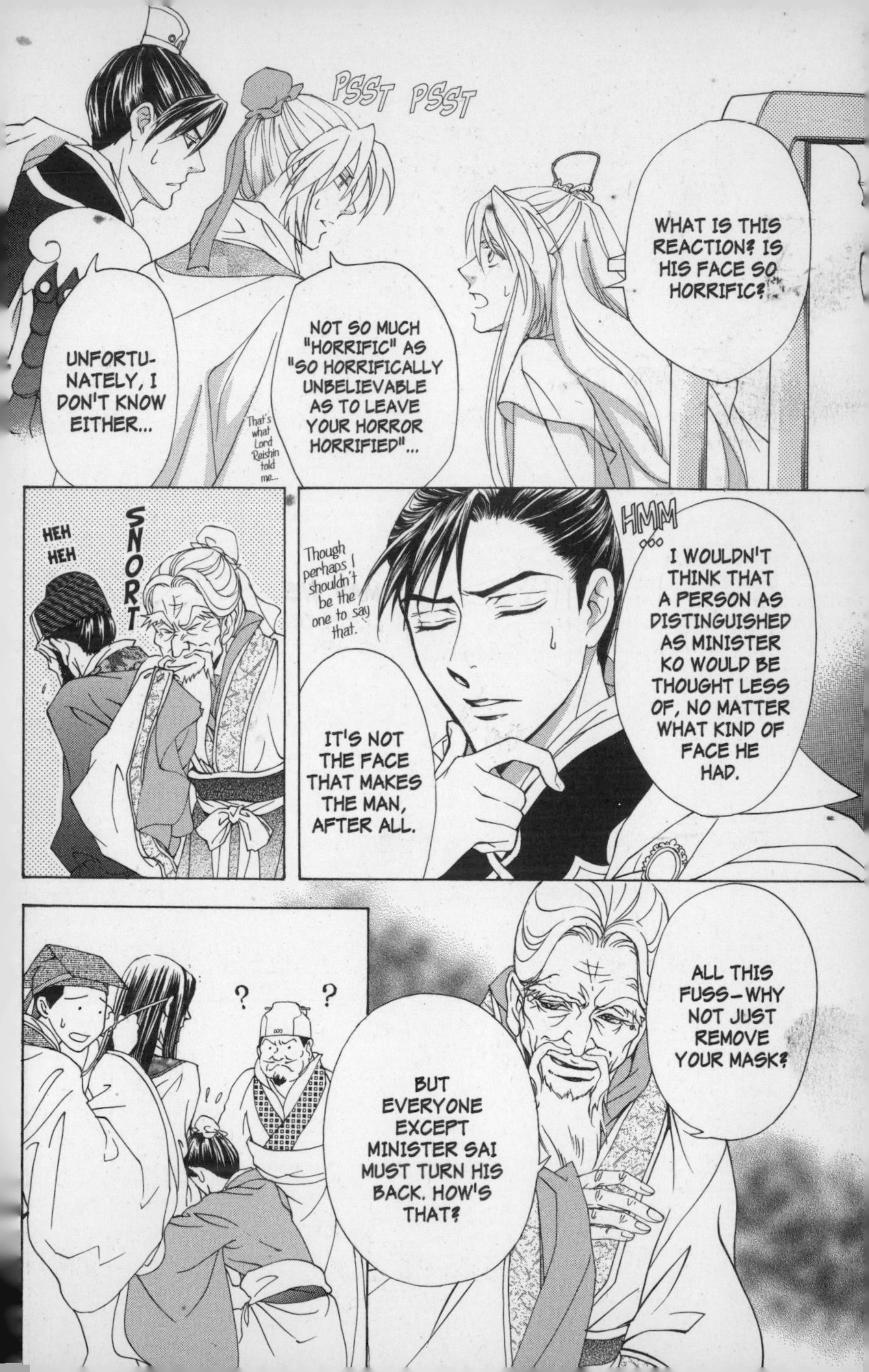
PSST PSST
WHAT IS THIS REACTION? IS HIS FACE SO HORRIFIC?
NOT SO MUCH "HORRIFIC" AS "SO HORRIFICALLY UNBELIEVABLE AS TO LEAVE YOUR HORROR HORRIFIED"...
That's what Lord Reishin told me...
UNFORTU-NATELY, I DON'T KNOW EITHER...
HMM
I WOULDN'T THINK THAT A PERSON AS DISTINGUISHED AS MINISTER KO WOULD BE THOUGHT LESS OF, NO MATTER WHAT KIND OF FACE HE HAD.
Though perhaps I shouldn't be the one to say that.
IT'S NOT THE FACE THAT MAKES THE MAN, AFTER ALL.
SNORT
HEH HEH
ALL THIS FUSS—WHY NOT JUST REMOVE YOUR MASK?
BUT EVERYONE EXCEPT MINISTER SAI MUST TURN HIS BACK. HOW'S THAT?
?
?

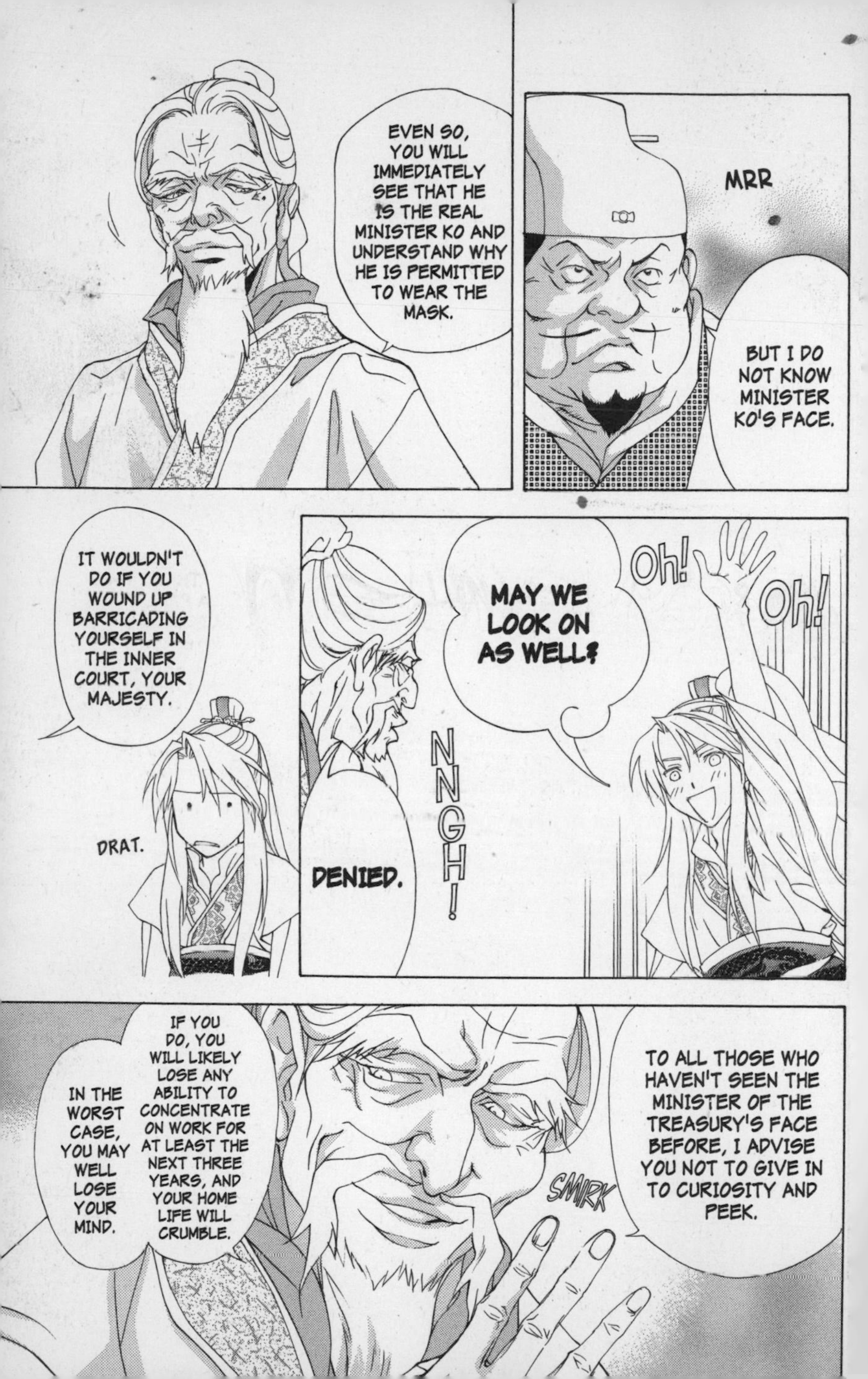
MRR
BUT I DO NOT KNOW MINISTER KO'S FACE.
EVEN SO, YOU WILL IMMEDIATELY SEE THAT HE IS THE REAL MINISTER KO AND UNDERSTAND WHY HE IS PERMITTED TO WEAR THE MASK.
Oh!
Oh!
MAY WE LOOK ON AS WELL?
NNGH!
DENIED.
IT WOULDN'T DO IF YOU WOUND UP BARRICADING YOURSELF IN THE INNER COURT, YOUR MAJESTY.
DRAT.
TO ALL THOSE WHO HAVEN'T SEEN THE MINISTER OF THE TREASURY'S FACE BEFORE, I ADVISE YOU NOT TO GIVE IN TO CURIOSITY AND PEEK.
SMIRK
IF YOU DO, YOU WILL LIKELY LOSE ANY ABILITY TO CONCENTRATE ON WORK FOR AT LEAST THE NEXT THREE YEARS, AND YOUR HOME LIFE WILL CRUMBLE.
IN THE WORST CASE, YOU MAY WELL LOSE YOUR MIND.

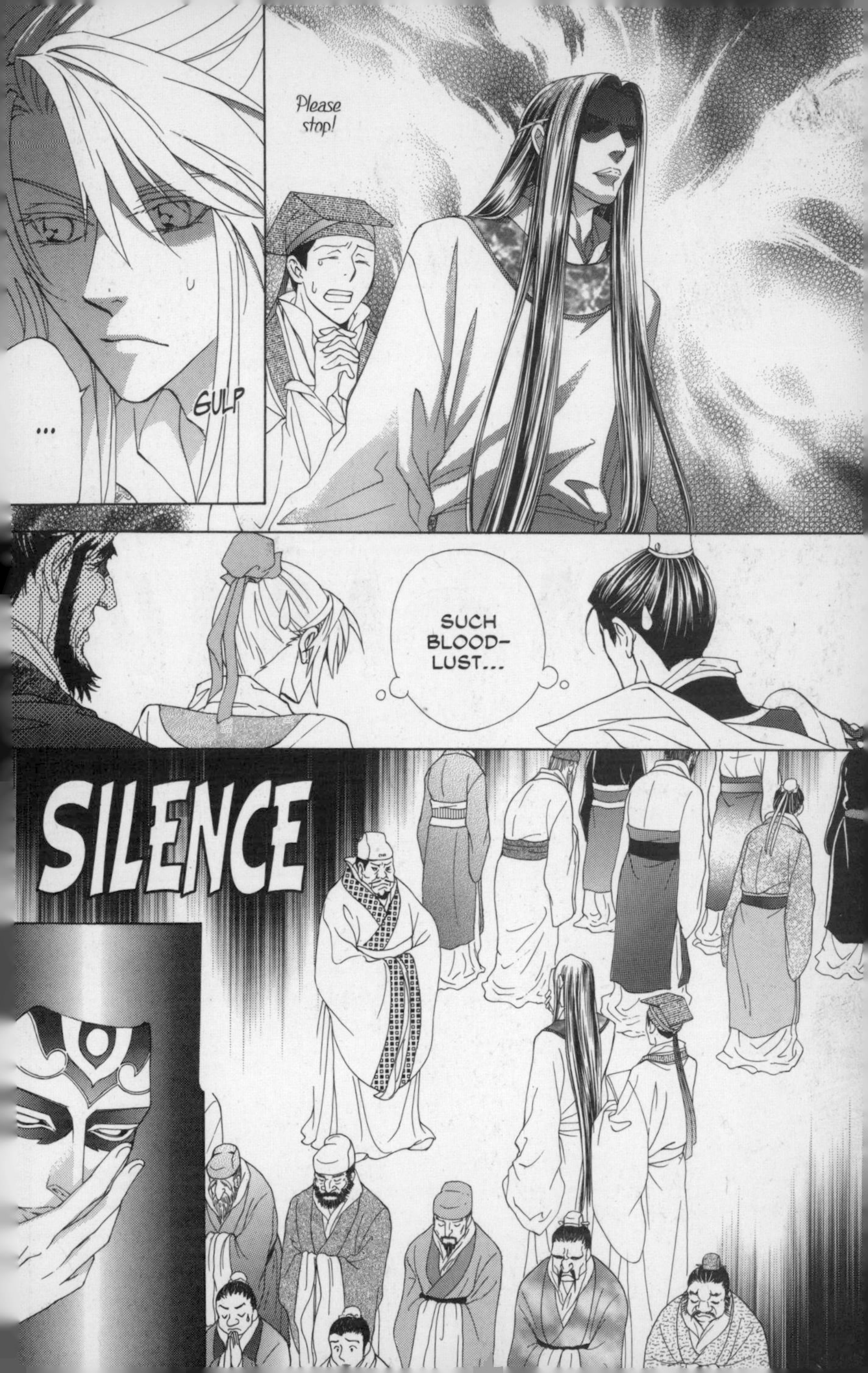
Please stop!
GULP
...
SUCH BLOOD-LUST...
SILENCE

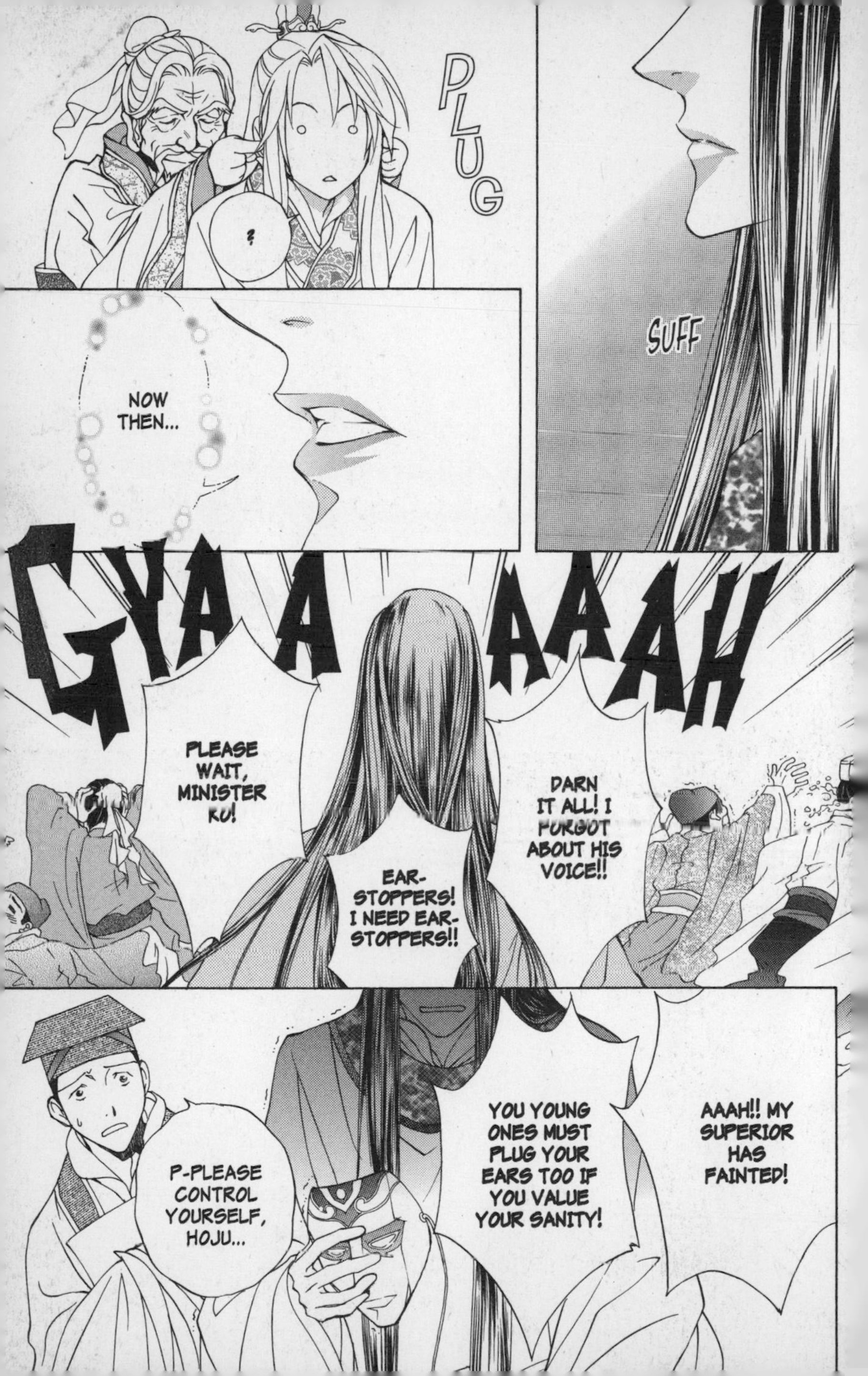
SUFF
PLUG
?
NOW THEN...
GYAAAAAH
DARN IT ALL! I FORGOT ABOUT HIS VOICE!!
EAR-STOPPERS! I NEED EAR-STOPPERS!!
PLEASE WAIT, MINISTER KO!
AAAH!! MY SUPERIOR HAS FAINTED!
YOU YOUNG ONES MUST PLUG YOUR EARS TOO IF YOU VALUE YOUR SANITY!
P-PLEASE CONTROL YOURSELF, HOJU...

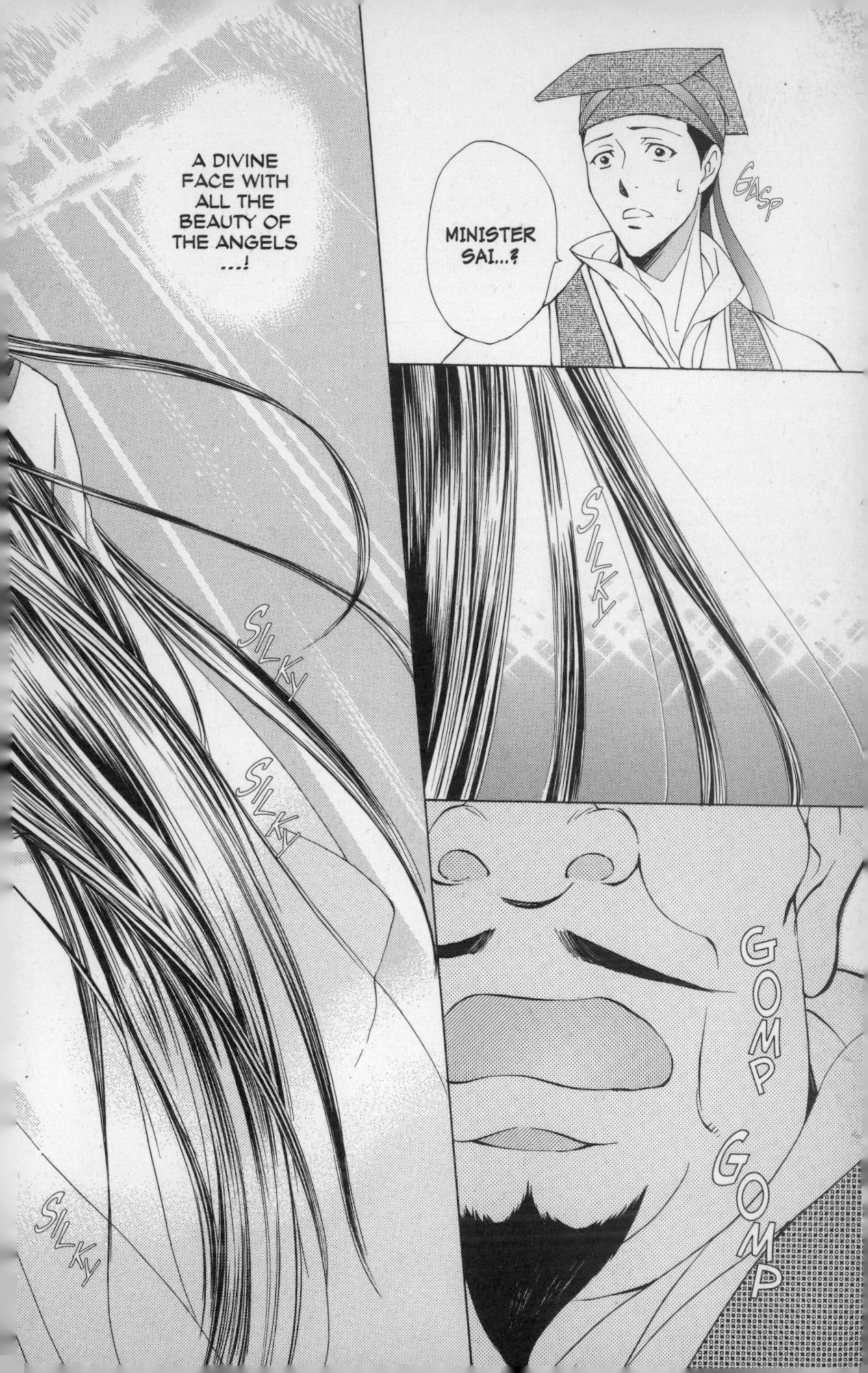
GASP
MINISTER SAI...?
SILKY
GOMP
GOMP
A DIVINE FACE WITH ALL THE BEAUTY OF THE ANGELS ...!
SILKY
SILKY
SILKY

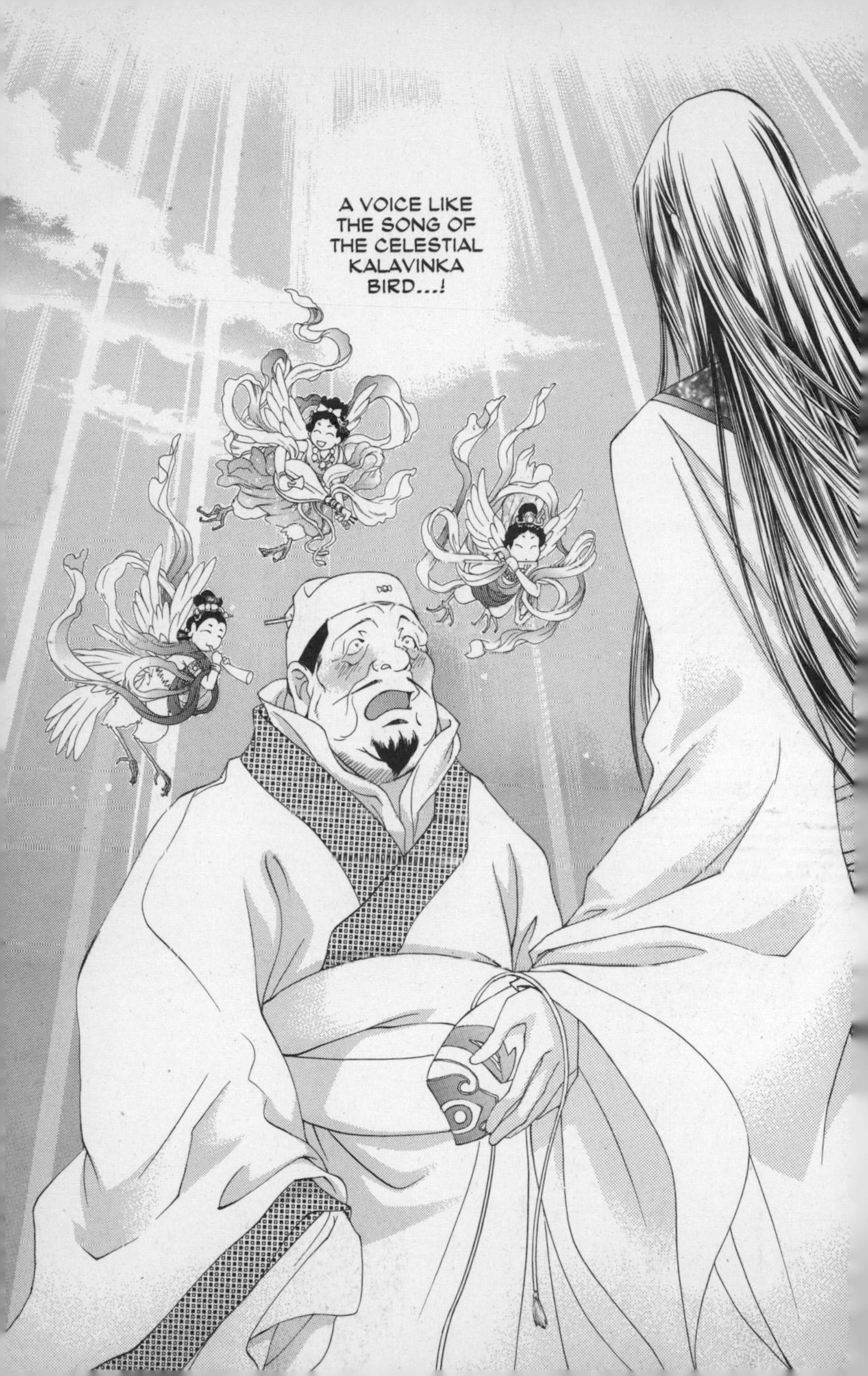
A VOICE LIKE THE SONG OF THE CELESTIAL KALAVINKA BIRD...!

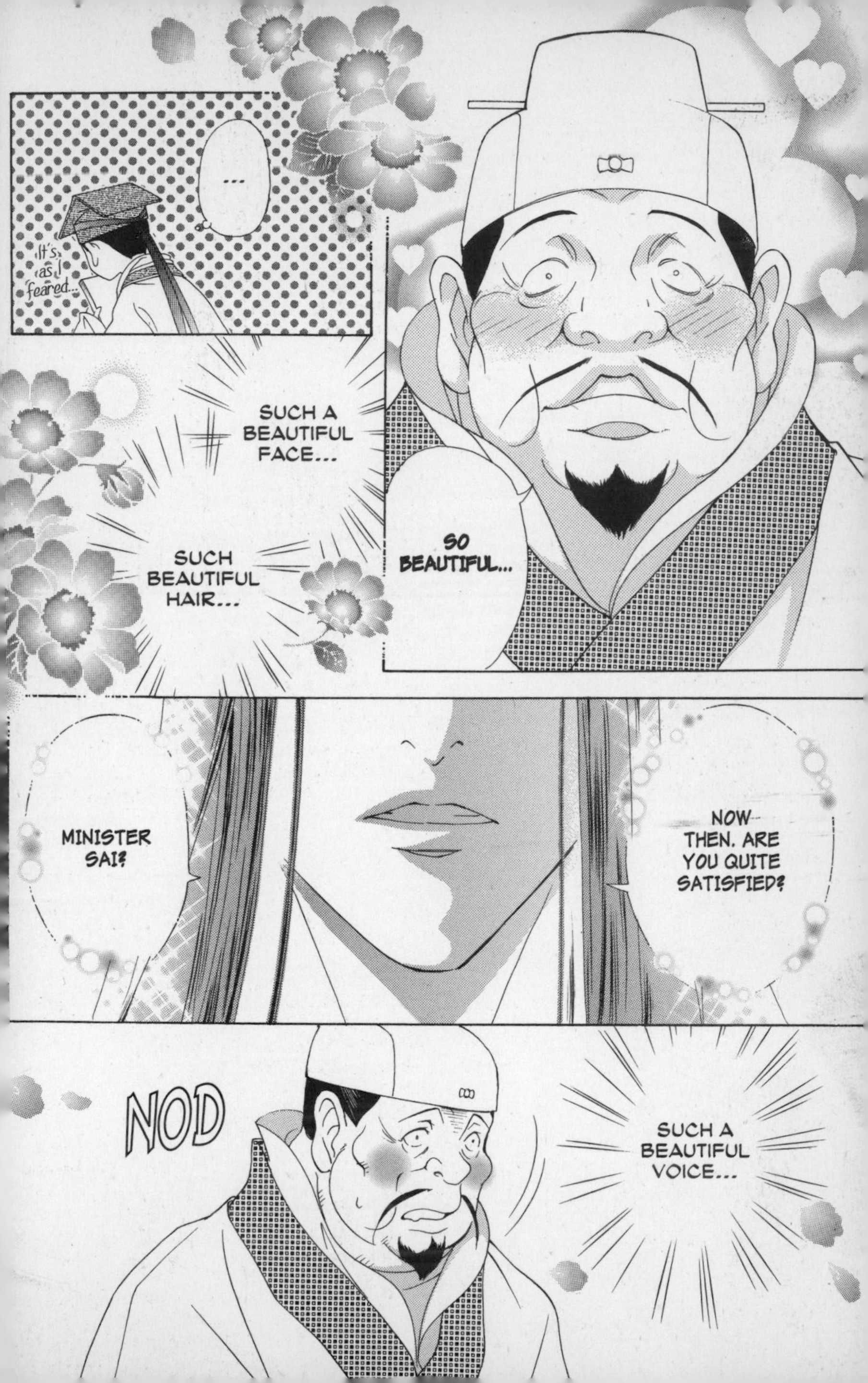
SO BEAUTIFUL...
...
It's as I feared...
SUCH A BEAUTIFUL FACE...
SUCH BEAUTIFUL HAIR...
NOW THEN. ARE YOU QUITE SATISFIED?
MINISTER SAI?
SUCH A BEAUTIFUL VOICE...
NOD

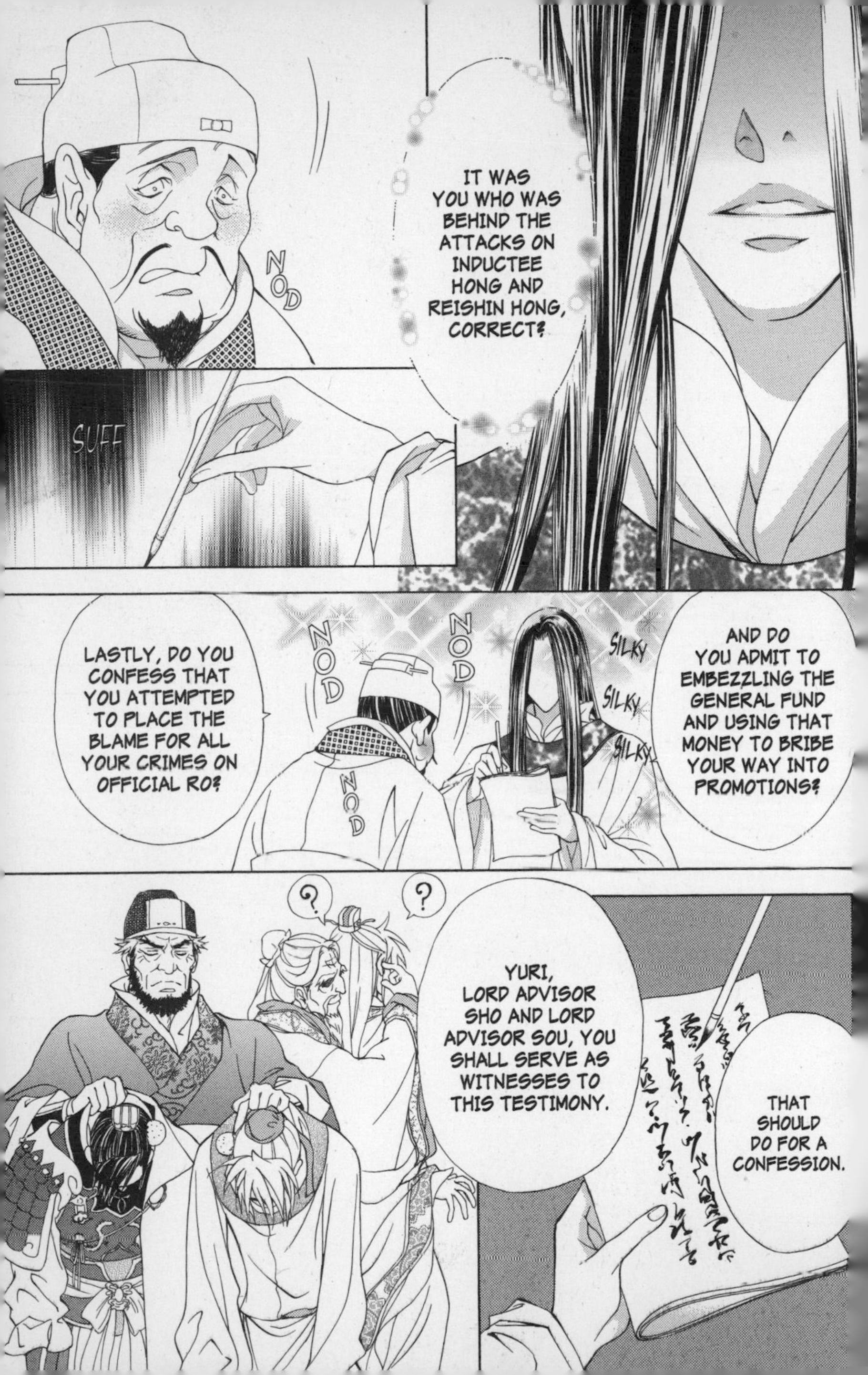
IT WAS YOU WHO WAS BEHIND THE ATTACKS ON INDUCTEE HONG AND REISHIN HONG, CORRECT?
NOD
SUFF
AND DO YOU ADMIT TO EMBEZZLING THE GENERAL FUND AND USING THAT MONEY TO BRIBE YOUR WAY INTO PROMOTIONS?
SILKY SILKY SILKY
NOD NOD NOD
LASTLY, DO YOU CONFESS THAT YOU ATTEMPTED TO PLACE THE BLAME FOR ALL YOUR CRIMES ON OFFICIAL RO?
THAT SHOULD DO FOR A CONFESSION.
YURI, LORD ADVISOR SHO AND LORD ADVISOR SOU, YOU SHALL SERVE AS WITNESSES TO THIS TESTIMONY.
?
?

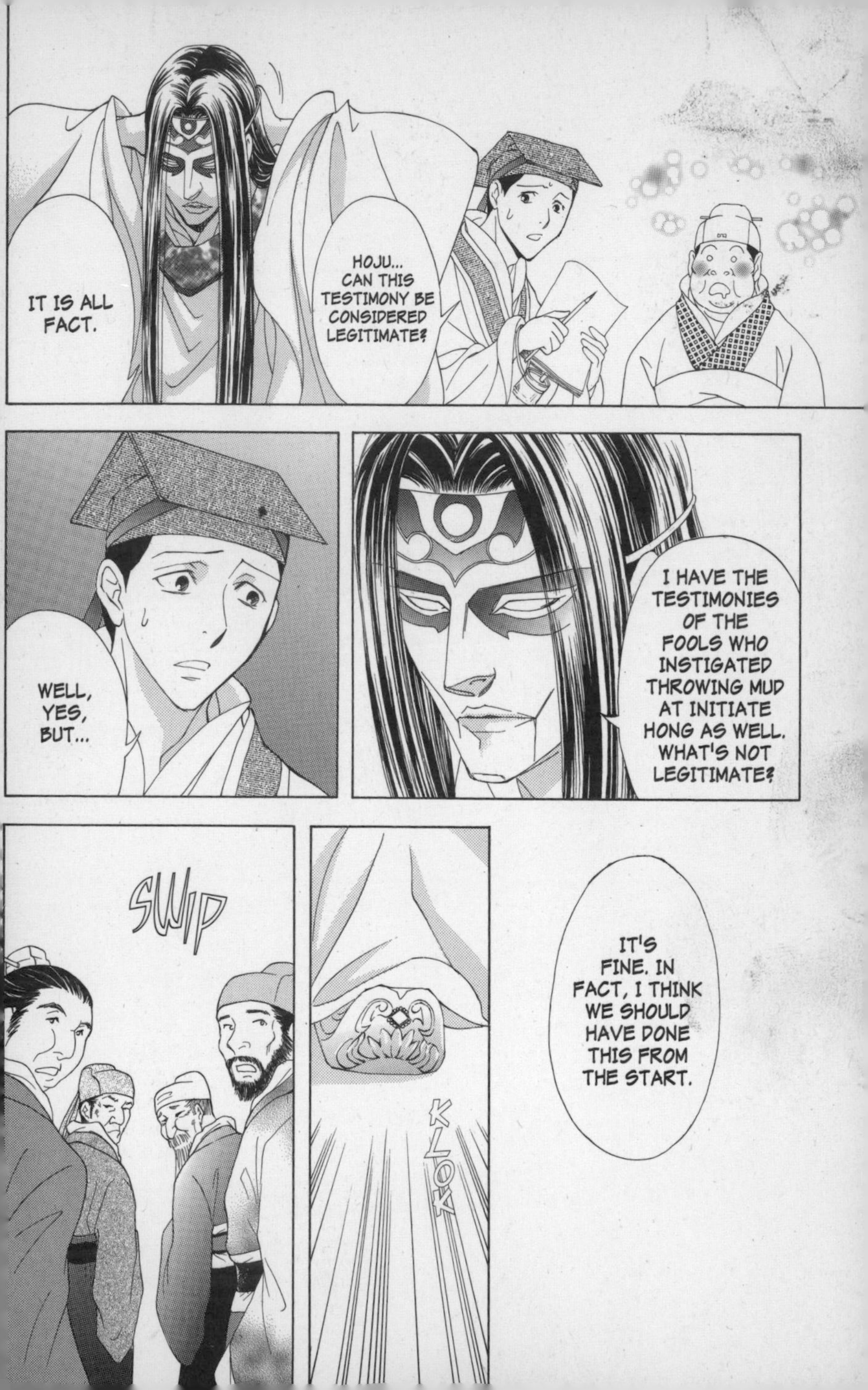
HOJU... CAN THIS TESTIMONY BE CONSIDERED LEGITIMATE?
IT IS ALL FACT.
I HAVE THE TESTIMONIES OF THE FOOLS WHO INSTIGATED THROWING MUD AT INITIATE HONG AS WELL. WHAT'S NOT LEGITIMATE?
WELL, YES, BUT...
IT'S FINE. IN FACT, I THINK WE SHOULD HAVE DONE THIS FROM THE START.
KLOK
SWIP

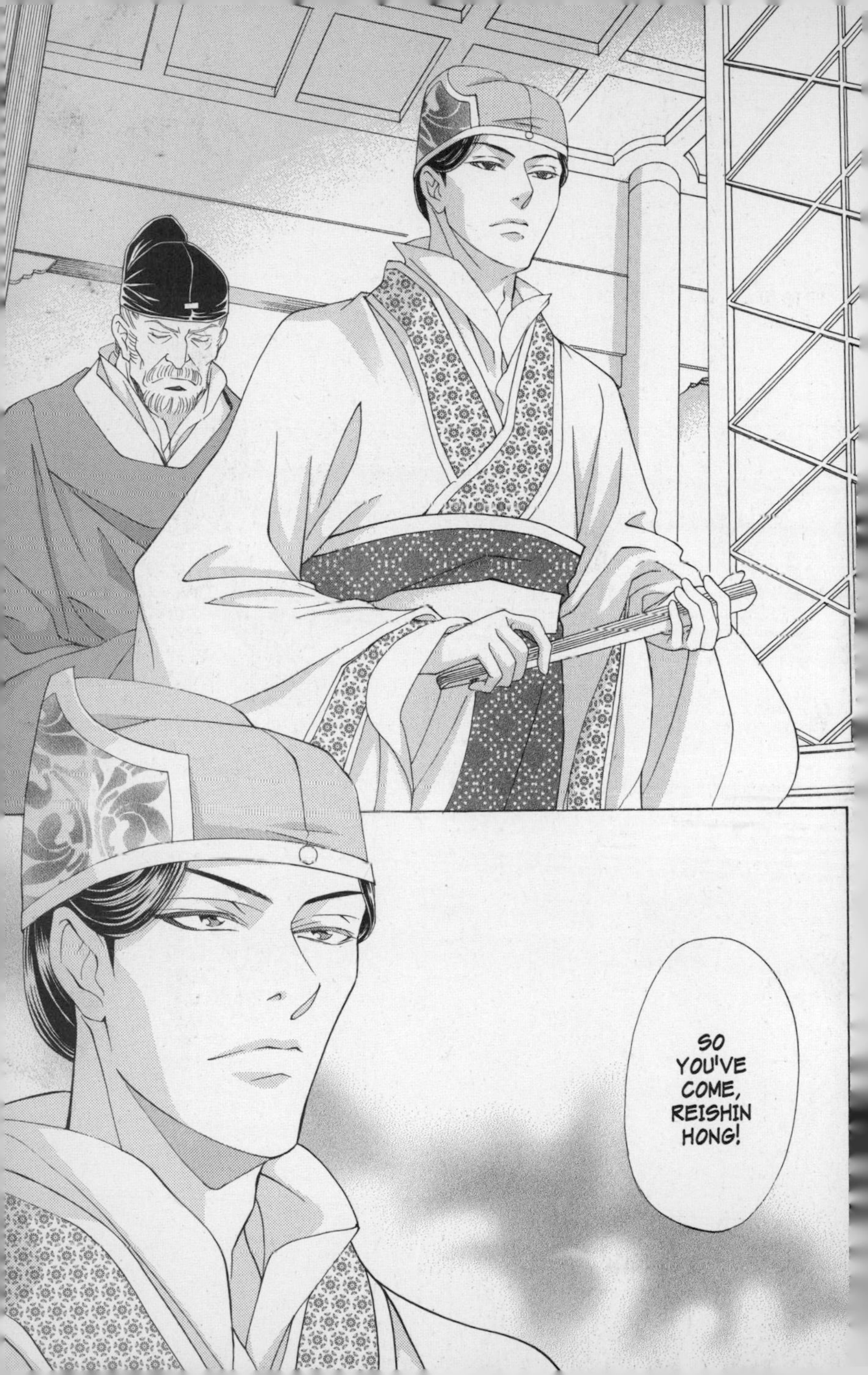
SO YOU'VE COME, REISHIN HONG!

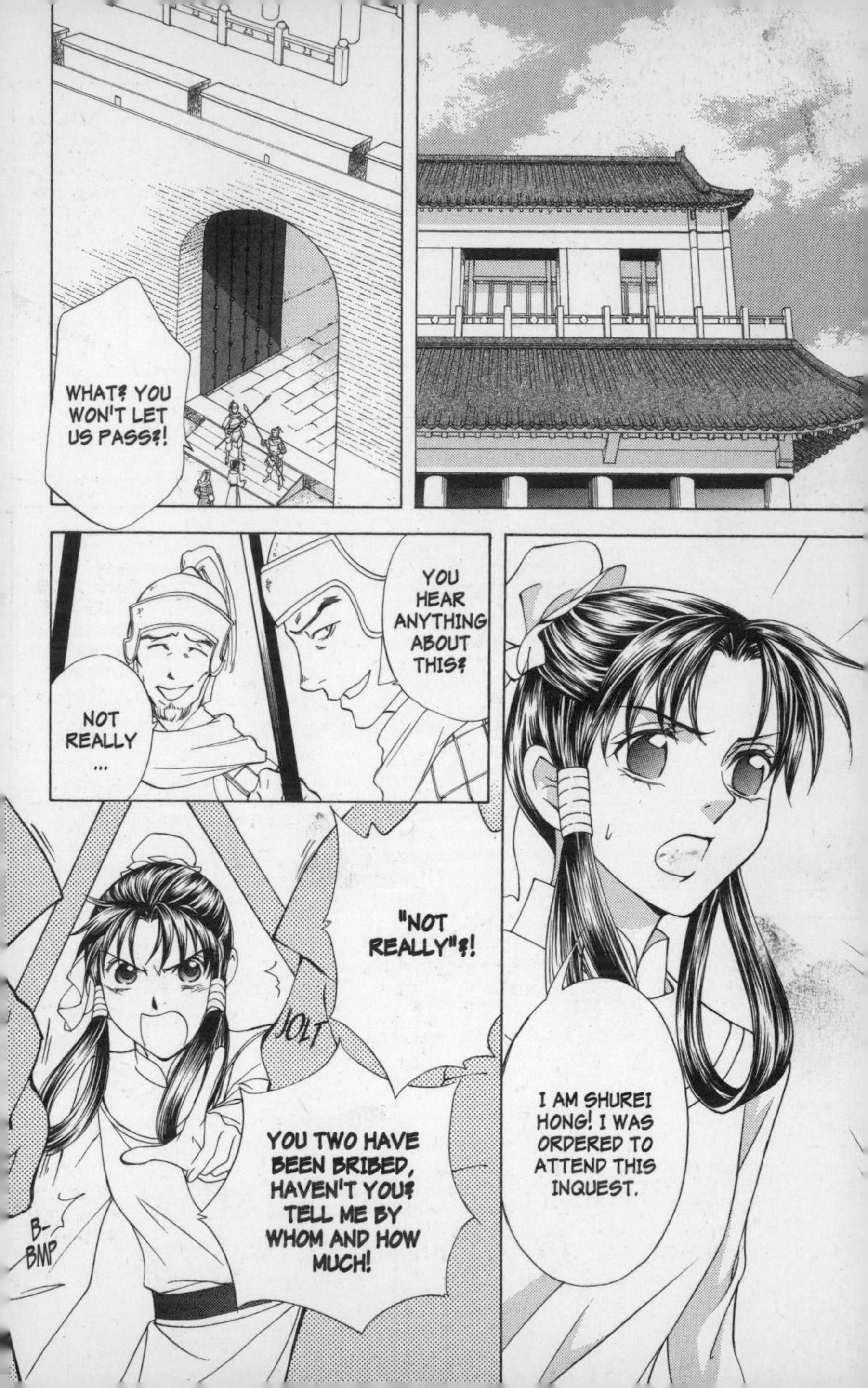
WHAT? YOU WON'T LET US PASS?!
I AM SHUREI HONG! I WAS ORDERED TO ATTEND THIS INQUEST.
YOU HEAR ANYTHING ABOUT THIS?
NOT REALLY ...
"NOT REALLY"?!
JOLT
YOU TWO HAVE BEEN BRIBED, HAVEN'T YOU? TELL ME BY WHOM AND HOW MUCH!
B-BMP

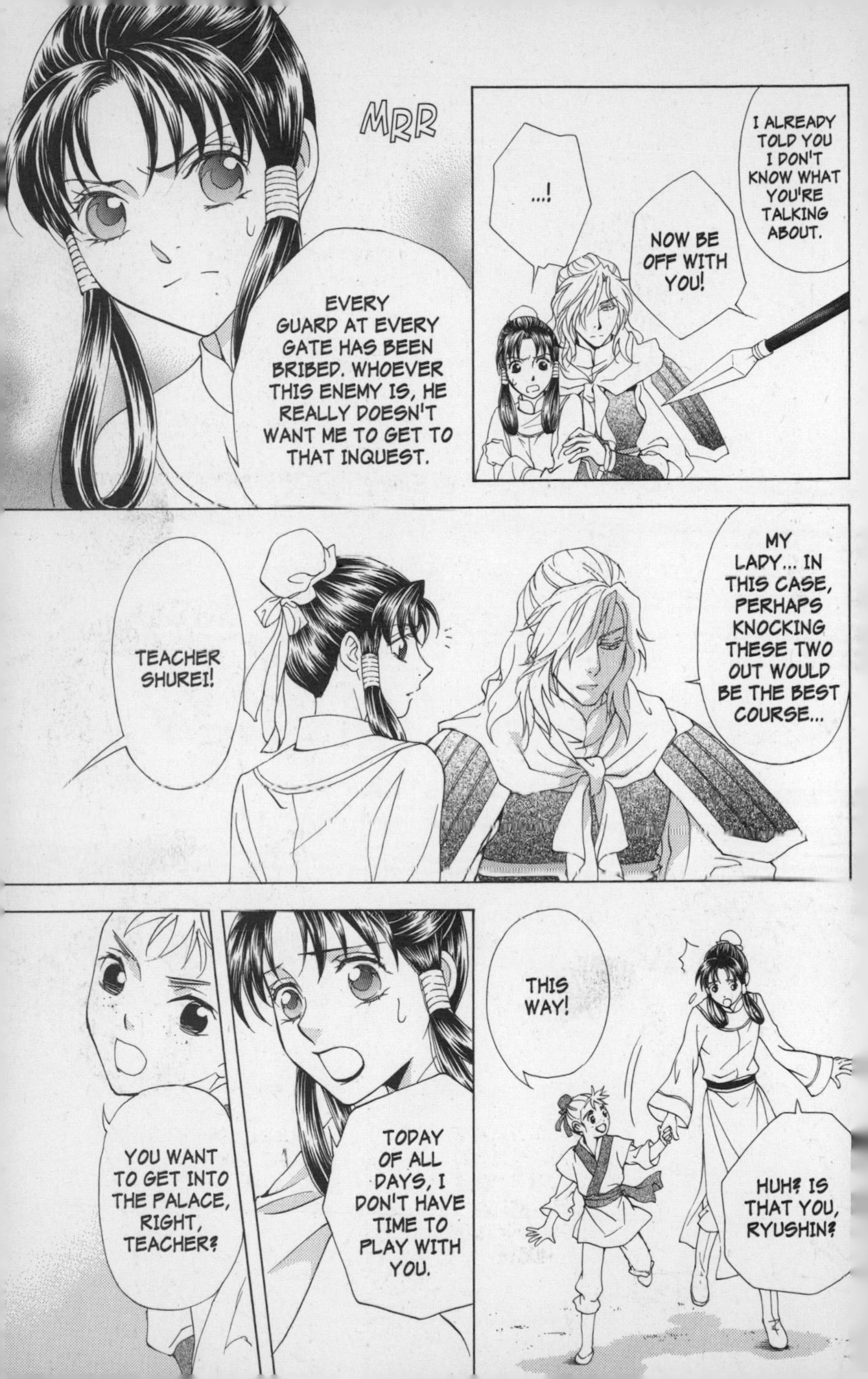
I ALREADY TOLD YOU I DON'T KNOW WHAT YOU'RE TALKING ABOUT.
NOW BE OFF WITH YOU!
...!
MRR
EVERY GUARD AT EVERY GATE HAS BEEN BRIBED. WHOEVER THIS ENEMY IS, HE REALLY DOESN'T WANT ME TO GET TO THAT INQUEST.
MY LADY... IN THIS CASE, PERHAPS KNOCKING THESE TWO OUT WOULD BE THE BEST COURSE...
TEACHER SHUREI!
THIS WAY!
HUH? IS THAT YOU, RYUSHIN?
TODAY OF ALL DAYS, I DON'T HAVE TIME TO PLAY WITH YOU.
YOU WANT TO GET INTO THE PALACE, RIGHT, TEACHER?

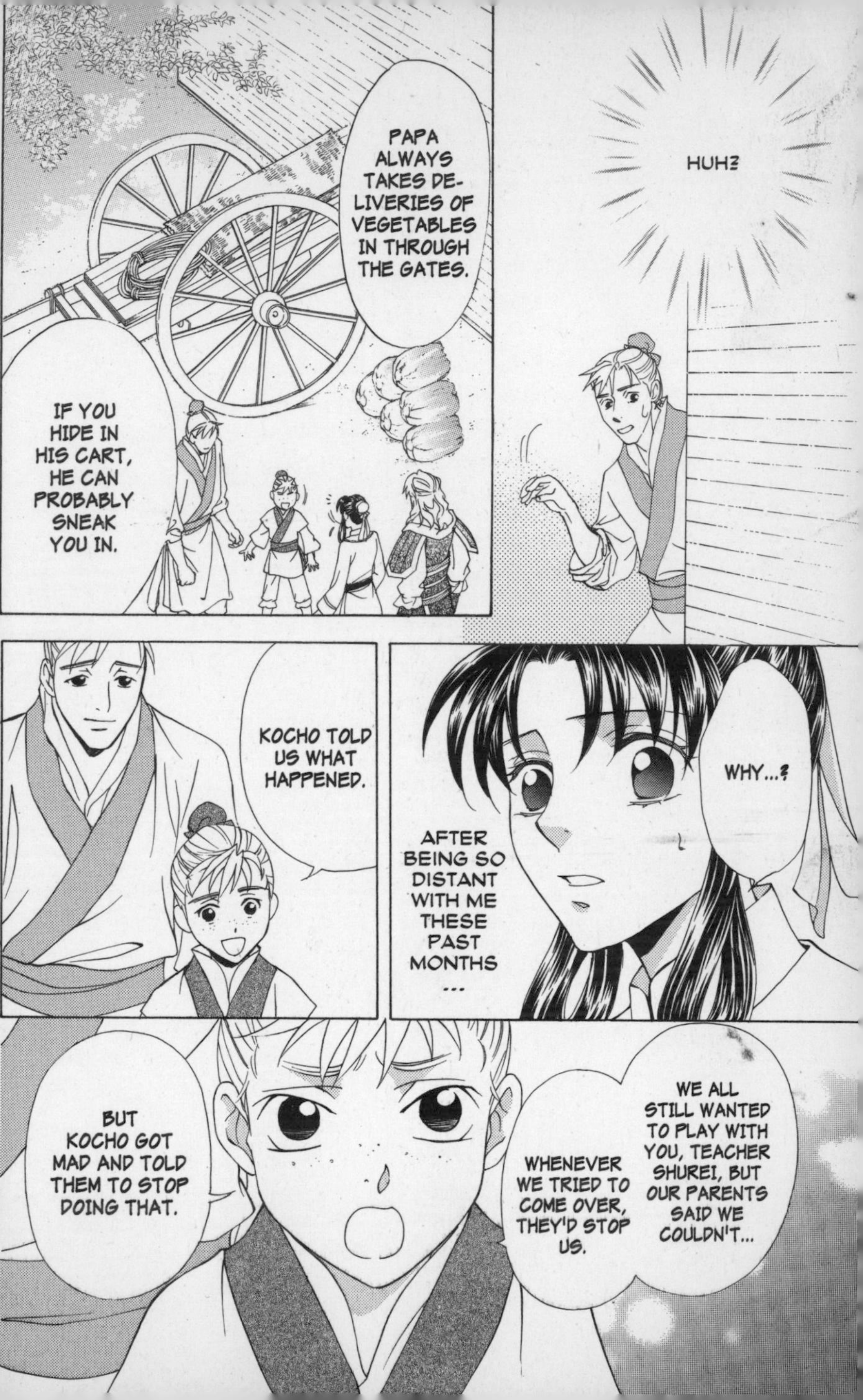
HUH?
PAPA ALWAYS TAKES DE-LIVERIES OF VEGETABLES IN THROUGH THE GATES.
IF YOU HIDE IN HIS CART, HE CAN PROBABLY SNEAK YOU IN.
WHY...?
AFTER BEING SO DISTANT WITH ME THESE PAST MONTHS ...
KOCHO TOLD US WHAT HAPPENED.
WE ALL STILL WANTED TO PLAY WITH YOU, TEACHER SHUREI, BUT OUR PARENTS SAID WE COULDN'T...
WHENEVER WE TRIED TO COME OVER, THEY'D STOP US.
BUT KOCHO GOT MAD AND TOLD THEM TO STOP DOING THAT.

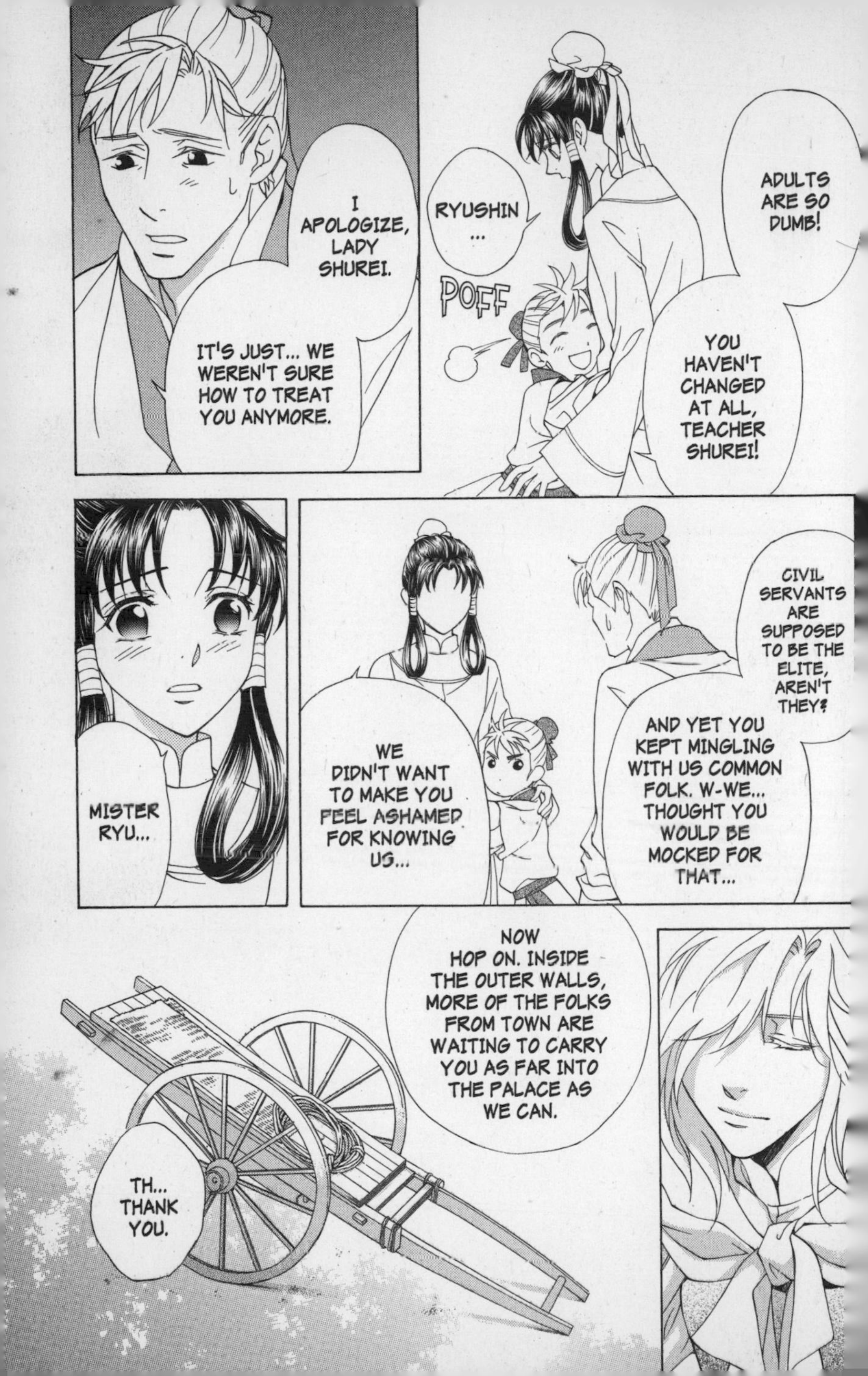
ADULTS ARE SO DUMB!
RYUSHIN ...
POFF
YOU HAVEN'T CHANGED AT ALL, TEACHER SHUREI!
I APOLOGIZE, LADY SHUREI.
IT'S JUST... WE WEREN'T SURE HOW TO TREAT YOU ANYMORE.
CIVIL SERVANTS ARE SUPPOSED TO BE THE ELITE, AREN'T THEY?
AND YET YOU KEPT MINGLING WITH US COMMON FOLK. W-WE... THOUGHT YOU WOULD BE MOCKED FOR THAT...
WE DIDN'T WANT TO MAKE YOU FEEL ASHAMED FOR KNOWING US...
MISTER RYU...
NOW HOP ON. INSIDE THE OUTER WALLS, MORE OF THE FOLKS FROM TOWN ARE WAITING TO CARRY YOU AS FAR INTO THE PALACE AS WE CAN.
TH... THANK YOU.

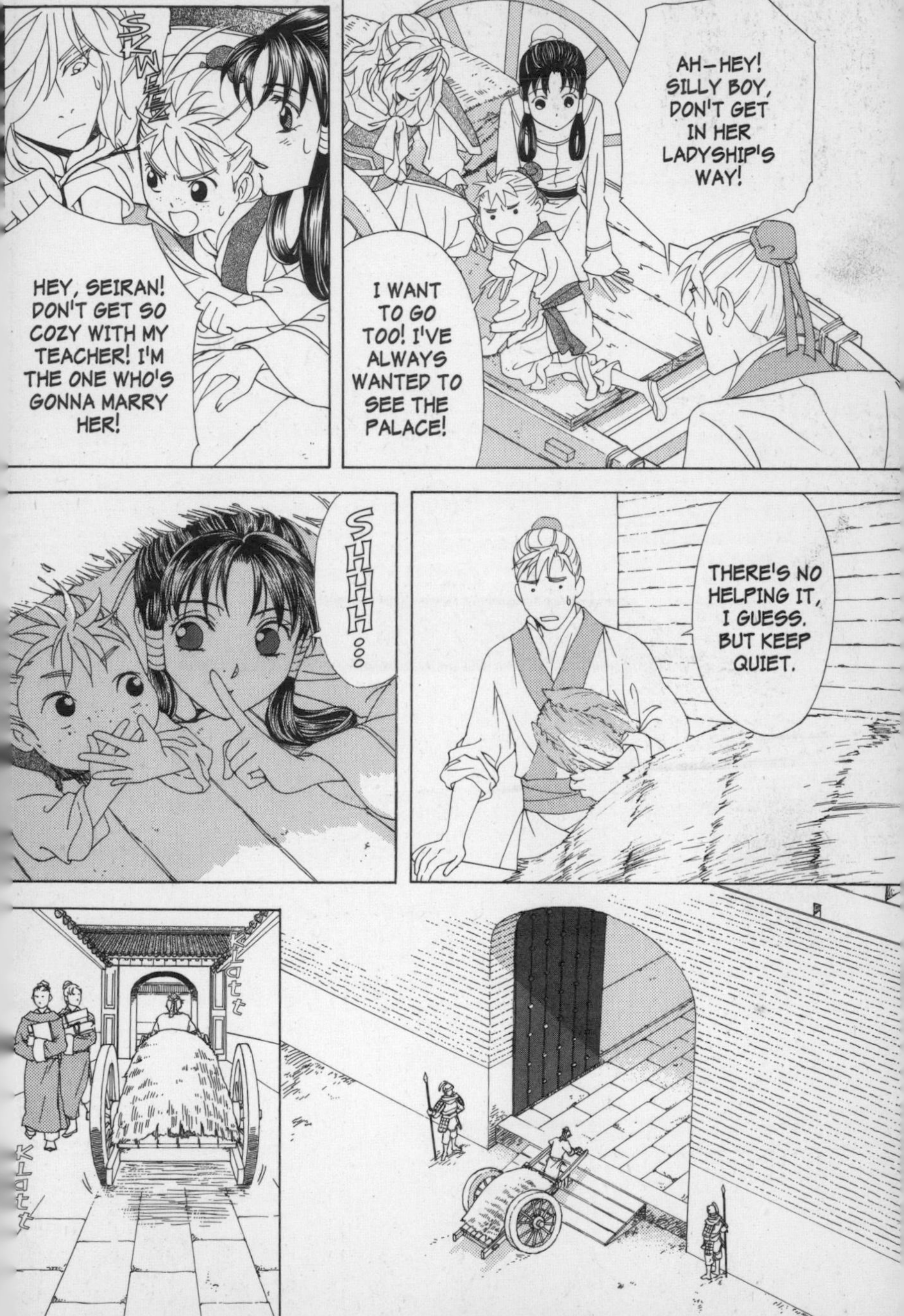
AH—HEY! SILLY BOY, DON'T GET IN HER LADYSHIP'S WAY!
I WANT TO GO TOO! I'VE ALWAYS WANTED TO SEE THE PALACE!
SKWEEZ
HEY, SEIRAN! DON'T GET SO COZY WITH MY TEACHER! I'M THE ONE WHO'S GONNA MARRY HER!
THERE'S NO HELPING IT, I GUESS. BUT KEEP QUIET.
SHHHH...
KLOTT
KLOTT

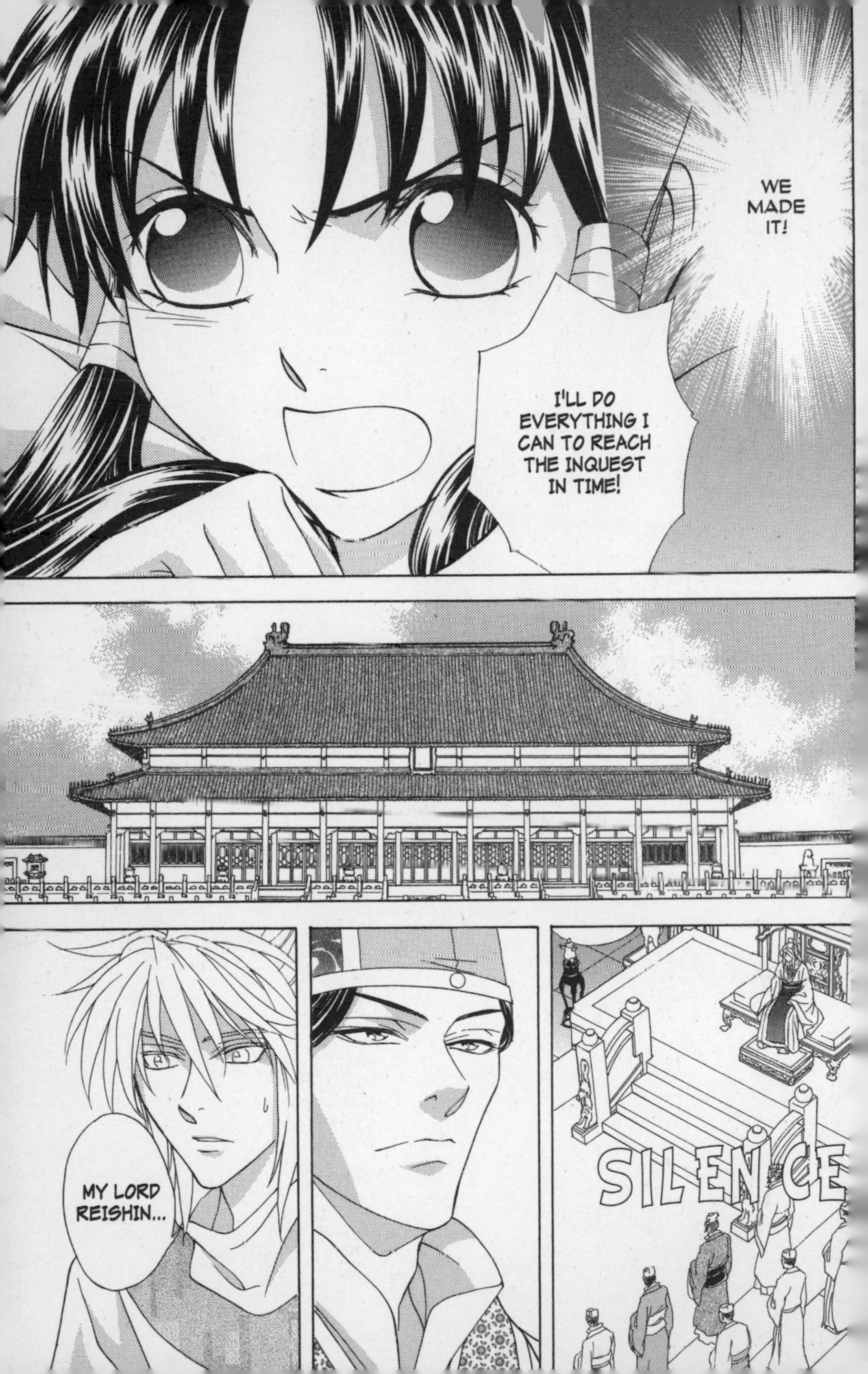
WE MADE IT!
I'LL DO EVERYTHING I CAN TO REACH THE INQUEST IN TIME!
SILENCE
MY LORD REISHIN...

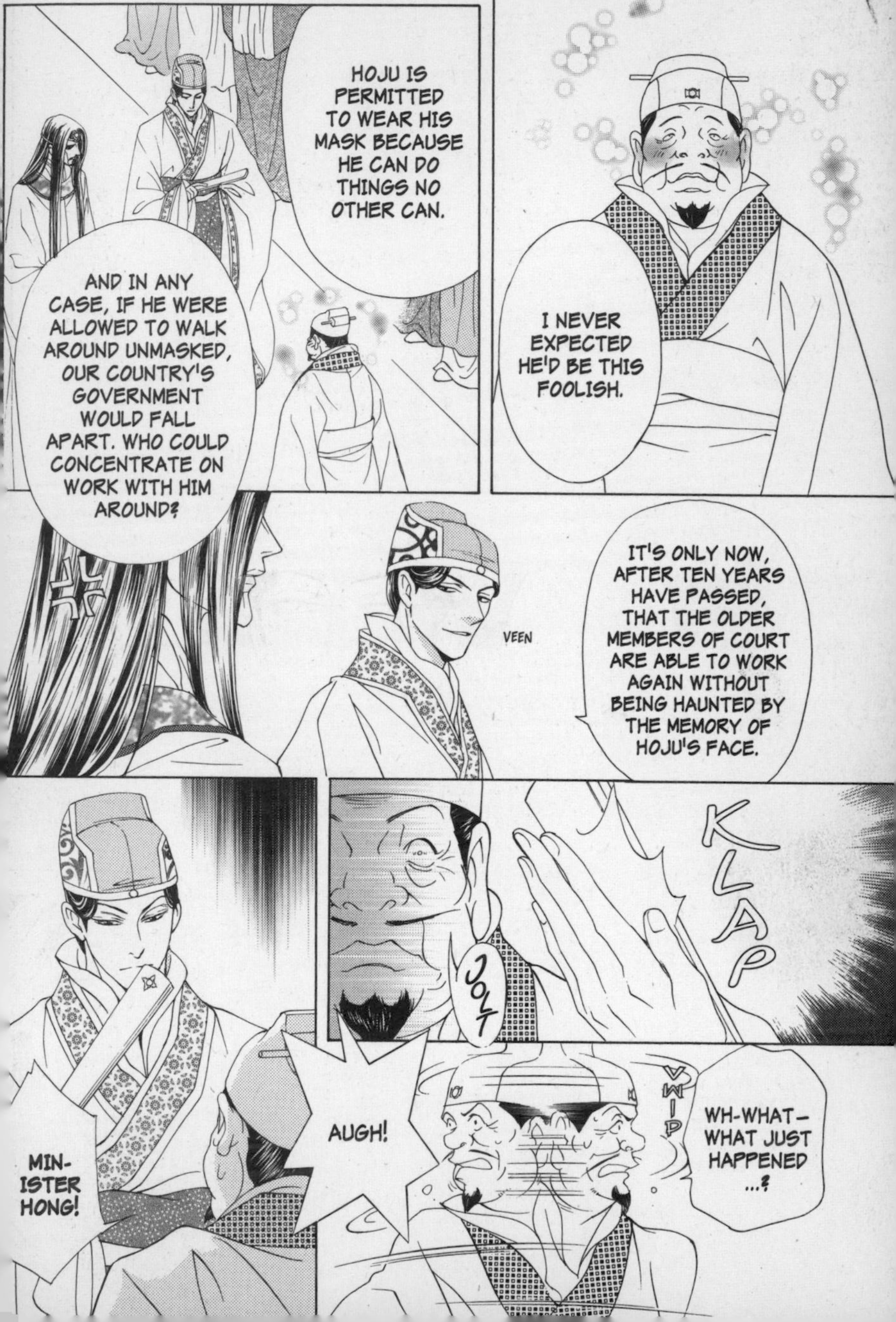
I NEVER EXPECTED HE'D BE THIS FOOLISH.
HOJU IS PERMITTED TO WEAR HIS MASK BECAUSE HE CAN DO THINGS NO OTHER CAN.
AND IN ANY CASE, IF HE WERE ALLOWED TO WALK AROUND UNMASKED, OUR COUNTRY'S GOVERNMENT WOULD FALL APART. WHO COULD CONCENTRATE ON WORK WITH HIM AROUND?
IT'S ONLY NOW, AFTER TEN YEARS HAVE PASSED, THAT THE OLDER MEMBERS OF COURT ARE ABLE TO WORK AGAIN WITHOUT BEING HAUNTED BY THE MEMORY OF HOJU'S FACE.
VEEN
KLAP
JOLT
WH-WHAT-WHAT JUST HAPPENED ...?
WHIP
AUGH!
MIN-ISTER HONG!

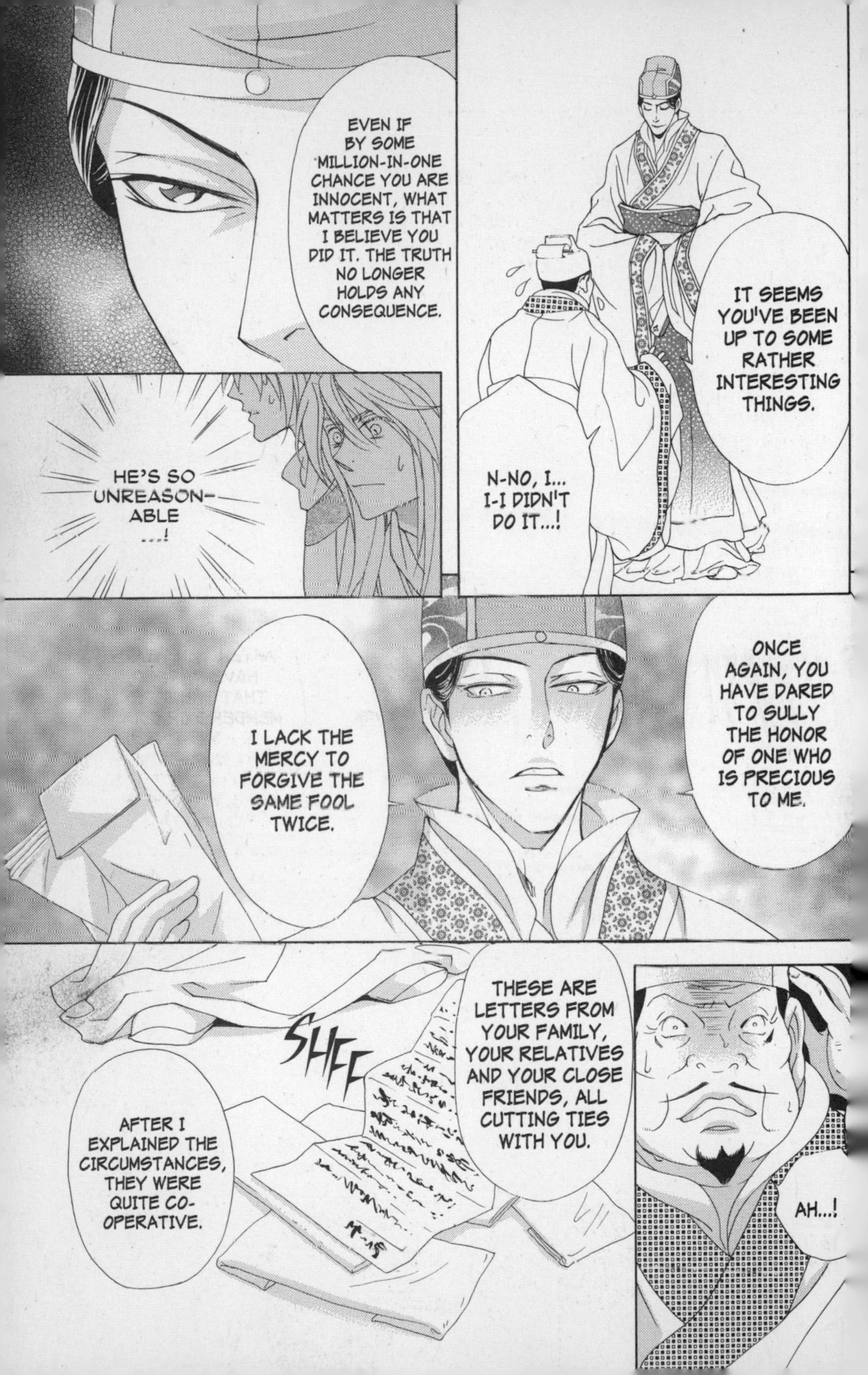
IT SEEMS YOU'VE BEEN UP TO SOME RATHER INTERESTING THINGS.
N-NO, I... I-I DIDN'T DO IT...!
EVEN IF BY SOME MILLION-IN-ONE CHANCE YOU ARE INNOCENT, WHAT MATTERS IS THAT I BELIEVE YOU DID IT. THE TRUTH NO LONGER HOLDS ANY CONSEQUENCE.
HE'S SO UNREASON-ABLE ...!
ONCE AGAIN, YOU HAVE DARED TO SULLY THE HONOR OF ONE WHO IS PRECIOUS TO ME.
I LACK THE MERCY TO FORGIVE THE SAME FOOL TWICE.
AH...!
THESE ARE LETTERS FROM YOUR FAMILY, YOUR RELATIVES AND YOUR CLOSE FRIENDS, ALL CUTTING TIES WITH YOU.
SHFF
AFTER I EXPLAINED THE CIRCUMSTANCES, THEY WERE QUITE CO-OPERATIVE.

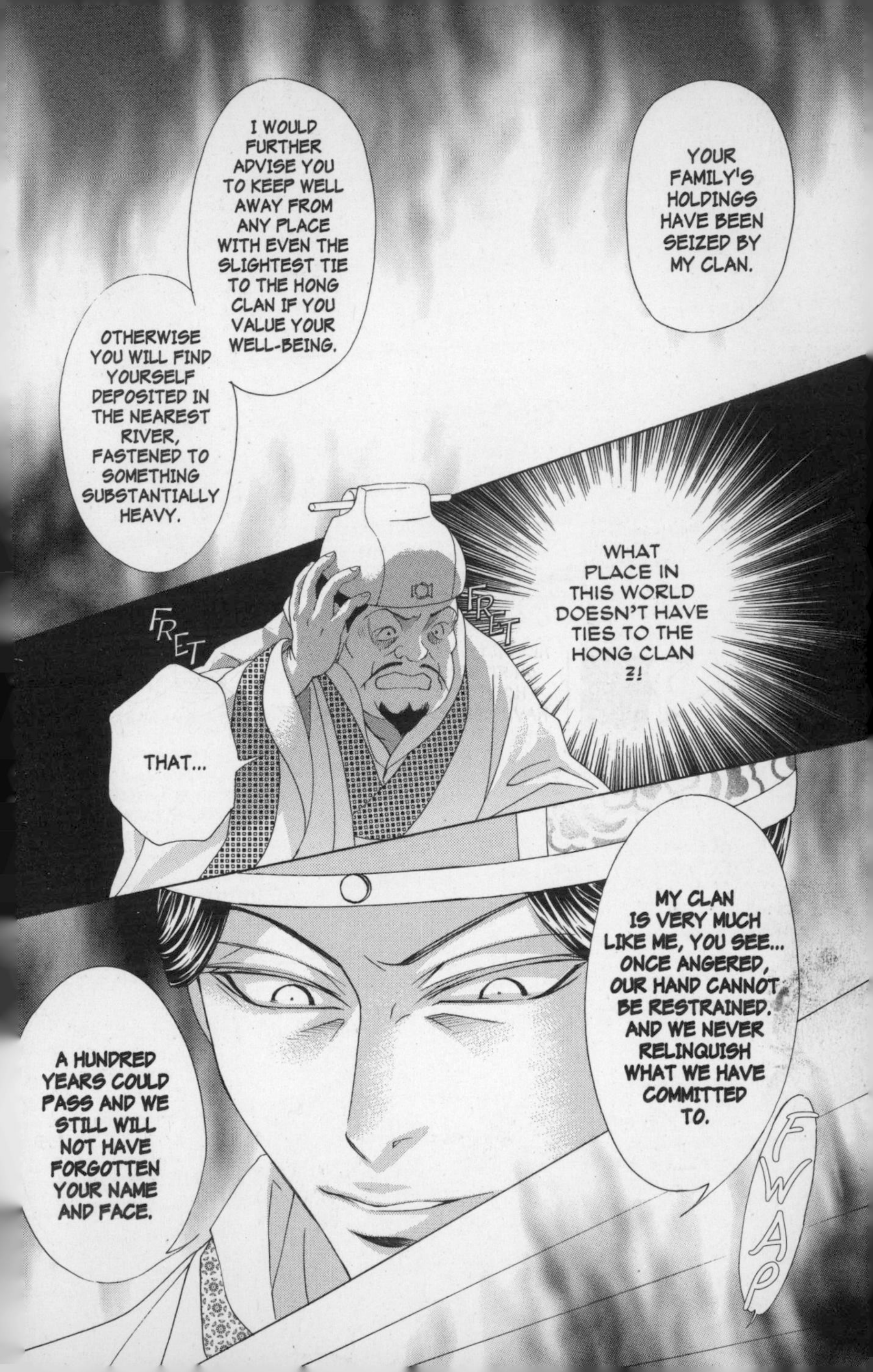
YOUR FAMILY'S HOLDINGS HAVE BEEN SEIZED BY MY CLAN.
I WOULD FURTHER ADVISE YOU TO KEEP WELL AWAY FROM ANY PLACE WITH EVEN THE SLIGHTEST TIE TO THE HONG CLAN IF YOU VALUE YOUR WELL-BEING.
OTHERWISE YOU WILL FIND YOURSELF DEPOSITED IN THE NEAREST RIVER, FASTENED TO SOMETHING SUBSTANTIALLY HEAVY.
WHAT PLACE IN THIS WORLD DOESN'T HAVE TIES TO THE HONG CLAN ?!
FRET
FRET
THAT...
MY CLAN IS VERY MUCH LIKE ME, YOU SEE... ONCE ANGERED, OUR HAND CANNOT BE RESTRAINED. AND WE NEVER RELINQUISH WHAT WE HAVE COMMITTED TO.
A HUNDRED YEARS COULD PASS AND WE STILL WILL NOT HAVE FORGOTTEN YOUR NAME AND FACE.
FWAP

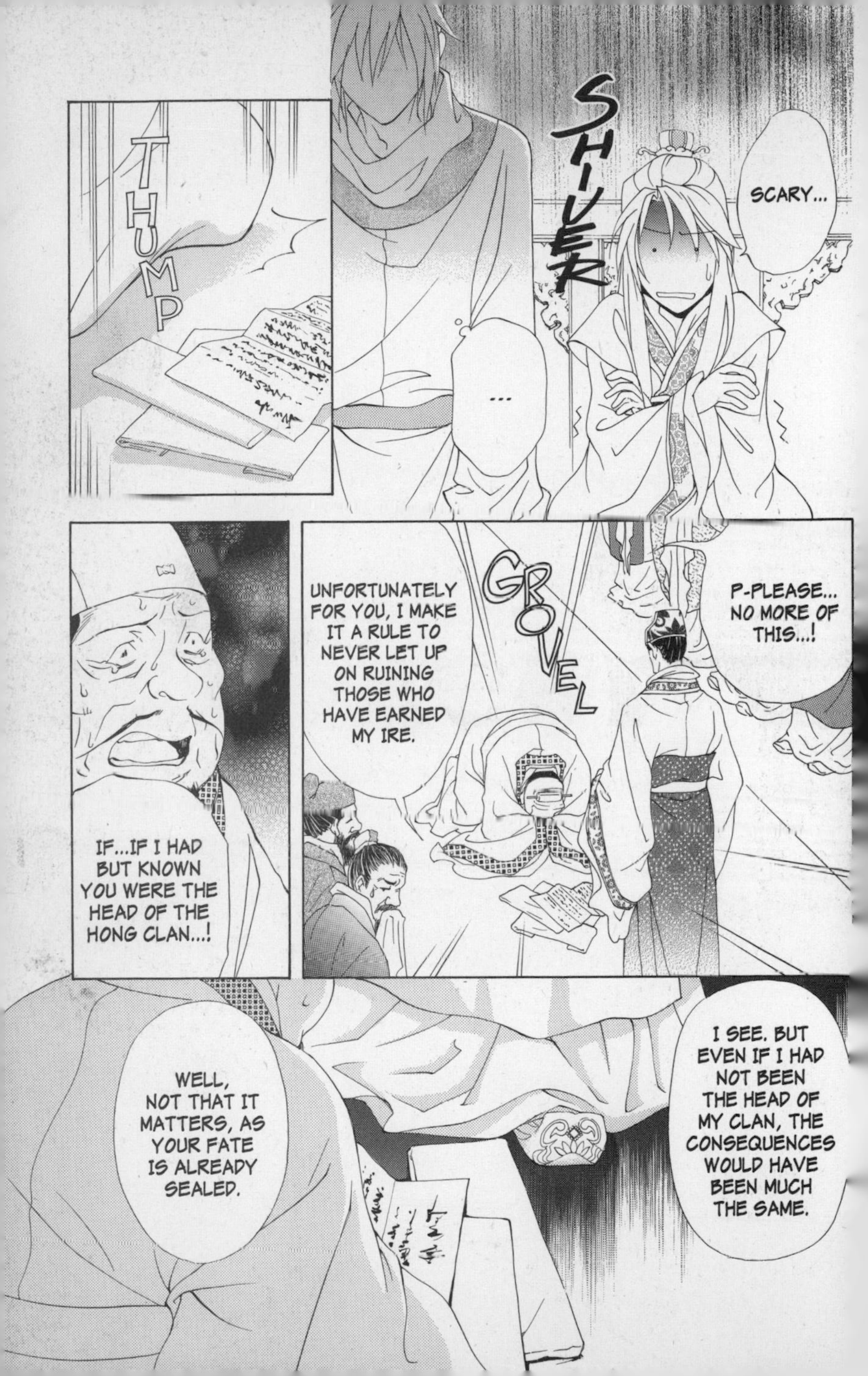
SHIVER
SCARY...
...
THUMP
P-PLEASE... NO MORE OF THIS...!
GROVEL
UNFORTUNATELY FOR YOU, I MAKE IT A RULE TO NEVER LET UP ON RUINING THOSE WHO HAVE EARNED MY IRE.
IF...IF I HAD BUT KNOWN YOU WERE THE HEAD OF THE HONG CLAN...!
I SEE. BUT EVEN IF I HAD NOT BEEN THE HEAD OF MY CLAN, THE CONSEQUENCES WOULD HAVE BEEN MUCH THE SAME.
WELL, NOT THAT IT MATTERS, AS YOUR FATE IS ALREADY SEALED.

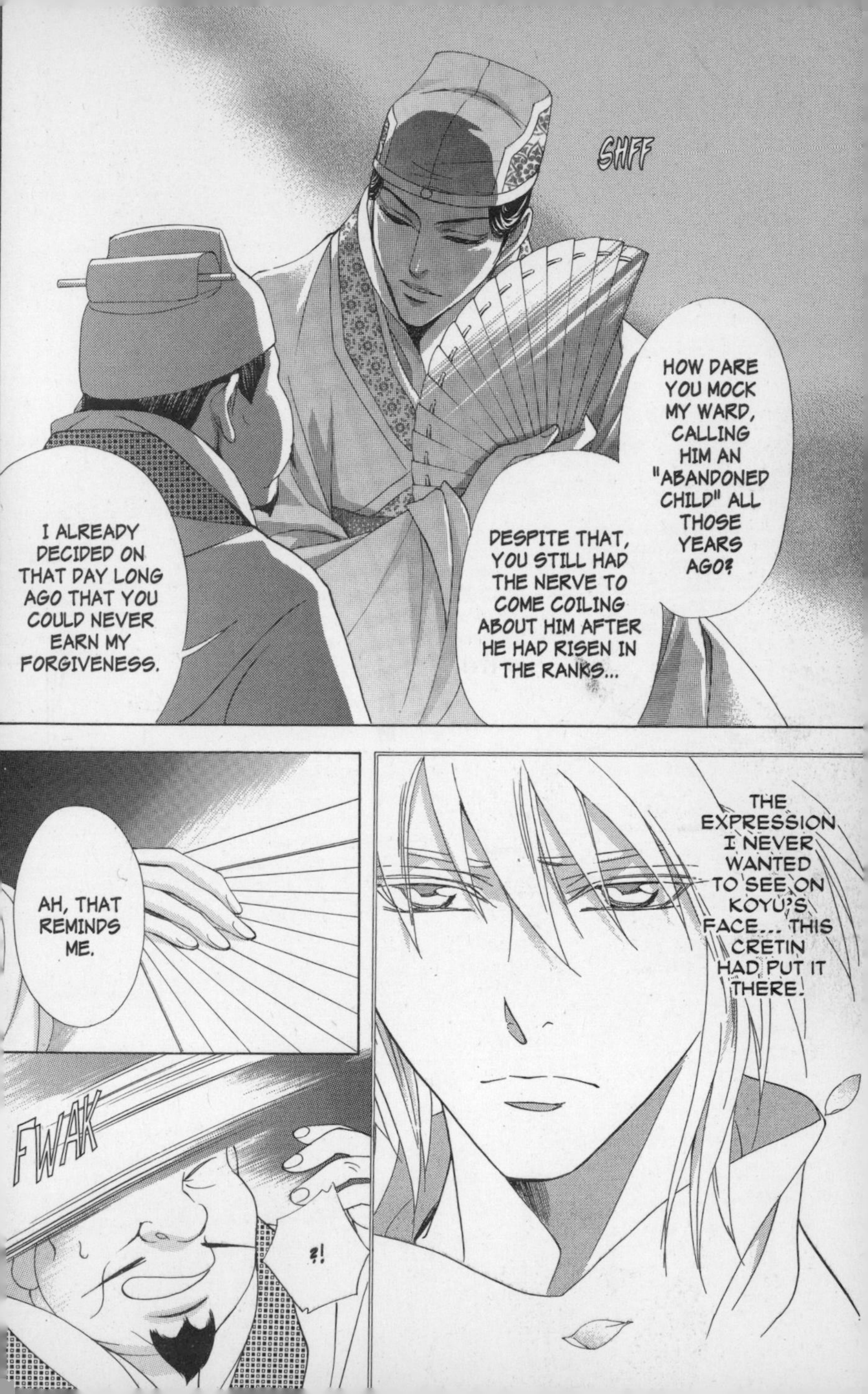
SHFF
HOW DARE YOU MOCK MY WARD, CALLING HIM AN "ABANDONED CHILD" ALL THOSE YEARS AGO?
DESPITE THAT, YOU STILL HAD THE NERVE TO COME COILING ABOUT HIM AFTER HE HAD RISEN IN THE RANKS...
I ALREADY DECIDED ON THAT DAY LONG AGO THAT YOU COULD NEVER EARN MY FORGIVENESS.
THE EXPRESSION I NEVER WANTED TO SEE ON KOYU'S FACE... THIS CRETIN HAD PUT IT THERE.
AH, THAT REMINDS ME.
FWAK
?!

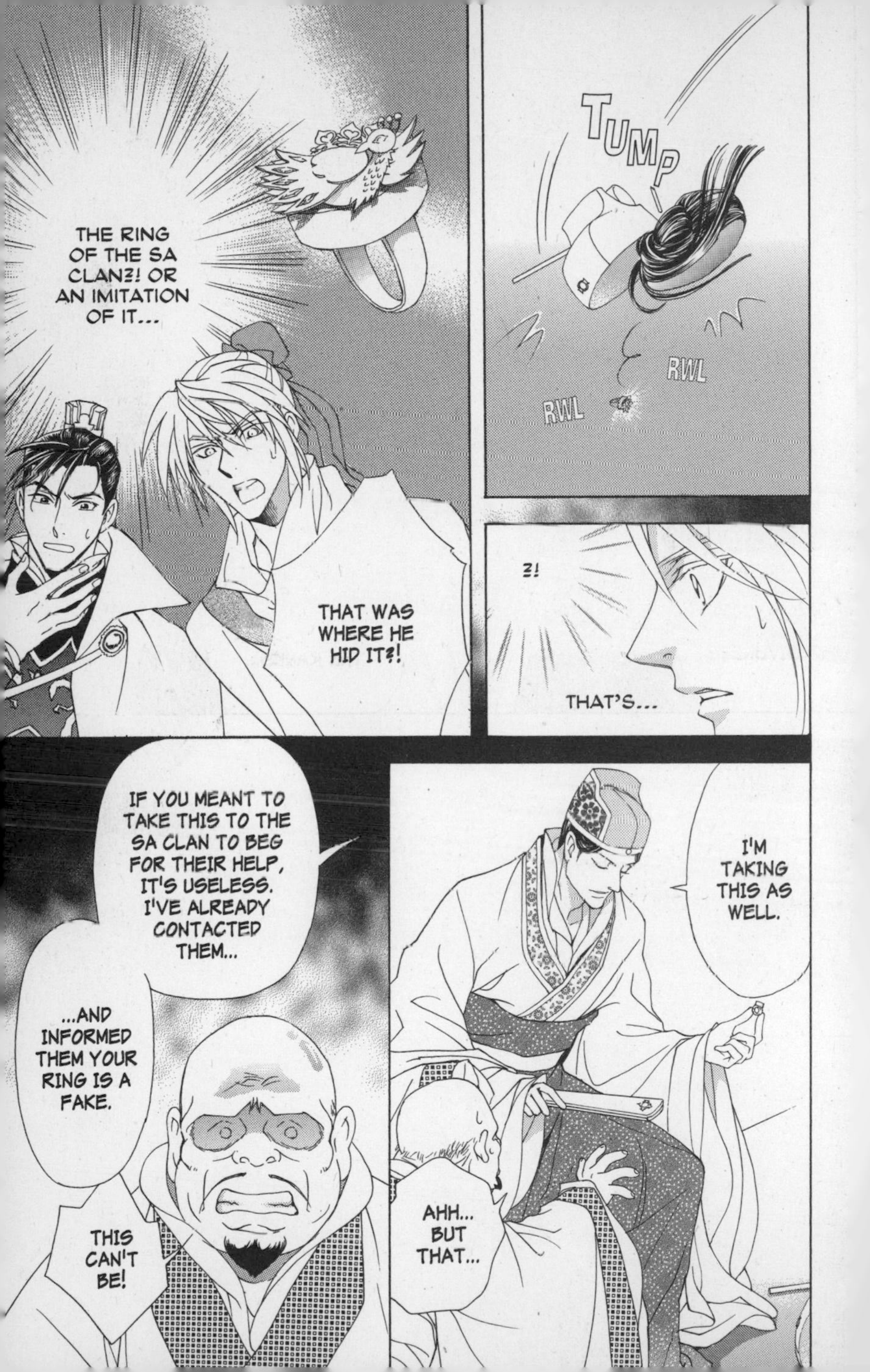
TUMP
RWL
RWL
?!
THAT'S...
THE RING OF THE SA CLAN?! OR AN IMITATION OF IT...
THAT WAS WHERE HE HID IT?!
I'M TAKING THIS AS WELL.
AHH... BUT THAT...
IF YOU MEANT TO TAKE THIS TO THE SA CLAN TO BEG FOR THEIR HELP, IT'S USELESS. I'VE ALREADY CONTACTED THEM...
...AND INFORMED THEM YOUR RING IS A FAKE.
THIS CAN'T BE!

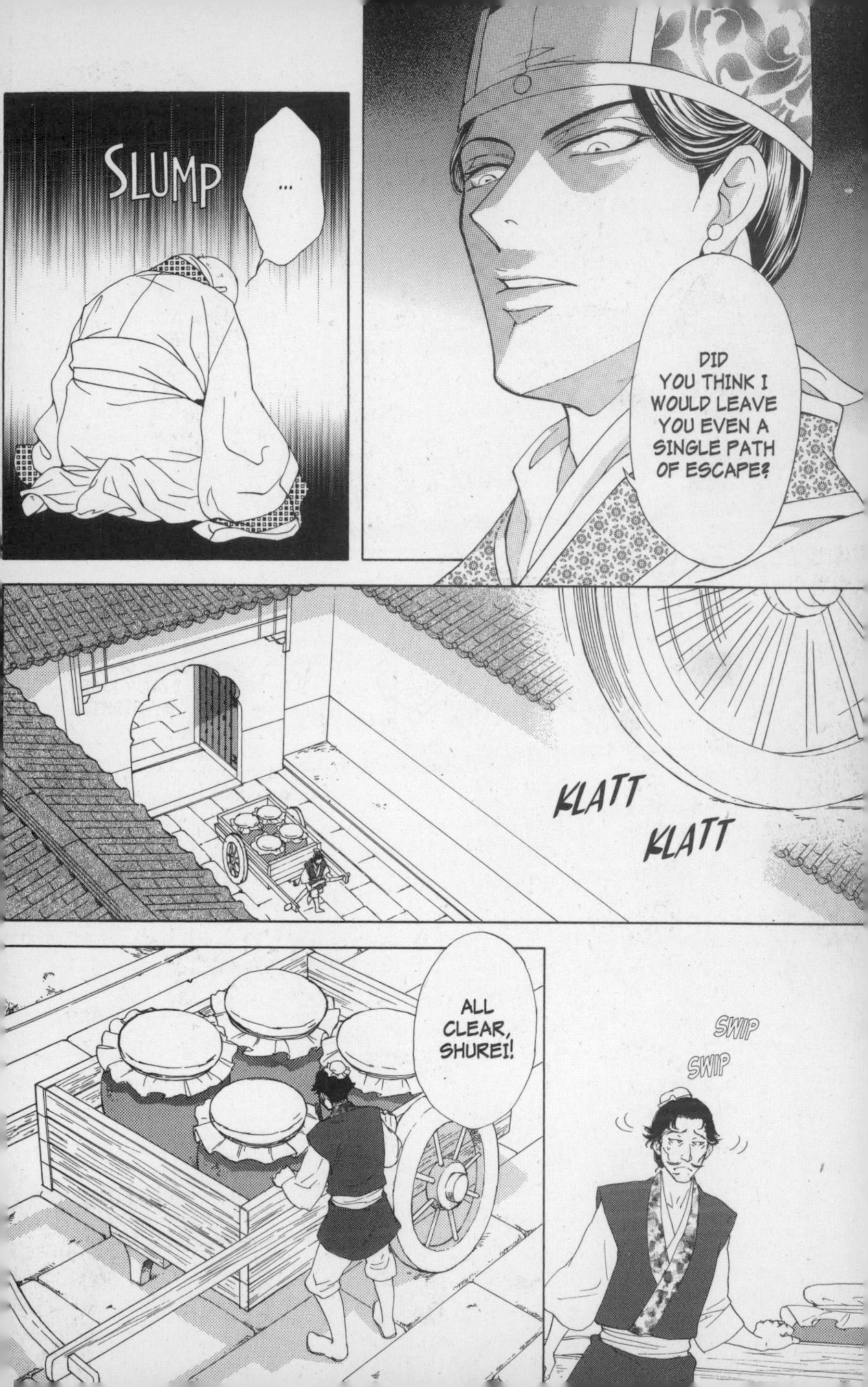
DID YOU THINK I WOULD LEAVE YOU EVEN A SINGLE PATH OF ESCAPE?
SLUMP
...
KLATT
KLATT
SWIP
SWIP
ALL CLEAR, SHUREI!

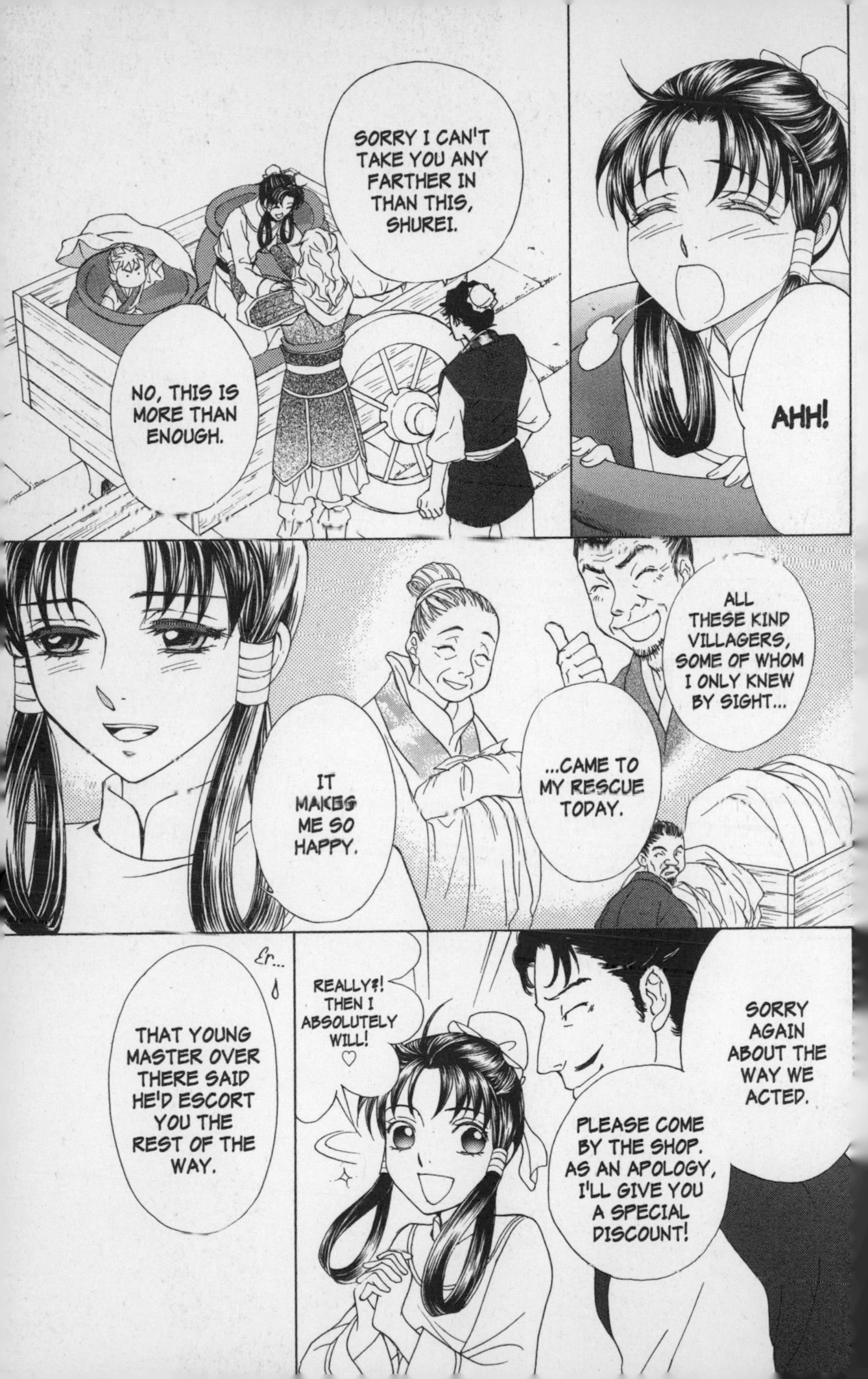
AHH!
SORRY I CAN'T TAKE YOU ANY FARTHER IN THAN THIS, SHUREI.
NO, THIS IS MORE THAN ENOUGH.
ALL THESE KIND VILLAGERS, SOME OF WHOM I ONLY KNEW BY SIGHT...
...CAME TO MY RESCUE TODAY.
IT MAKES ME SO HAPPY.
SORRY AGAIN ABOUT THE WAY WE ACTED.
PLEASE COME BY THE SHOP. AS AN APOLOGY, I'LL GIVE YOU A SPECIAL DISCOUNT!
REALLY?! THEN I ABSOLUTELY WILL! ♡
Er...
THAT YOUNG MASTER OVER THERE SAID HE'D ESCORT YOU THE REST OF THE WAY.

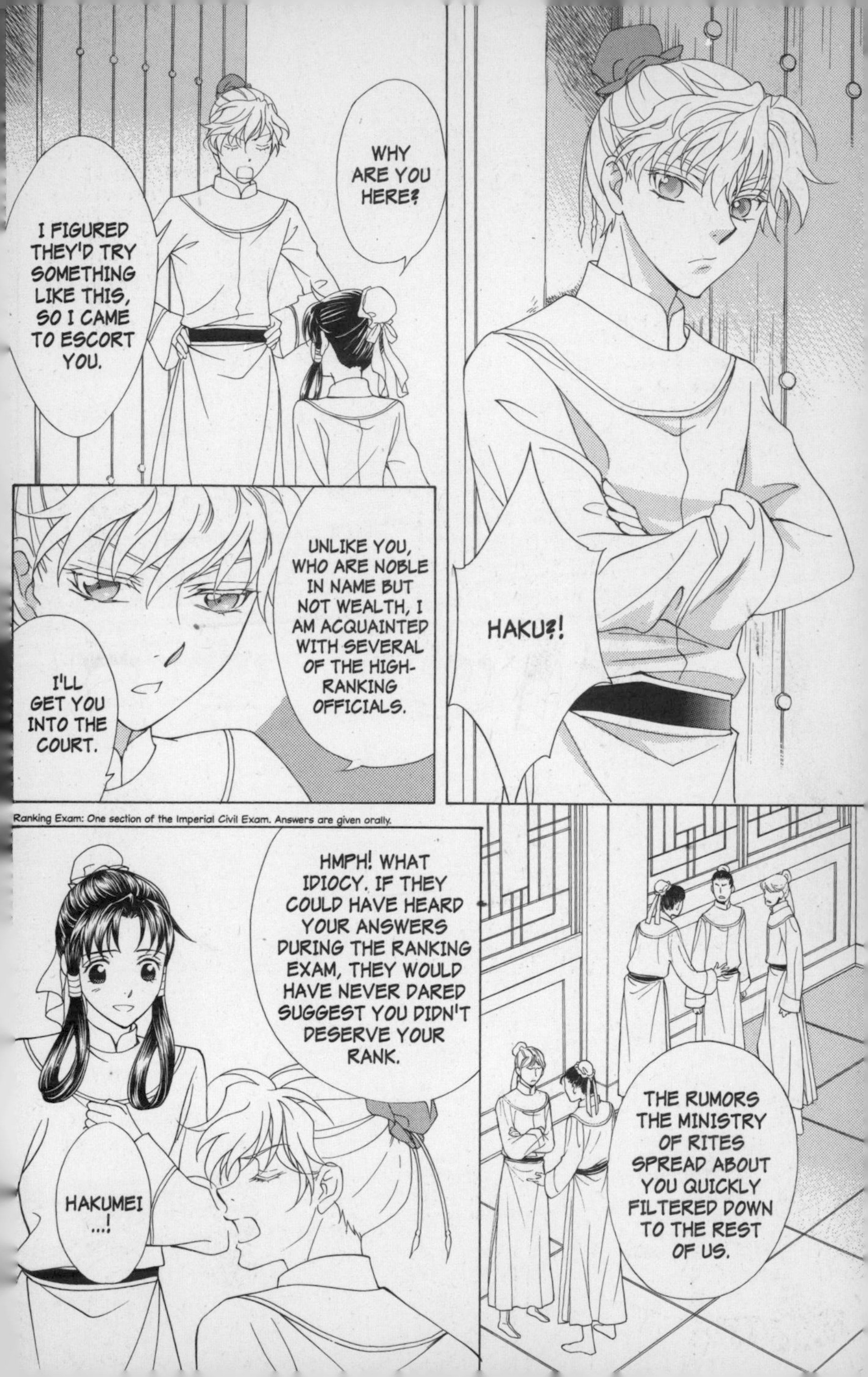
HAKU?!
WHY ARE YOU HERE?
I FIGURED THEY'D TRY SOMETHING LIKE THIS, SO I CAME TO ESCORT YOU.
UNLIKE YOU, WHO ARE NOBLE IN NAME BUT NOT WEALTH, I AM ACQUAINTED WITH SEVERAL OF THE HIGH-RANKING OFFICIALS.
I'LL GET YOU INTO THE COURT.
THE RUMORS THE MINISTRY OF RITES SPREAD ABOUT YOU QUICKLY FILTERED DOWN TO THE REST OF US.
HMPH! WHAT IDIOCY. IF THEY COULD HAVE HEARD YOUR ANSWERS DURING THE RANKING EXAM, THEY WOULD HAVE NEVER DARED SUGGEST YOU DIDN'T DESERVE YOUR RANK.
HAKUMEI ...!
Ranking Exam: One section of the Imperial Civil Exam. Answers are given orally.

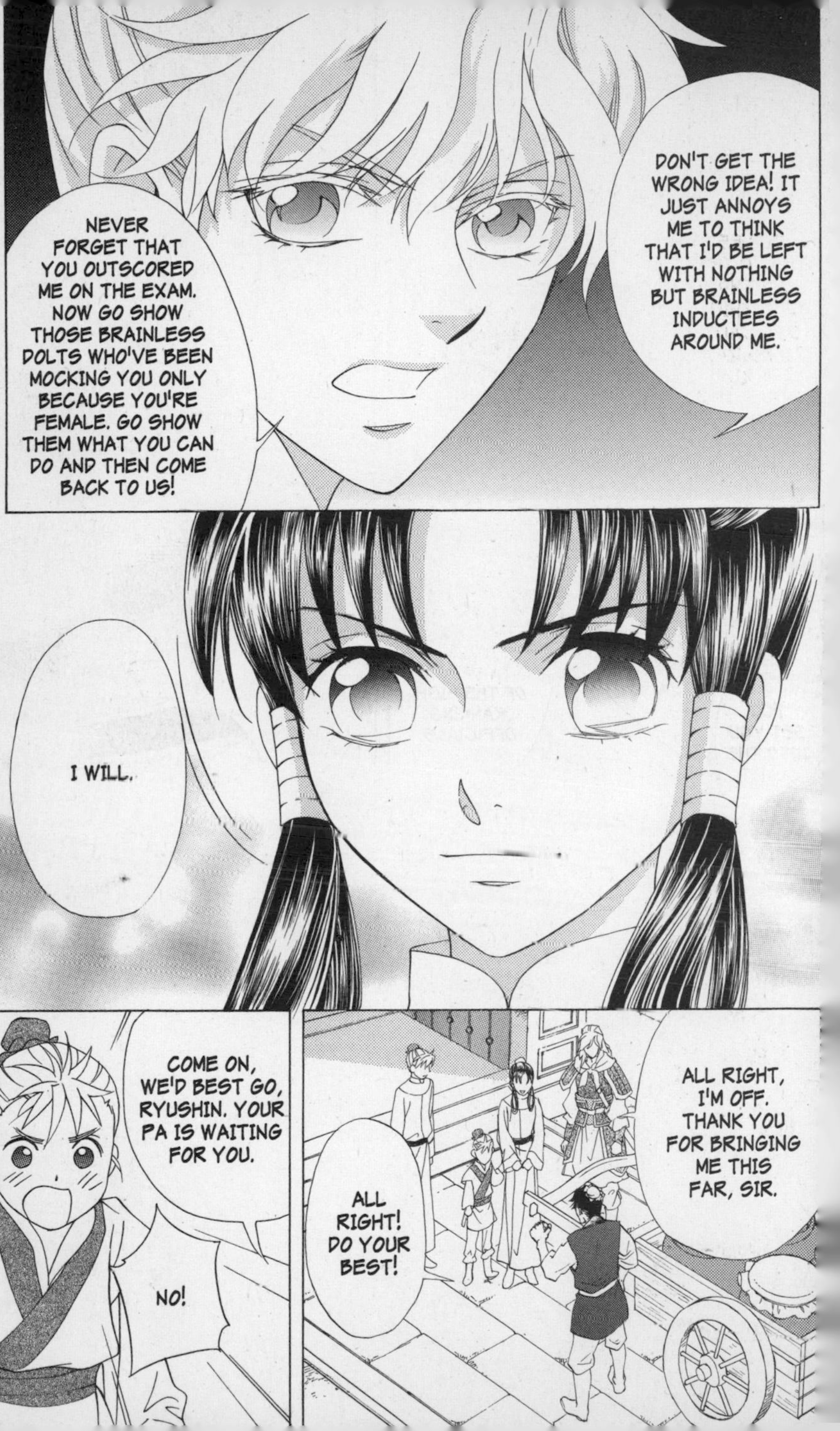
DON'T GET THE WRONG IDEA! IT JUST ANNOYS ME TO THINK THAT I'D BE LEFT WITH NOTHING BUT BRAINLESS INDUCTEES AROUND ME.
NEVER FORGET THAT YOU OUTSCORED ME ON THE EXAM. NOW GO SHOW THOSE BRAINLESS DOLTS WHO'VE BEEN MOCKING YOU ONLY BECAUSE YOU'RE FEMALE. GO SHOW THEM WHAT YOU CAN DO AND THEN COME BACK TO US!
I WILL.
ALL RIGHT, I'M OFF. THANK YOU FOR BRINGING ME THIS FAR, SIR.
ALL RIGHT! DO YOUR BEST!
COME ON, WE'D BEST GO, RYUSHIN. YOUR PA IS WAITING FOR YOU.
NO!

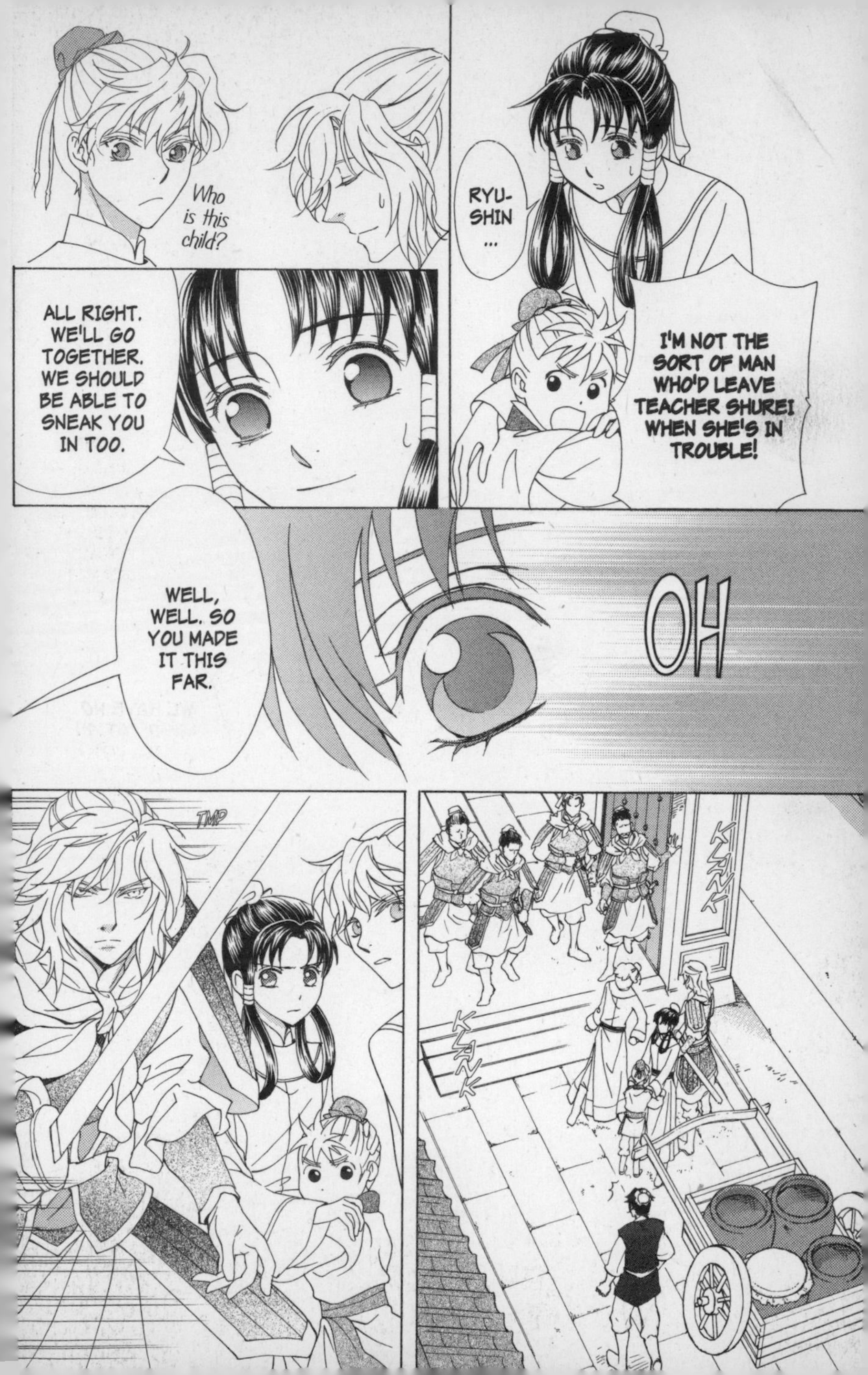
RYU-SHIN ...
I'M NOT THE SORT OF MAN WHO'D LEAVE TEACHER SHUREI WHEN SHE'S IN TROUBLE!
Who is this child?
ALL RIGHT. WE'LL GO TOGETHER. WE SHOULD BE ABLE TO SNEAK YOU IN TOO.
OH
WELL, WELL. SO YOU MADE IT THIS FAR.
KLANK
KLANK
TMP

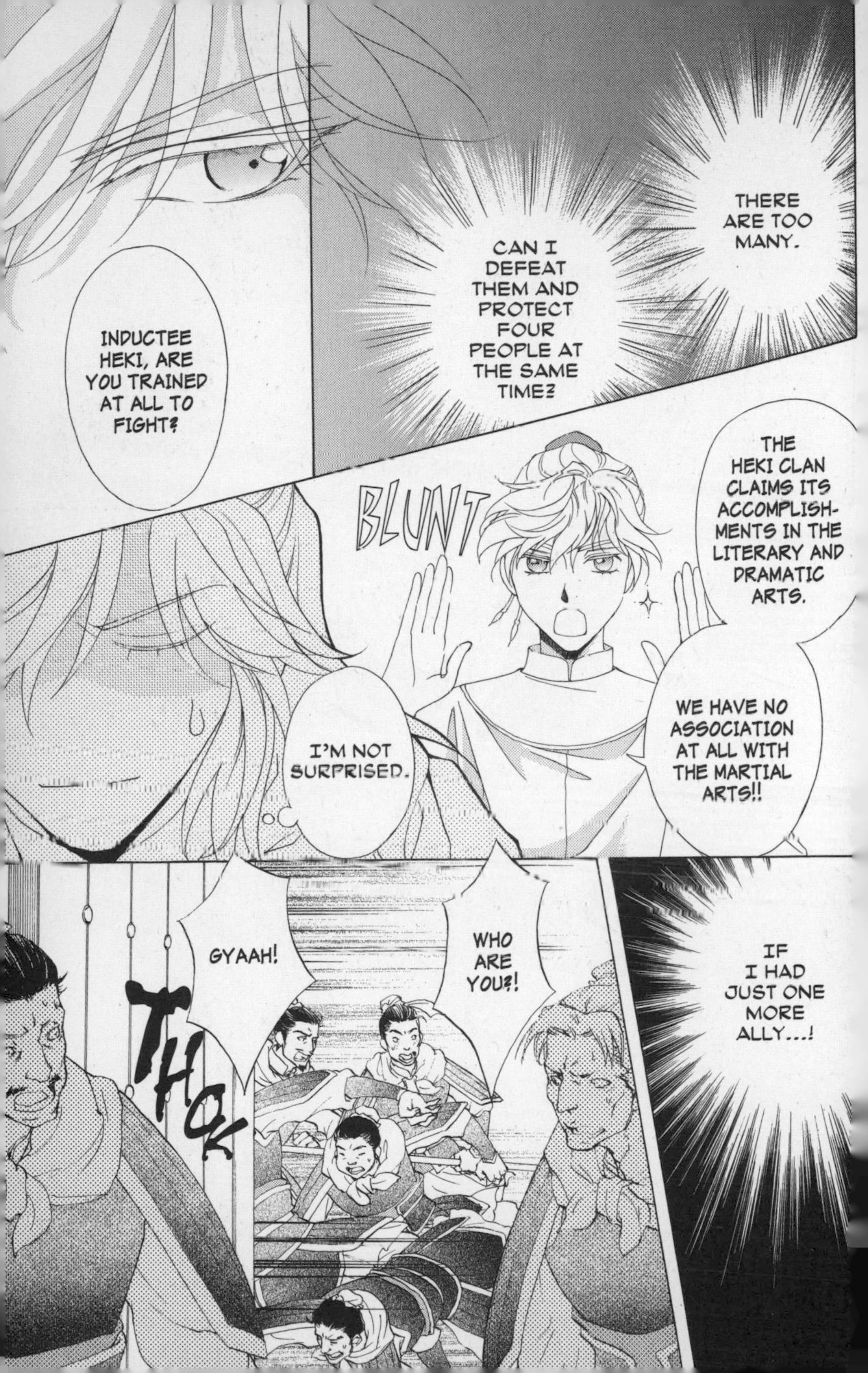
THERE ARE TOO MANY.
CAN I DEFEAT THEM AND PROTECT FOUR PEOPLE AT THE SAME TIME?
INDUCTEE HEKI, ARE YOU TRAINED AT ALL TO FIGHT?
THE HEKI CLAN CLAIMS ITS ACCOMPLISH-MENTS IN THE LITERARY AND DRAMATIC ARTS.
BLUNT
WE HAVE NO ASSOCIATION AT ALL WITH THE MARTIAL ARTS!!
I'M NOT SURPRISED.
IF I HAD JUST ONE MORE ALLY...!
WHO ARE YOU?!
GYAAH!
THOK

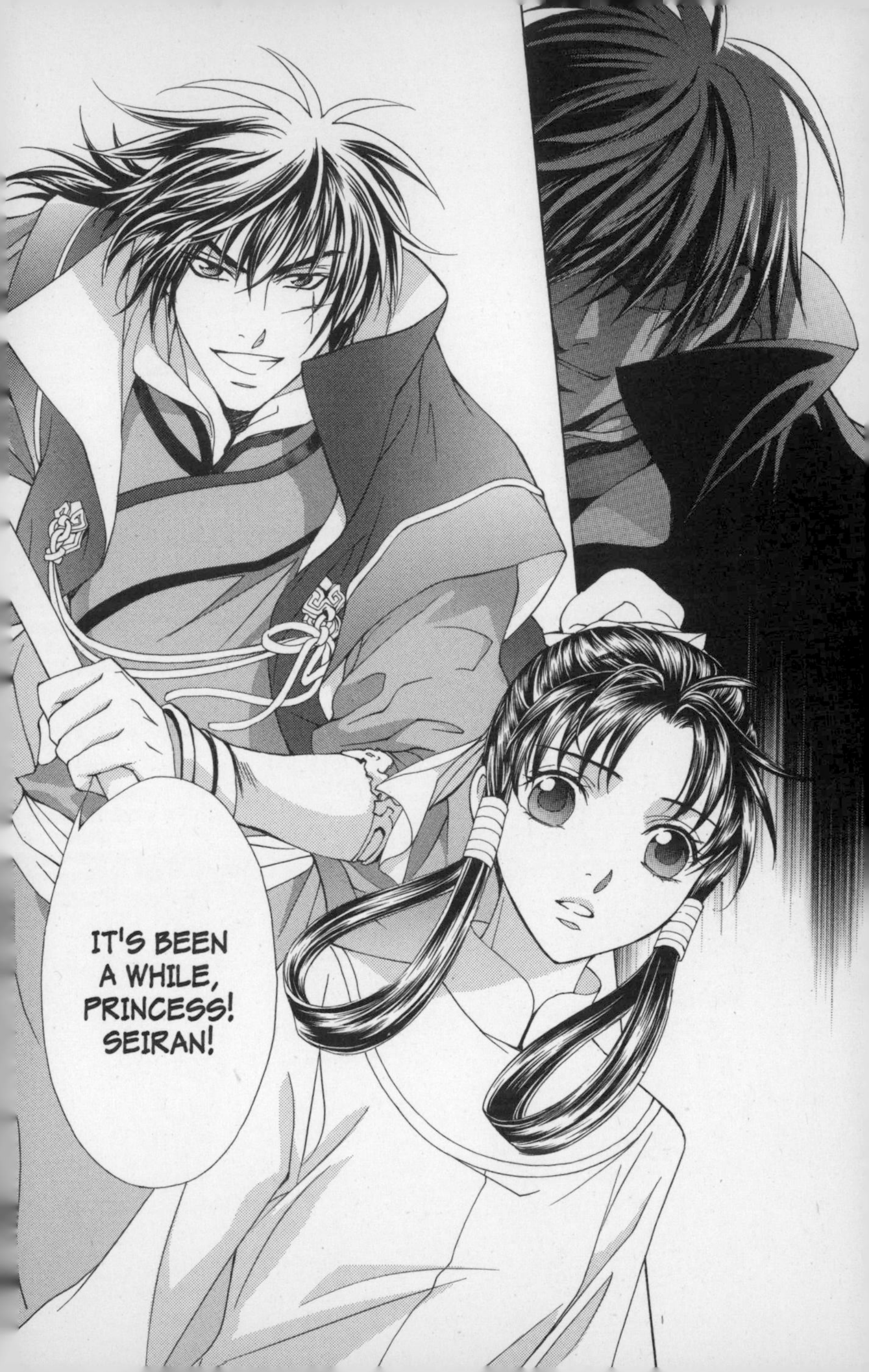
IT'S BEEN A WHILE, PRINCESS! SEIRAN!

SLUMP

The Story of
SAIUNKOKU

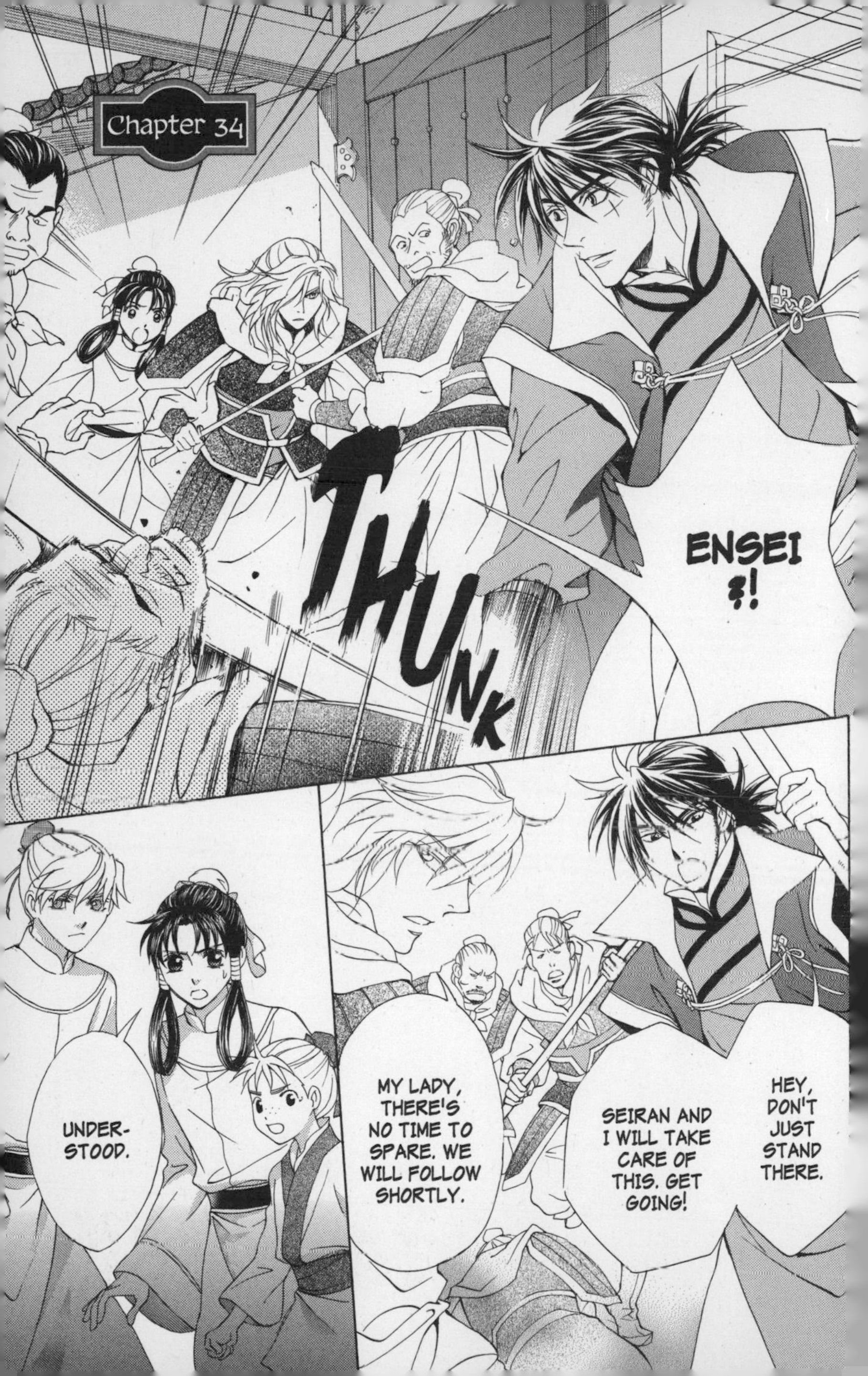
Chapter 34
ENSEI ?!
THUNK
HEY, DON'T JUST STAND THERE.
SEIRAN AND I WILL TAKE CARE OF THIS. GET GOING!
MY LADY, THERE'S NO TIME TO SPARE. WE WILL FOLLOW SHORTLY.
UNDER-STOOD.

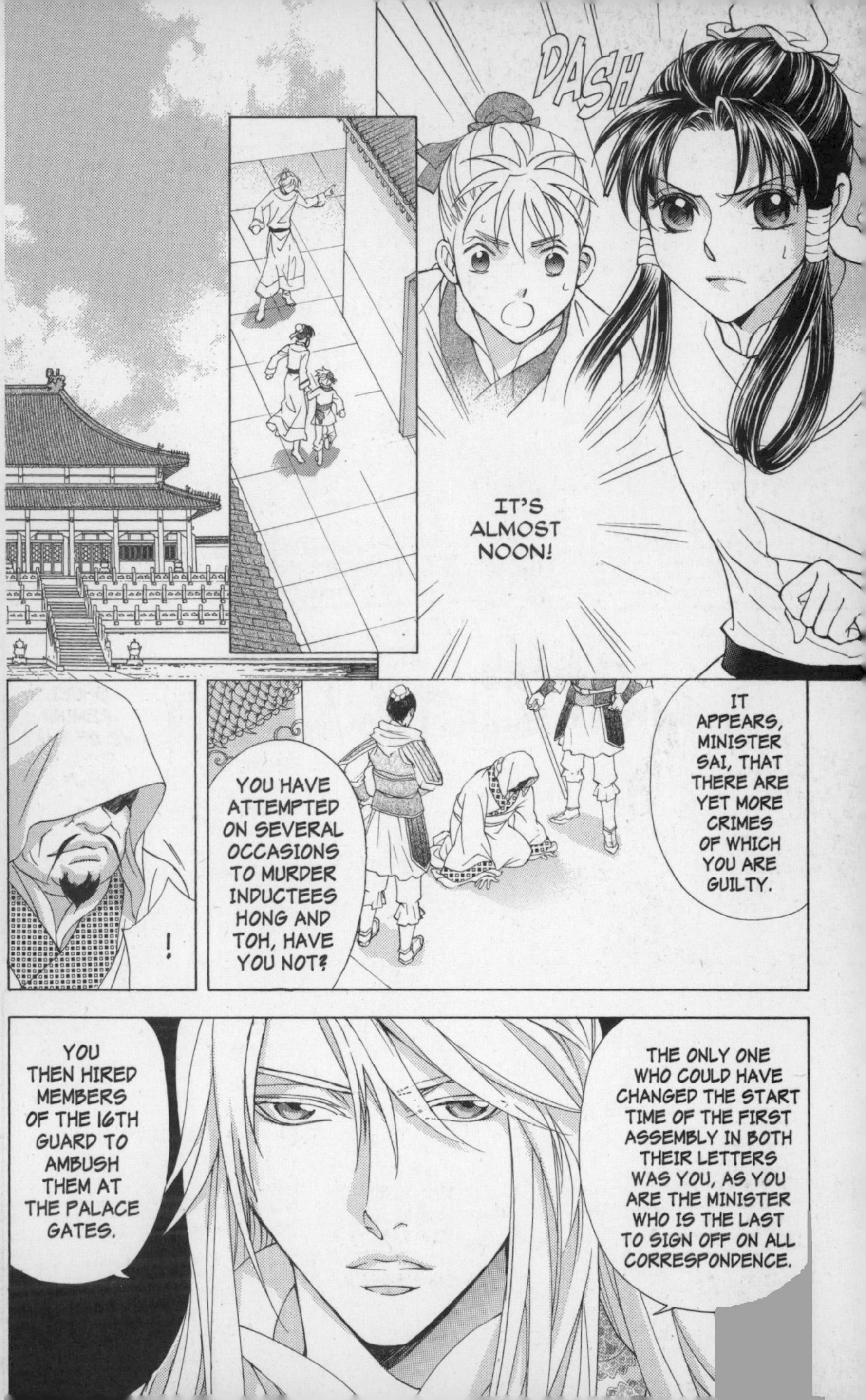
DASH
IT'S ALMOST NOON!
IT APPEARS, MINISTER SAI, THAT THERE ARE YET MORE CRIMES OF WHICH YOU ARE GUILTY.
YOU HAVE ATTEMPTED ON SEVERAL OCCASIONS TO MURDER INDUCTEES HONG AND TOH, HAVE YOU NOT?
!
THE ONLY ONE WHO COULD HAVE CHANGED THE START TIME OF THE FIRST ASSEMBLY IN BOTH THEIR LETTERS WAS YOU, AS YOU ARE THE MINISTER WHO IS THE LAST TO SIGN OFF ON ALL CORRESPONDENCE.
YOU THEN HIRED MEMBERS OF THE 16TH GUARD TO AMBUSH THEM AT THE PALACE GATES.

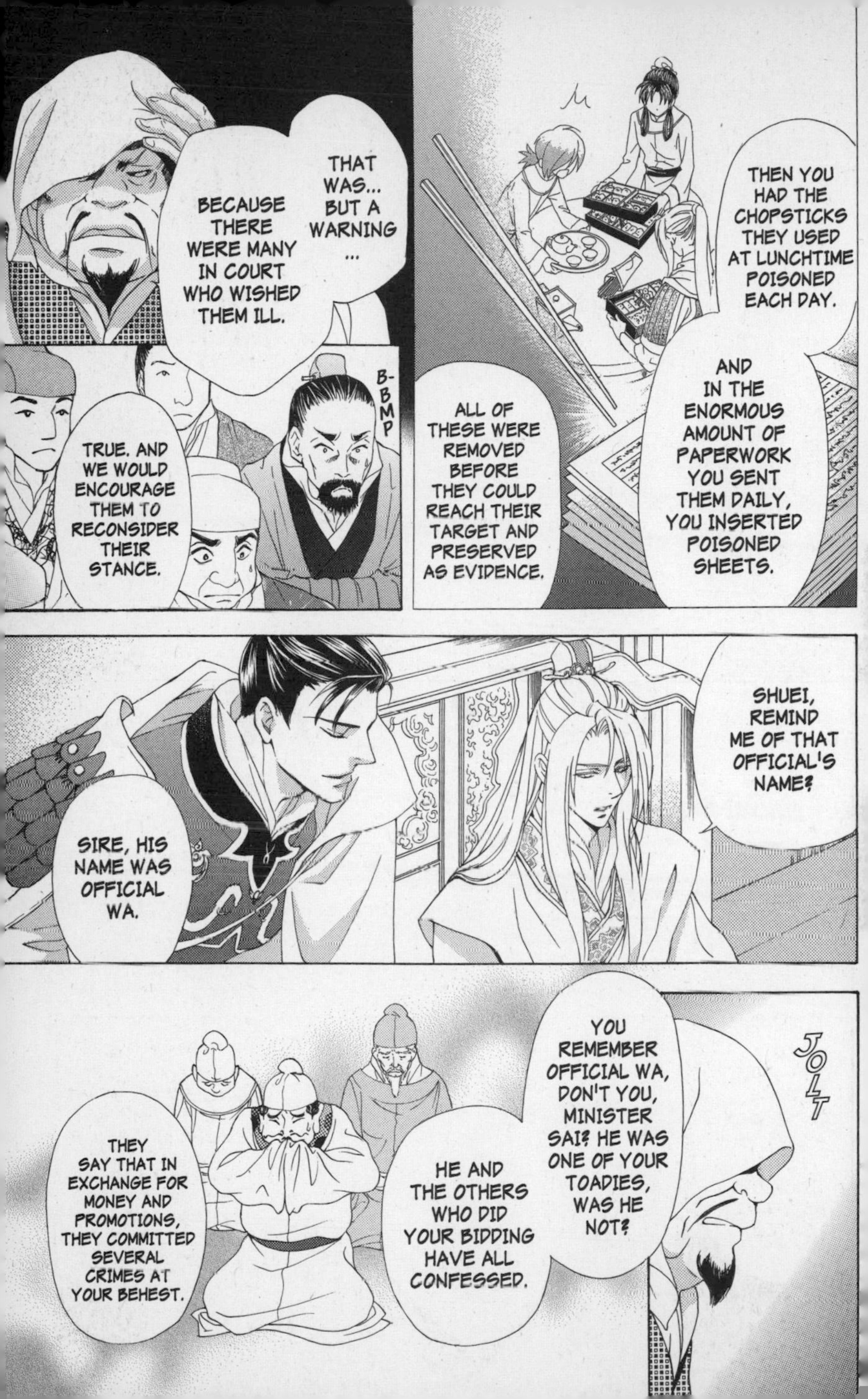
THEN YOU HAD THE CHOPSTICKS THEY USED AT LUNCHTIME POISONED EACH DAY.
AND IN THE ENORMOUS AMOUNT OF PAPERWORK YOU SENT THEM DAILY, YOU INSERTED POISONED SHEETS.
ALL OF THESE WERE REMOVED BEFORE THEY COULD REACH THEIR TARGET AND PRESERVED AS EVIDENCE.
THAT WAS... BUT A WARNING...
BECAUSE THERE WERE MANY IN COURT WHO WISHED THEM ILL.
B-BMP
TRUE. AND WE WOULD ENCOURAGE THEM TO RECONSIDER THEIR STANCE.
SHUEI, REMIND ME OF THAT OFFICIAL'S NAME?
SIRE, HIS NAME WAS OFFICIAL WA.
JOLT
YOU REMEMBER OFFICIAL WA, DON'T YOU, MINISTER SAI? HE WAS ONE OF YOUR TOADIES, WAS HE NOT?
HE AND THE OTHERS WHO DID YOUR BIDDING HAVE ALL CONFESSED.
THEY SAY THAT IN EXCHANGE FOR MONEY AND PROMOTIONS, THEY COMMITTED SEVERAL CRIMES AT YOUR BEHEST.

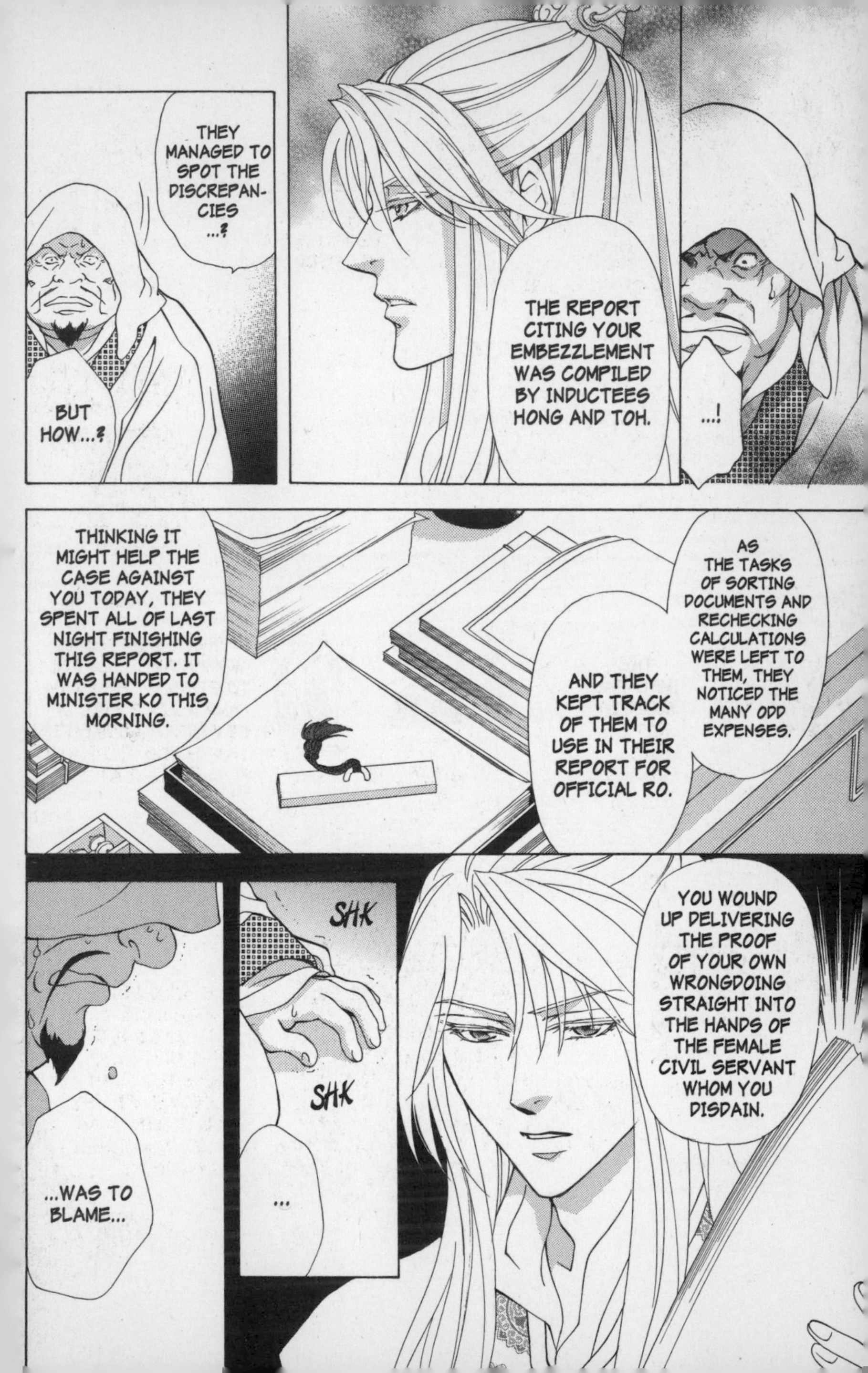
THE REPORT CITING YOUR EMBEZZLEMENT WAS COMPILED BY INDUCTEES HONG AND TOH.
...!
THEY MANAGED TO SPOT THE DISCREPAN-CIES ...?
BUT HOW...?
AS THE TASKS OF SORTING DOCUMENTS AND RECHECKING CALCULATIONS WERE LEFT TO THEM, THEY NOTICED THE MANY ODD EXPENSES.
AND THEY KEPT TRACK OF THEM TO USE IN THEIR REPORT FOR OFFICIAL RO.
THINKING IT MIGHT HELP THE CASE AGAINST YOU TODAY, THEY SPENT ALL OF LAST NIGHT FINISHING THIS REPORT. IT WAS HANDED TO MINISTER KO THIS MORNING.
YOU WOUND UP DELIVERING THE PROOF OF YOUR OWN WRONGDOING STRAIGHT INTO THE HANDS OF THE FEMALE CIVIL SERVANT WHOM YOU DISDAIN.
SHK
SHK
...
...WAS TO BLAME...

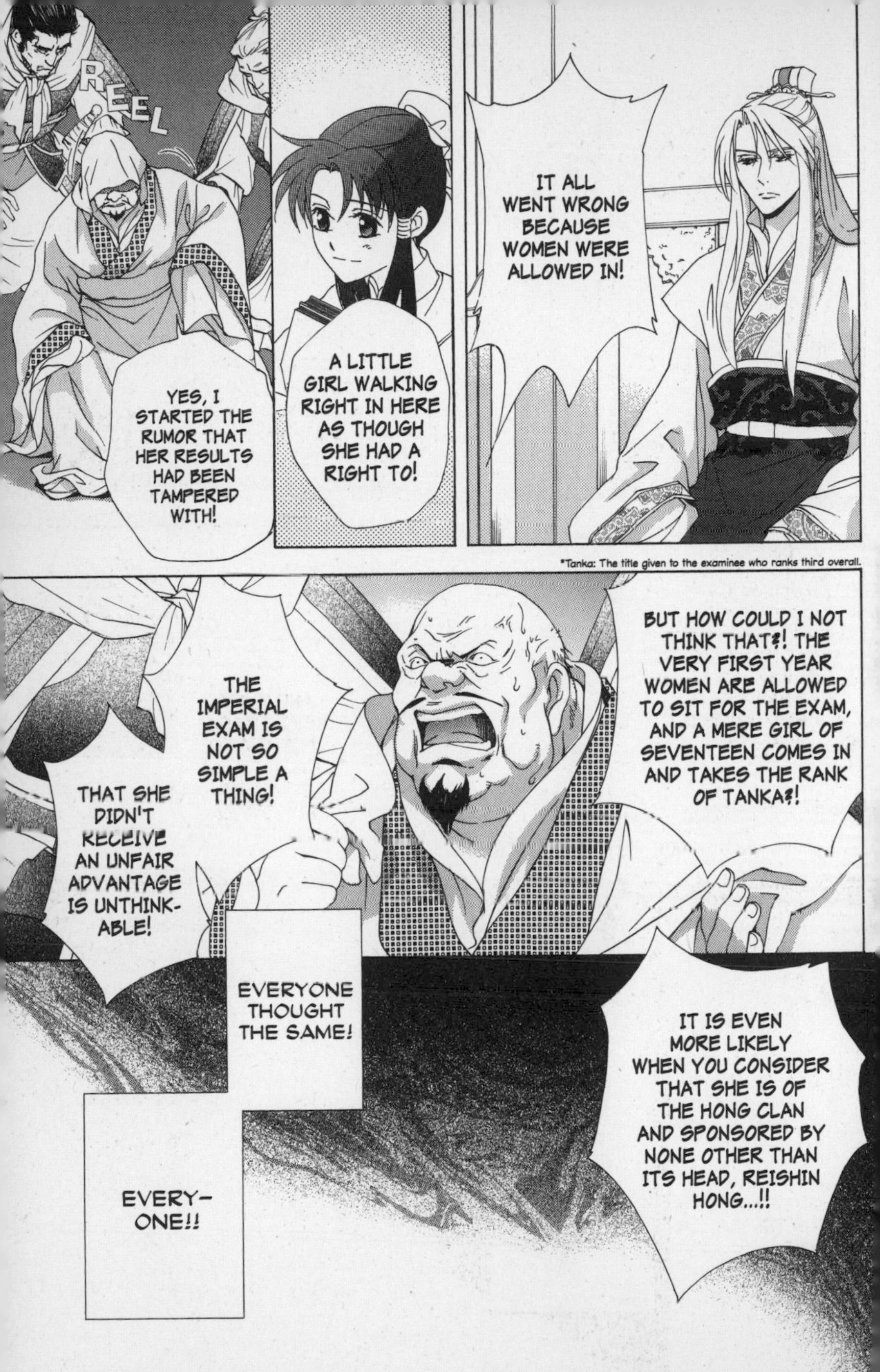
IT ALL WENT WRONG BECAUSE WOMEN WERE ALLOWED IN!
A LITTLE GIRL WALKING RIGHT IN HERE AS THOUGH SHE HAD A RIGHT TO!
REEL
YES, I STARTED THE RUMOR THAT HER RESULTS HAD BEEN TAMPERED WITH!
BUT HOW COULD I NOT THINK THAT?! THE VERY FIRST YEAR WOMEN ARE ALLOWED TO SIT FOR THE EXAM, AND A MERE GIRL OF SEVENTEEN COMES IN AND TAKES THE RANK OF TANKA?!
THE IMPERIAL EXAM IS NOT SO SIMPLE A THING!
THAT SHE DIDN'T RECEIVE AN UNFAIR ADVANTAGE IS UNTHINK-ABLE!
IT IS EVEN MORE LIKELY WHEN YOU CONSIDER THAT SHE IS OF THE HONG CLAN AND SPONSORED BY NONE OTHER THAN ITS HEAD, REISHIN HONG...!!
EVERYONE THOUGHT THE SAME!
EVERY-ONE!!

*Tanka: The title given to the examinee who ranks third overall.

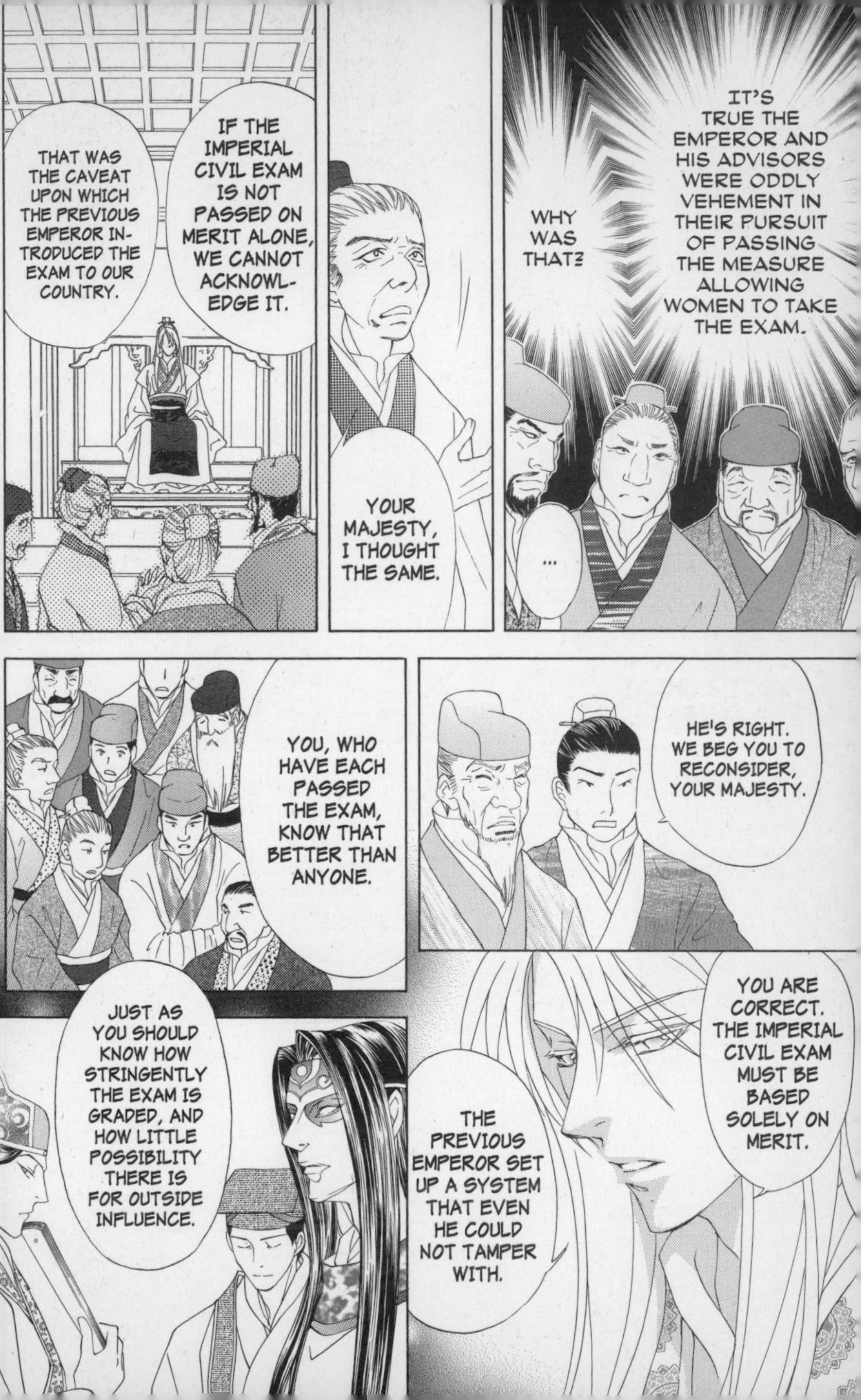

IT'S TRUE THE EMPEROR AND HIS ADVISORS WERE ODDLY VEHEMENT IN THEIR PURSUIT OF PASSING THE MEASURE ALLOWING WOMEN TO TAKE THE EXAM.
WHY WAS THAT?
...
YOUR MAJESTY, I THOUGHT THE SAME.
IF THE IMPERIAL CIVIL EXAM IS NOT PASSED ON MERIT ALONE, WE CANNOT ACKNOWLEDGE IT.
THAT WAS THE CAVEAT UPON WHICH THE PREVIOUS EMPEROR INTRODUCED THE EXAM TO OUR COUNTRY.
HE'S RIGHT. WE BEG YOU TO RECONSIDER, YOUR MAJESTY.
YOU, WHO HAVE EACH PASSED THE EXAM, KNOW THAT BETTER THAN ANYONE.
YOU ARE CORRECT. THE IMPERIAL CIVIL EXAM MUST BE BASED SOLELY ON MERIT.
THE PREVIOUS EMPEROR SET UP A SYSTEM THAT EVEN HE COULD NOT TAMPER WITH.
JUST AS YOU SHOULD KNOW HOW STRINGENTLY THE EXAM IS GRADED, AND HOW LITTLE POSSIBILITY THERE IS FOR OUTSIDE INFLUENCE.

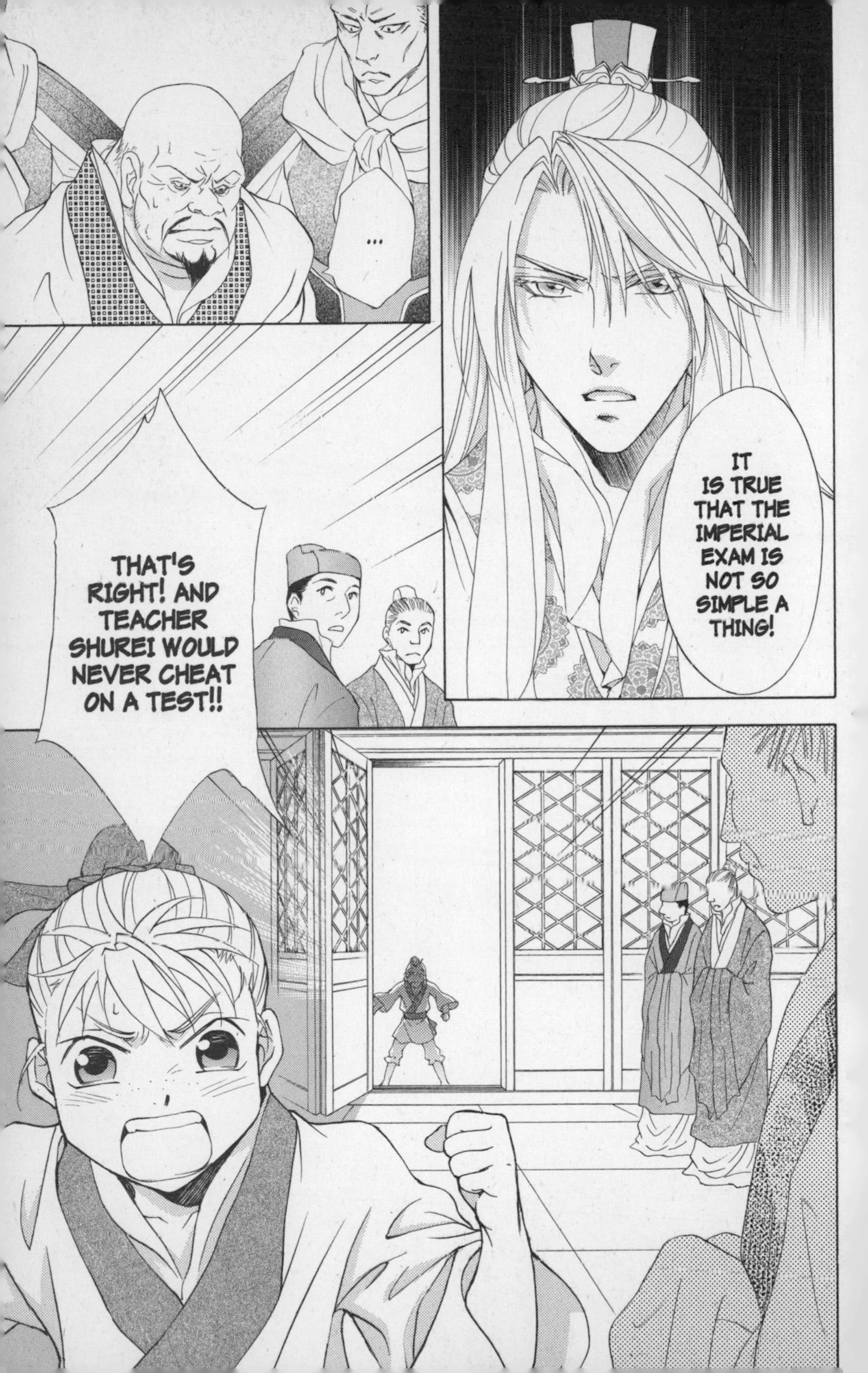
IT IS TRUE THAT THE IMPERIAL EXAM IS NOT SO SIMPLE A THING!
...
THAT'S RIGHT! AND TEACHER SHUREI WOULD NEVER CHEAT ON A TEST!!

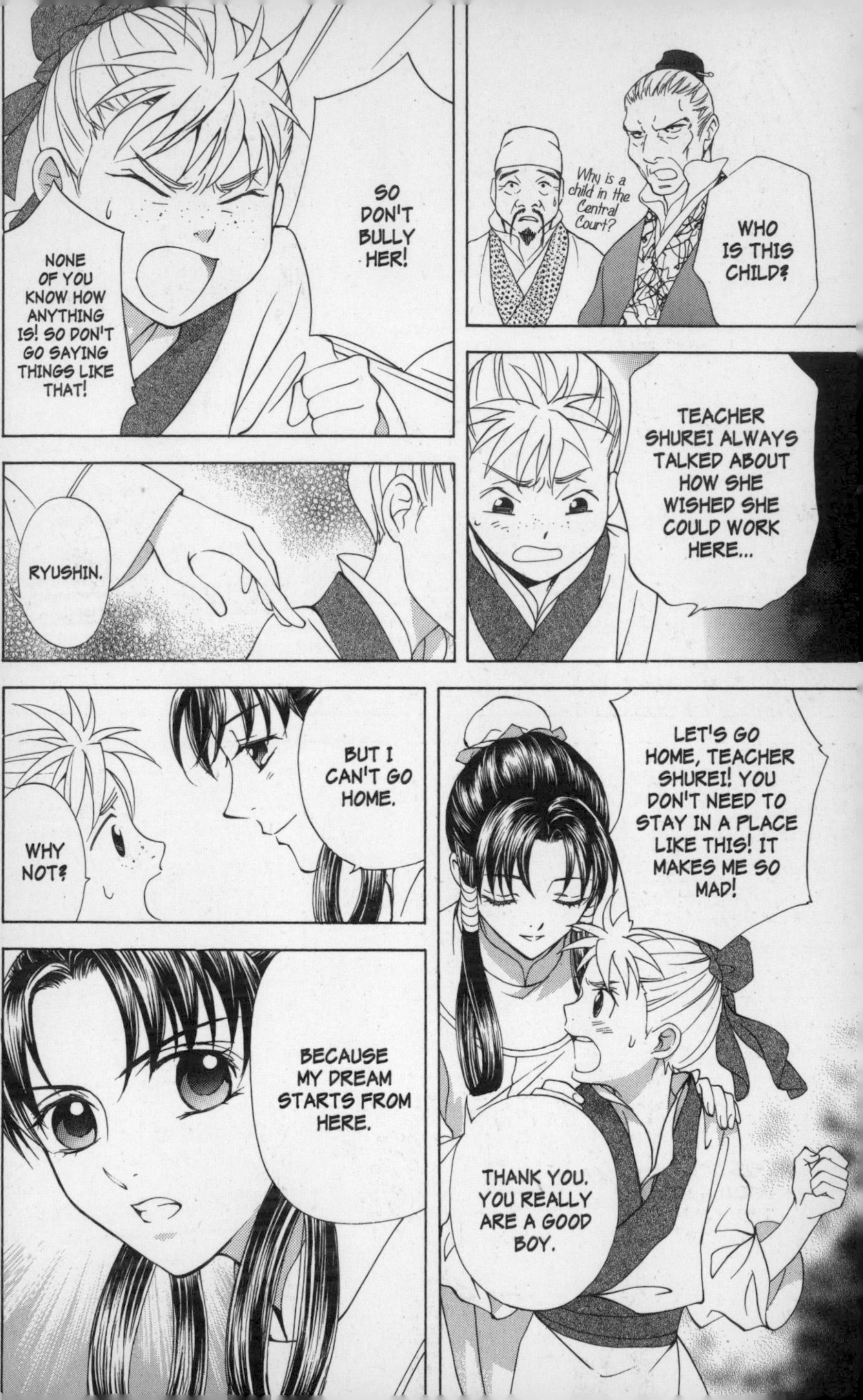
WHO IS THIS CHILD?
Why is a child in the Central Court?
SO DON'T BULLY HER!
NONE OF YOU KNOW HOW ANYTHING IS! SO DON'T GO SAYING THINGS LIKE THAT!
TEACHER SHUREI ALWAYS TALKED ABOUT HOW SHE WISHED SHE COULD WORK HERE...
RYUSHIN.
LET'S GO HOME, TEACHER SHUREI! YOU DON'T NEED TO STAY IN A PLACE LIKE THIS! IT MAKES ME SO MAD!
THANK YOU. YOU REALLY ARE A GOOD BOY.
BUT I CAN'T GO HOME.
WHY NOT?
BECAUSE MY DREAM STARTS FROM HERE.

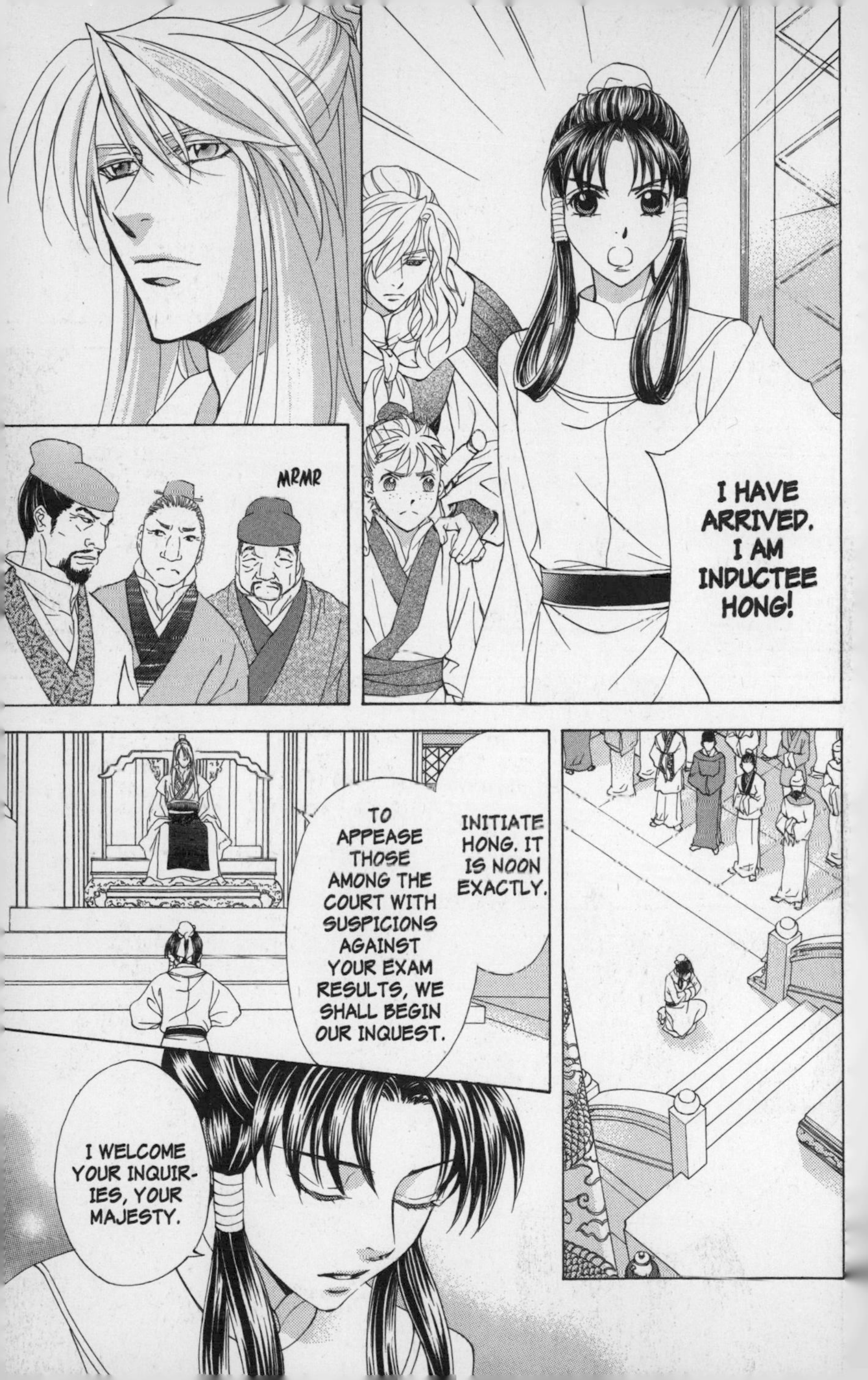
I HAVE ARRIVED. I AM INDUCTEE HONG!
MRMR
INITIATE HONG. IT IS NOON EXACTLY.
TO APPEASE THOSE AMONG THE COURT WITH SUSPICIONS AGAINST YOUR EXAM RESULTS, WE SHALL BEGIN OUR INQUEST.
I WELCOME YOUR INQUIR-IES, YOUR MAJESTY.

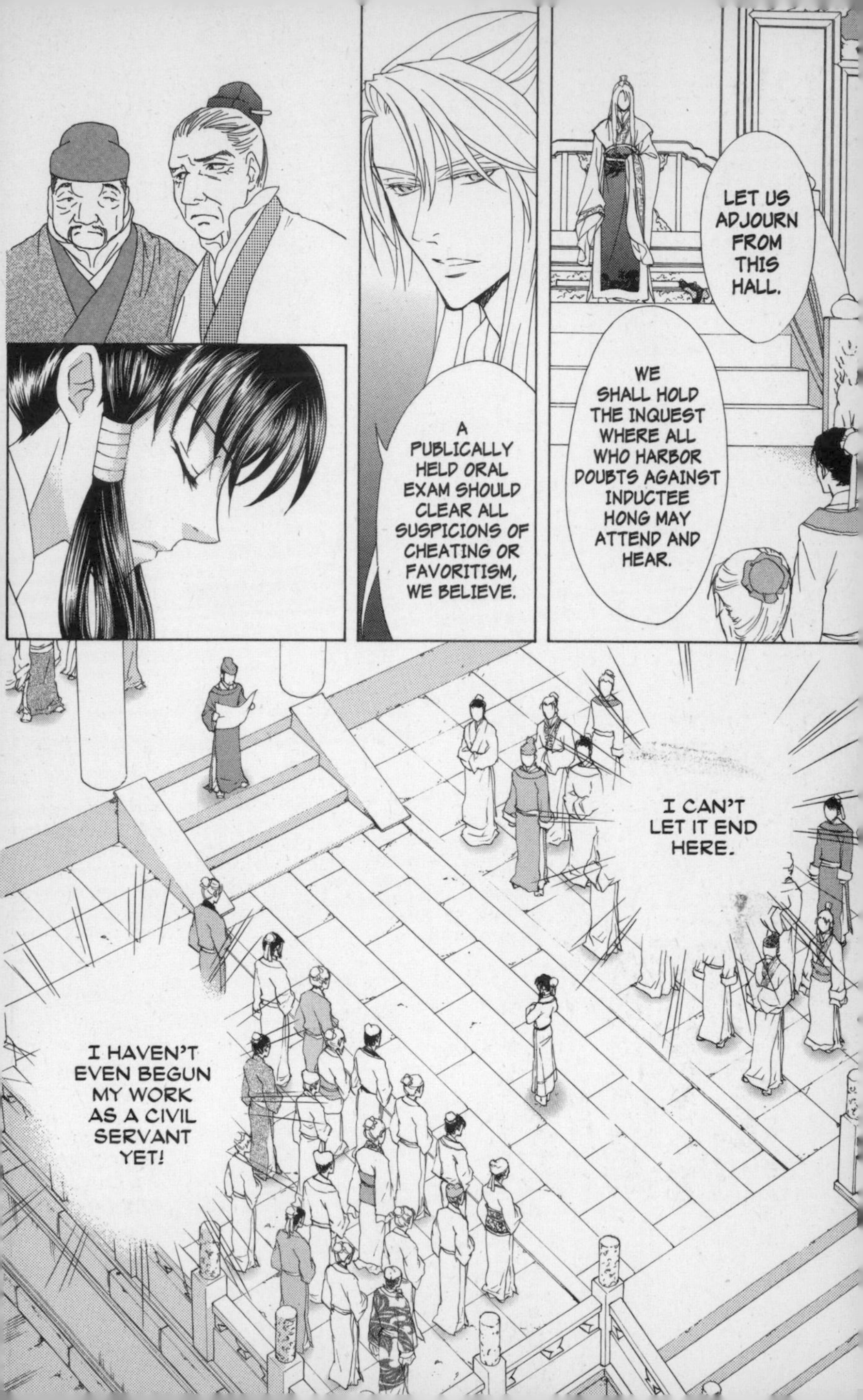
LET US ADJOURN FROM THIS HALL.
WE SHALL HOLD THE INQUEST WHERE ALL WHO HARBOR DOUBTS AGAINST INDUCTEE HONG MAY ATTEND AND HEAR.
A PUBLICALLY HELD ORAL EXAM SHOULD CLEAR ALL SUSPICIONS OF CHEATING OR FAVORITISM, WE BELIEVE.
I CAN'T LET IT END HERE.
I HAVEN'T EVEN BEGUN MY WORK AS A CIVIL SERVANT YET!

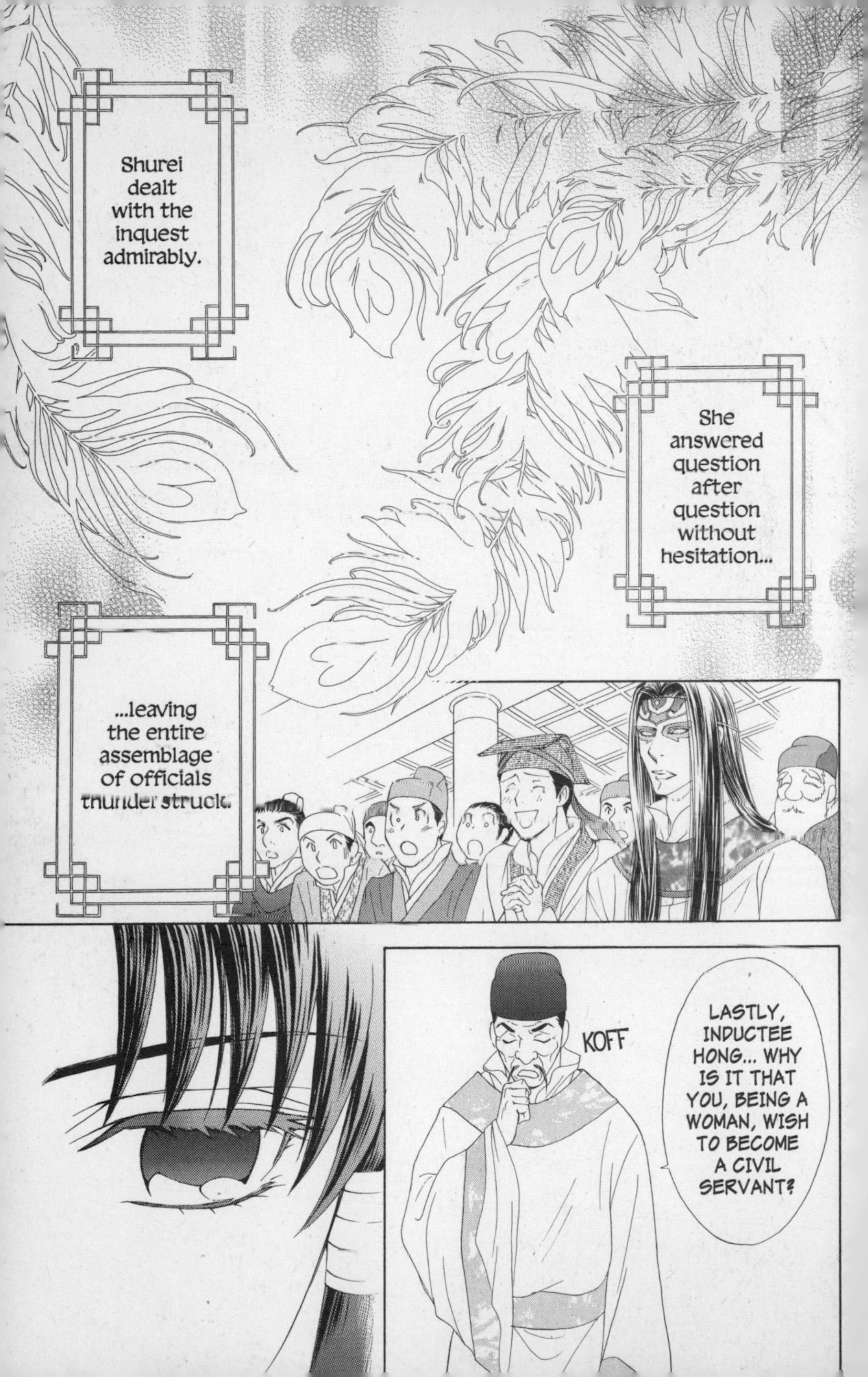

Shurei dealt with the inquest admirably.
She answered question after question without hesitation...
...leaving the entire assemblage of officials thunderstruck.
LASTLY, INDUCTEE HONG... WHY IS IT THAT YOU, BEING A WOMAN, WISH TO BECOME A CIVIL SERVANT?
KOFF

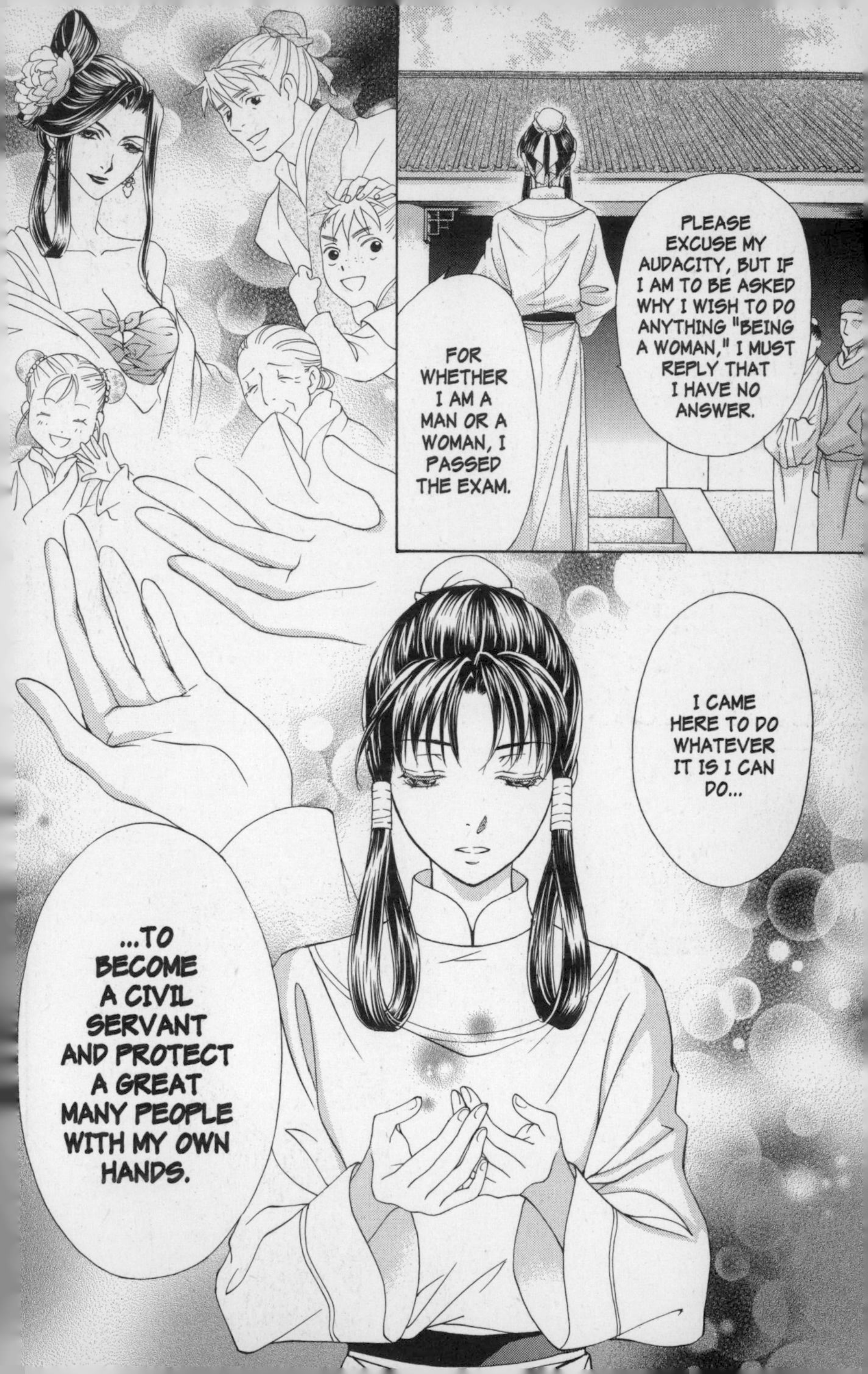
PLEASE EXCUSE MY AUDACITY, BUT IF I AM TO BE ASKED WHY I WISH TO DO ANYTHING "BEING A WOMAN," I MUST REPLY THAT I HAVE NO ANSWER.
FOR WHETHER I AM A MAN OR A WOMAN, I PASSED THE EXAM.
I CAME HERE TO DO WHATEVER IT IS I CAN DO...
...TO BECOME A CIVIL SERVANT AND PROTECT A GREAT MANY PEOPLE WITH MY OWN HANDS.

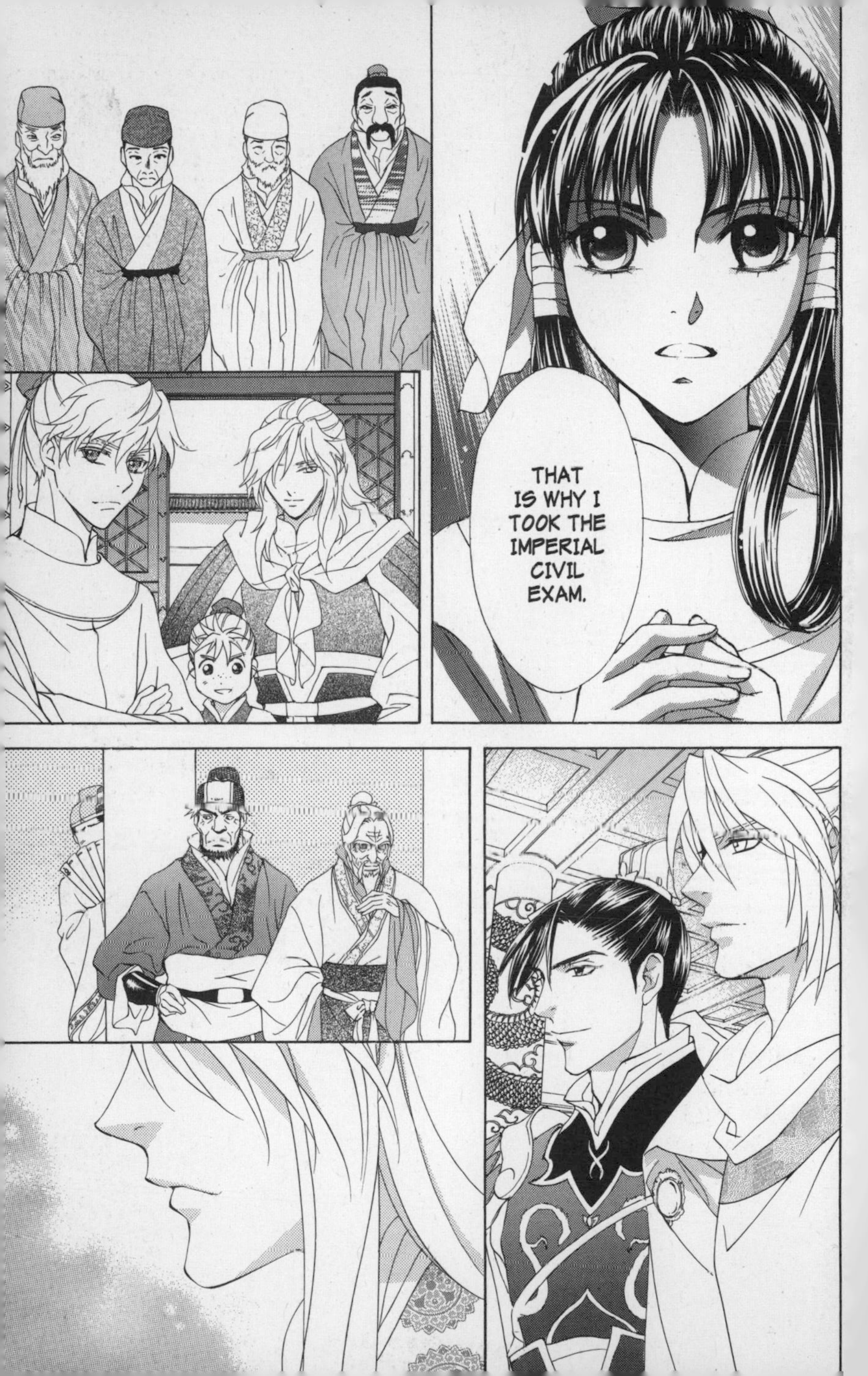
THAT IS WHY I TOOK THE IMPERIAL CIVIL EXAM.

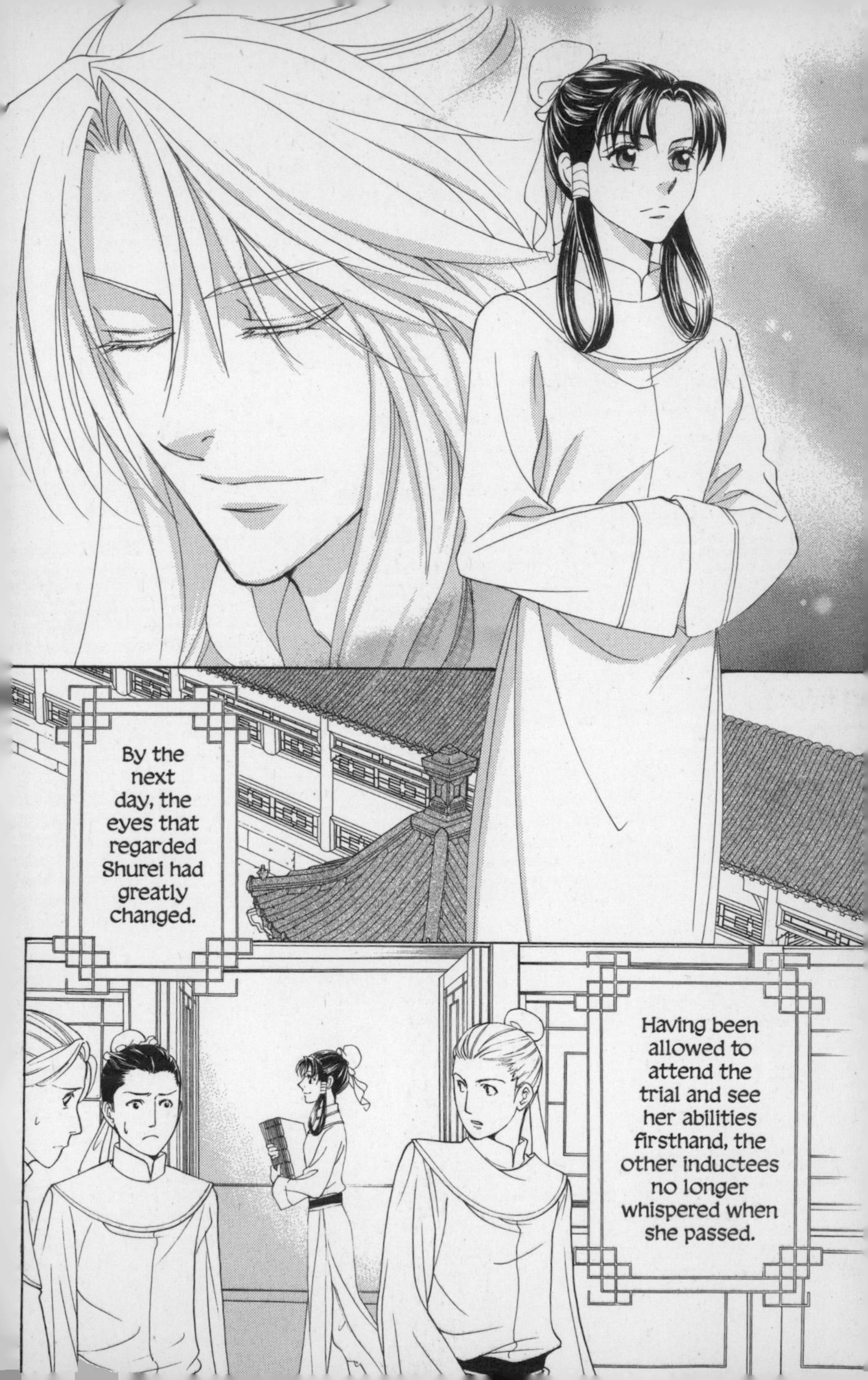
By the next day, the eyes that regarded Shurei had greatly changed.
Having been allowed to attend the trial and see her abilities firsthand, the other inductees no longer whispered when she passed.

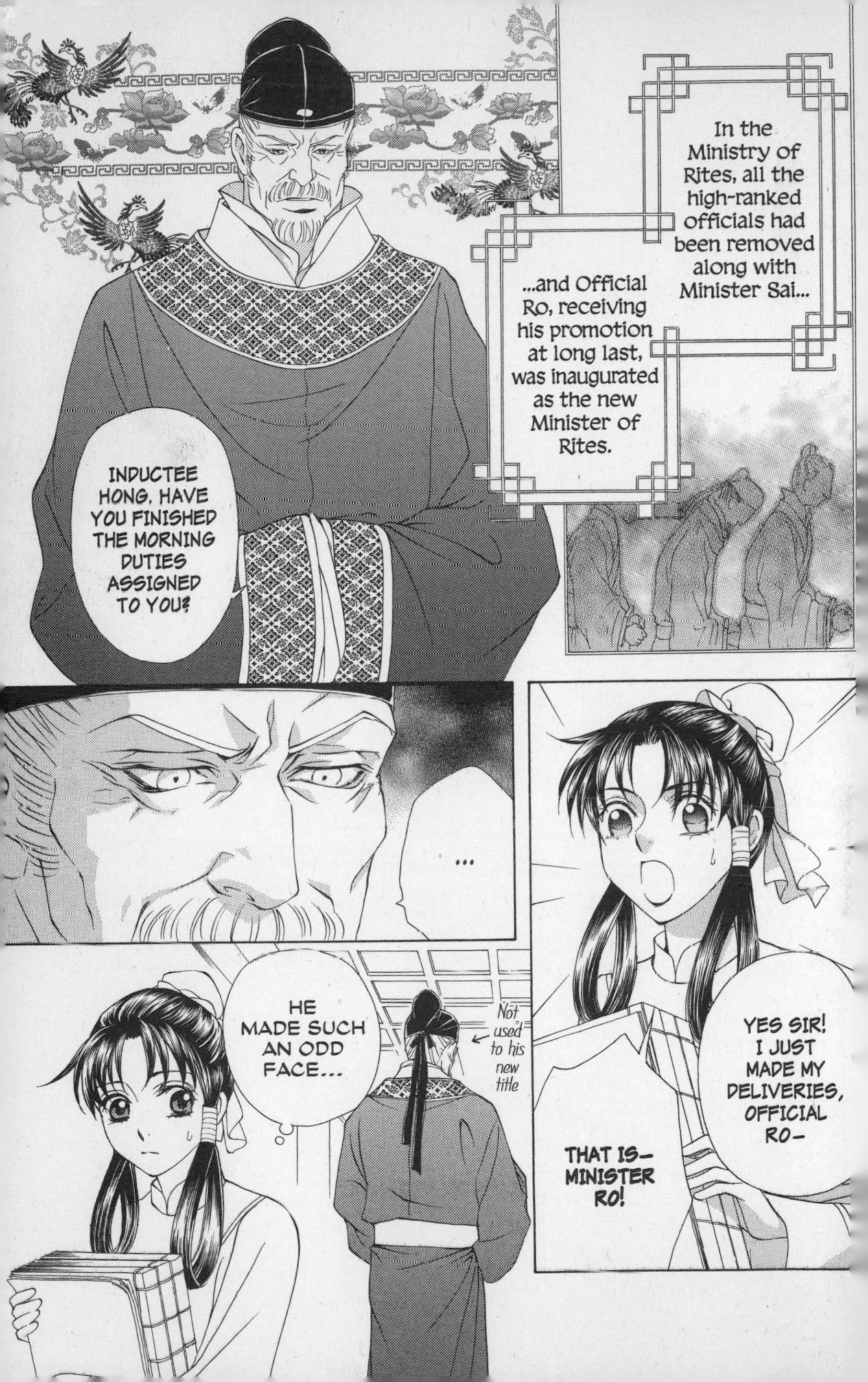
In the Ministry of Rites, all the high-ranked officials had been removed along with Minister Sai...
...and Official Ro, receiving his promotion at long last, was inaugurated as the new Minister of Rites.
INDUCTEE HONG. HAVE YOU FINISHED THE MORNING DUTIES ASSIGNED TO YOU?
YES SIR! I JUST MADE MY DELIVERIES, OFFICIAL RO—
THAT IS— MINISTER RO!
...
HE MADE SUCH AN ODD FACE...
Not used to his new title

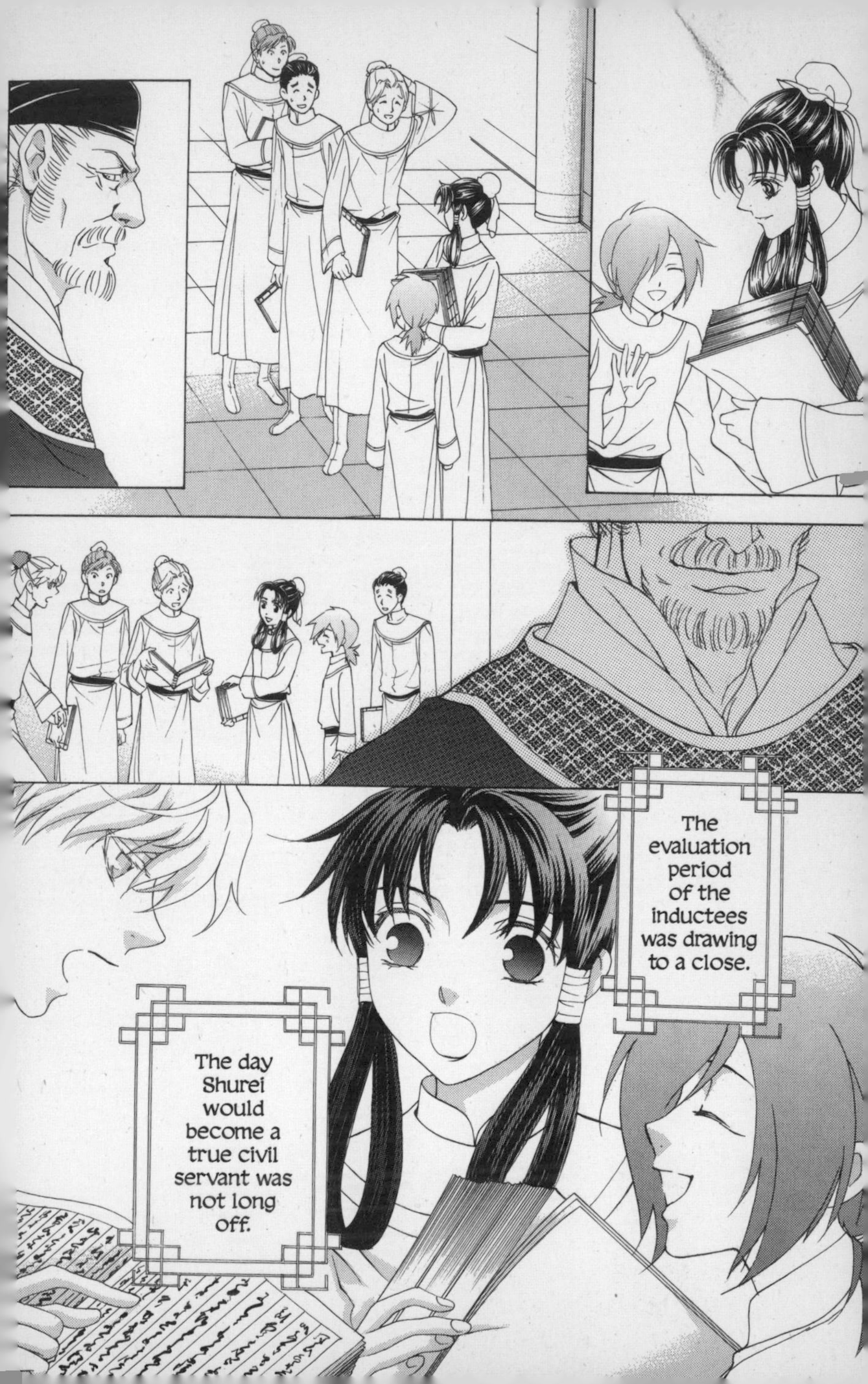
The evaluation period of the inductees was drawing to a close.
The day Shurei would become a true civil servant was not long off.

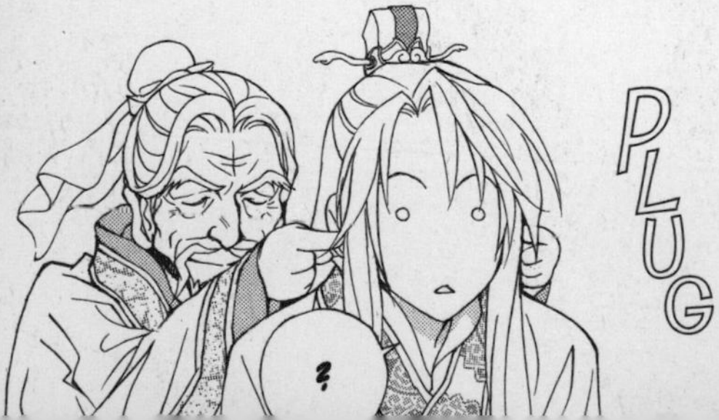
PLUG
?

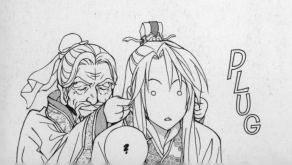

The Story of
SAIUNKOKU

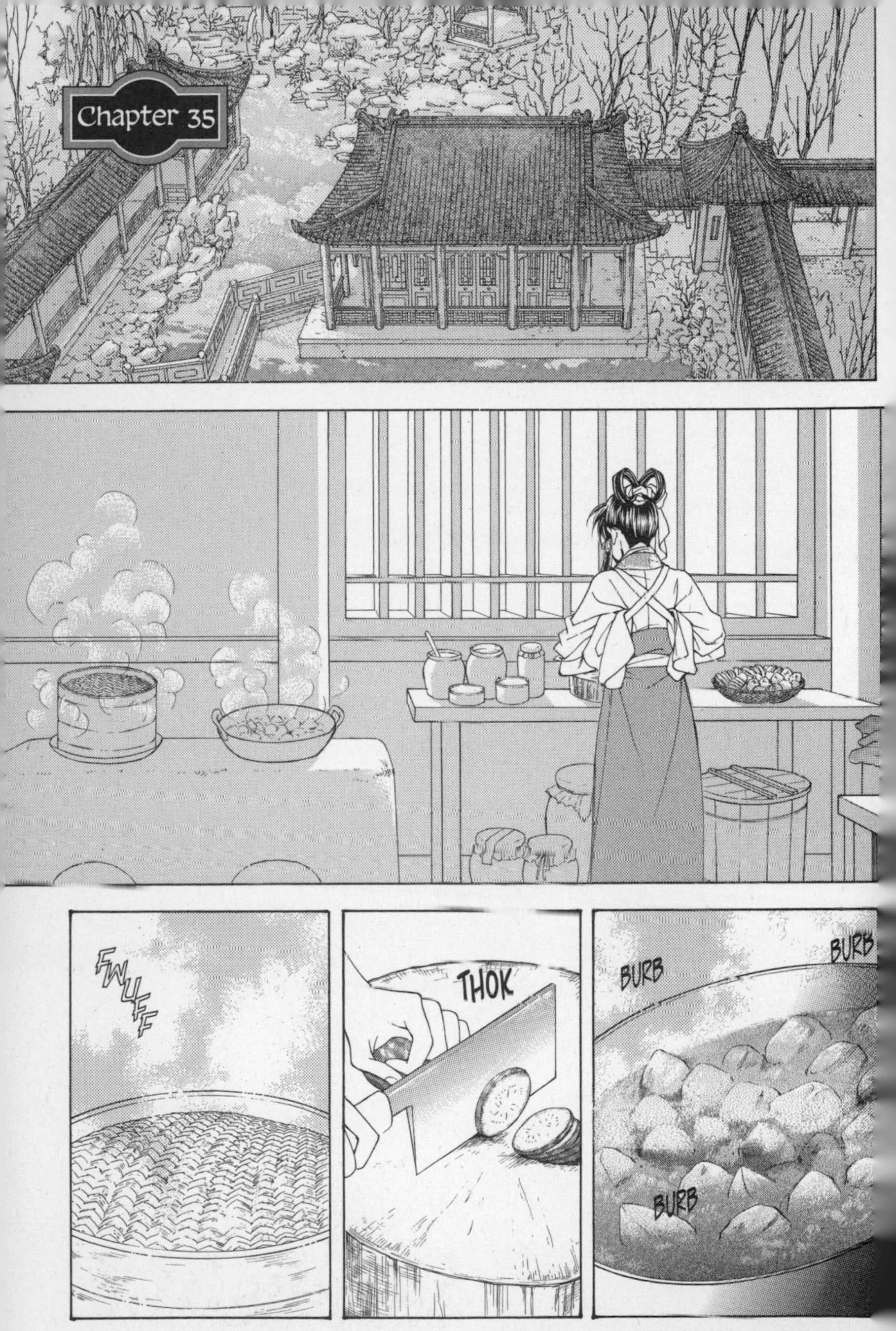
Chapter 35
BURB
BURB
BURB
THOK
FWUFF

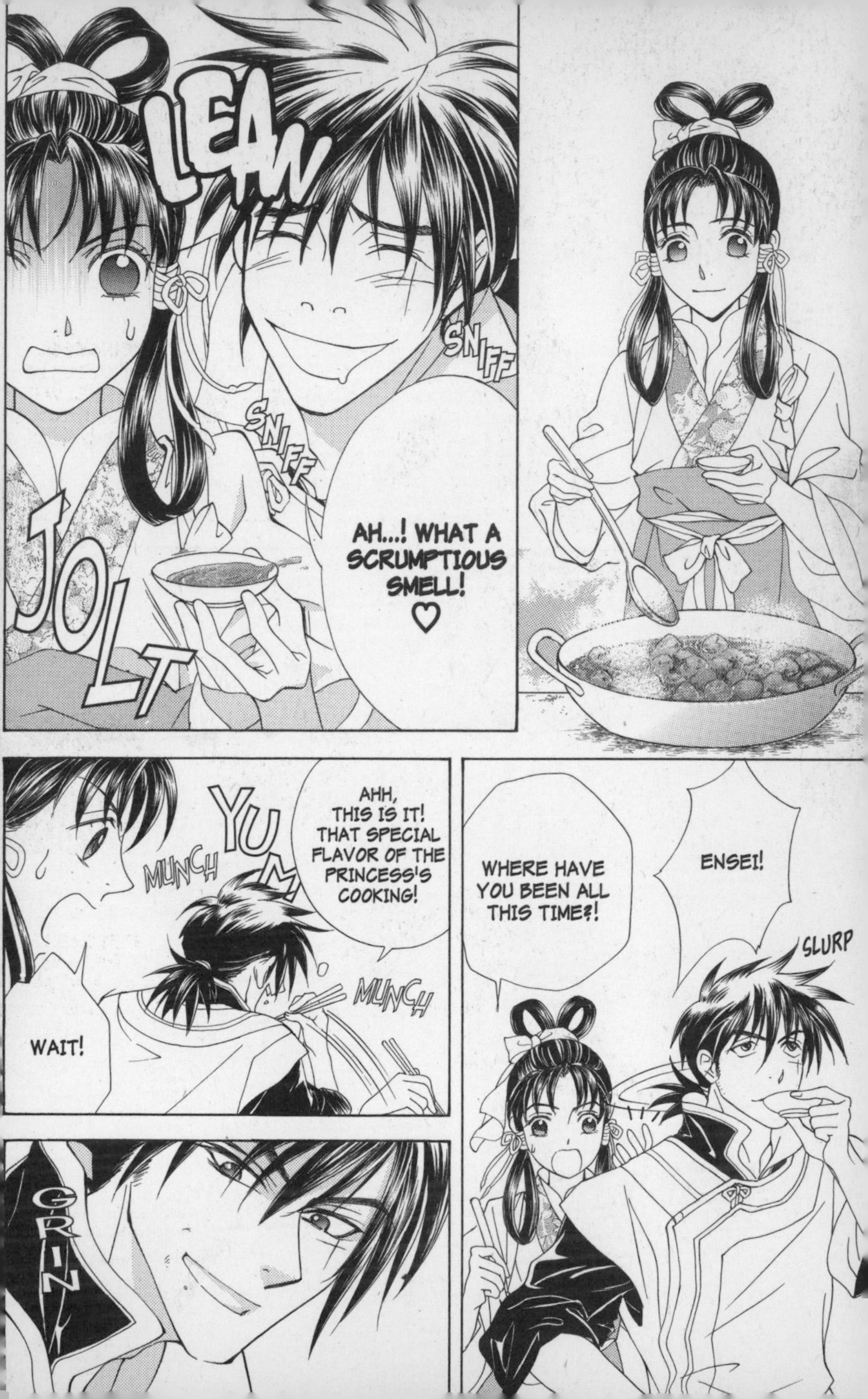
LEAN
SNIFF
SNIFF
AH...! WHAT A SCRUMPTIOUS SMELL! ♡
JOLT
ENSEI!
WHERE HAVE YOU BEEN ALL THIS TIME?!
SLURP
AHH, THIS IS IT! THAT SPECIAL FLAVOR OF THE PRINCESS'S COOKING!
YUM
MUNCH
MUNCH
WAIT!
GRIN

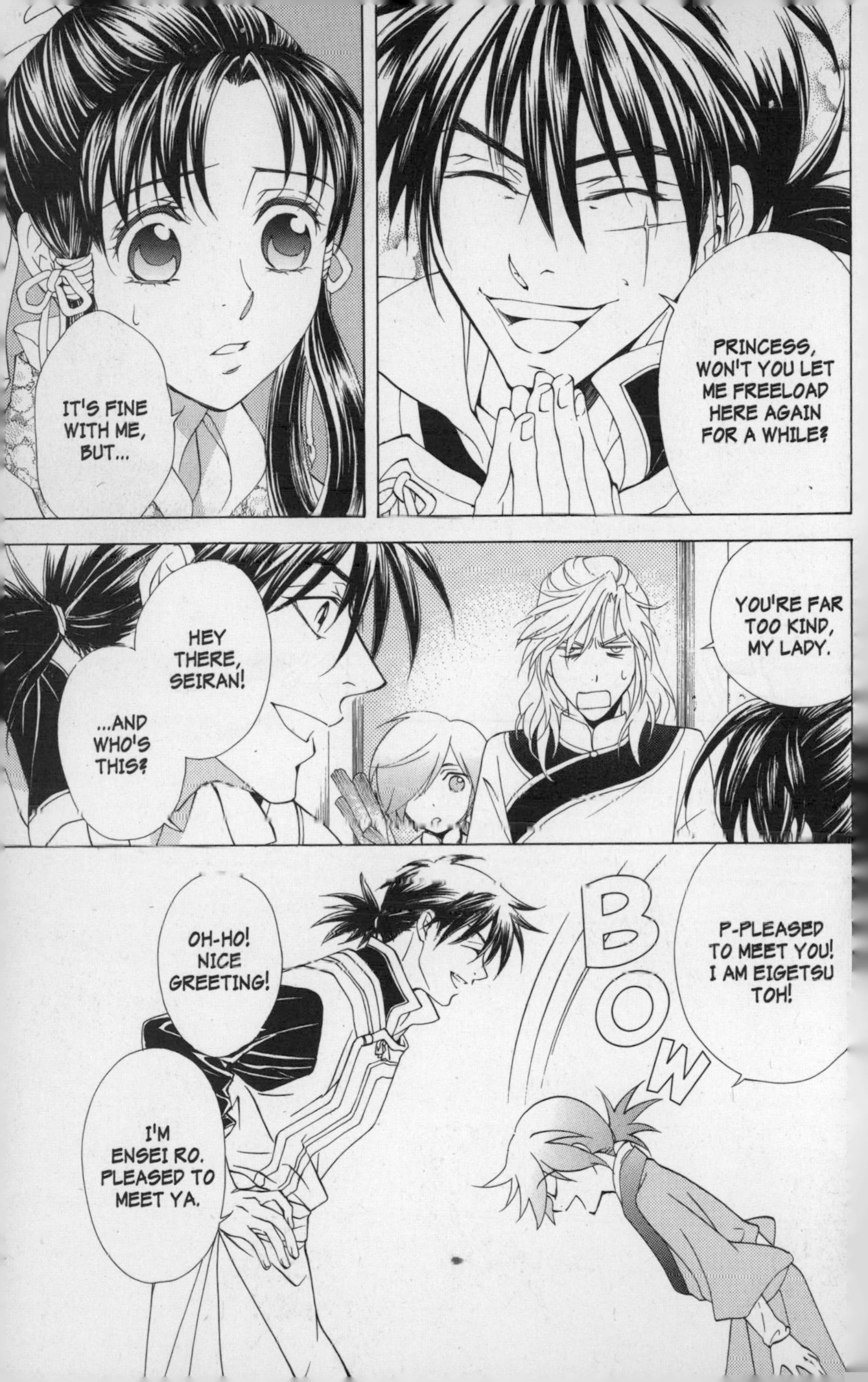
PRINCESS, WON'T YOU LET ME FREELOAD HERE AGAIN FOR A WHILE?
IT'S FINE WITH ME, BUT...
YOU'RE FAR TOO KIND, MY LADY.
HEY THERE, SEIRAN!
...AND WHO'S THIS?
P-PLEASED TO MEET YOU! I AM EIGETSU TOH!
BOW
OH-HO! NICE GREETING!
I'M ENSEI RO. PLEASED TO MEET YA.

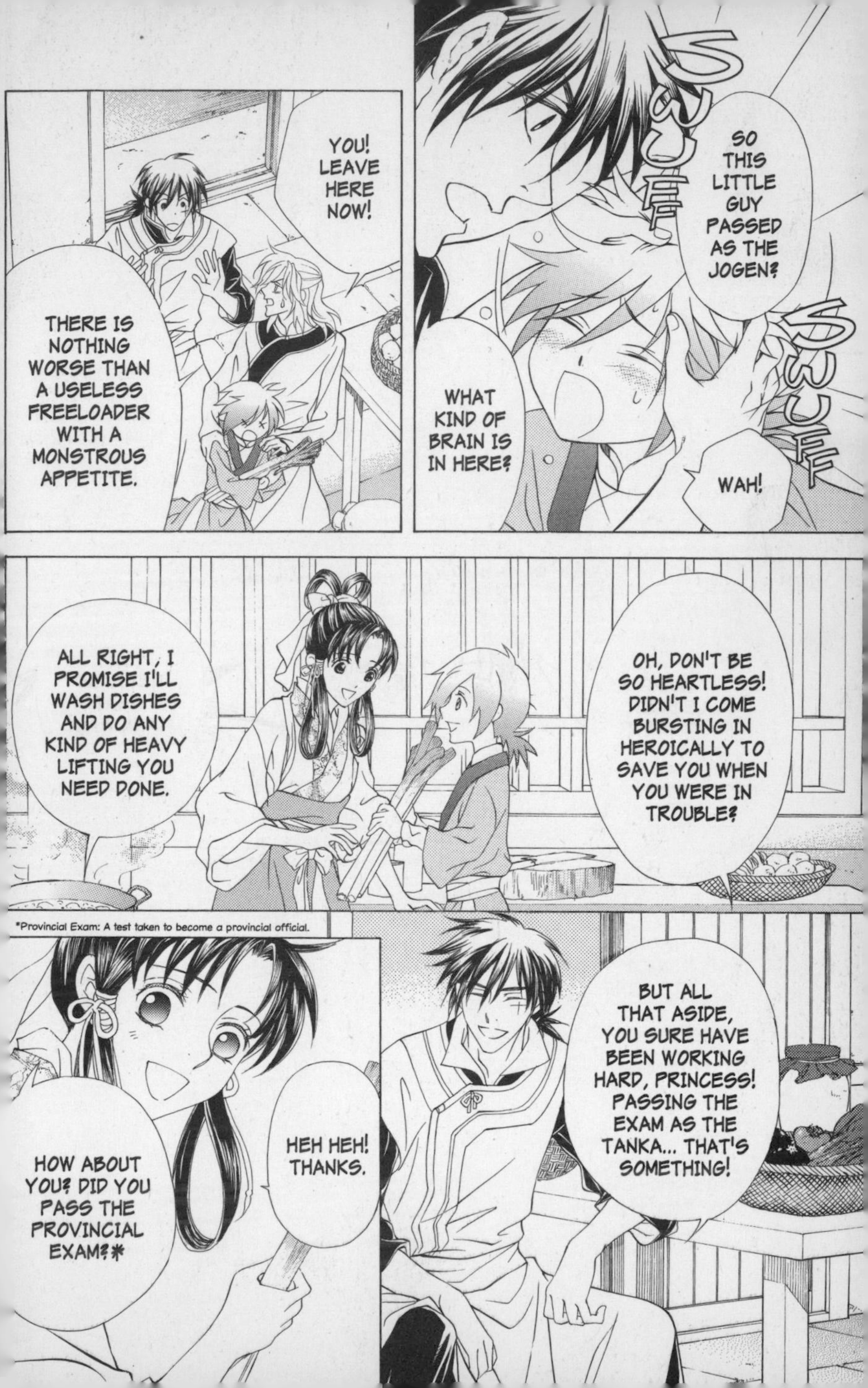
SWUFF
SO THIS LITTLE GUY PASSED AS THE JOGEN?
SWUFF
WHAT KIND OF BRAIN IS IN HERE?
WAH!
YOU! LEAVE HERE NOW!
THERE IS NOTHING WORSE THAN A USELESS FREELOADER WITH A MONSTROUS APPETITE.
OH, DON'T BE SO HEARTLESS! DIDN'T I COME BURSTING IN HEROICALLY TO SAVE YOU WHEN YOU WERE IN TROUBLE?
ALL RIGHT, I PROMISE I'LL WASH DISHES AND DO ANY KIND OF HEAVY LIFTING YOU NEED DONE.
BUT ALL THAT ASIDE, YOU SURE HAVE BEEN WORKING HARD, PRINCESS! PASSING THE EXAM AS THE TANKA... THAT'S SOMETHING!
HEH HEH! THANKS.
HOW ABOUT YOU? DID YOU PASS THE PROVINCIAL EXAM?*

*Provincial Exam: A test taken to become a provincial official.

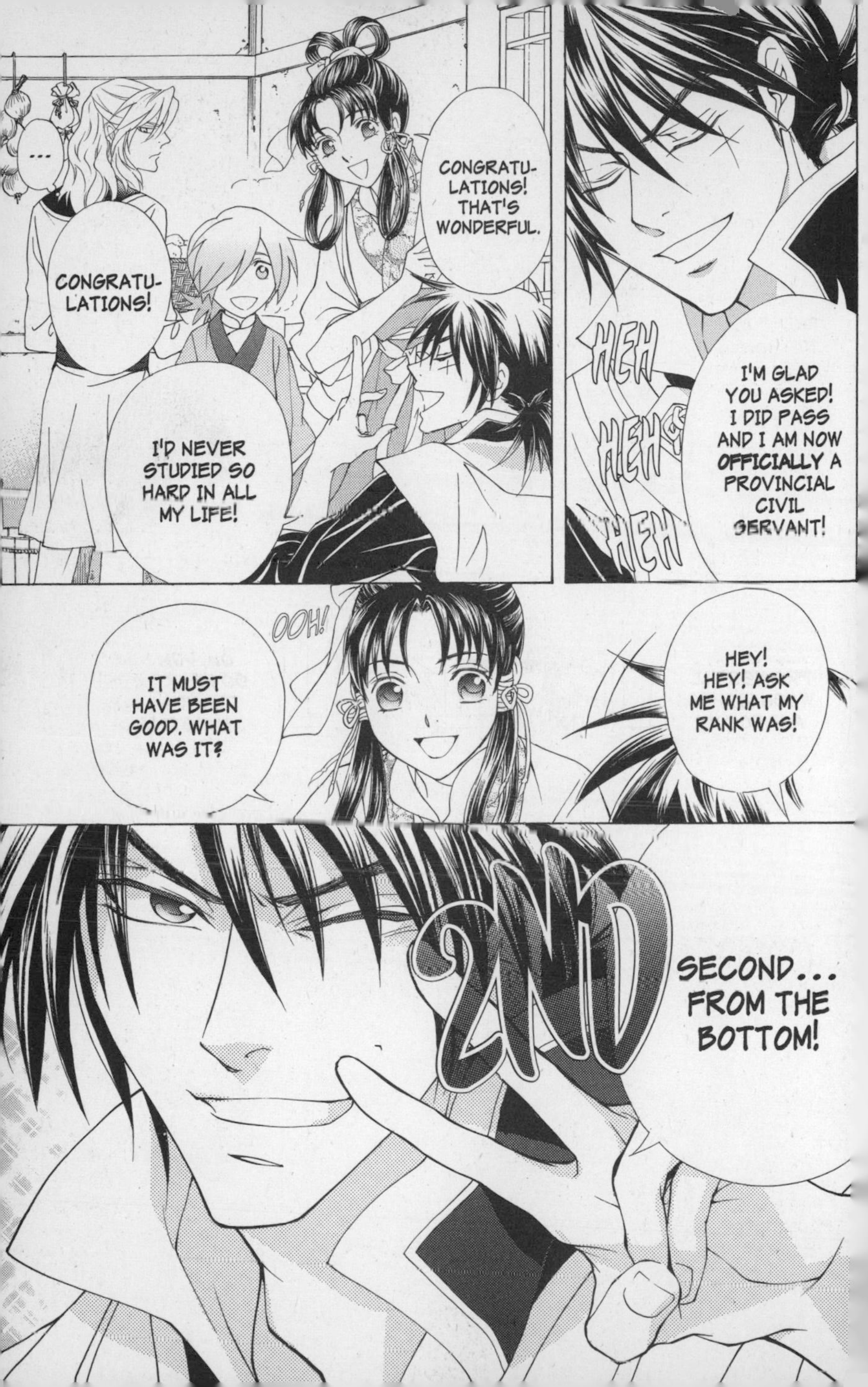
HEH HEH HEH
I'M GLAD YOU ASKED! I DID PASS AND I AM NOW OFFICIALLY A PROVINCIAL CIVIL SERVANT!
CONGRATULATIONS! THAT'S WONDERFUL.
...
CONGRATULATIONS!
I'D NEVER STUDIED SO HARD IN ALL MY LIFE!
HEY! HEY! ASK ME WHAT MY RANK WAS!
OOH!
IT MUST HAVE BEEN GOOD. WHAT WAS IT?
2ND
SECOND... FROM THE BOTTOM!

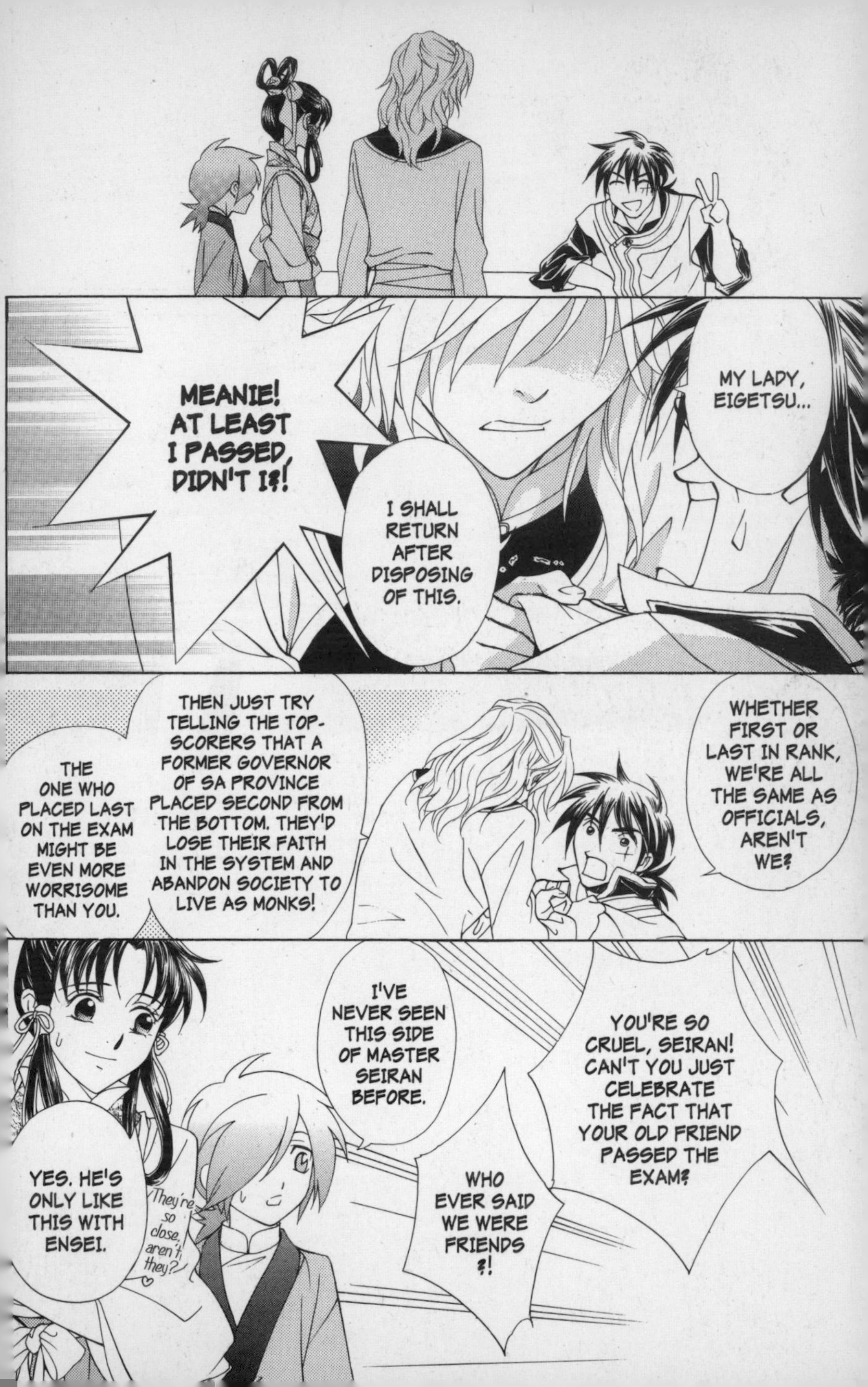
MY LADY, EIGETSU...
I SHALL RETURN AFTER DISPOSING OF THIS.
MEANIE! AT LEAST I PASSED, DIDN'T I?!
WHETHER FIRST OR LAST IN RANK, WE'RE ALL THE SAME AS OFFICIALS, AREN'T WE?
THEN JUST TRY TELLING THE TOP-SCORERS THAT A FORMER GOVERNOR OF SA PROVINCE PLACED SECOND FROM THE BOTTOM. THEY'D LOSE THEIR FAITH IN THE SYSTEM AND ABANDON SOCIETY TO LIVE AS MONKS!
THE ONE WHO PLACED LAST ON THE EXAM MIGHT BE EVEN MORE WORRISOME THAN YOU.
YOU'RE SO CRUEL, SEIRAN! CAN'T YOU JUST CELEBRATE THE FACT THAT YOUR OLD FRIEND PASSED THE EXAM?
WHO EVER SAID WE WERE FRIENDS?!
I'VE NEVER SEEN THIS SIDE OF MASTER SEIRAN BEFORE.
YES. HE'S ONLY LIKE THIS WITH ENSEI.
They're so close, aren't they?

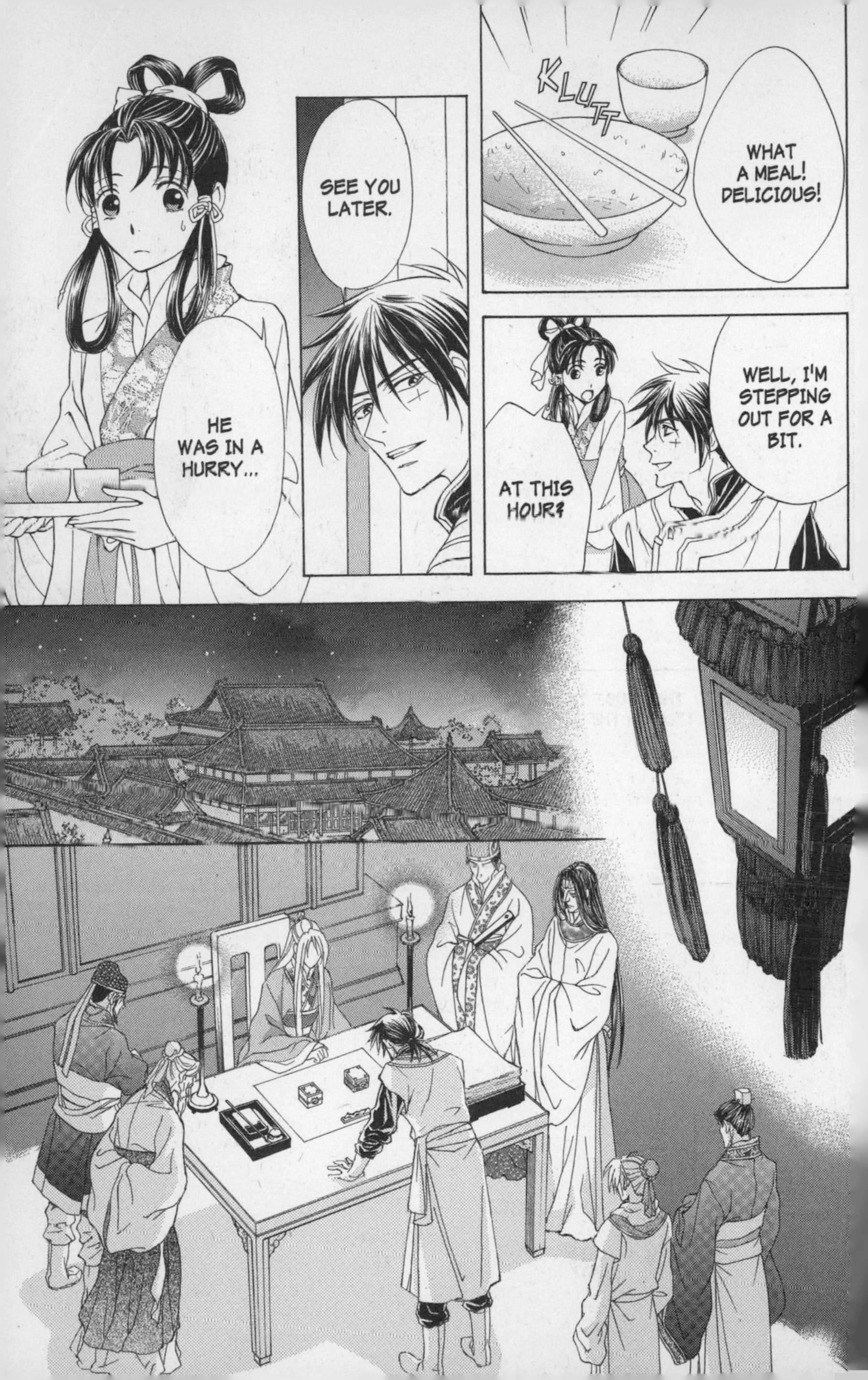
KLUTT
WHAT A MEAL! DELICIOUS!
WELL, I'M STEPPING OUT FOR A BIT.
AT THIS HOUR?
SEE YOU LATER.
HE WAS IN A HURRY...

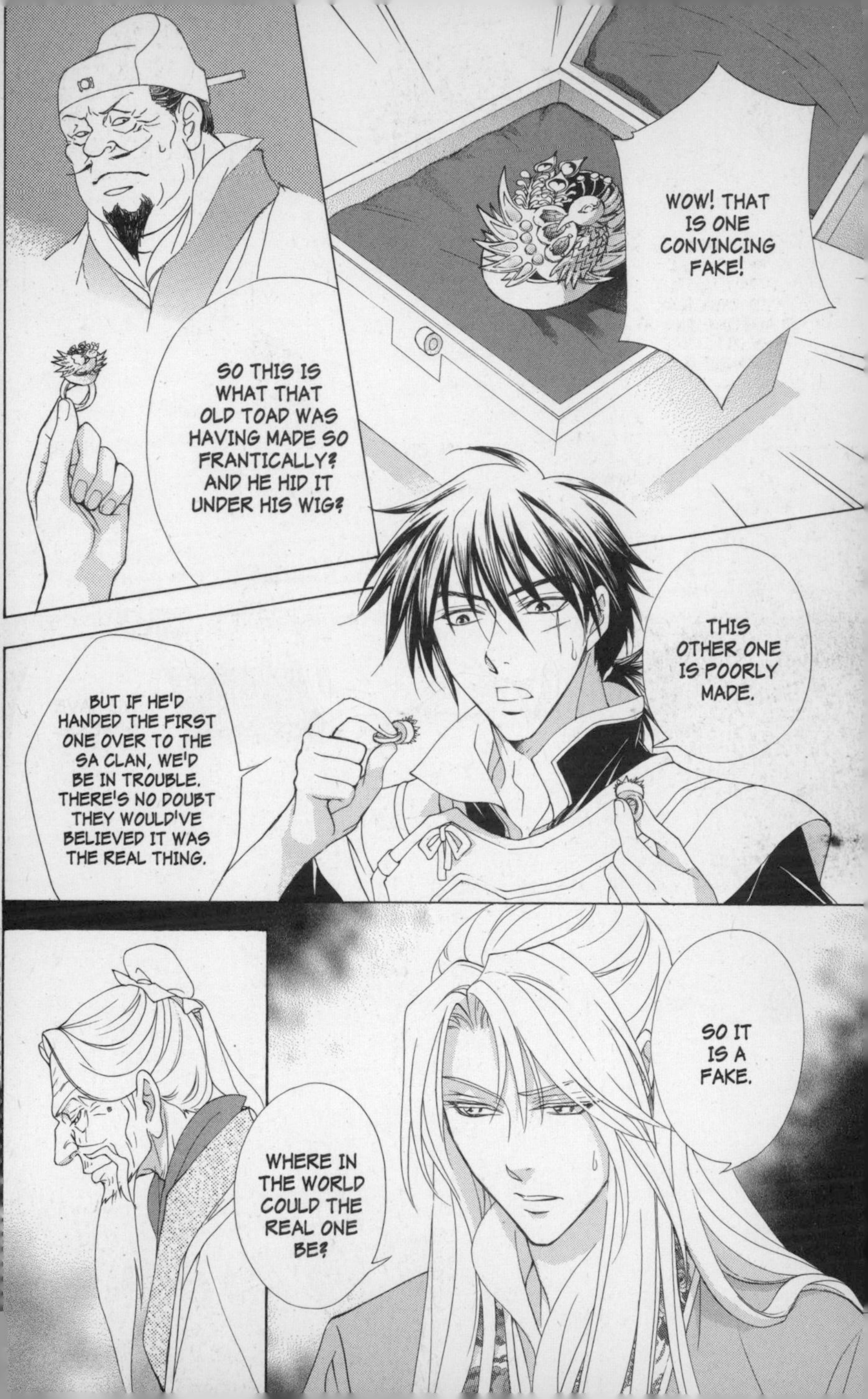
WOW! THAT IS ONE CONVINCING FAKE!
SO THIS IS WHAT THAT OLD TOAD WAS HAVING MADE SO FRANTICALLY? AND HE HID IT UNDER HIS WIG?
THIS OTHER ONE IS POORLY MADE.
BUT IF HE'D HANDED THE FIRST ONE OVER TO THE SA CLAN, WE'D BE IN TROUBLE. THERE'S NO DOUBT THEY WOULD'VE BELIEVED IT WAS THE REAL THING.
SO IT IS A FAKE.
WHERE IN THE WORLD COULD THE REAL ONE BE?

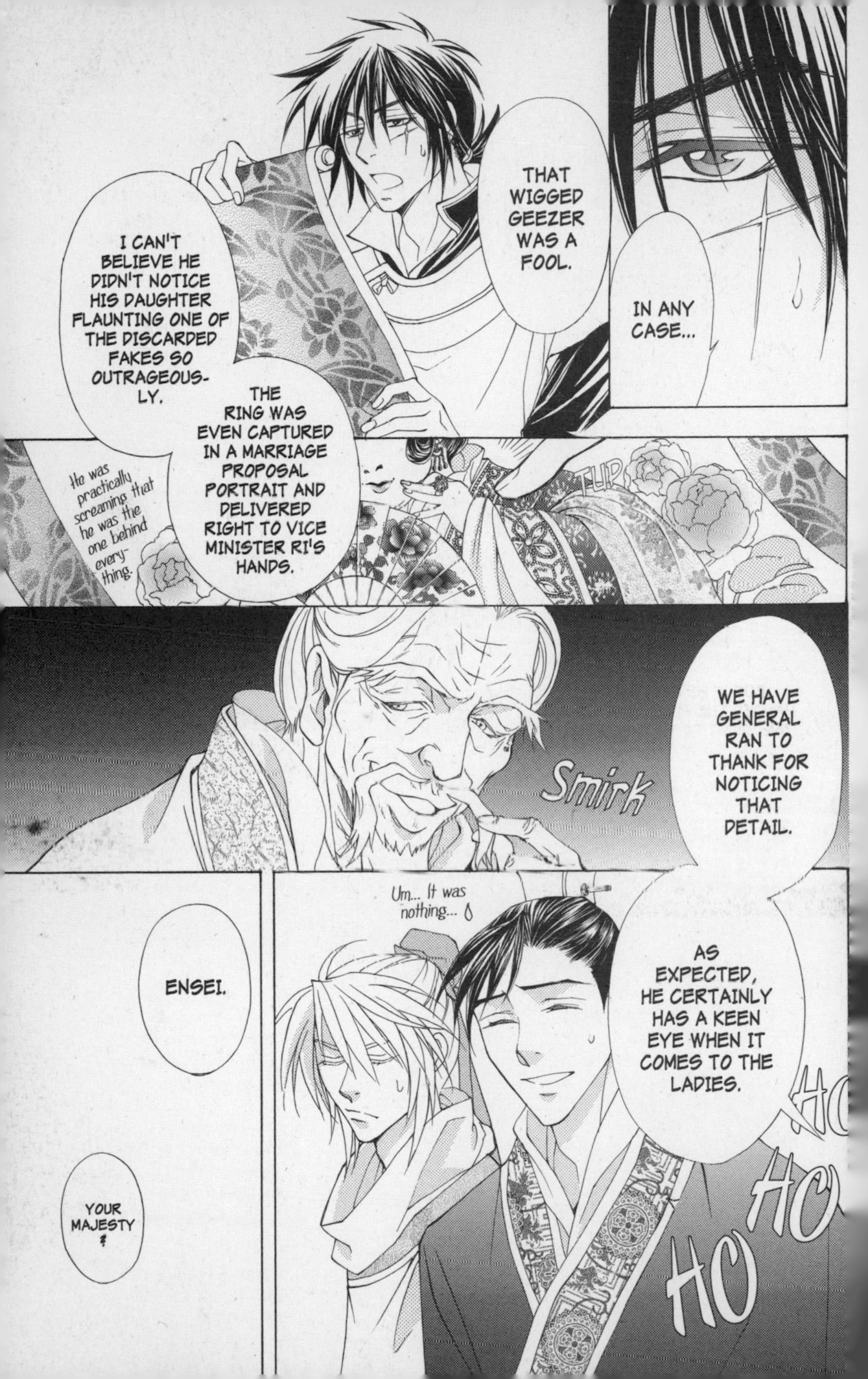
THAT WIGGED GEEZER WAS A FOOL.
IN ANY CASE...
I CAN'T BELIEVE HE DIDN'T NOTICE HIS DAUGHTER FLAUNTING ONE OF THE DISCARDED FAKES SO OUTRAGEOUS-LY.
THE RING WAS EVEN CAPTURED IN A MARRIAGE PROPOSAL PORTRAIT AND DELIVERED RIGHT TO VICE MINISTER RI'S HANDS.
He was practically screaming that he was the one behind every-thing.
TUP
WE HAVE GENERAL RAN TO THANK FOR NOTICING THAT DETAIL.
Smirk
AS EXPECTED, HE CERTAINLY HAS A KEEN EYE WHEN IT COMES TO THE LADIES.
Um... It was nothing...
HO HO HO HO
ENSEI.
YOUR MAJESTY?

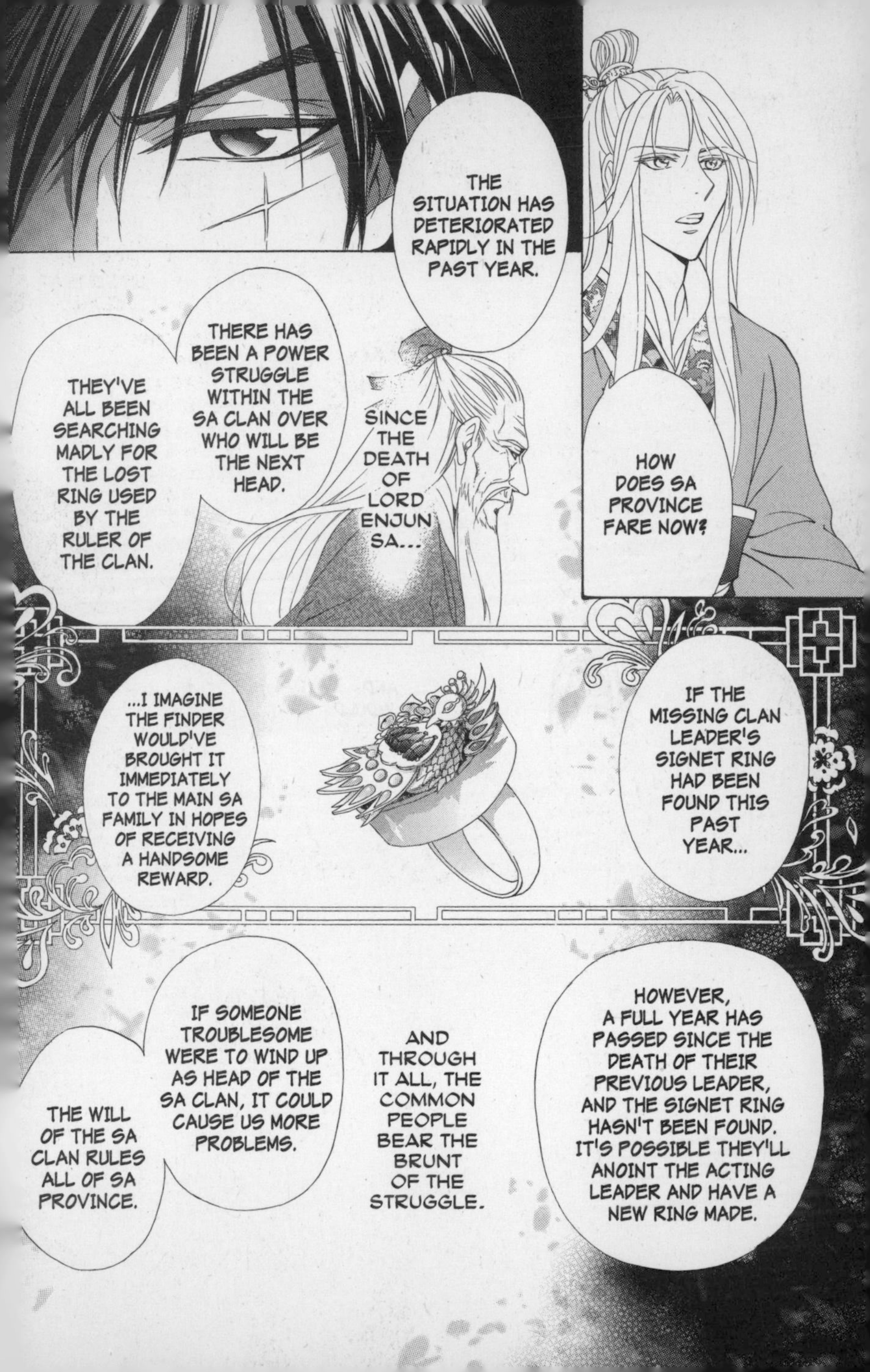
HOW DOES SA PROVINCE FARE NOW?
THE SITUATION HAS DETERIORATED RAPIDLY IN THE PAST YEAR.
SINCE THE DEATH OF LORD ENJUN SA...
THERE HAS BEEN A POWER STRUGGLE WITHIN THE SA CLAN OVER WHO WILL BE THE NEXT HEAD.
THEY'VE ALL BEEN SEARCHING MADLY FOR THE LOST RING USED BY THE RULER OF THE CLAN.
IF THE MISSING CLAN LEADER'S SIGNET RING HAD BEEN FOUND THIS PAST YEAR...
...I IMAGINE THE FINDER WOULD'VE BROUGHT IT IMMEDIATELY TO THE MAIN SA FAMILY IN HOPES OF RECEIVING A HANDSOME REWARD.
HOWEVER, A FULL YEAR HAS PASSED SINCE THE DEATH OF THEIR PREVIOUS LEADER, AND THE SIGNET RING HASN'T BEEN FOUND. IT'S POSSIBLE THEY'LL ANOINT THE ACTING LEADER AND HAVE A NEW RING MADE.
AND THROUGH IT ALL, THE COMMON PEOPLE BEAR THE BRUNT OF THE STRUGGLE.
IF SOMEONE TROUBLESOME WERE TO WIND UP AS HEAD OF THE SA CLAN, IT COULD CAUSE US MORE PROBLEMS.
THE WILL OF THE SA CLAN RULES ALL OF SA PROVINCE.

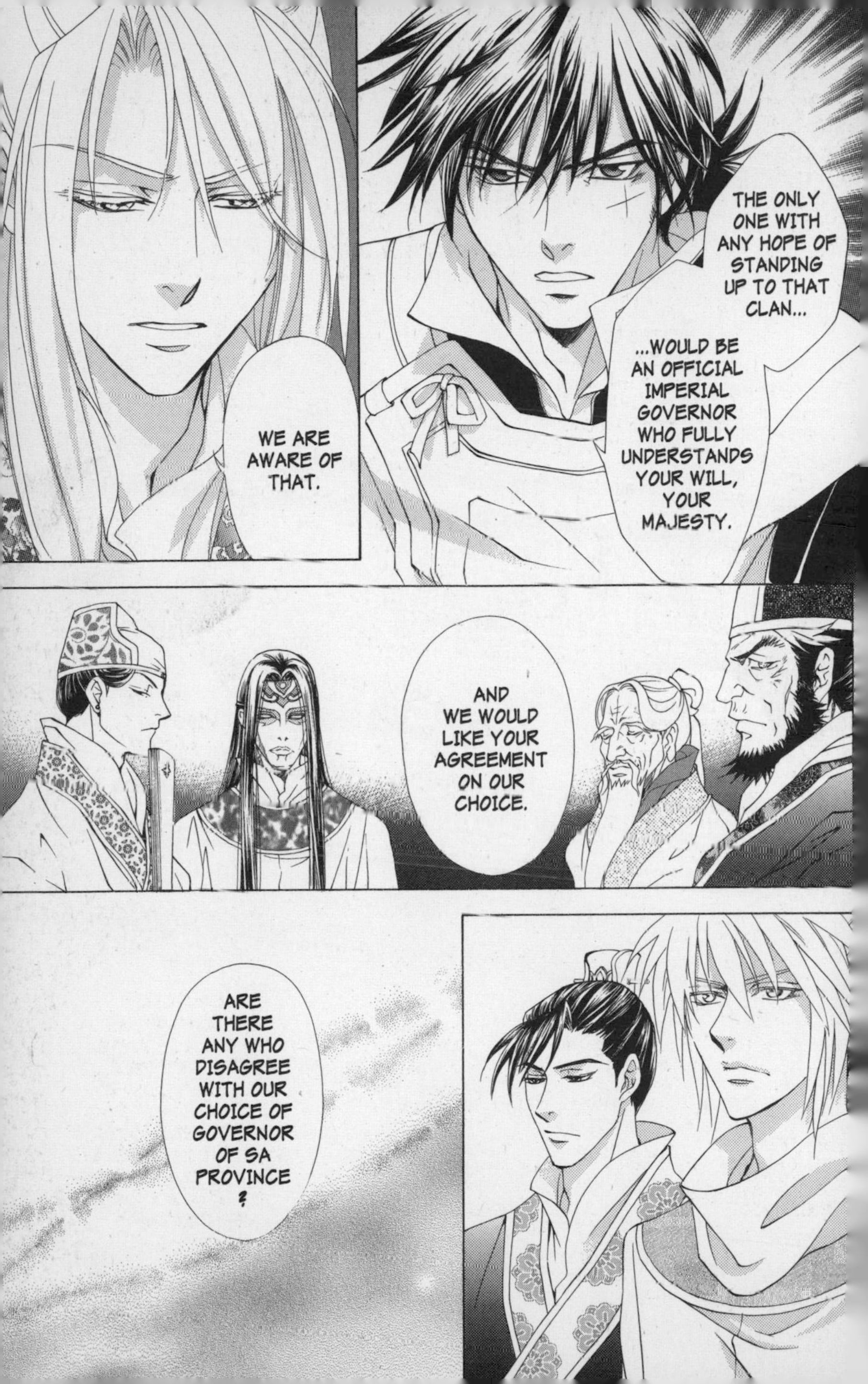
THE ONLY ONE WITH ANY HOPE OF STANDING UP TO THAT CLAN...
...WOULD BE AN OFFICIAL IMPERIAL GOVERNOR WHO FULLY UNDERSTANDS YOUR WILL, YOUR MAJESTY.
WE ARE AWARE OF THAT.
AND WE WOULD LIKE YOUR AGREEMENT ON OUR CHOICE.
ARE THERE ANY WHO DISAGREE WITH OUR CHOICE OF GOVERNOR OF SA PROVINCE ?

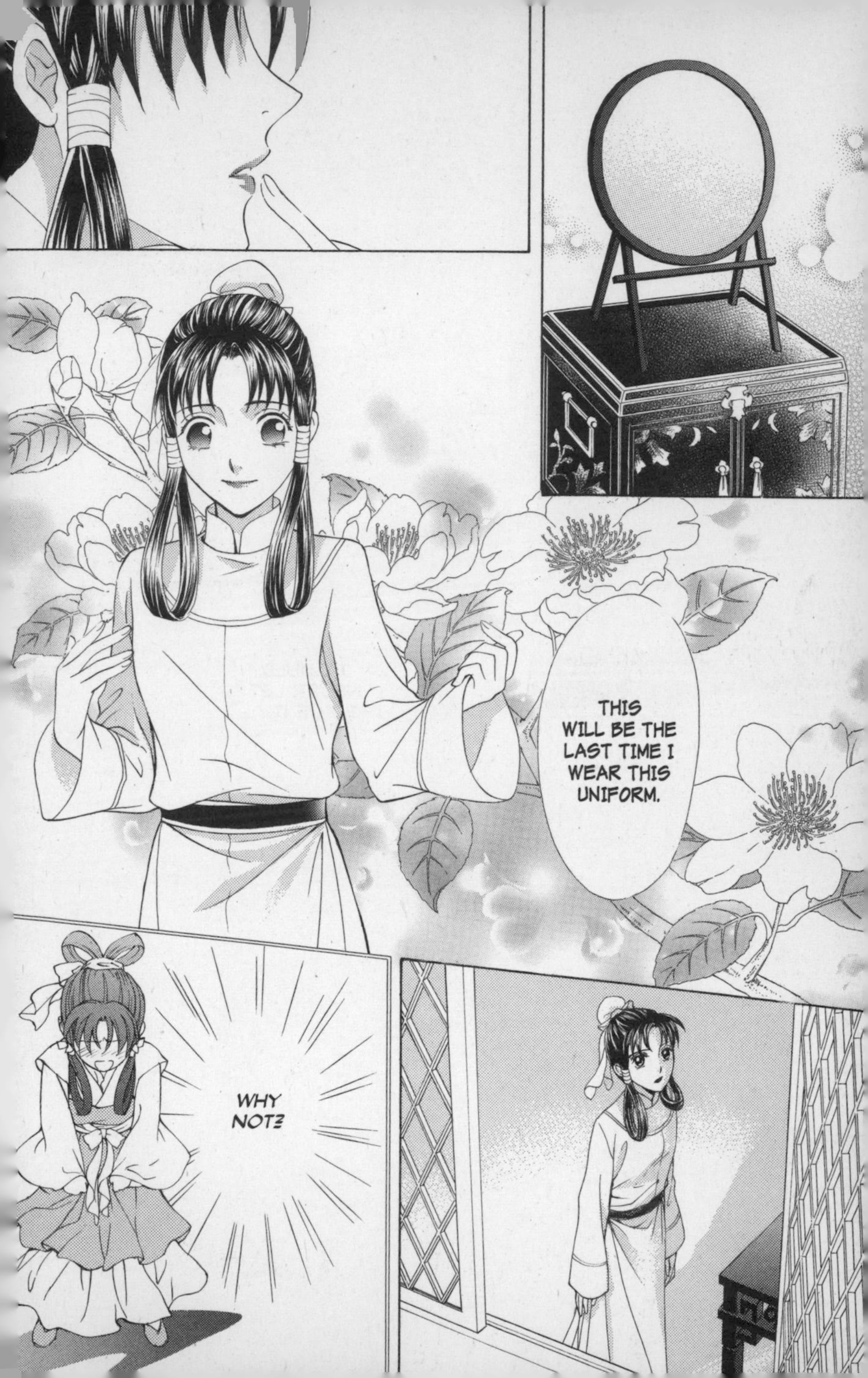
THIS WILL BE THE LAST TIME I WEAR THIS UNIFORM.
WHY NOT?

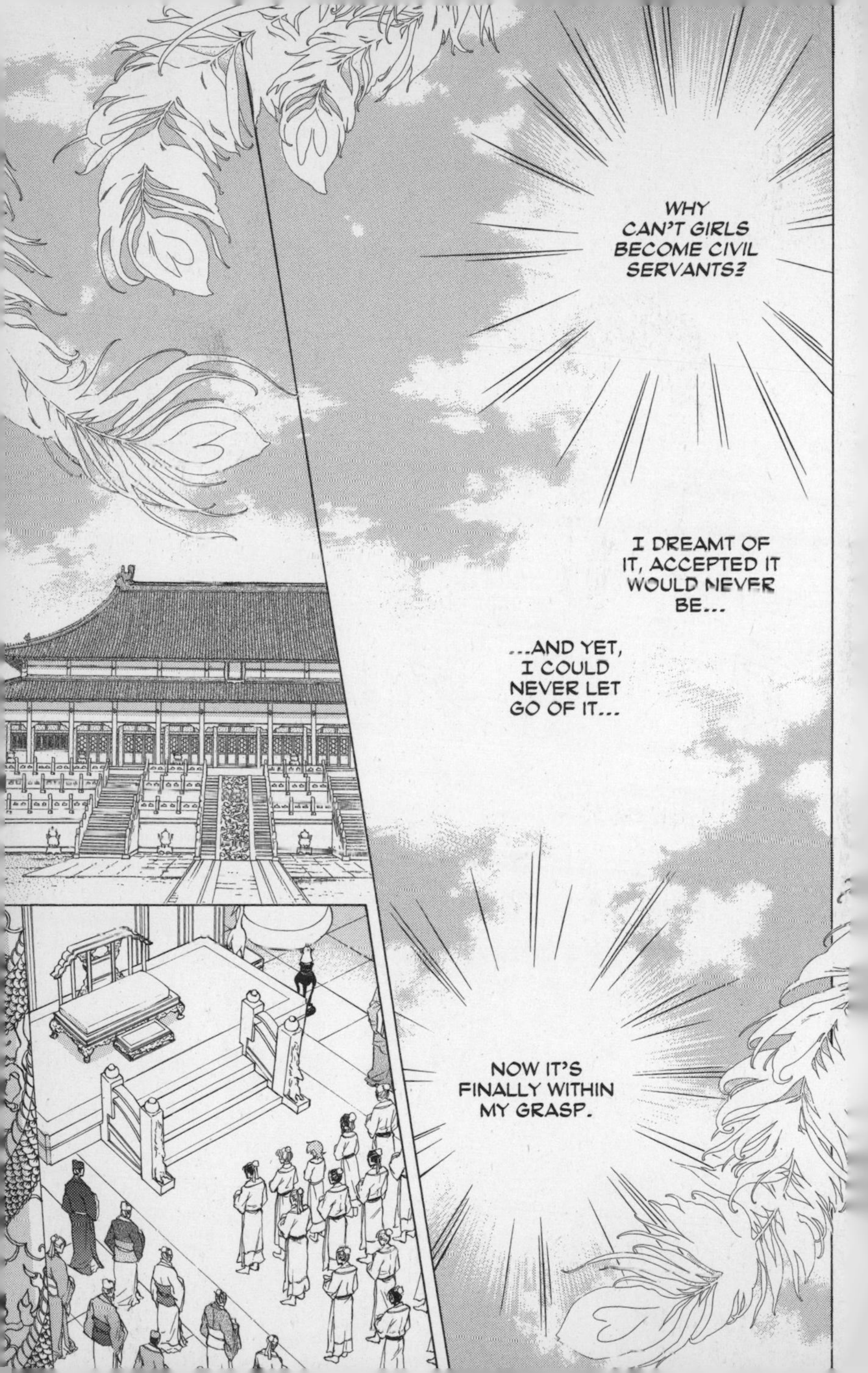
WHY CAN'T GIRLS BECOME CIVIL SERVANTS?
I DREAMT OF IT, ACCEPTED IT WOULD NEVER BE...
...AND YET, I COULD NEVER LET GO OF IT...
NOW IT'S FINALLY WITHIN MY GRASP.

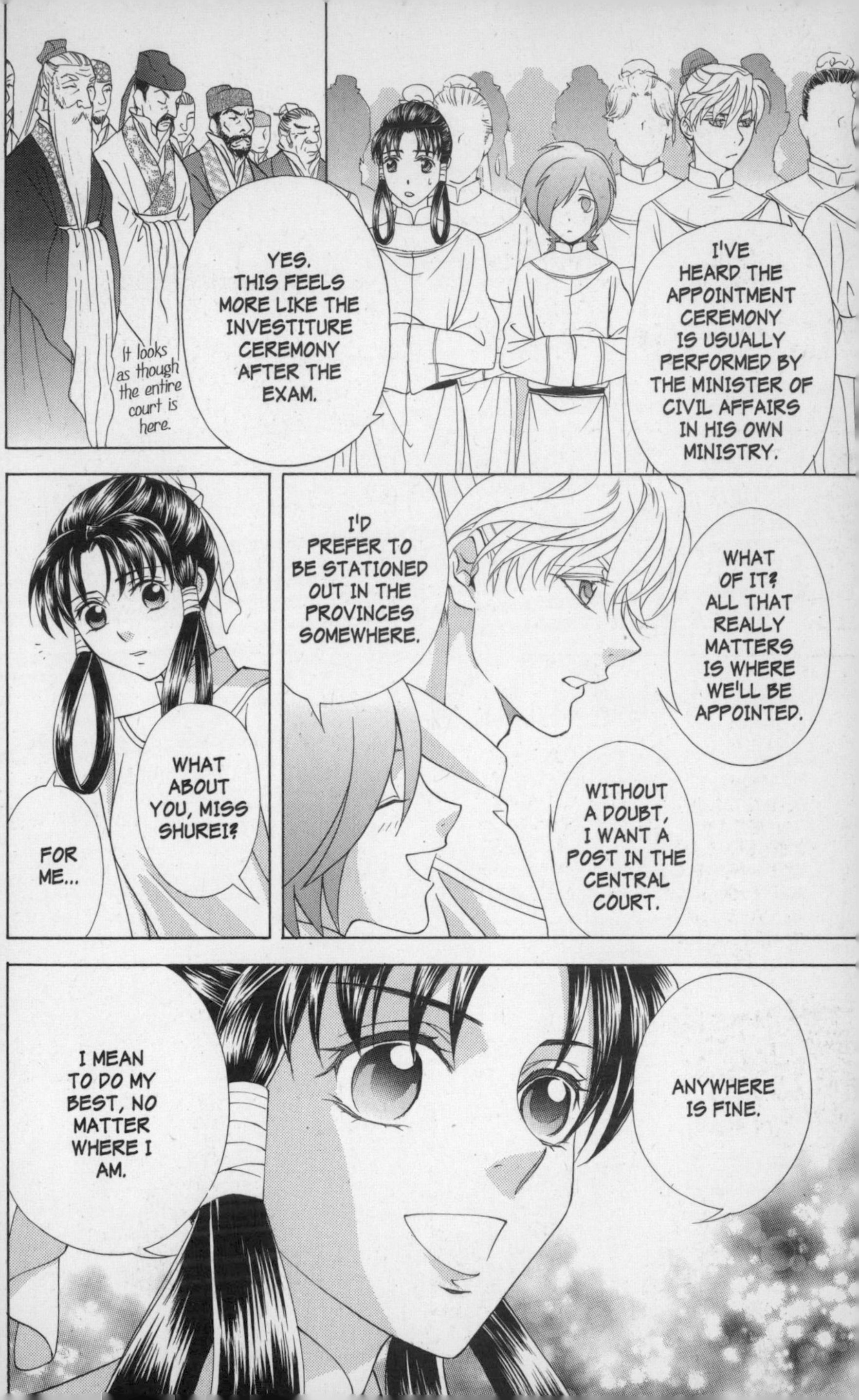
I'VE HEARD THE APPOINTMENT CEREMONY IS USUALLY PERFORMED BY THE MINISTER OF CIVIL AFFAIRS IN HIS OWN MINISTRY.
YES. THIS FEELS MORE LIKE THE INVESTITURE CEREMONY AFTER THE EXAM.
It looks as though the entire court is here.
WHAT OF IT? ALL THAT REALLY MATTERS IS WHERE WE'LL BE APPOINTED.
I'D PREFER TO BE STATIONED OUT IN THE PROVINCES SOMEWHERE.
WITHOUT A DOUBT, I WANT A POST IN THE CENTRAL COURT.
WHAT ABOUT YOU, MISS SHUREI?
FOR ME...
ANYWHERE IS FINE.
I MEAN TO DO MY BEST, NO MATTER WHERE I AM.

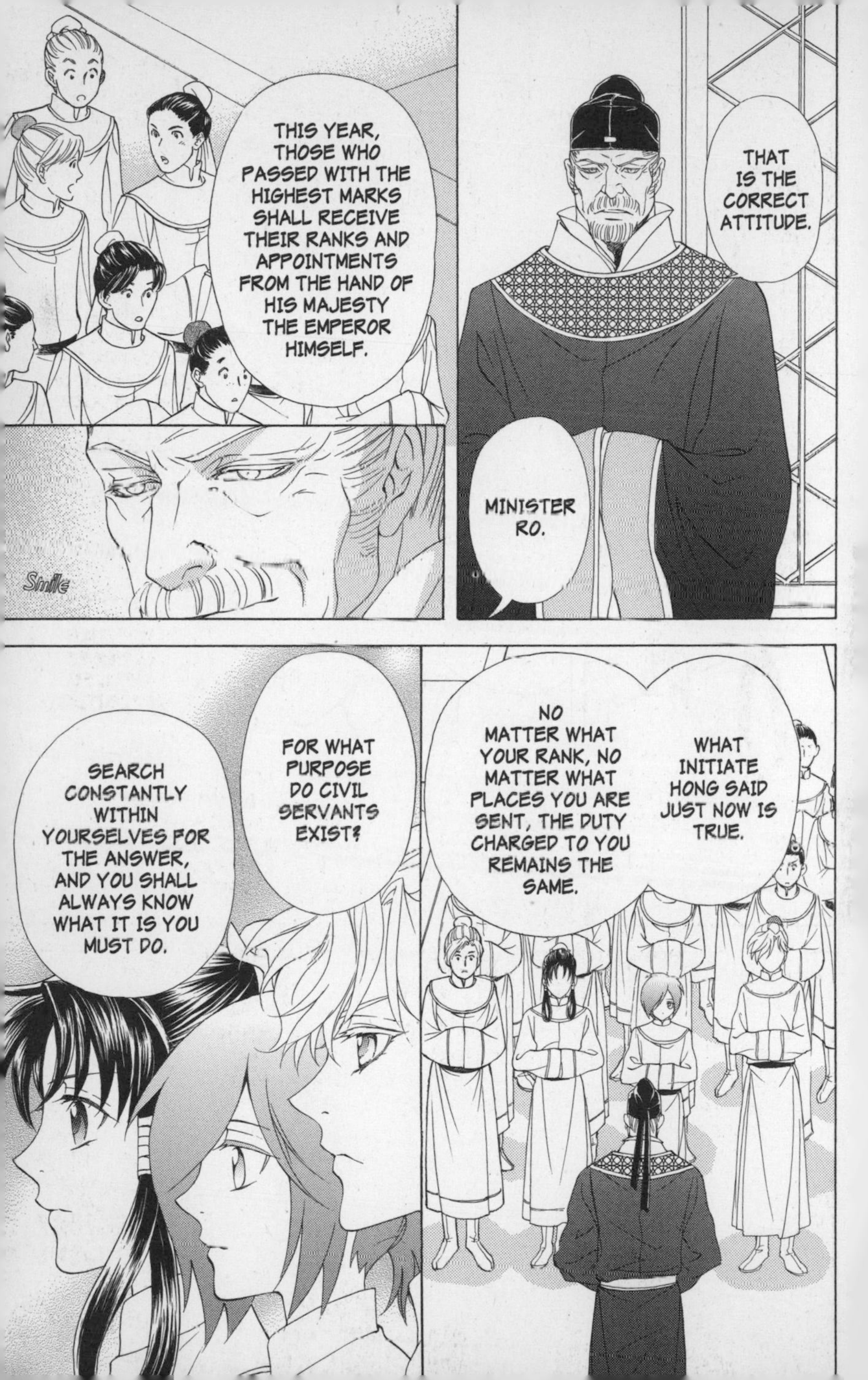
THAT IS THE CORRECT ATTITUDE.
MINISTER RO.
THIS YEAR, THOSE WHO PASSED WITH THE HIGHEST MARKS SHALL RECEIVE THEIR RANKS AND APPOINTMENTS FROM THE HAND OF HIS MAJESTY THE EMPEROR HIMSELF.
Smile
WHAT INITIATE HONG SAID JUST NOW IS TRUE.
NO MATTER WHAT YOUR RANK, NO MATTER WHAT PLACES YOU ARE SENT, THE DUTY CHARGED TO YOU REMAINS THE SAME.
FOR WHAT PURPOSE DO CIVIL SERVANTS EXIST?
SEARCH CONSTANTLY WITHIN YOURSELVES FOR THE ANSWER, AND YOU SHALL ALWAYS KNOW WHAT IT IS YOU MUST DO.

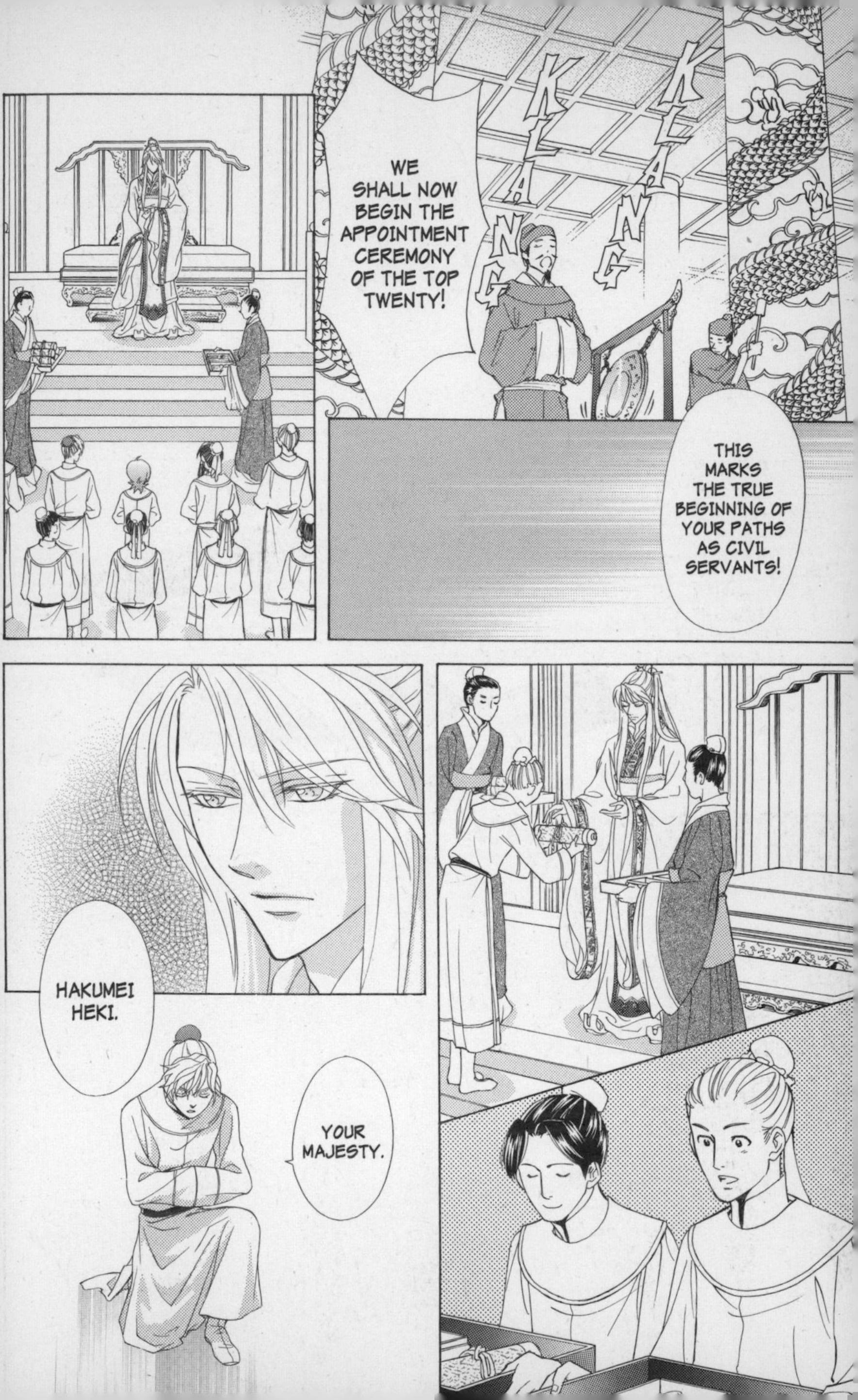
KLANG
KLANG
WE SHALL NOW BEGIN THE APPOINTMENT CEREMONY OF THE TOP TWENTY!
THIS MARKS THE TRUE BEGINNING OF YOUR PATHS AS CIVIL SERVANTS!
HAKUMEI HEKI.
YOUR MAJESTY.

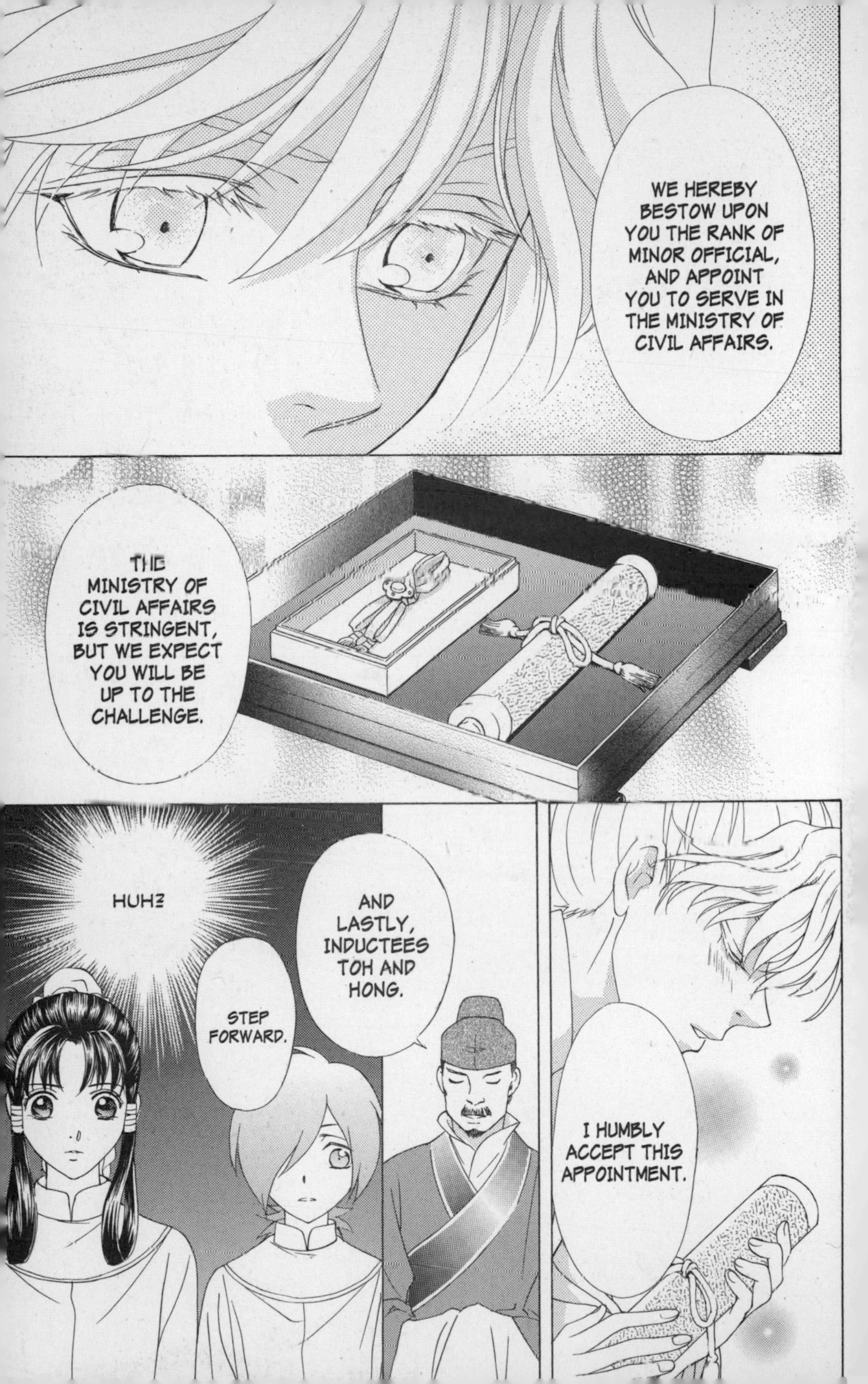
WE HEREBY BESTOW UPON YOU THE RANK OF MINOR OFFICIAL, AND APPOINT YOU TO SERVE IN THE MINISTRY OF CIVIL AFFAIRS.
THE MINISTRY OF CIVIL AFFAIRS IS STRINGENT, BUT WE EXPECT YOU WILL BE UP TO THE CHALLENGE.
I HUMBLY ACCEPT THIS APPOINTMENT.
AND LASTLY, INDUCTEES TOH AND HONG.
STEP FORWARD.
HUH?

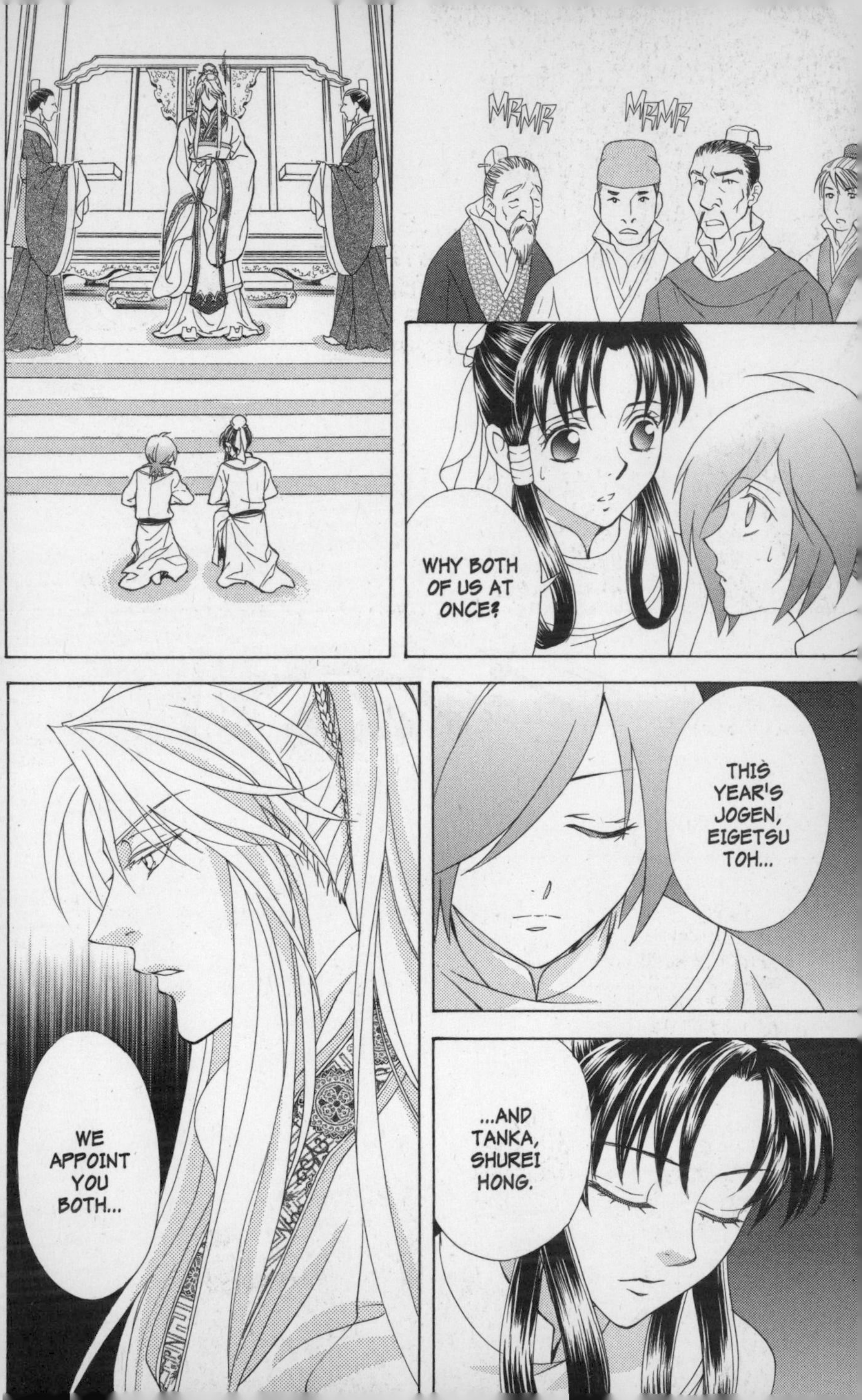
MRMR
MRMR
WHY BOTH OF US AT ONCE?
THIS YEAR'S JOGEN, EIGETSU TOH...
...AND TANKA, SHUREI HONG.
WE APPOINT YOU BOTH...

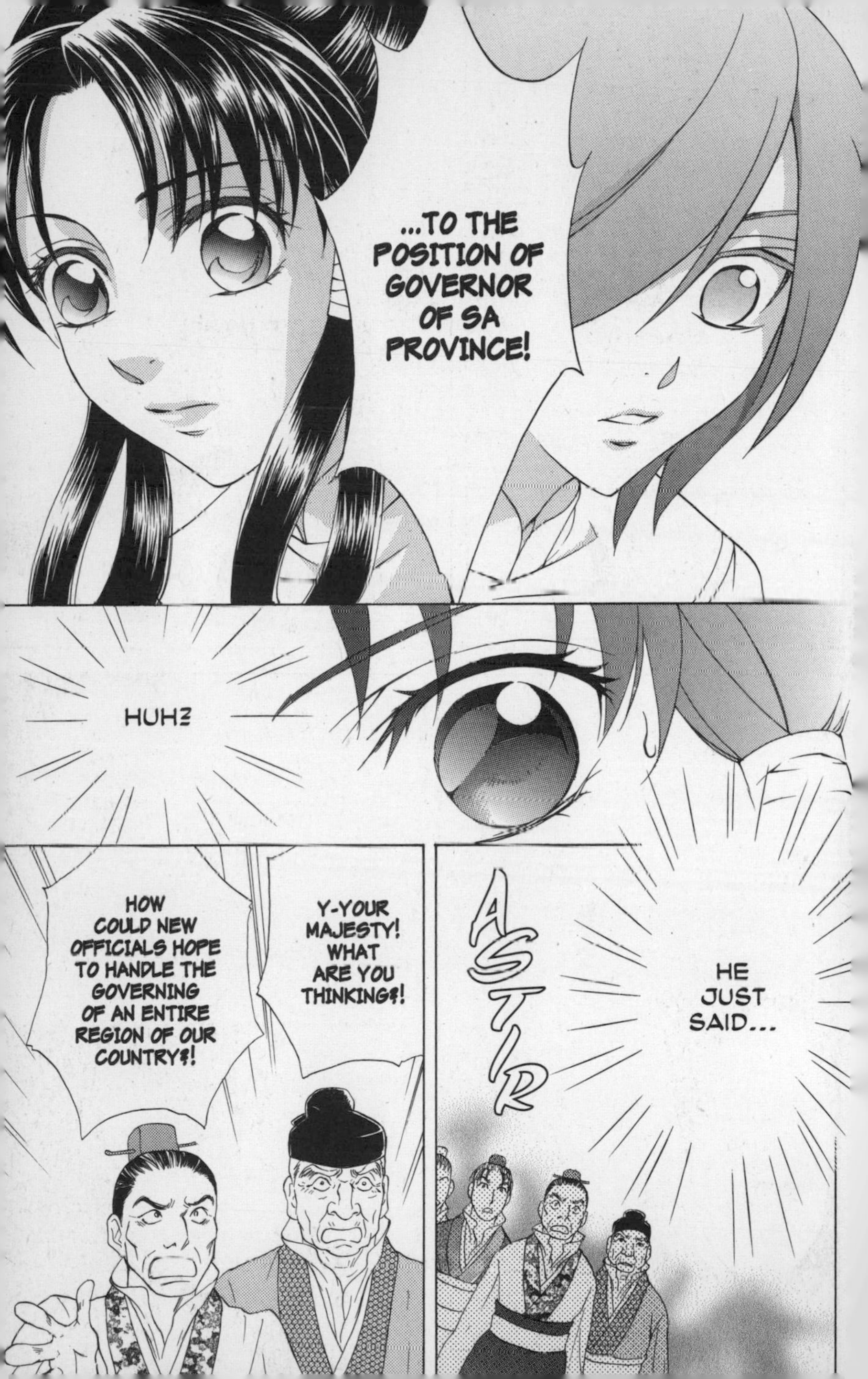
...TO THE POSITION OF GOVERNOR OF SA PROVINCE!
HUH?
ASTIR
HE JUST SAID...
Y-YOUR MAJESTY! WHAT ARE YOU THINKING?!
HOW COULD NEW OFFICIALS HOPE TO HANDLE THE GOVERNING OF AN ENTIRE REGION OF OUR COUNTRY?!

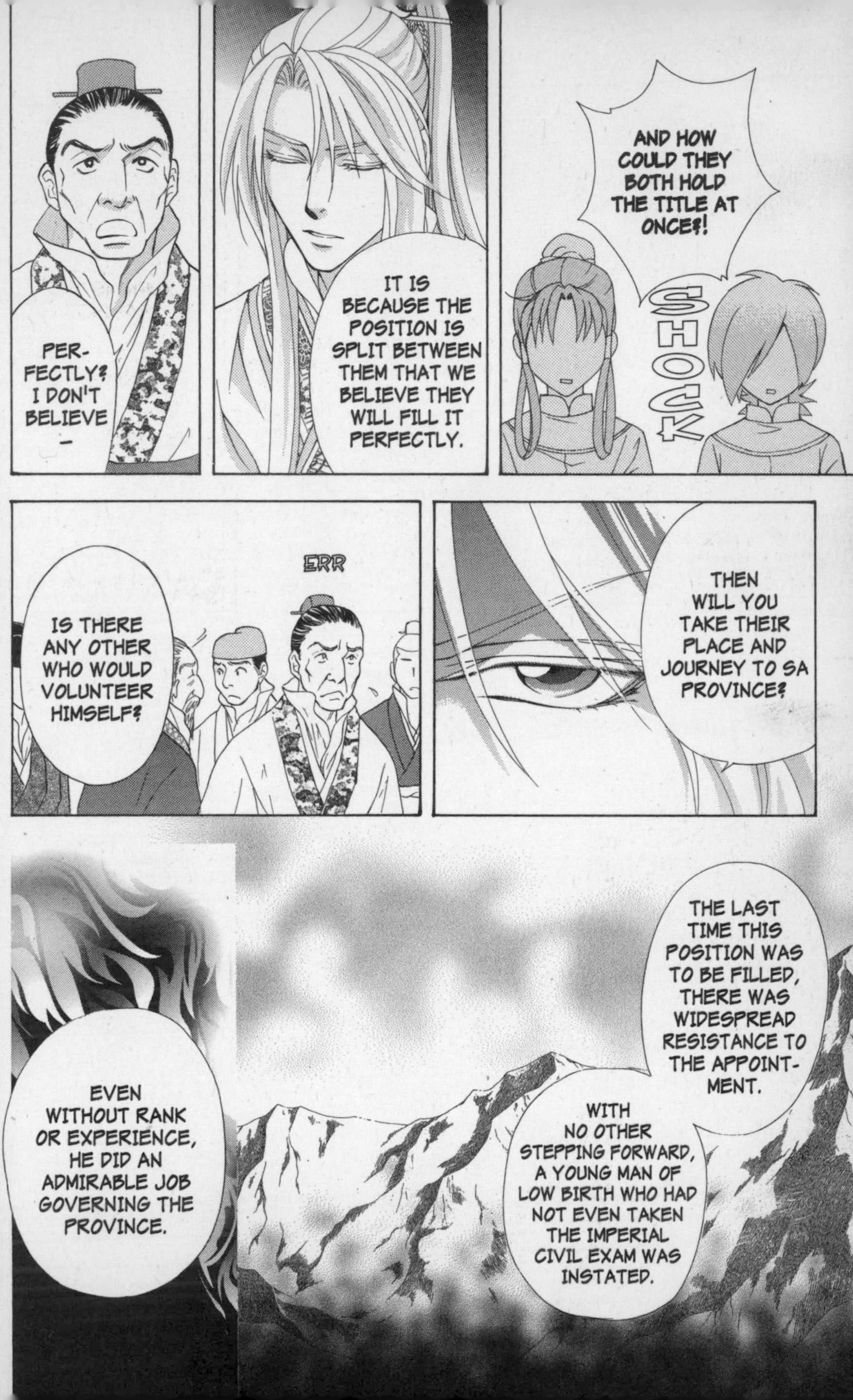
AND HOW COULD THEY BOTH HOLD THE TITLE AT ONCE?!
SHOCK
IT IS BECAUSE THE POSITION IS SPLIT BETWEEN THEM THAT WE BELIEVE THEY WILL FILL IT PERFECTLY.
PER-FECTLY? I DON'T BELIEVE –
THEN WILL YOU TAKE THEIR PLACE AND JOURNEY TO SA PROVINCE?
ERR
IS THERE ANY OTHER WHO WOULD VOLUNTEER HIMSELF?
THE LAST TIME THIS POSITION WAS TO BE FILLED, THERE WAS WIDESPREAD RESISTANCE TO THE APPOINT-MENT.
WITH NO OTHER STEPPING FORWARD, A YOUNG MAN OF LOW BIRTH WHO HAD NOT EVEN TAKEN THE IMPERIAL CIVIL EXAM WAS INSTATED.
EVEN WITHOUT RANK OR EXPERIENCE, HE DID AN ADMIRABLE JOB GOVERNING THE PROVINCE.

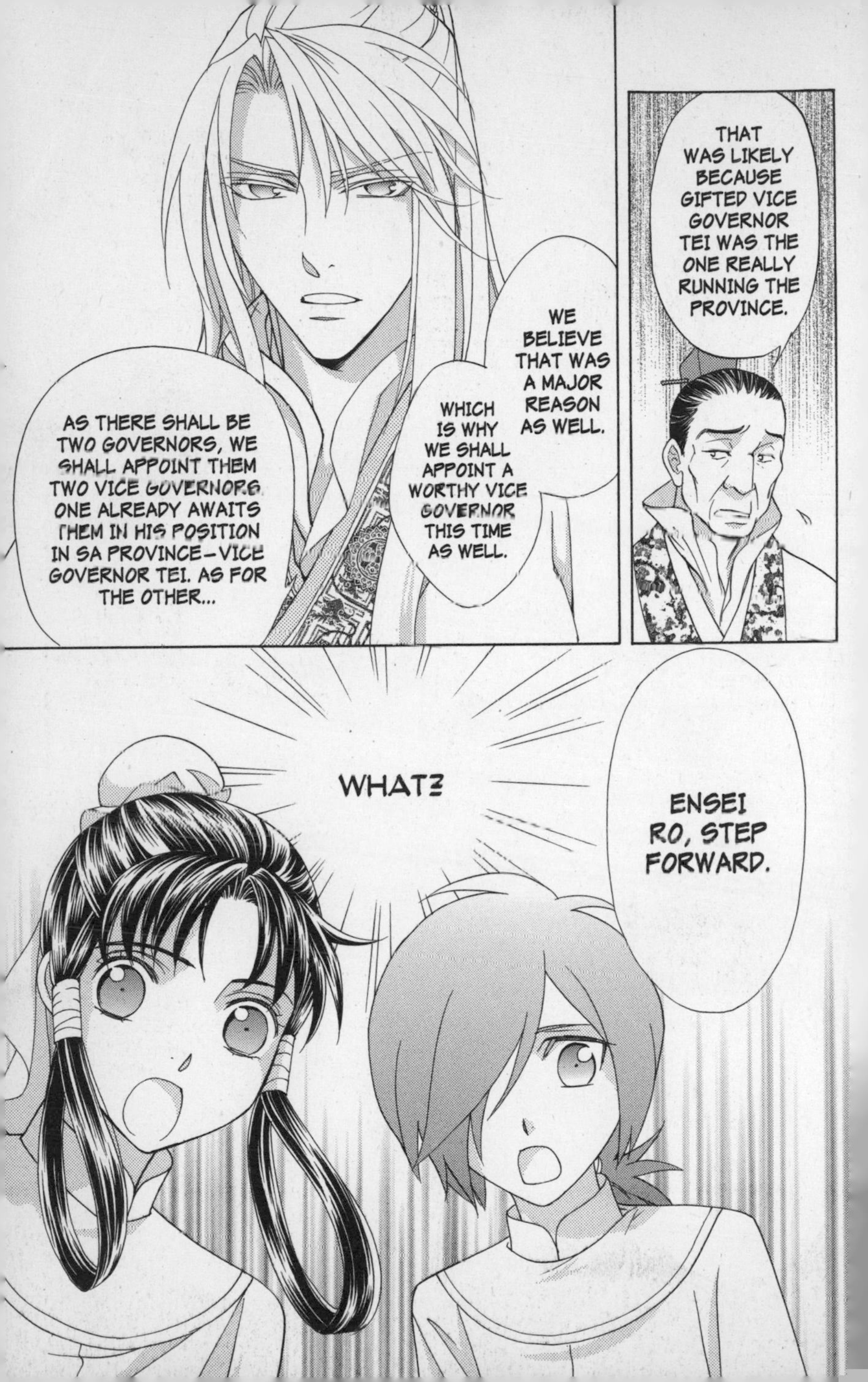
THAT WAS LIKELY BECAUSE GIFTED VICE GOVERNOR TEI WAS THE ONE REALLY RUNNING THE PROVINCE.
WE BELIEVE THAT WAS A MAJOR REASON AS WELL.
WHICH IS WHY WE SHALL APPOINT A WORTHY VICE GOVERNOR THIS TIME AS WELL.
AS THERE SHALL BE TWO GOVERNORS, WE SHALL APPOINT THEM TWO VICE GOVERNORS. ONE ALREADY AWAITS THEM IN HIS POSITION IN SA PROVINCE—VICE GOVERNOR TEI. AS FOR THE OTHER...
ENSEI RO, STEP FORWARD.
WHAT?

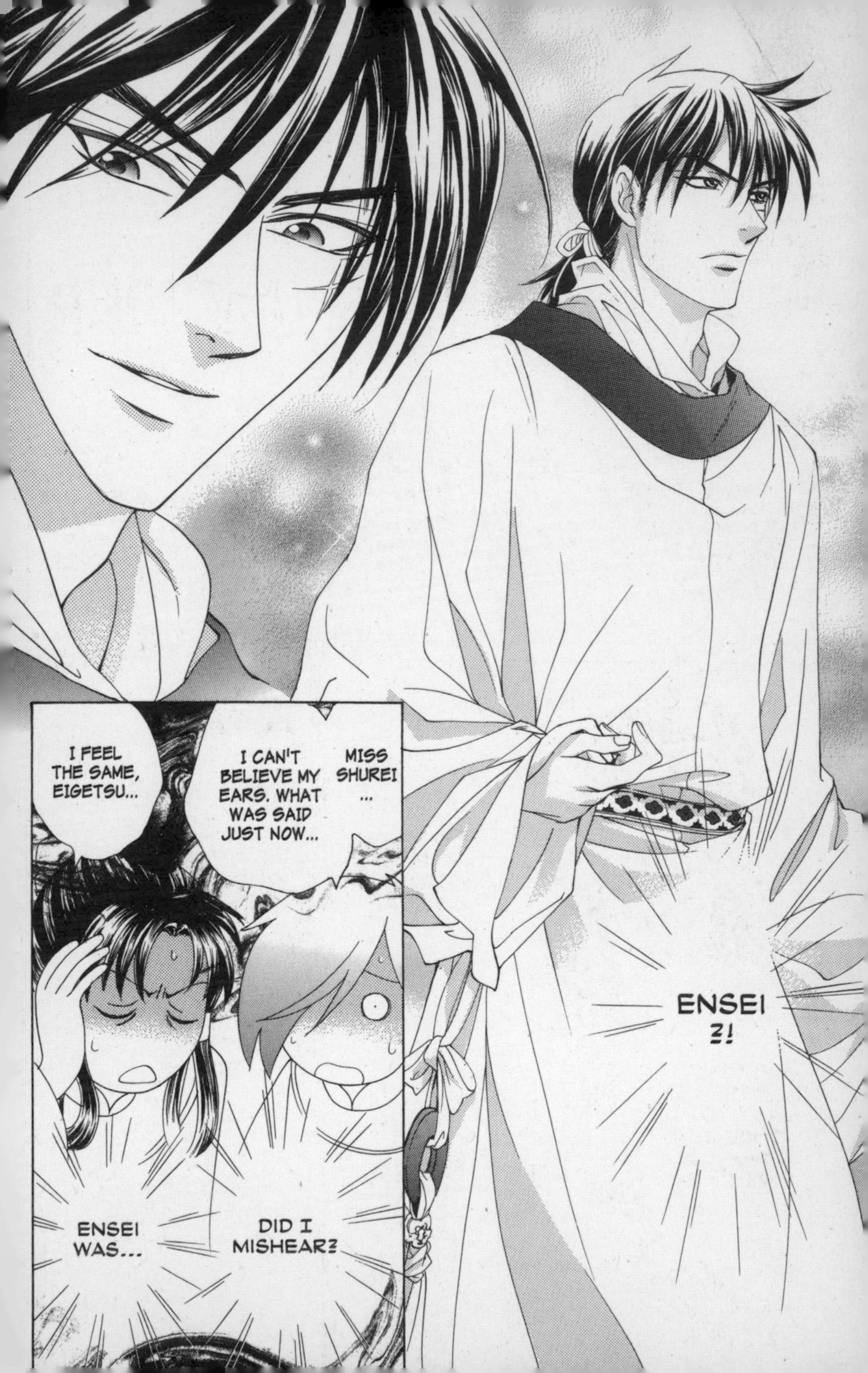
ENSEI ?!
MISS SHUREI ...
I CAN'T BELIEVE MY EARS. WHAT WAS SAID JUST NOW...
I FEEL THE SAME, EIGETSU...
DID I MISHEAR?
ENSEI WAS...

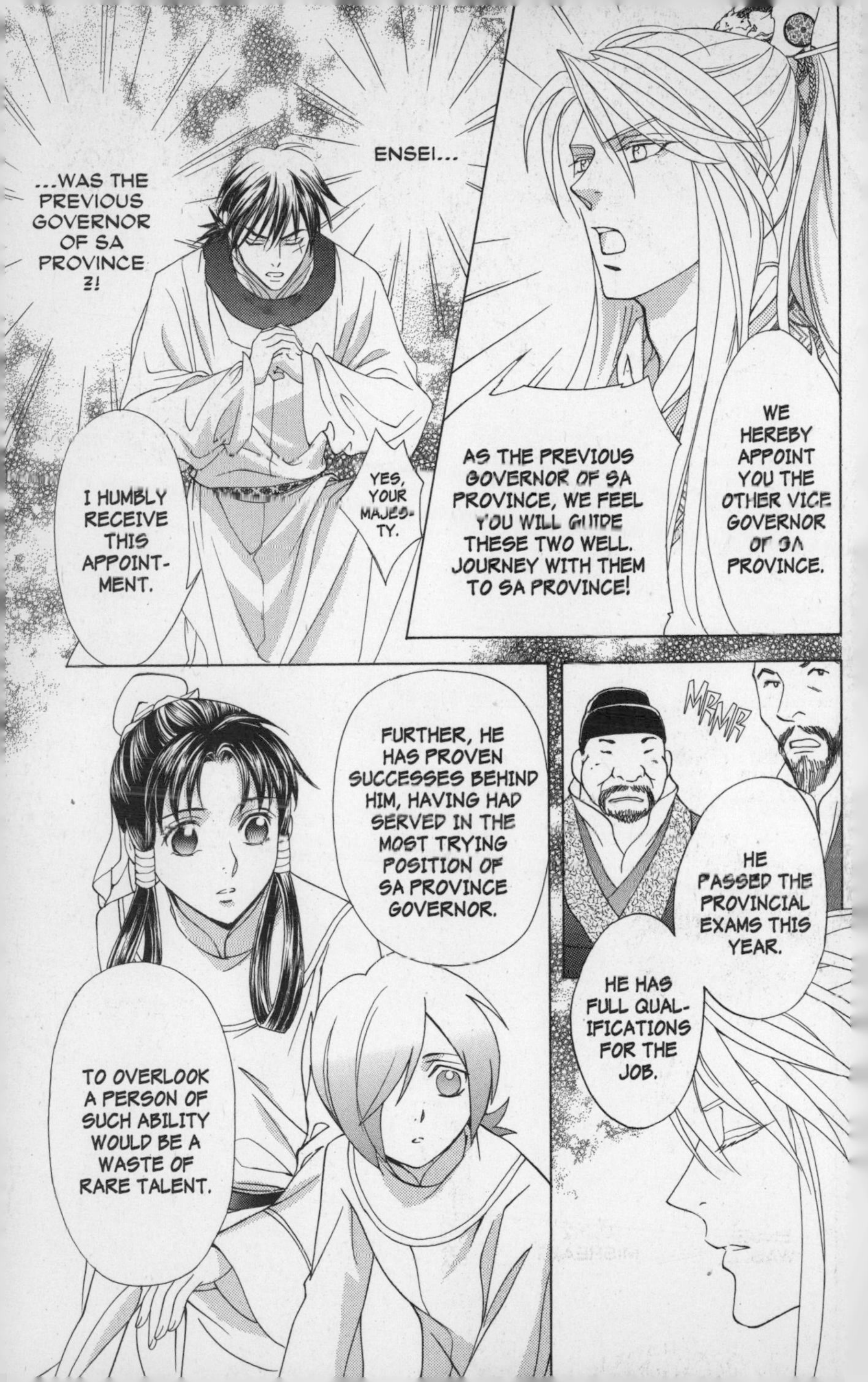

WE HEREBY APPOINT YOU THE OTHER VICE GOVERNOR OF SA PROVINCE.
AS THE PREVIOUS GOVERNOR OF SA PROVINCE, WE FEEL YOU WILL GUIDE THESE TWO WELL. JOURNEY WITH THEM TO SA PROVINCE!
ENSEI...
...WAS THE PREVIOUS GOVERNOR OF SA PROVINCE?!
YES, YOUR MAJESTY.
I HUMBLY RECEIVE THIS APPOINTMENT.
MRMR
HE PASSED THE PROVINCIAL EXAMS THIS YEAR.
HE HAS FULL QUALIFICATIONS FOR THE JOB.
FURTHER, HE HAS PROVEN SUCCESSES BEHIND HIM, HAVING HAD SERVED IN THE MOST TRYING POSITION OF SA PROVINCE GOVERNOR.
TO OVERLOOK A PERSON OF SUCH ABILITY WOULD BE A WASTE OF RARE TALENT.

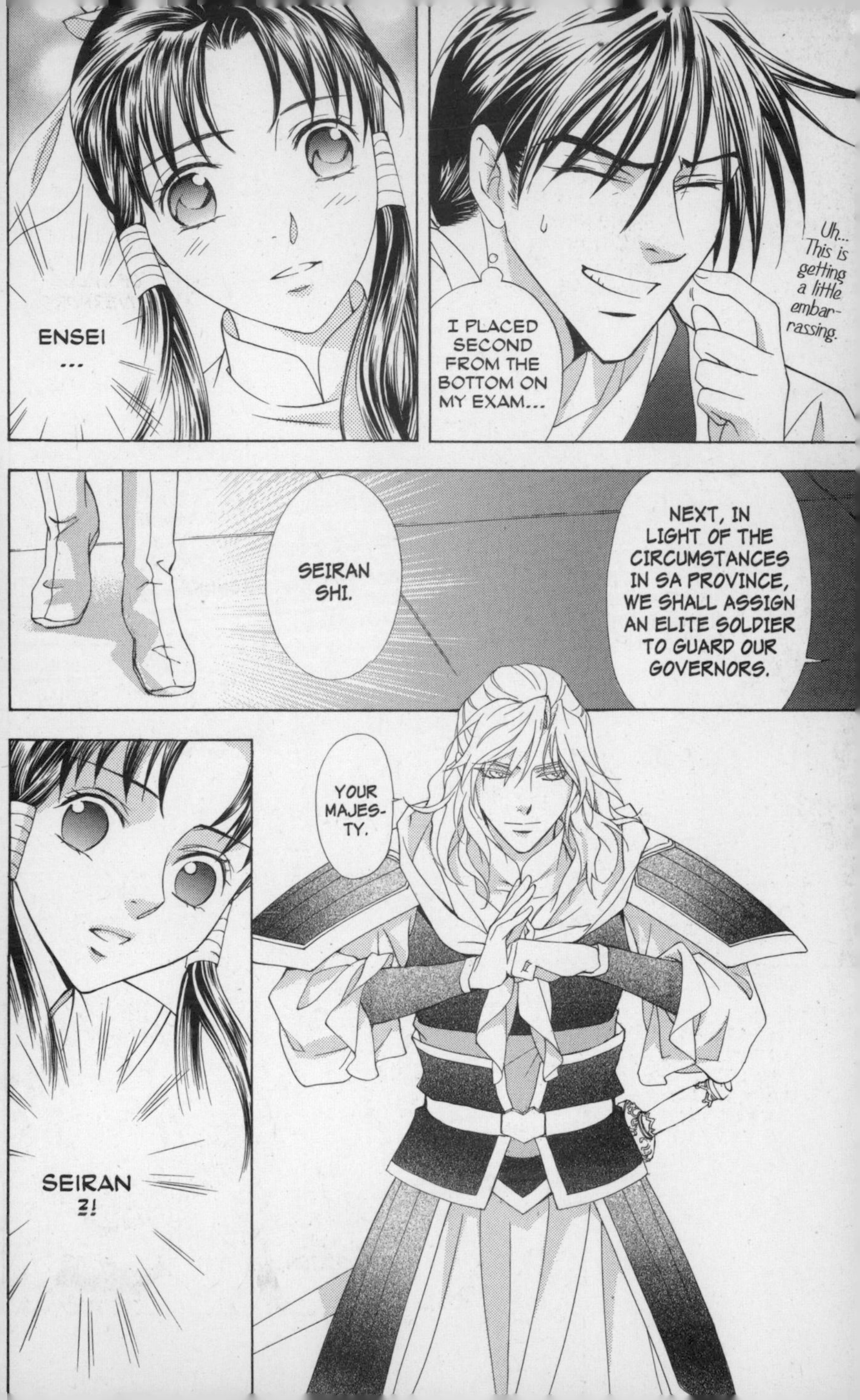
Uh... This is getting a little embar-rassing.
I PLACED SECOND FROM THE BOTTOM ON MY EXAM...
ENSEI ...
NEXT, IN LIGHT OF THE CIRCUMSTANCES IN SA PROVINCE, WE SHALL ASSIGN AN ELITE SOLDIER TO GUARD OUR GOVERNORS.
SEIRAN SHI.
YOUR MAJES-TY.
SEIRAN ?!

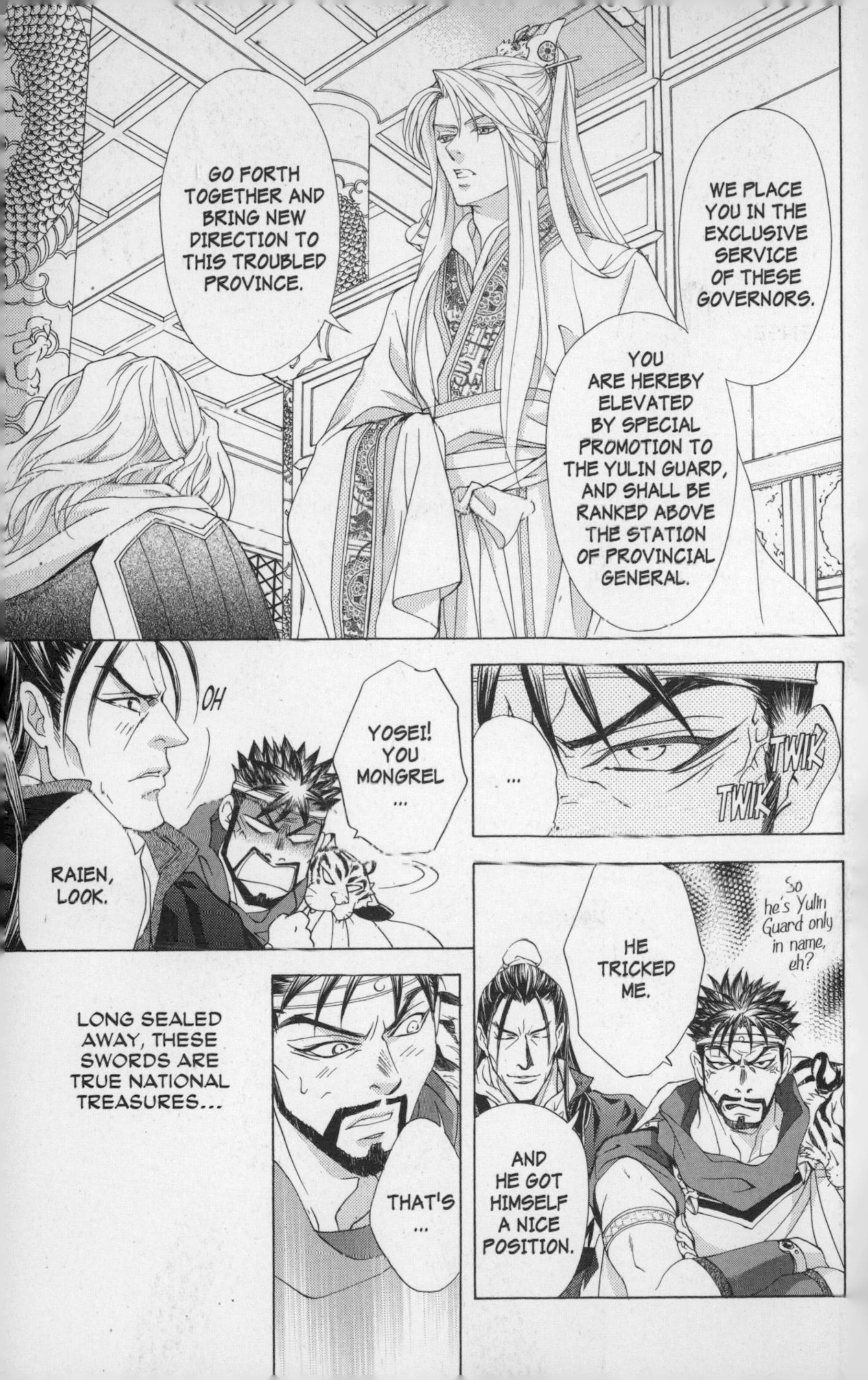
WE PLACE YOU IN THE EXCLUSIVE SERVICE OF THESE GOVERNORS.
YOU ARE HEREBY ELEVATED BY SPECIAL PROMOTION TO THE YULIN GUARD, AND SHALL BE RANKED ABOVE THE STATION OF PROVINCIAL GENERAL.
GO FORTH TOGETHER AND BRING NEW DIRECTION TO THIS TROUBLED PROVINCE.
...
TWIK
TWIK
YOSEI! YOU MONGREL ...
OH
RAIEN, LOOK.
So he's Yulin Guard only in name, eh?
HE TRICKED ME.
AND HE GOT HIMSELF A NICE POSITION.
THAT'S ...
LONG SEALED AWAY, THESE SWORDS ARE TRUE NATIONAL TREASURES...

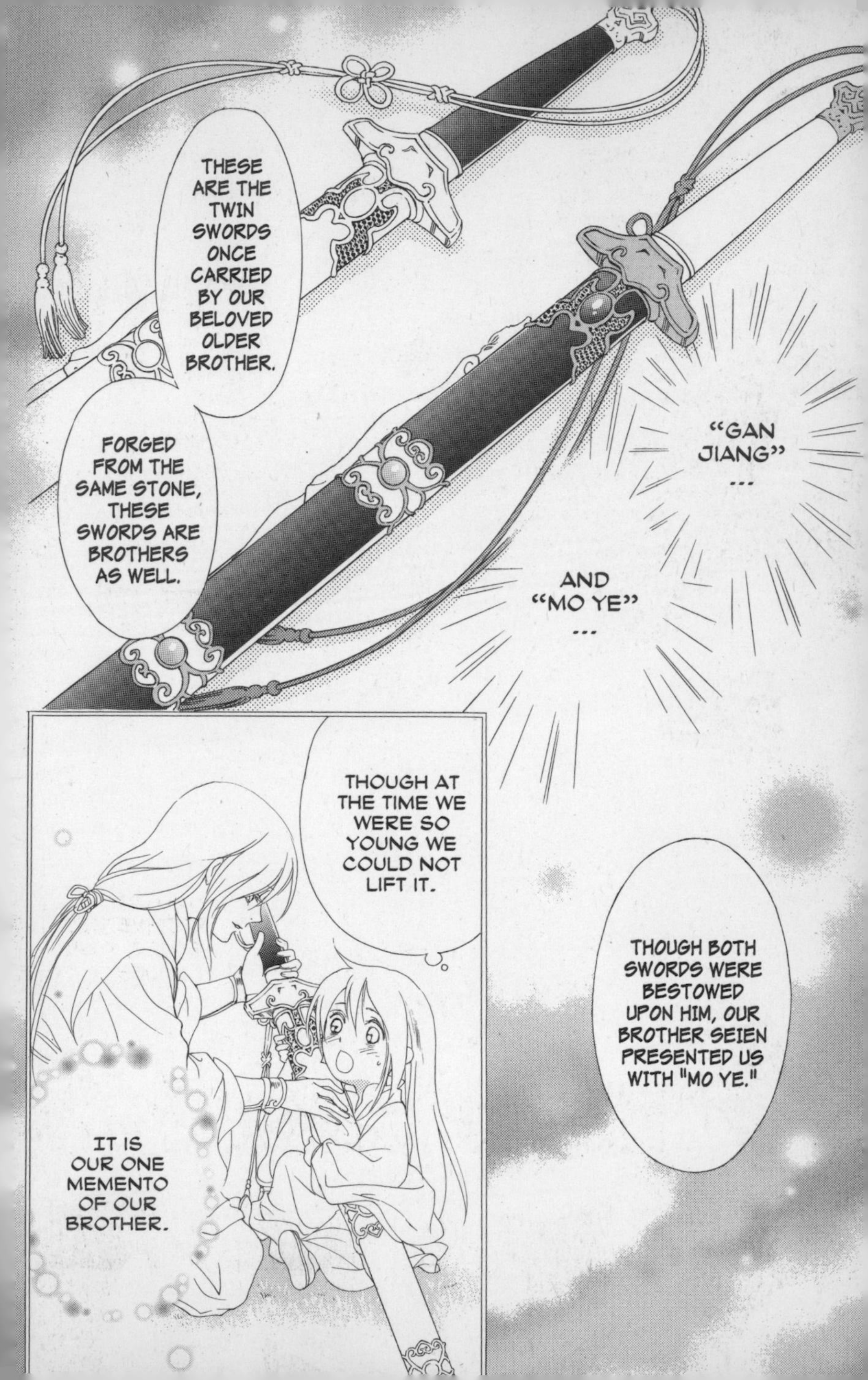
THESE ARE THE TWIN SWORDS ONCE CARRIED BY OUR BELOVED OLDER BROTHER.
"GAN JIANG" ...
AND "MO YE" ...
FORGED FROM THE SAME STONE, THESE SWORDS ARE BROTHERS AS WELL.
THOUGH BOTH SWORDS WERE BESTOWED UPON HIM, OUR BROTHER SEIEN PRESENTED US WITH "MO YE."
THOUGH AT THE TIME WE WERE SO YOUNG WE COULD NOT LIFT IT.
IT IS OUR ONE MEMENTO OF OUR BROTHER.

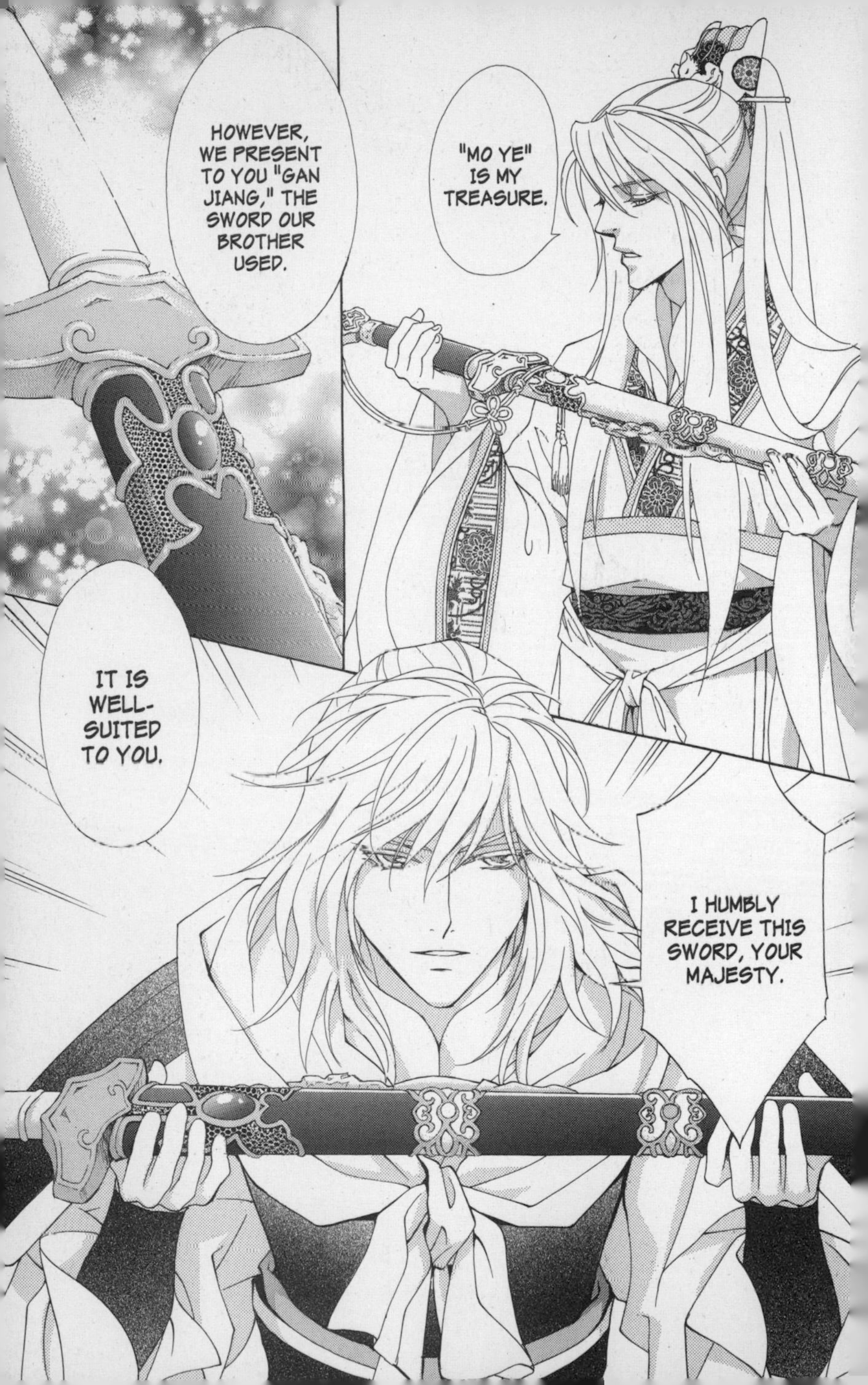
"MO YE" IS MY TREASURE.
HOWEVER, WE PRESENT TO YOU "GAN JIANG," THE SWORD OUR BROTHER USED.
IT IS WELL-SUITED TO YOU.
I HUMBLY RECEIVE THIS SWORD, YOUR MAJESTY.

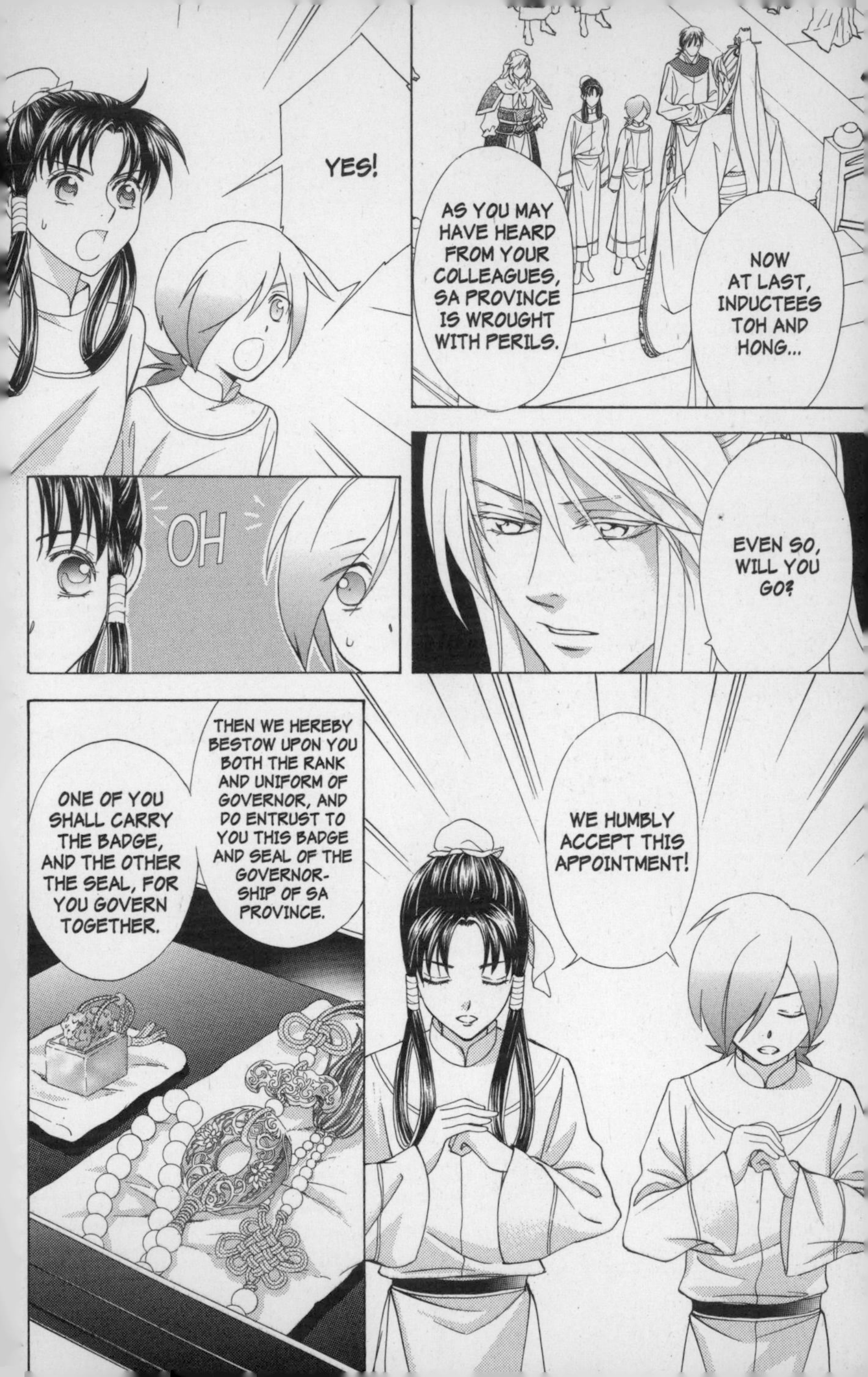
NOW AT LAST, INDUCTEES TOH AND HONG...
AS YOU MAY HAVE HEARD FROM YOUR COLLEAGUES, SA PROVINCE IS WROUGHT WITH PERILS.
EVEN SO, WILL YOU GO?
YES!
OH
WE HUMBLY ACCEPT THIS APPOINTMENT!
THEN WE HEREBY BESTOW UPON YOU BOTH THE RANK AND UNIFORM OF GOVERNOR, AND DO ENTRUST TO YOU THIS BADGE AND SEAL OF THE GOVERNOR-SHIP OF SA PROVINCE.
ONE OF YOU SHALL CARRY THE BADGE, AND THE OTHER THE SEAL, FOR YOU GOVERN TOGETHER.

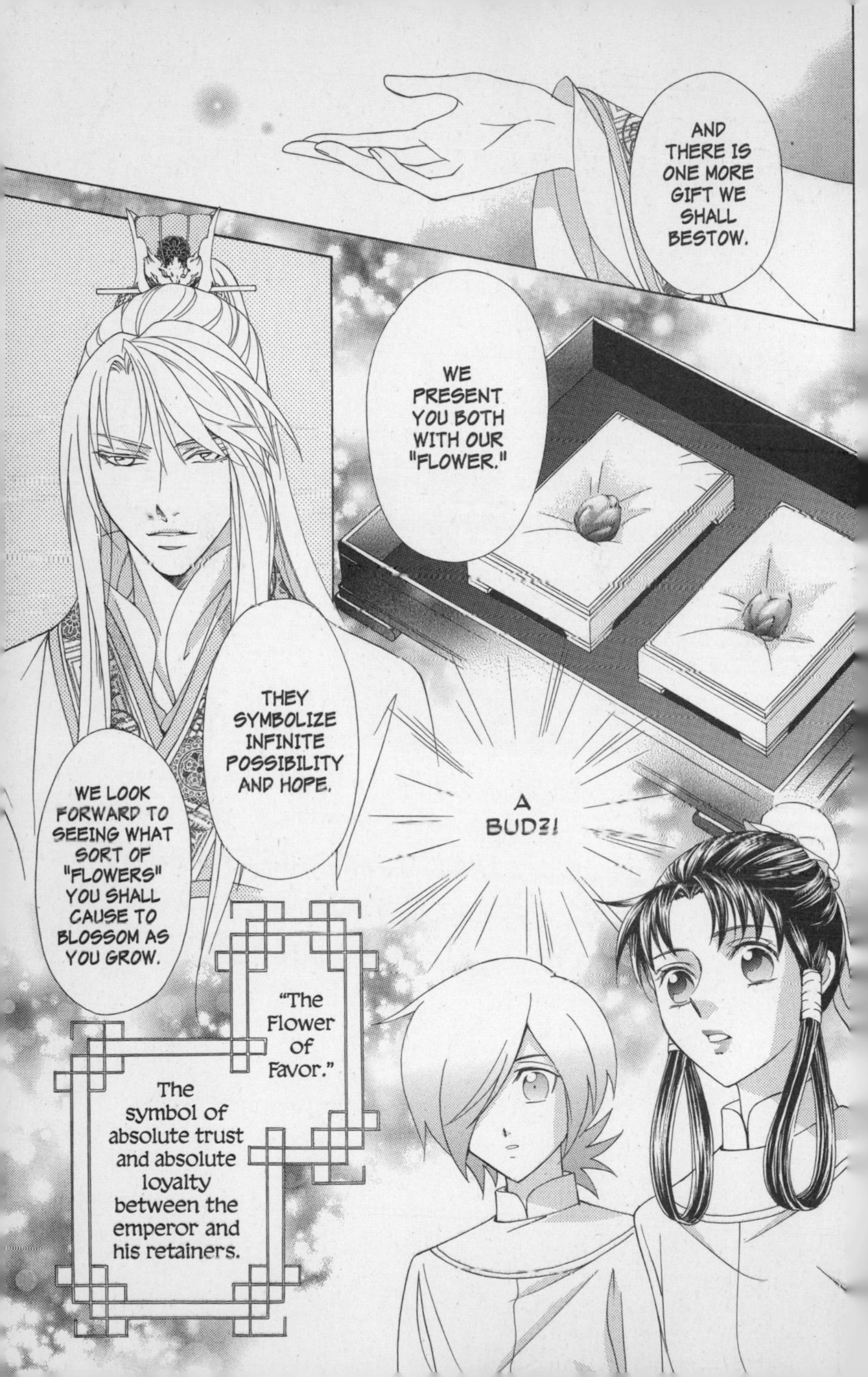
AND THERE IS ONE MORE GIFT WE SHALL BESTOW.
WE PRESENT YOU BOTH WITH OUR "FLOWER."
A BUD?!
THEY SYMBOLIZE INFINITE POSSIBILITY AND HOPE.
WE LOOK FORWARD TO SEEING WHAT SORT OF "FLOWERS" YOU SHALL CAUSE TO BLOSSOM AS YOU GROW.
"The Flower of Favor."
The symbol of absolute trust and absolute loyalty between the emperor and his retainers.

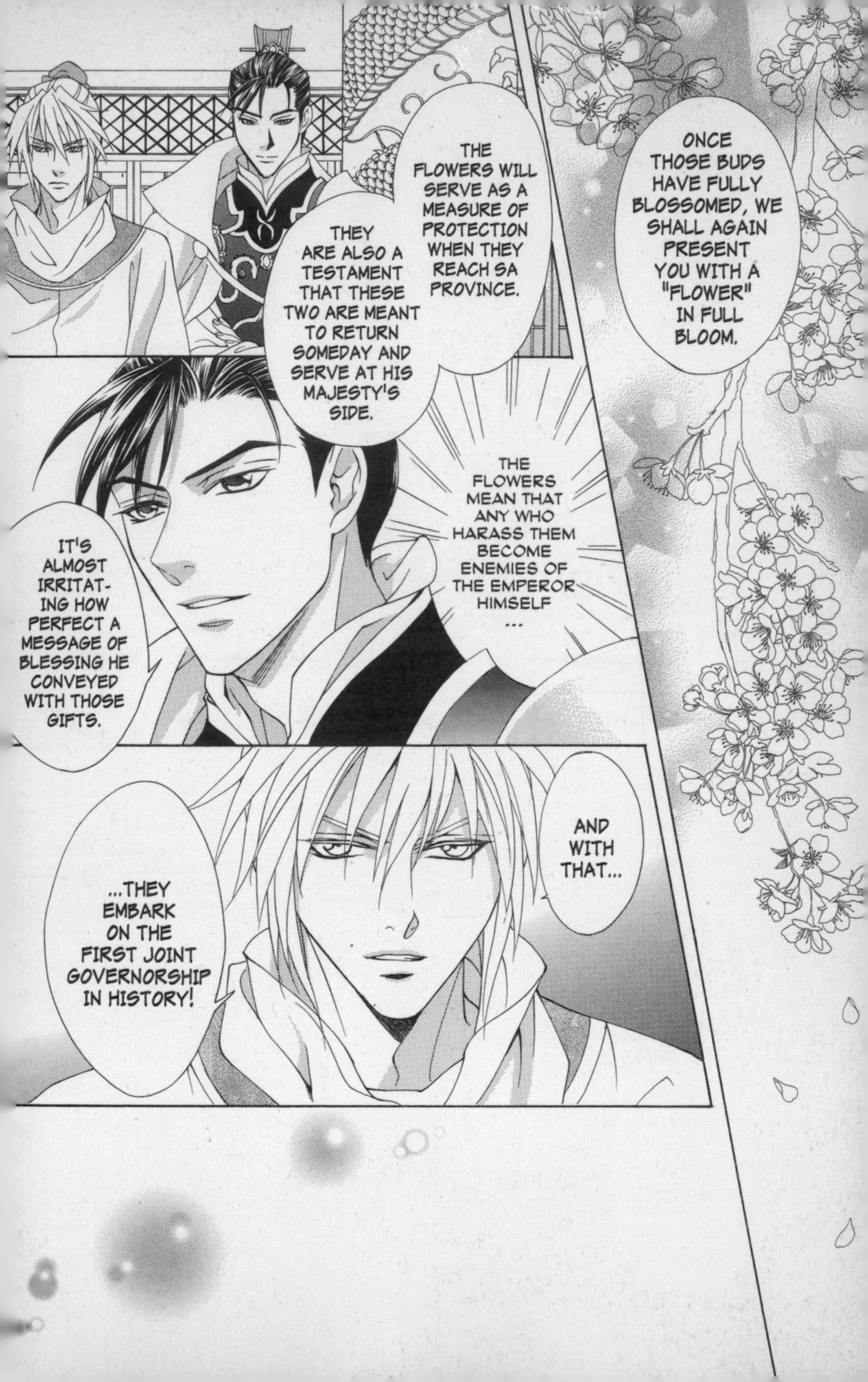
ONCE THOSE BUDS HAVE FULLY BLOSSOMED, WE SHALL AGAIN PRESENT YOU WITH A "FLOWER" IN FULL BLOOM.
THE FLOWERS WILL SERVE AS A MEASURE OF PROTECTION WHEN THEY REACH SA PROVINCE.
THEY ARE ALSO A TESTAMENT THAT THESE TWO ARE MEANT TO RETURN SOMEDAY AND SERVE AT HIS MAJESTY'S SIDE.
THE FLOWERS MEAN THAT ANY WHO HARASS THEM BECOME ENEMIES OF THE EMPEROR HIMSELF ...
IT'S ALMOST IRRITATING HOW PERFECT A MESSAGE OF BLESSING HE CONVEYED WITH THOSE GIFTS.
AND WITH THAT...
...THEY EMBARK ON THE FIRST JOINT GOVERNORSHIP IN HISTORY!

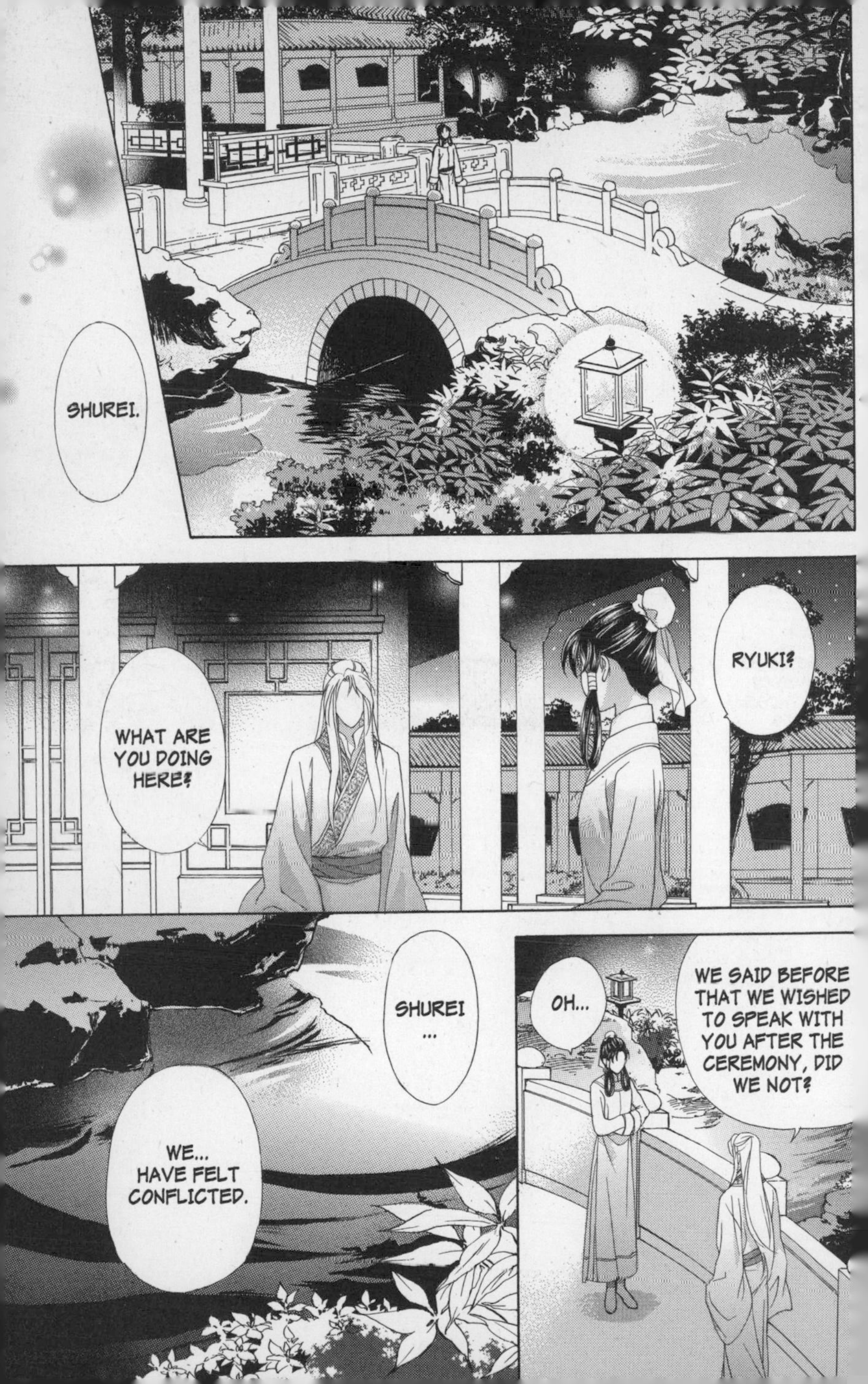
SHUREI.
RYUKI?
WHAT ARE YOU DOING HERE?
WE SAID BEFORE THAT WE WISHED TO SPEAK WITH YOU AFTER THE CEREMONY, DID WE NOT?
OH...
SHUREI ...
WE... HAVE FELT CONFLICTED.

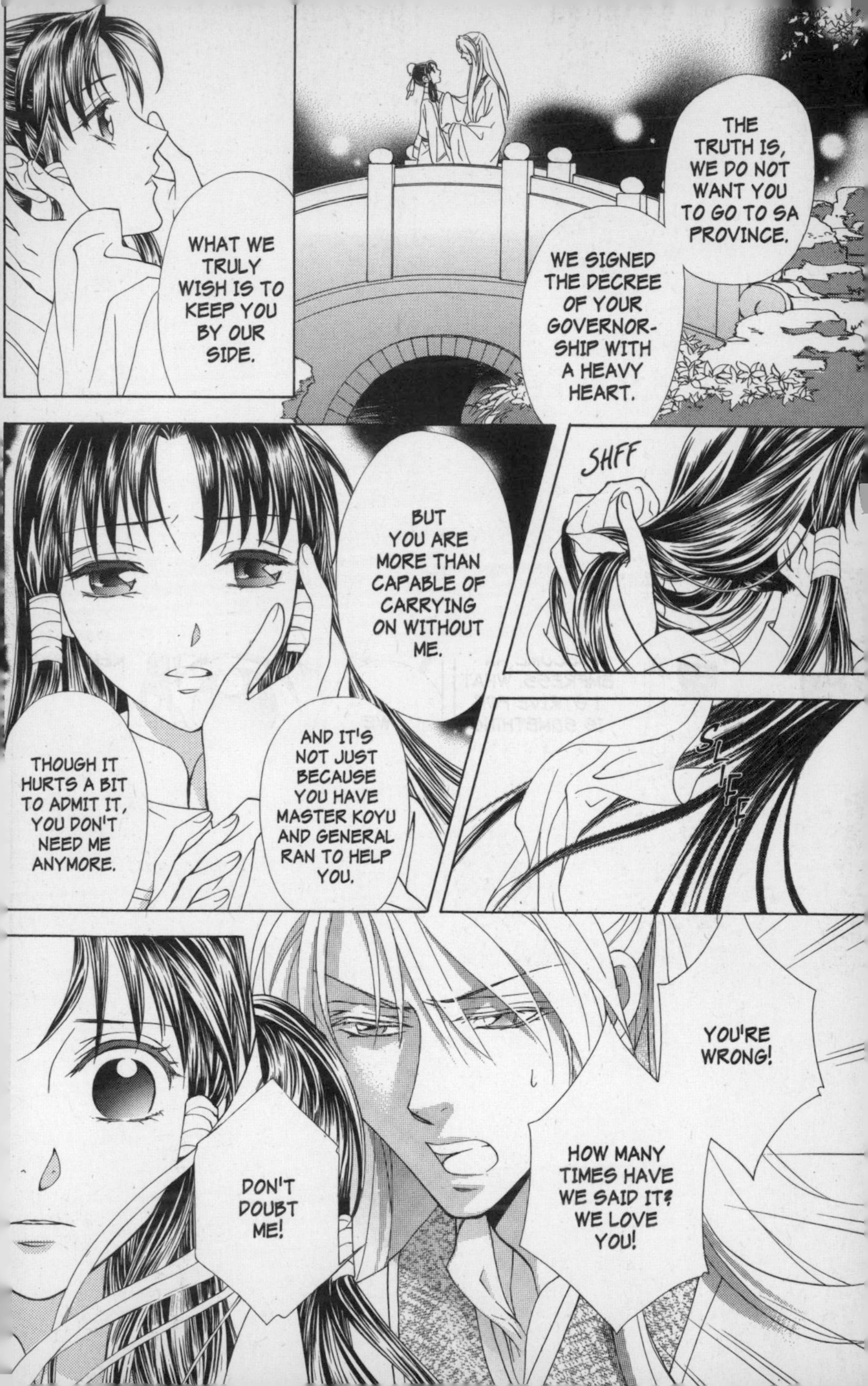
THE TRUTH IS, WE DO NOT WANT YOU TO GO TO SA PROVINCE.
WE SIGNED THE DECREE OF YOUR GOVERNOR-SHIP WITH A HEAVY HEART.
WHAT WE TRULY WISH IS TO KEEP YOU BY OUR SIDE.
SHFF
SLIFF
BUT YOU ARE MORE THAN CAPABLE OF CARRYING ON WITHOUT ME.
AND IT'S NOT JUST BECAUSE YOU HAVE MASTER KOYU AND GENERAL RAN TO HELP YOU.
THOUGH IT HURTS A BIT TO ADMIT IT, YOU DON'T NEED ME ANYMORE.
YOU'RE WRONG!
HOW MANY TIMES HAVE WE SAID IT? WE LOVE YOU!
DON'T DOUBT ME!

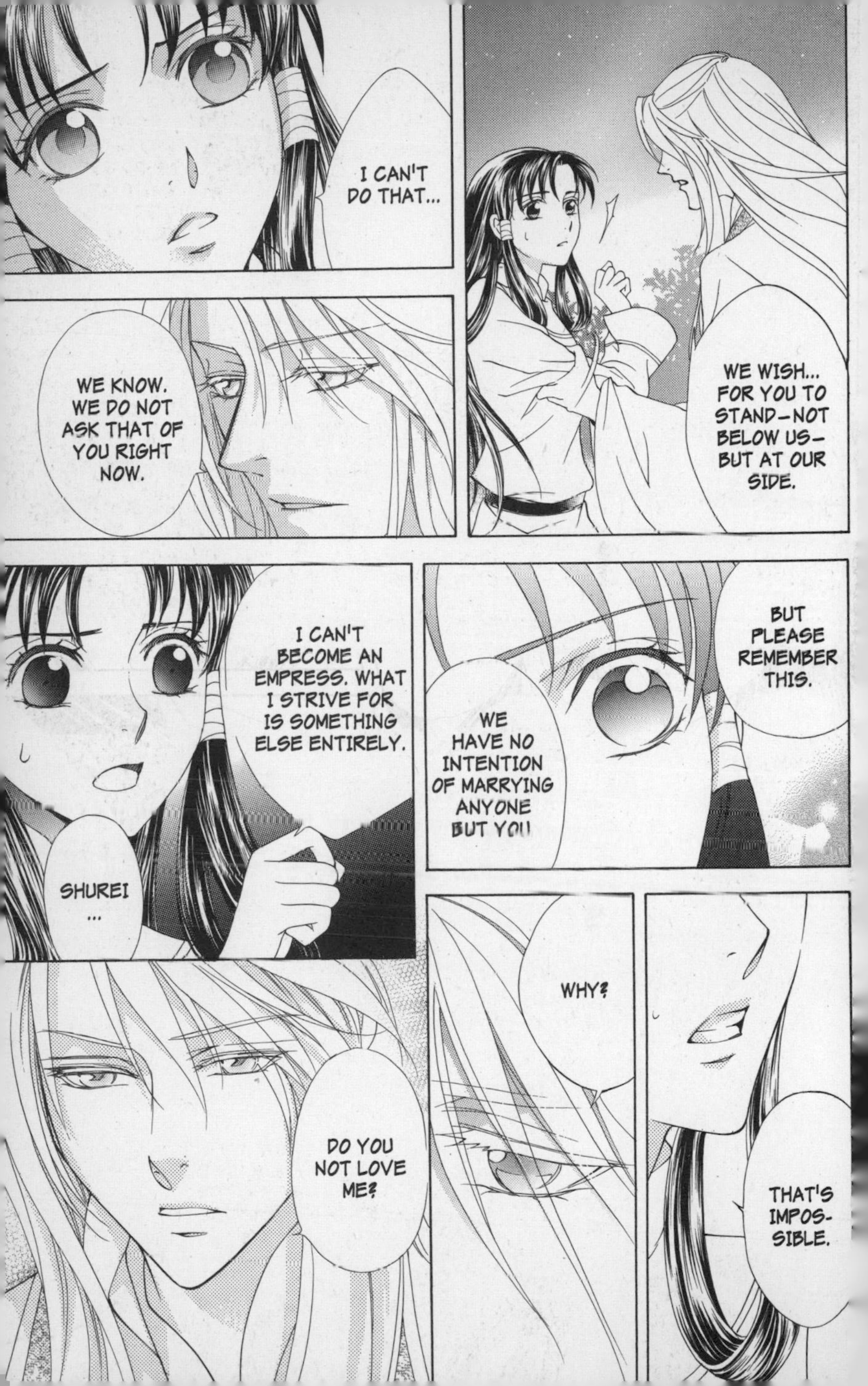
WE WISH... FOR YOU TO STAND—NOT BELOW US—BUT AT OUR SIDE.
I CAN'T DO THAT...
WE KNOW. WE DO NOT ASK THAT OF YOU RIGHT NOW.
BUT PLEASE REMEMBER THIS.
WE HAVE NO INTENTION OF MARRYING ANYONE BUT YOU
I CAN'T BECOME AN EMPRESS. WHAT I STRIVE FOR IS SOMETHING ELSE ENTIRELY.
SHUREI ...
THAT'S IMPOS-SIBLE.
WHY?
DO YOU NOT LOVE ME?

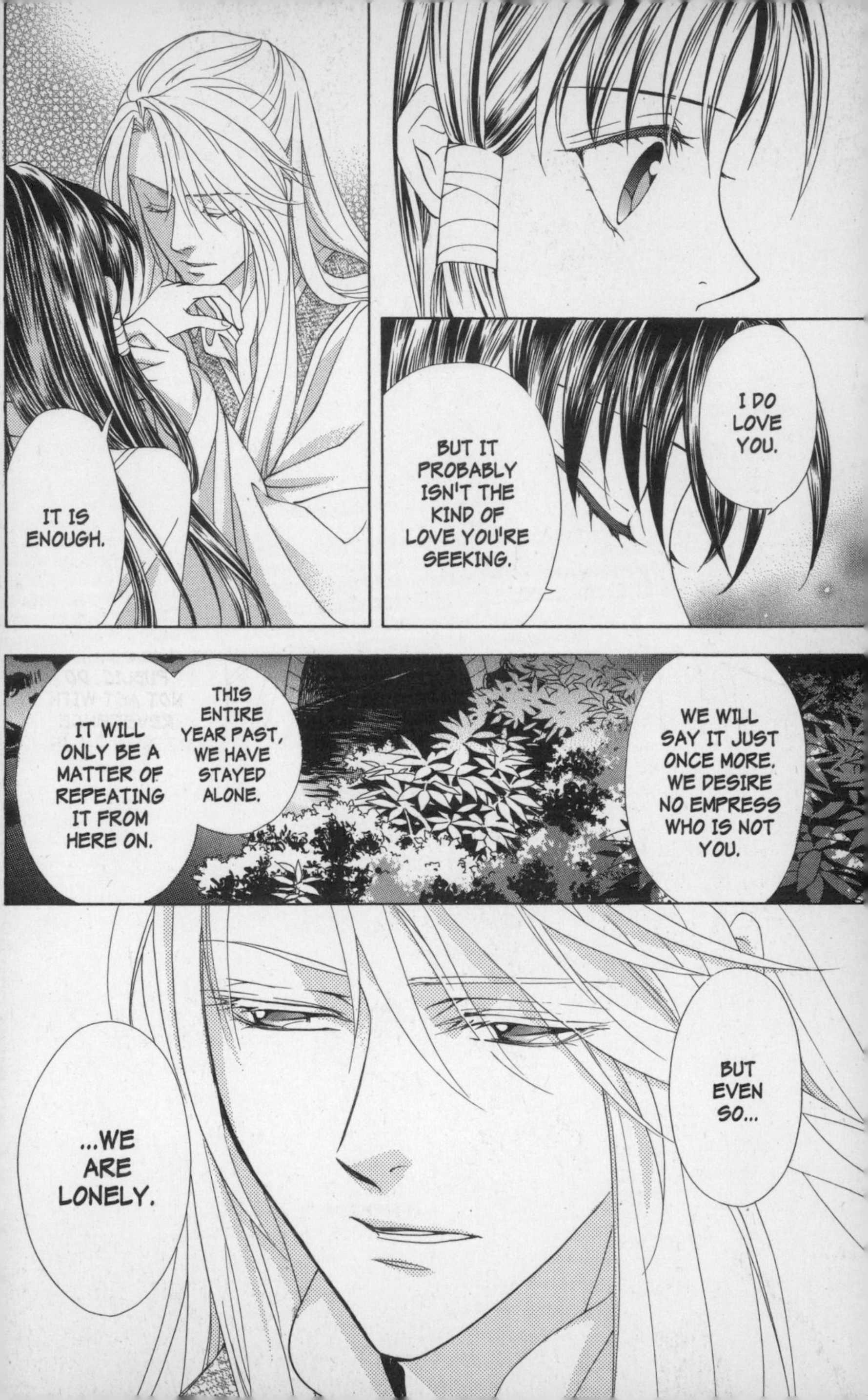
I DO LOVE YOU.
BUT IT PROBABLY ISN'T THE KIND OF LOVE YOU'RE SEEKING.
IT IS ENOUGH.
WE WILL SAY IT JUST ONCE MORE. WE DESIRE NO EMPRESS WHO IS NOT YOU.
THIS ENTIRE YEAR PAST, WE HAVE STAYED ALONE.
IT WILL ONLY BE A MATTER OF REPEATING IT FROM HERE ON.
BUT EVEN SO...
...WE ARE LONELY.

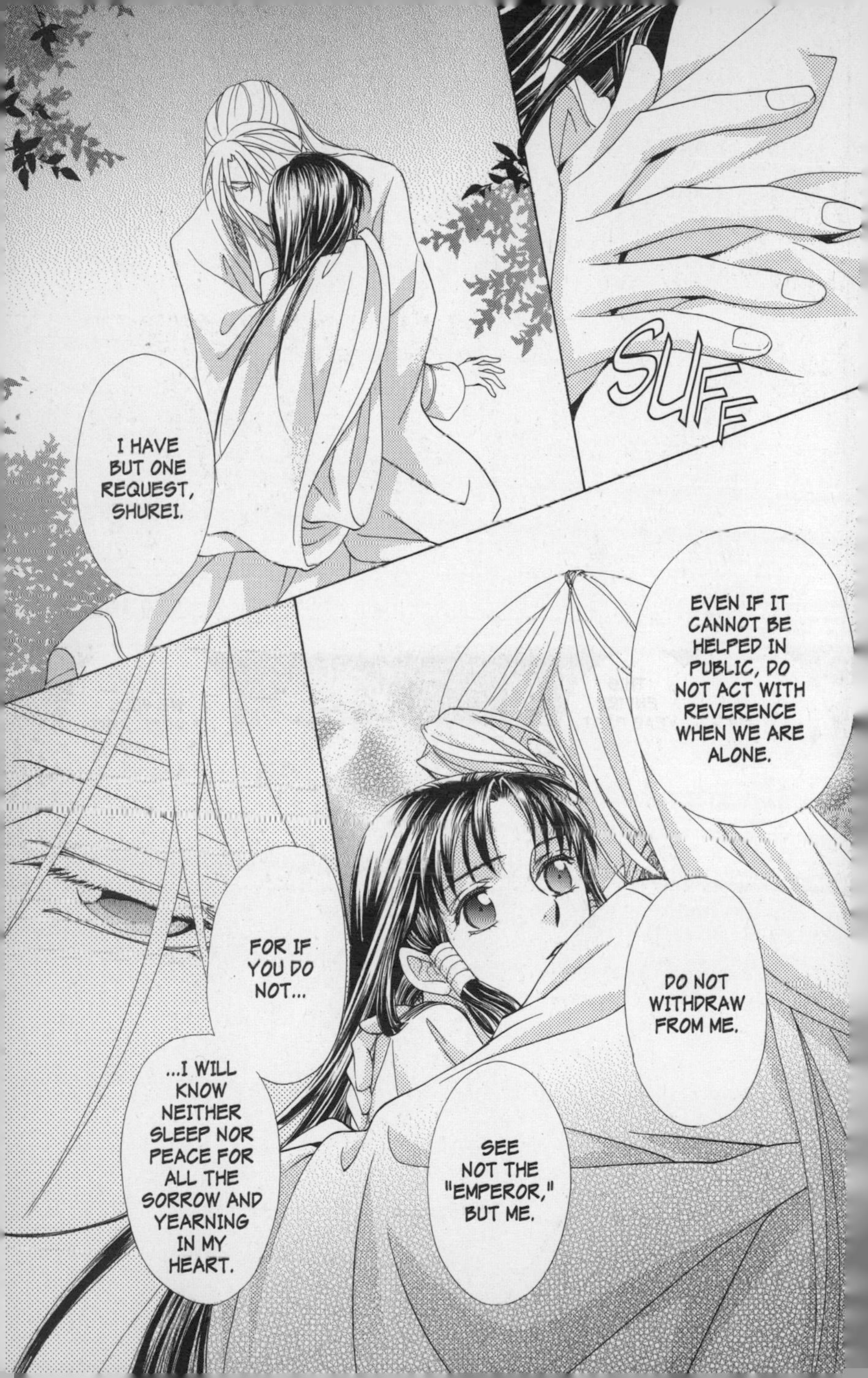
SUFF
I HAVE BUT ONE REQUEST, SHUREI.
EVEN IF IT CANNOT BE HELPED IN PUBLIC, DO NOT ACT WITH REVERENCE WHEN WE ARE ALONE.
DO NOT WITHDRAW FROM ME.
SEE NOT THE "EMPEROR," BUT ME.
FOR IF YOU DO NOT...
...I WILL KNOW NEITHER SLEEP NOR PEACE FOR ALL THE SORROW AND YEARNING IN MY HEART.

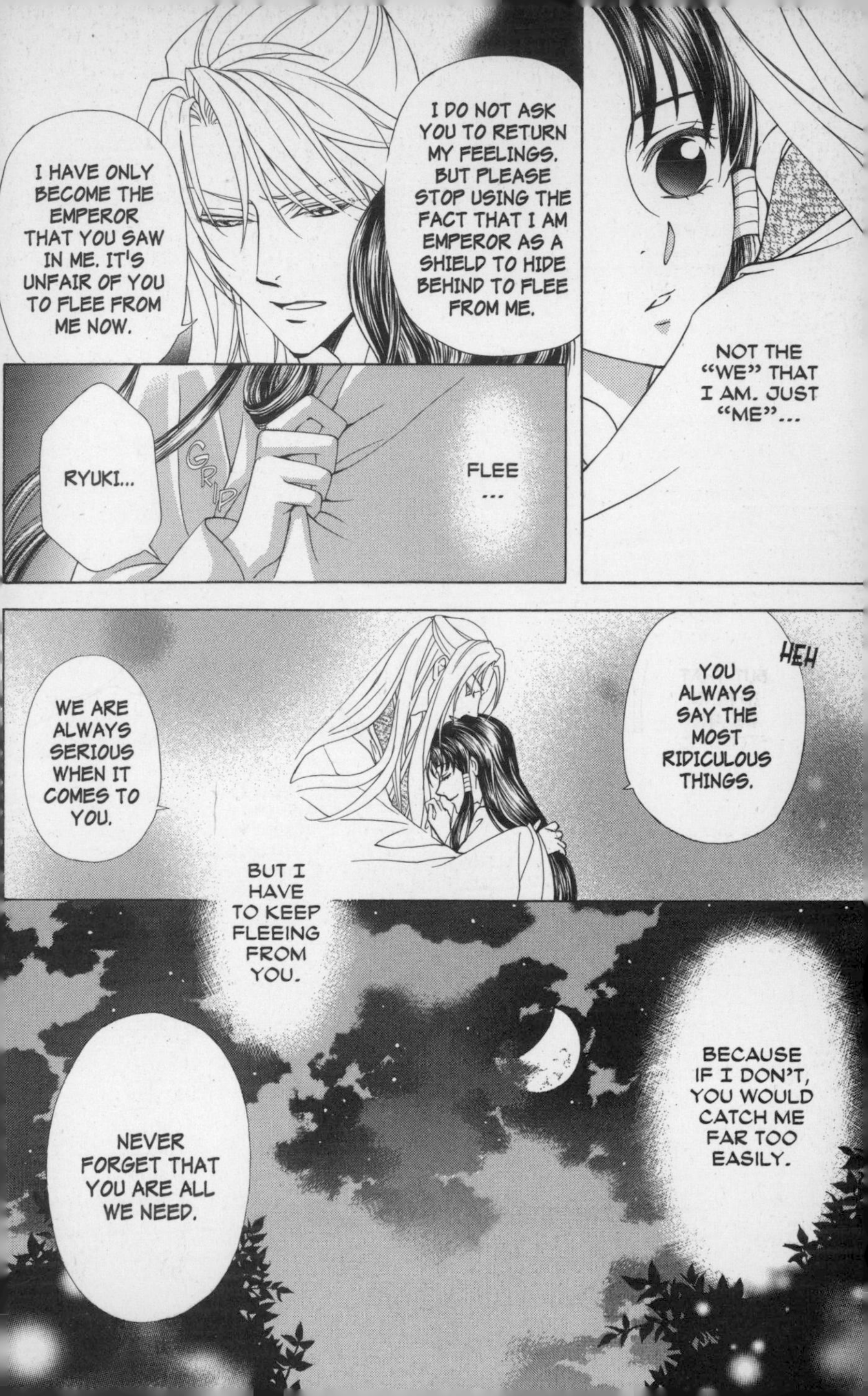
NOT THE "WE" THAT I AM. JUST "ME"...
I DO NOT ASK YOU TO RETURN MY FEELINGS. BUT PLEASE STOP USING THE FACT THAT I AM EMPEROR AS A SHIELD TO HIDE BEHIND TO FLEE FROM ME.
I HAVE ONLY BECOME THE EMPEROR THAT YOU SAW IN ME. IT'S UNFAIR OF YOU TO FLEE FROM ME NOW.
FLEE ...
GRIP
RYUKI...
HEH
YOU ALWAYS SAY THE MOST RIDICULOUS THINGS.
WE ARE ALWAYS SERIOUS WHEN IT COMES TO YOU.
BUT I HAVE TO KEEP FLEEING FROM YOU.
BECAUSE IF I DON'T, YOU WOULD CATCH ME FAR TOO EASILY.
NEVER FORGET THAT YOU ARE ALL WE NEED.

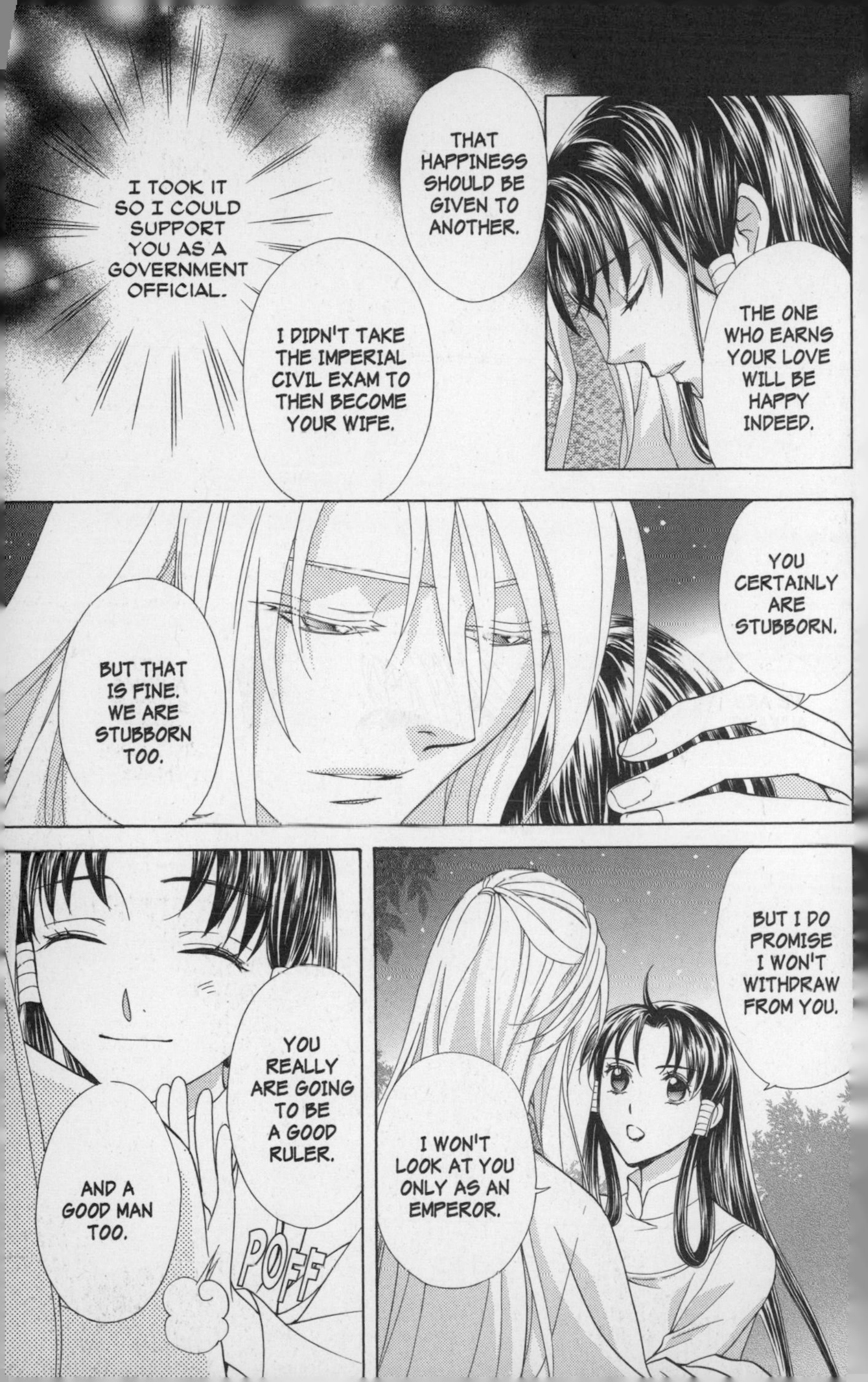
THE ONE WHO EARNS YOUR LOVE WILL BE HAPPY INDEED.
THAT HAPPINESS SHOULD BE GIVEN TO ANOTHER.
I DIDN'T TAKE THE IMPERIAL CIVIL EXAM TO THEN BECOME YOUR WIFE.
I TOOK IT SO I COULD SUPPORT YOU AS A GOVERNMENT OFFICIAL.
YOU CERTAINLY ARE STUBBORN.
BUT THAT IS FINE. WE ARE STUBBORN TOO.
BUT I DO PROMISE I WON'T WITHDRAW FROM YOU.
I WON'T LOOK AT YOU ONLY AS AN EMPEROR.
YOU REALLY ARE GOING TO BE A GOOD RULER.
AND A GOOD MAN TOO.
POFF

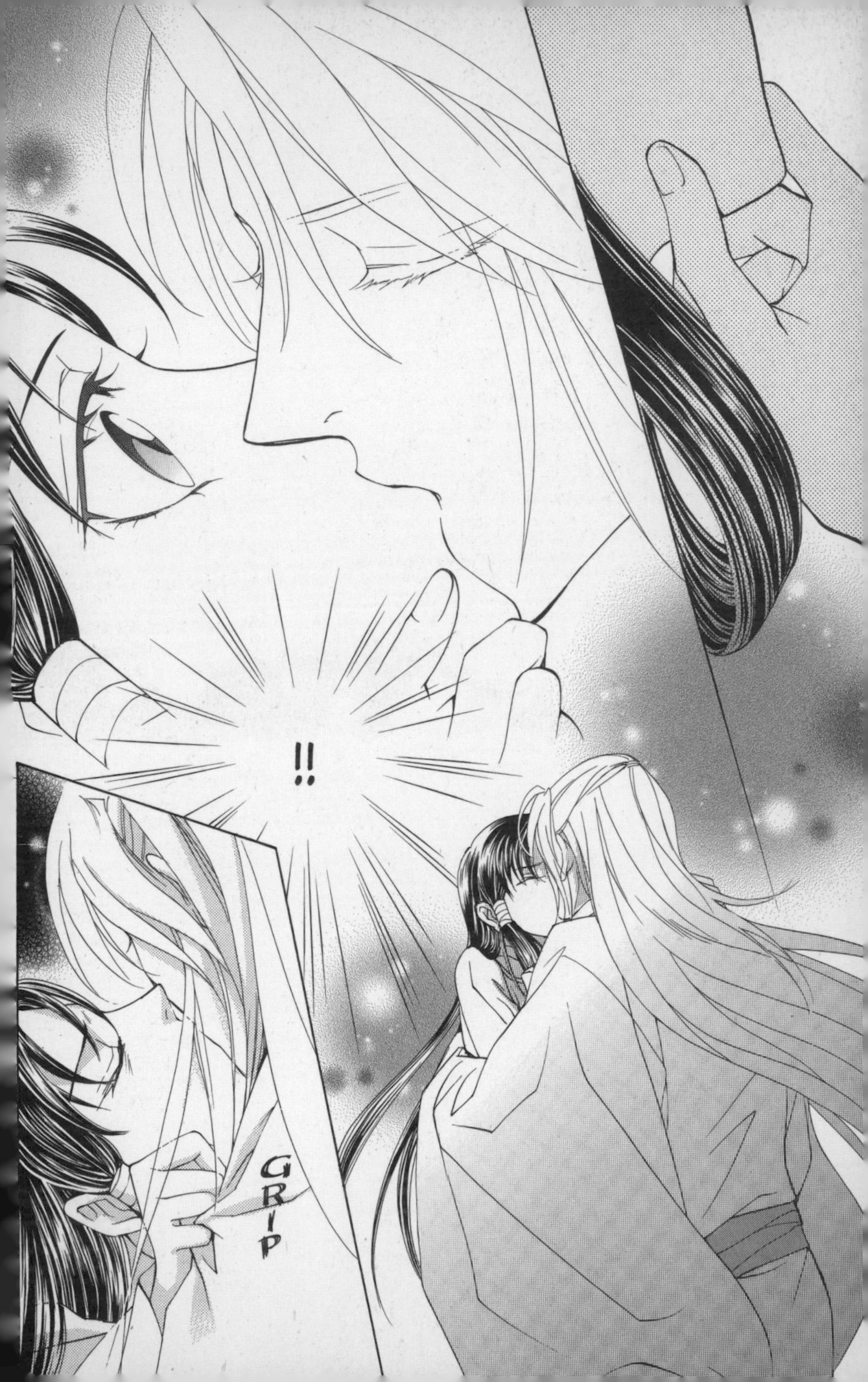
!!
GRIP

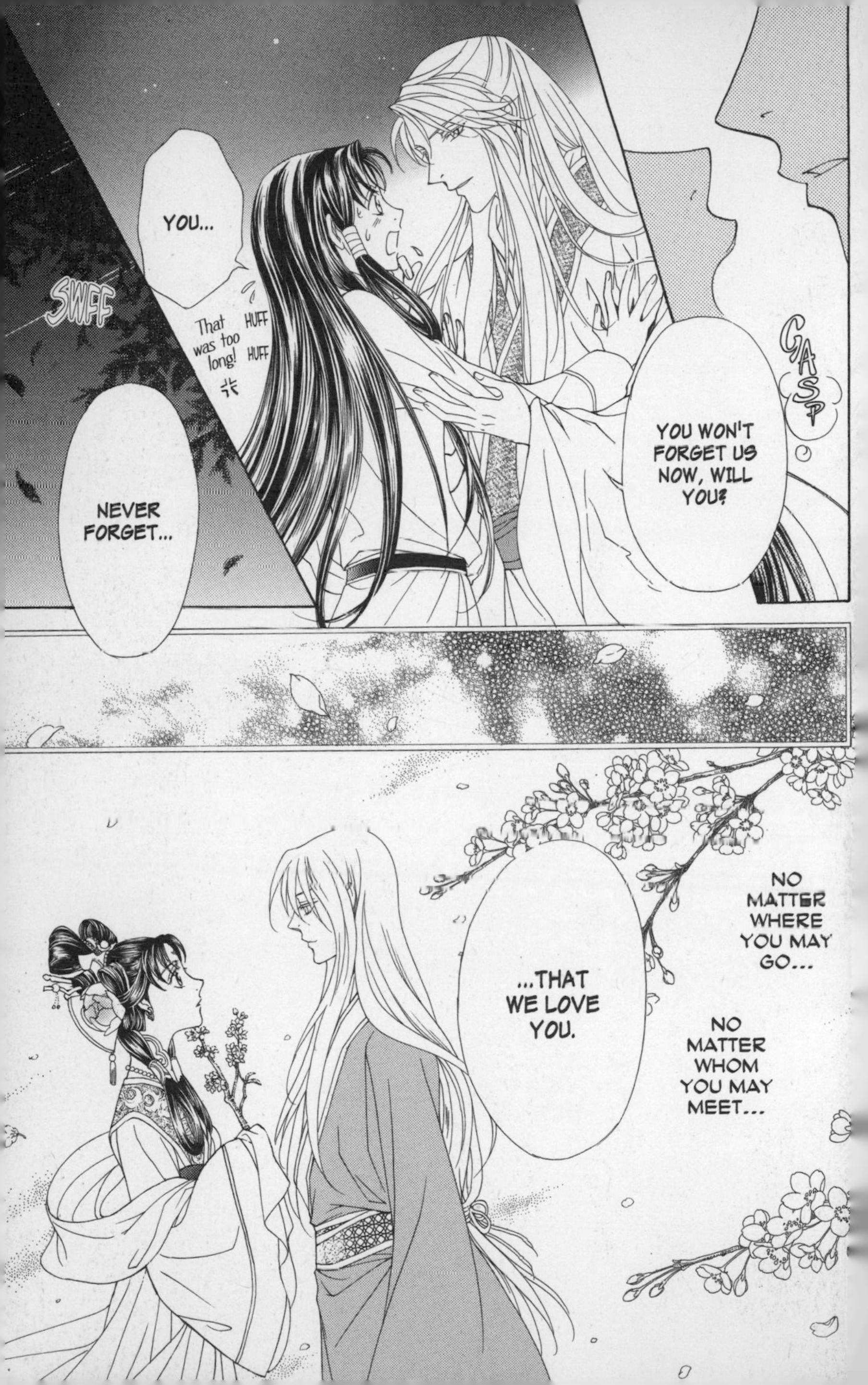
GASP
YOU WON'T FORGET US NOW, WILL YOU?
YOU...
That was too long!
HUFF HUFF
SWFF
NEVER FORGET...
NO MATTER WHERE YOU MAY GO...
NO MATTER WHOM YOU MAY MEET...
...THAT WE LOVE YOU.

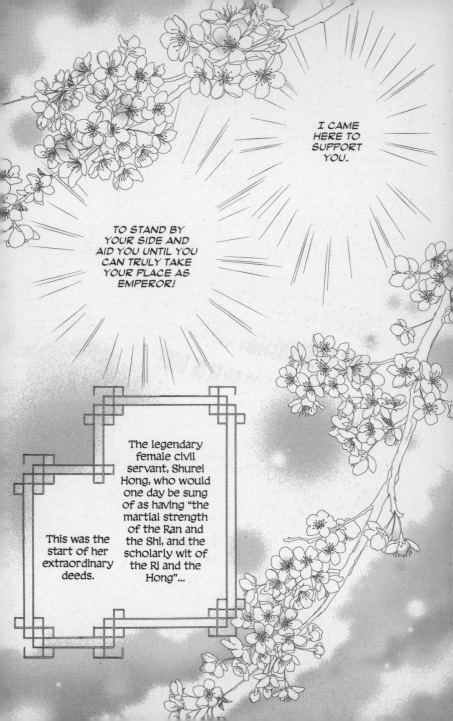

I CAME HERE TO SUPPORT YOU.

TO STAND BY YOUR SIDE AND AID YOU UNTIL YOU CAN TRULY TAKE YOUR PLACE AS EMPEROR!

The legendary female civil servant, Shurei Hong, who would one day be sung of as having "the martial strength of the Ran and the Shi, and the scholarly wit of the Ri and the Hong"...

This was the start of her extraordinary deeds.

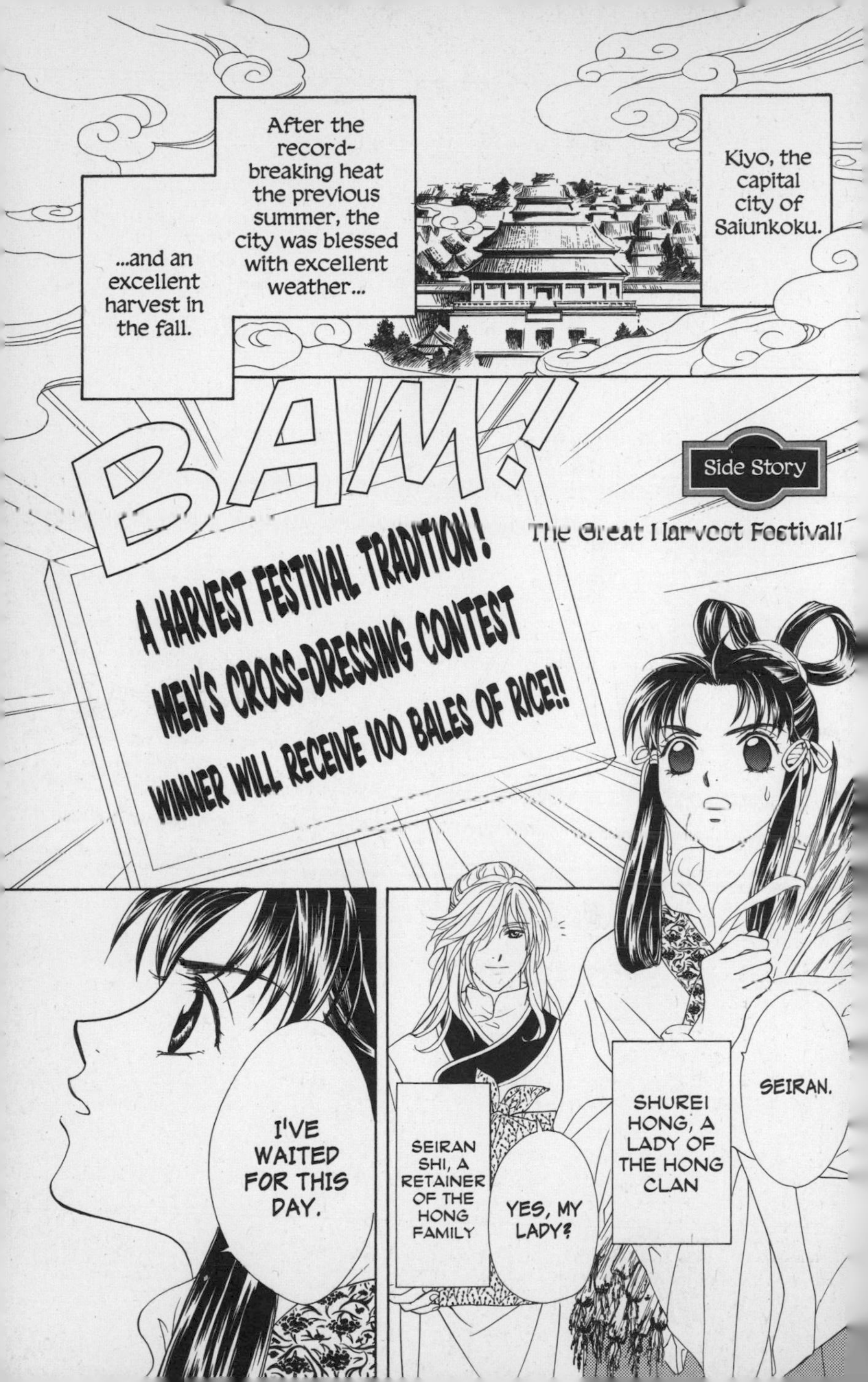
Kiyo, the capital city of Saiunkoku.
After the record-breaking heat the previous summer, the city was blessed with excellent weather...
...and an excellent harvest in the fall.
Side Story
The Great Harvest Festival!
BAM!
A HARVEST FESTIVAL TRADITION!
MEN'S CROSS-DRESSING CONTEST
WINNER WILL RECEIVE 100 BALES OF RICE!!
SEIRAN.
SHUREI HONG, A LADY OF THE HONG CLAN
YES, MY LADY?
SEIRAN SHI, A RETAINER OF THE HONG FAMILY
I'VE WAITED FOR THIS DAY.

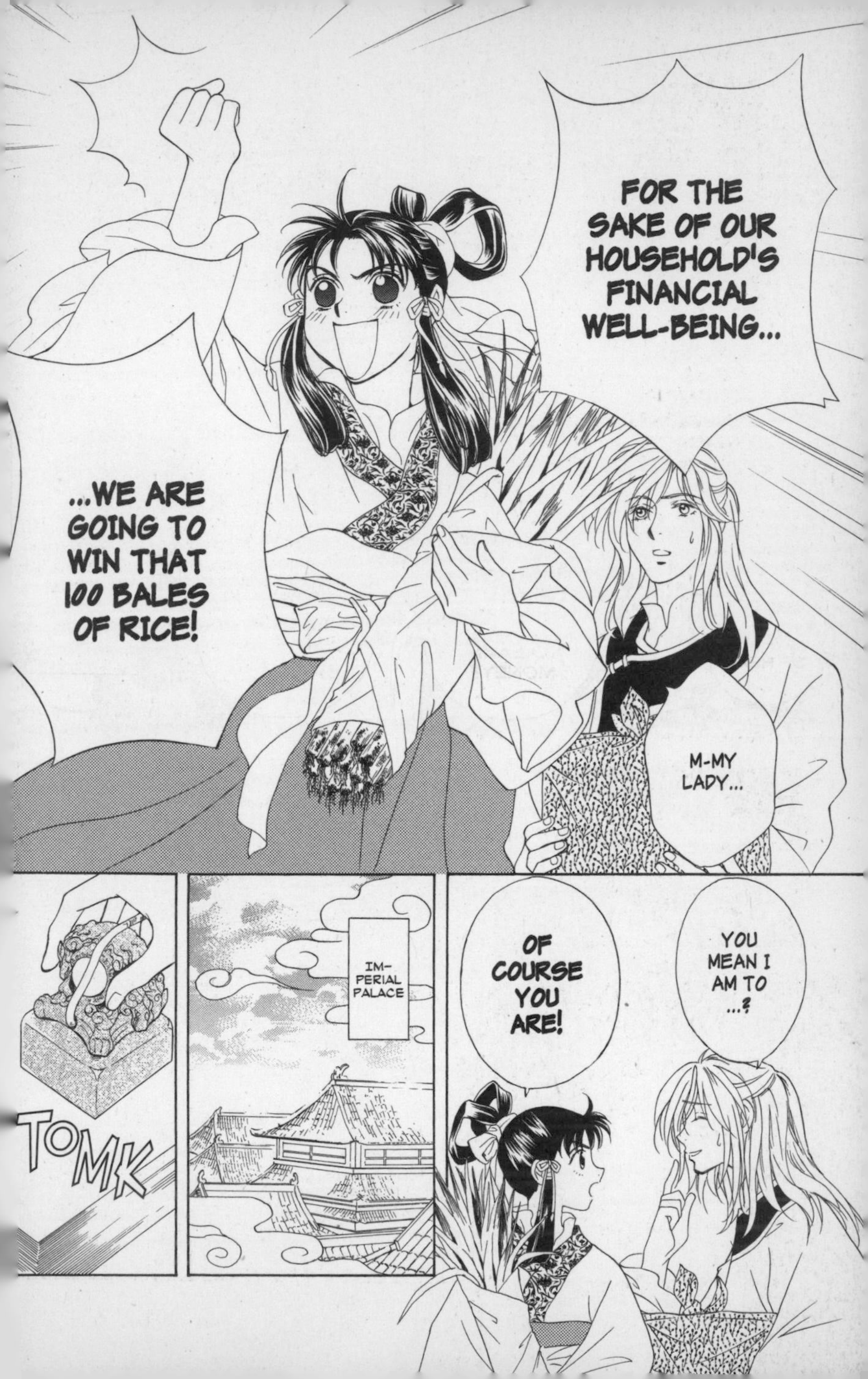
FOR THE SAKE OF OUR HOUSEHOLD'S FINANCIAL WELL-BEING...
...WE ARE GOING TO WIN THAT 100 BALES OF RICE!
M-MY LADY...
YOU MEAN I AM TO ...?
OF COURSE YOU ARE!
IMPERIAL PALACE
TOMK

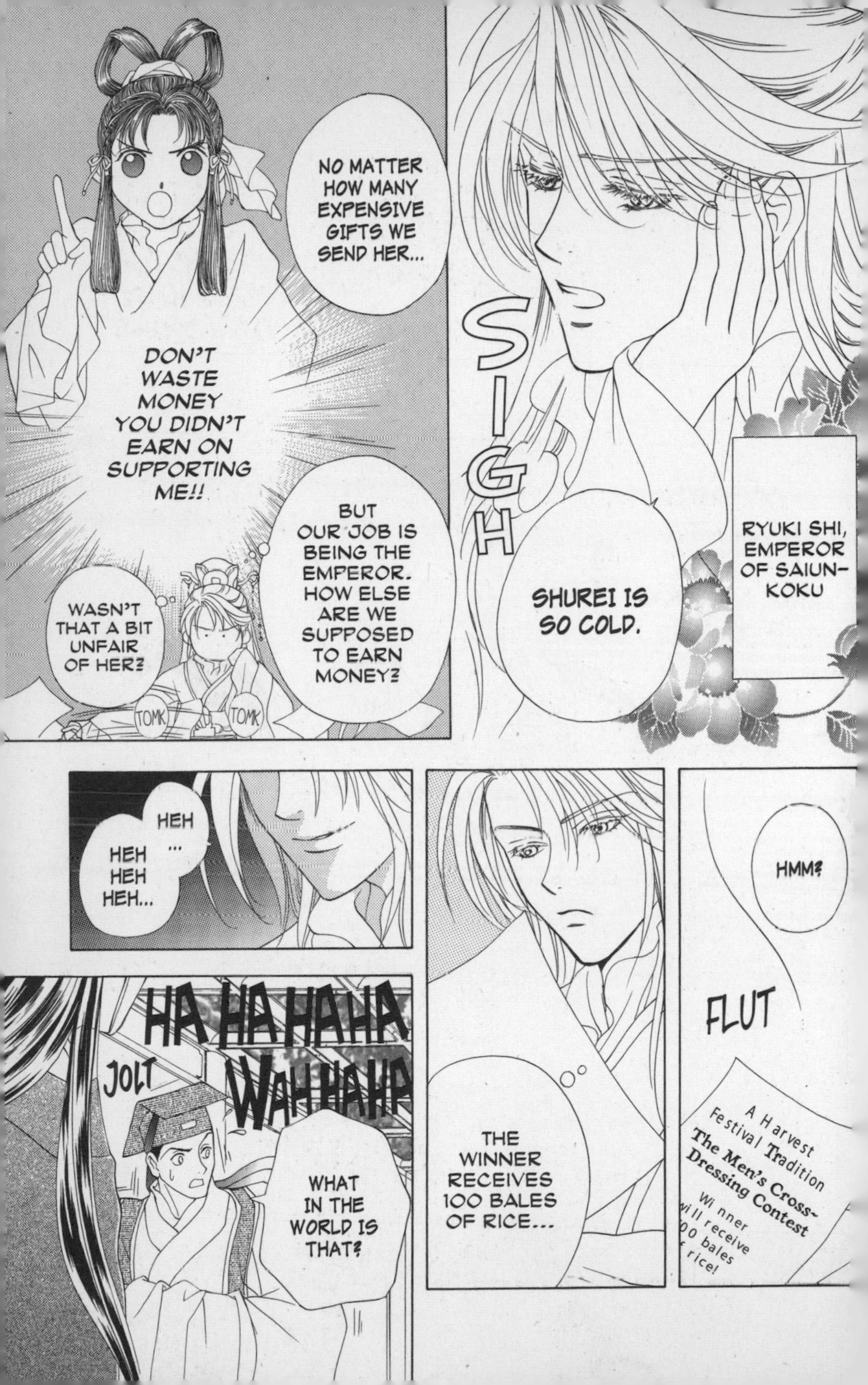
RYUKI SHI, EMPEROR OF SAIUN-KOKU
SIGH
SHUREI IS SO COLD.
NO MATTER HOW MANY EXPENSIVE GIFTS WE SEND HER...
DON'T WASTE MONEY YOU DIDN'T EARN ON SUPPORTING ME!!
BUT OUR JOB IS BEING THE EMPEROR. HOW ELSE ARE WE SUPPOSED TO EARN MONEY?
WASN'T THAT A BIT UNFAIR OF HER?
TOMK
TOMK
HMM?
FLUT
A Harvest Festival Tradition
The Men's Cross-Dressing Contest
Winner will receive 00 bales rice!
THE WINNER RECEIVES 100 BALES OF RICE...
HEH ... HEH HEH HEH...
HA HA HAHA
WAH HAHA
JOLT
WHAT IN THE WORLD IS THAT?

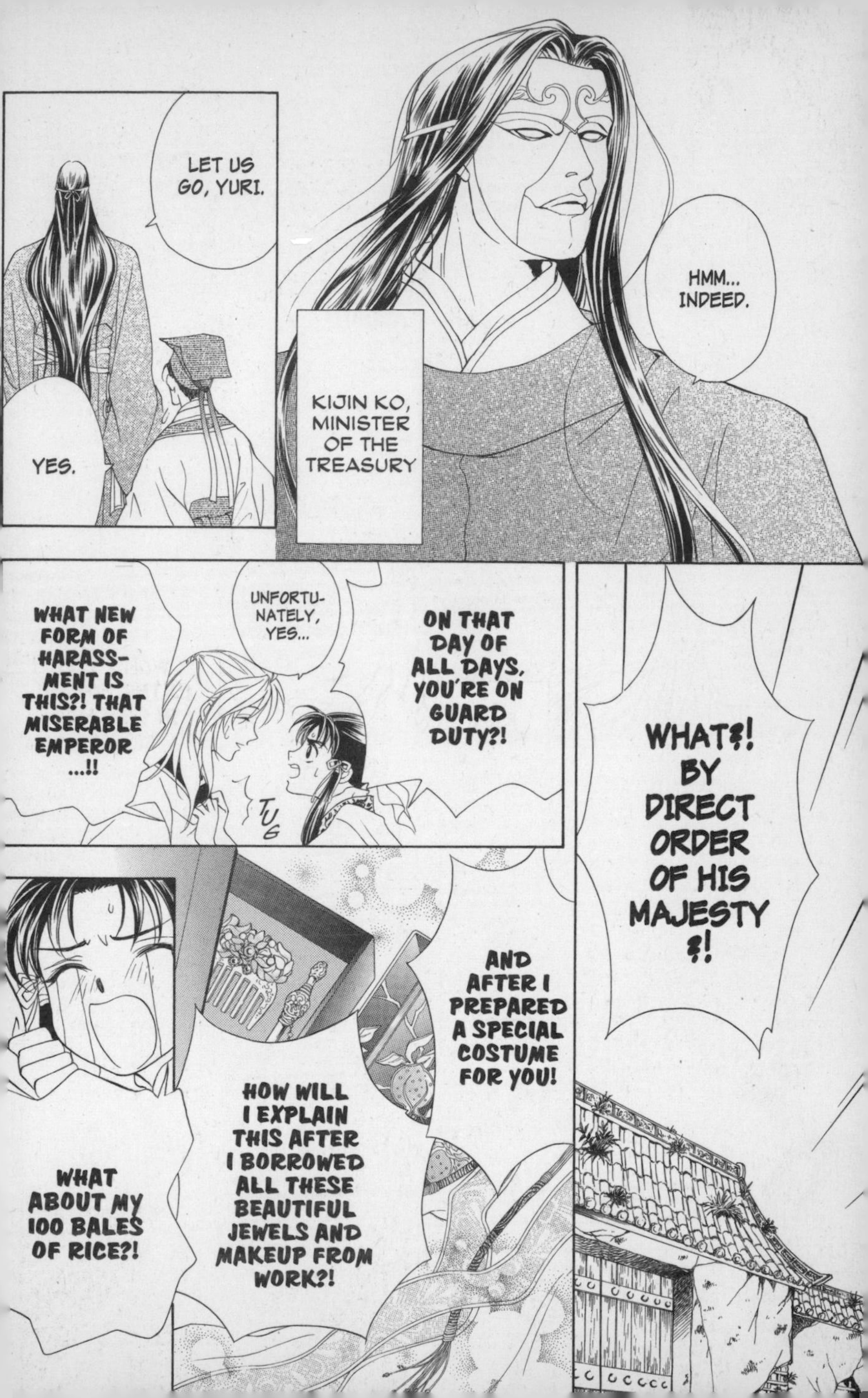
HMM... INDEED.
KIJIN KO, MINISTER OF THE TREASURY
LET US GO, YURI.
YES.
WHAT?! BY DIRECT ORDER OF HIS MAJESTY?!
ON THAT DAY OF ALL DAYS, YOU'RE ON GUARD DUTY?!
UNFORTU-NATELY, YES...
WHAT NEW FORM OF HARASS-MENT IS THIS?! THAT MISERABLE EMPEROR ...!!
TUG
AND AFTER I PREPARED A SPECIAL COSTUME FOR YOU!
HOW WILL I EXPLAIN THIS AFTER I BORROWED ALL THESE BEAUTIFUL JEWELS AND MAKEUP FROM WORK?!
WHAT ABOUT MY 100 BALES OF RICE?!

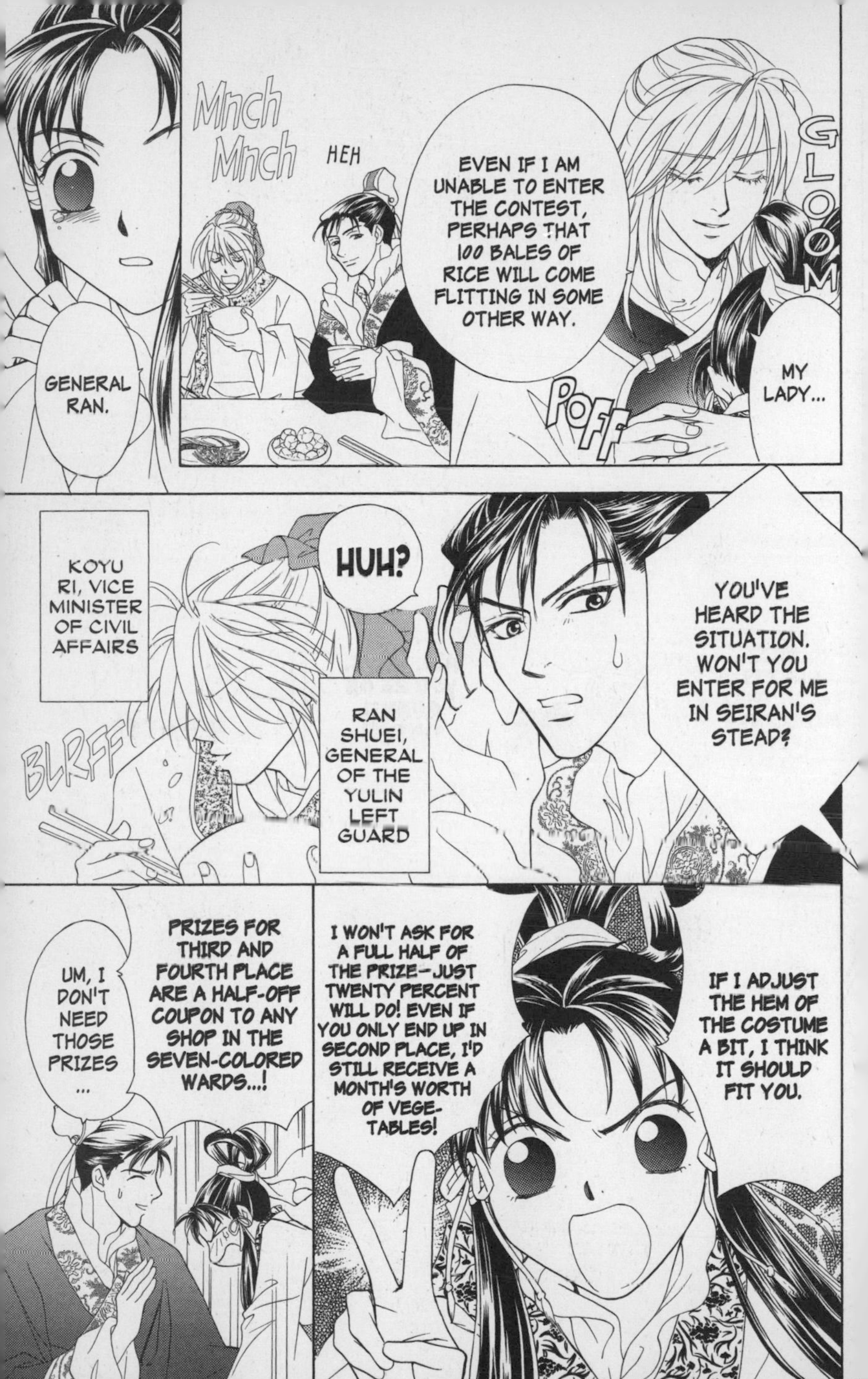
GLOOM
MY LADY...
POFF
EVEN IF I AM UNABLE TO ENTER THE CONTEST, PERHAPS THAT 100 BALES OF RICE WILL COME FLITTING IN SOME OTHER WAY.
HEH
Mnch Mnch
GENERAL RAN.
YOU'VE HEARD THE SITUATION. WON'T YOU ENTER FOR ME IN SEIRAN'S STEAD?
HUH?
RAN SHUEI, GENERAL OF THE YULIN LEFT GUARD
KOYU RI, VICE MINISTER OF CIVIL AFFAIRS
BLRFF
IF I ADJUST THE HEM OF THE COSTUME A BIT, I THINK IT SHOULD FIT YOU.
I WON'T ASK FOR A FULL HALF OF THE PRIZE—JUST TWENTY PERCENT WILL DO! EVEN IF YOU ONLY END UP IN SECOND PLACE, I'D STILL RECEIVE A MONTH'S WORTH OF VEGE-TABLES!
PRIZES FOR THIRD AND FOURTH PLACE ARE A HALF-OFF COUPON TO ANY SHOP IN THE SEVEN-COLORED WARDS...!
UM, I DON'T NEED THOSE PRIZES ...

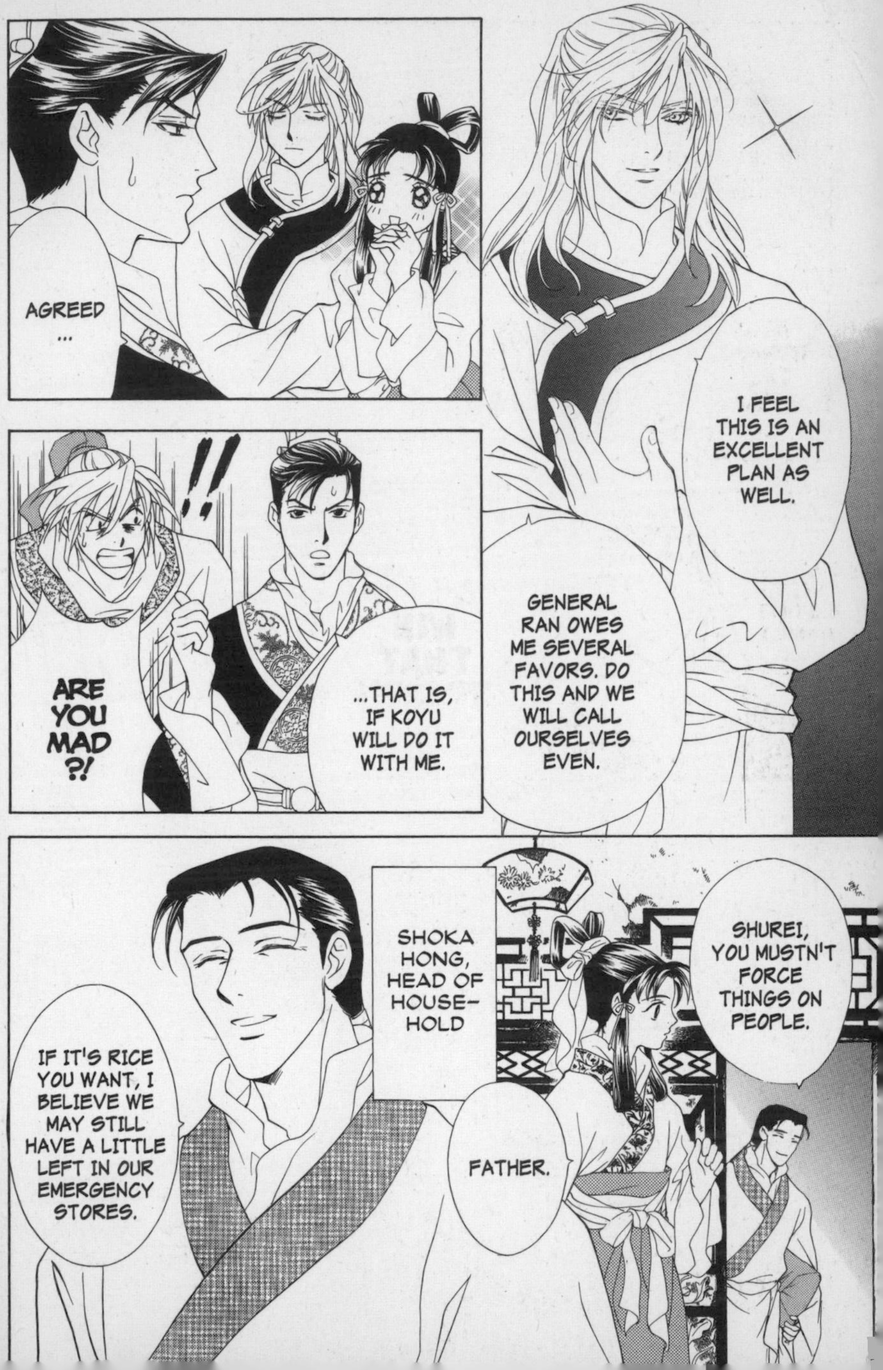
I FEEL THIS IS AN EXCELLENT PLAN AS WELL.
GENERAL RAN OWES ME SEVERAL FAVORS. DO THIS AND WE WILL CALL OURSELVES EVEN.
AGREED ...
...THAT IS, IF KOYU WILL DO IT WITH ME.
!!
ARE YOU MAD ?!
SHUREI, YOU MUSTN'T FORCE THINGS ON PEOPLE.
FATHER.
SHOKA HONG, HEAD OF HOUSE-HOLD
IF IT'S RICE YOU WANT, I BELIEVE WE MAY STILL HAVE A LITTLE LEFT IN OUR EMERGENCY STORES.

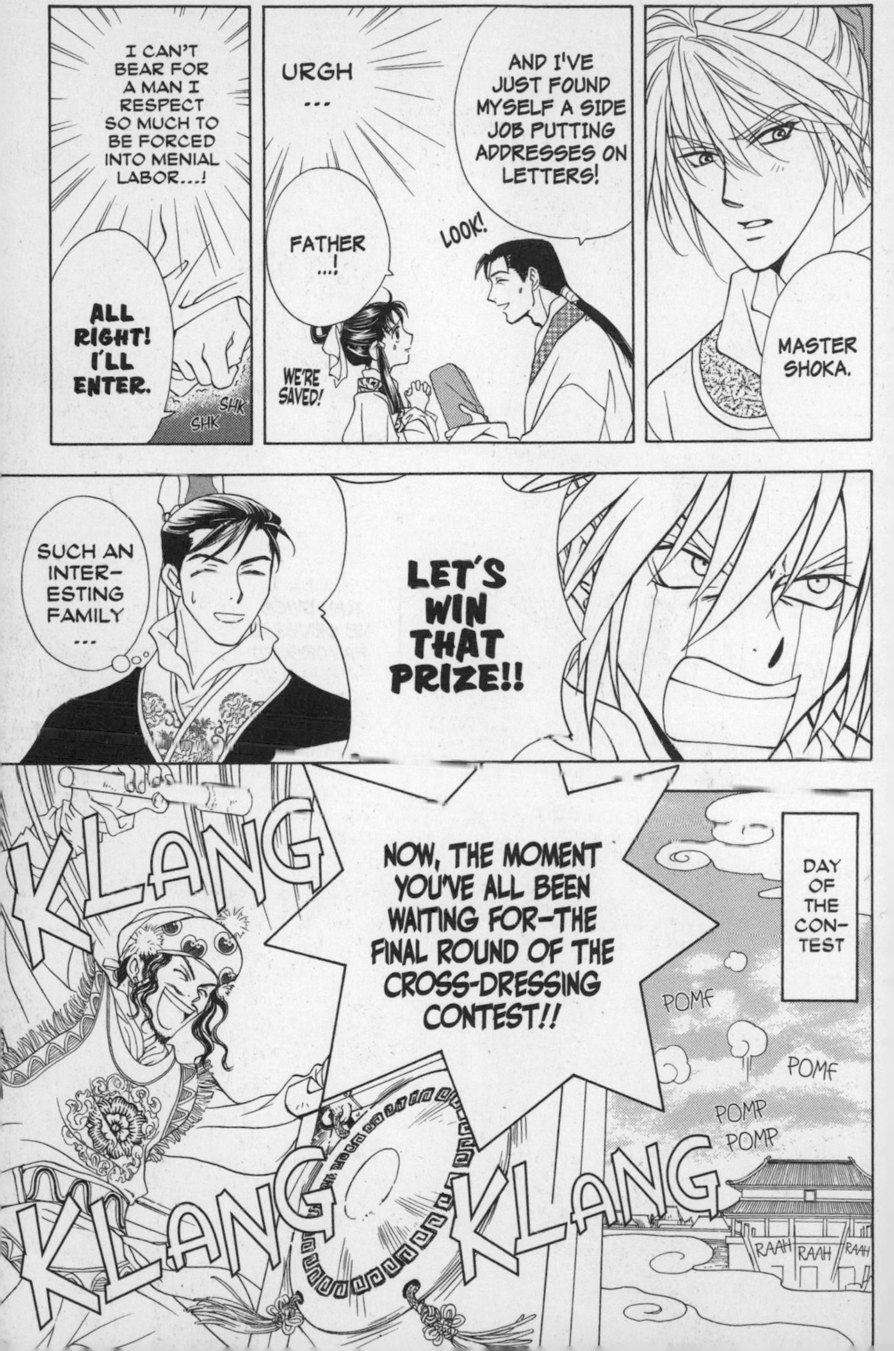
MASTER SHOKA.
AND I'VE JUST FOUND MYSELF A SIDE JOB PUTTING ADDRESSES ON LETTERS!
LOOK!
URGH ...
FATHER ...!
WE'RE SAVED!
I CAN'T BEAR FOR A MAN I RESPECT SO MUCH TO BE FORCED INTO MENIAL LABOR...!
ALL RIGHT! I'LL ENTER.
SHK
SHK
LET'S WIN THAT PRIZE!!
SUCH AN INTER-ESTING FAMILY ...
DAY OF THE CON-TEST
POMF
POMF
POMP
POMP
RAAH
RAAH
RAAH
NOW, THE MOMENT YOU'VE ALL BEEN WAITING FOR—THE FINAL ROUND OF THE CROSS-DRESSING CONTEST!!
KLANG
KLANG
KLANG

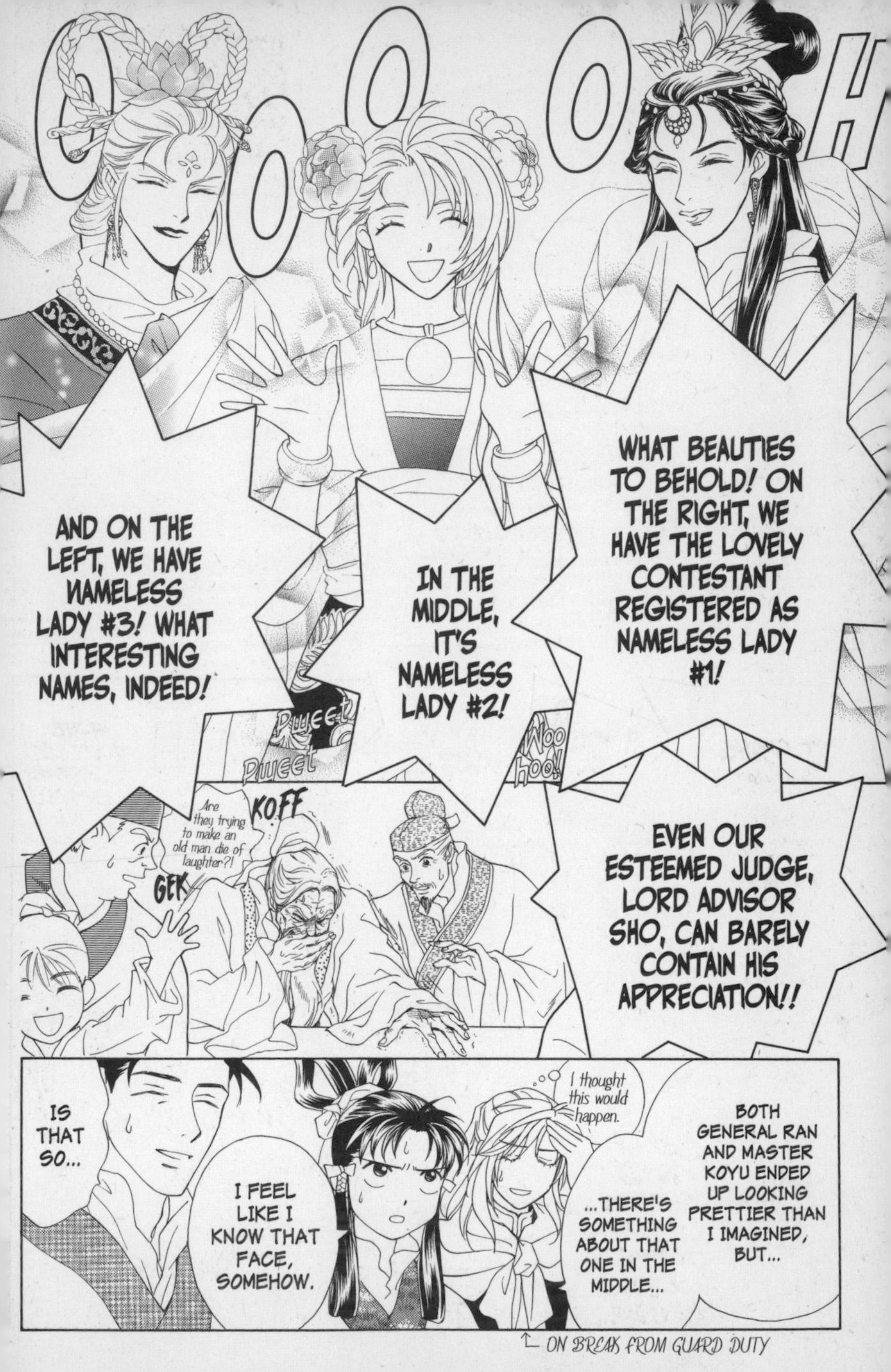
OOOOOH
WHAT BEAUTIES TO BEHOLD! ON THE RIGHT, WE HAVE THE LOVELY CONTESTANT REGISTERED AS NAMELESS LADY #1!
Woo hoo!
IN THE MIDDLE, IT'S NAMELESS LADY #2!
Pweet Pweet
AND ON THE LEFT, WE HAVE NAMELESS LADY #3! WHAT INTERESTING NAMES, INDEED!
EVEN OUR ESTEEMED JUDGE, LORD ADVISOR SHO, CAN BARELY CONTAIN HIS APPRECIATION!!
KOFF
Are they trying to make an old man die of laughter?!
GEK
BOTH GENERAL RAN AND MASTER KOYU ENDED UP LOOKING PRETTIER THAN I IMAGINED, BUT...
...THERE'S SOMETHING ABOUT THAT ONE IN THE MIDDLE...
I thought this would happen.
I FEEL LIKE I KNOW THAT FACE, SOMEHOW.
IS THAT SO...
ON BREAK FROM GUARD DUTY

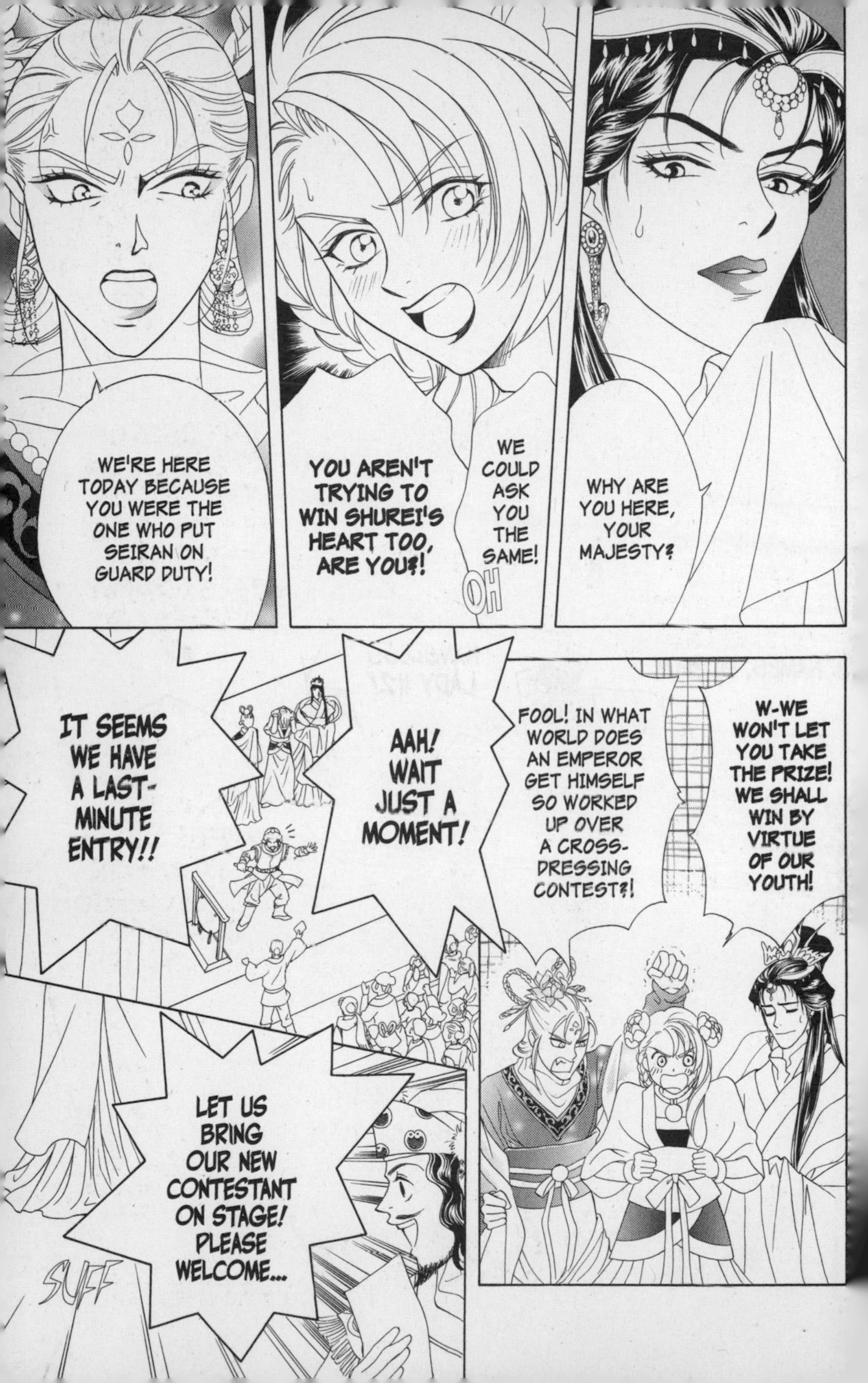
WHY ARE YOU HERE, YOUR MAJESTY?
WE COULD ASK YOU THE SAME!
OH
YOU AREN'T TRYING TO WIN SHUREI'S HEART TOO, ARE YOU?!
WE'RE HERE TODAY BECAUSE YOU WERE THE ONE WHO PUT SEIRAN ON GUARD DUTY!
W-WE WON'T LET YOU TAKE THE PRIZE! WE SHALL WIN BY VIRTUE OF OUR YOUTH!
FOOL! IN WHAT WORLD DOES AN EMPEROR GET HIMSELF SO WORKED UP OVER A CROSS-DRESSING CONTEST?!
AAH! WAIT JUST A MOMENT!
IT SEEMS WE HAVE A LAST-MINUTE ENTRY!!
LET US BRING OUR NEW CONTESTANT ON STAGE! PLEASE WELCOME...
SUFF

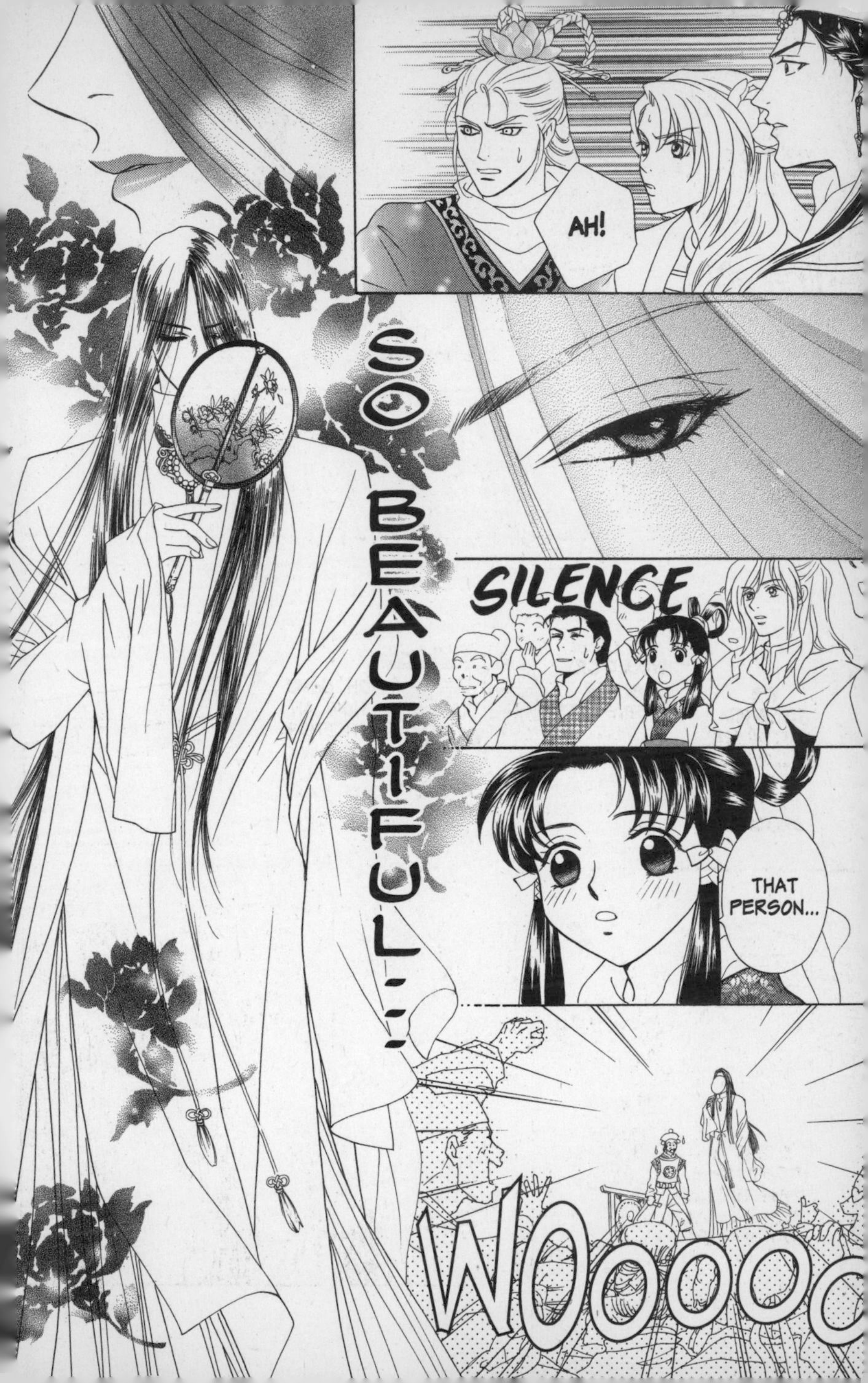
AH!
SILENCE
THAT PERSON...
WOOOOO
SO BEAUTIFUL...

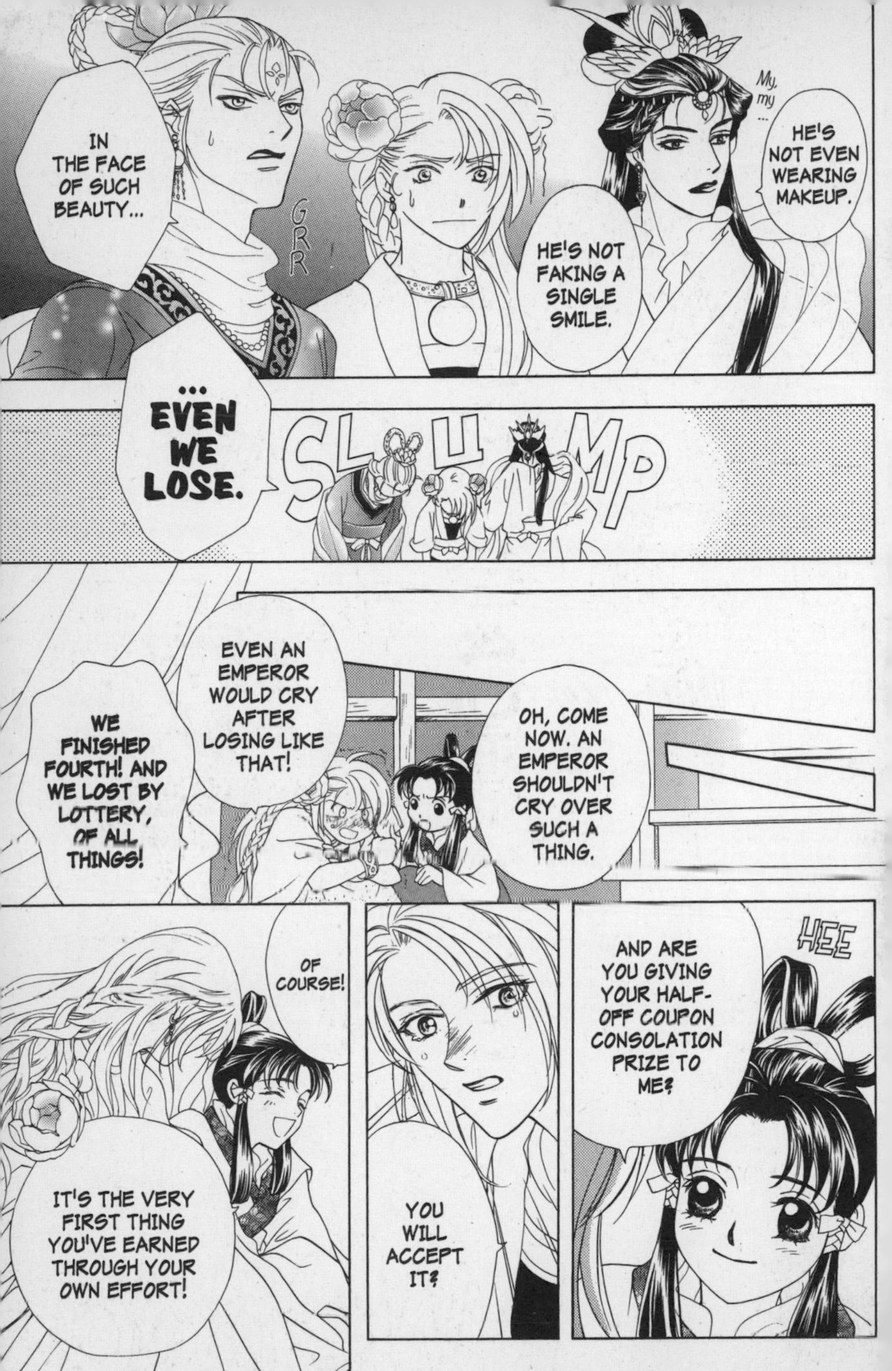
My, my...
HE'S NOT EVEN WEARING MAKEUP.
HE'S NOT FAKING A SINGLE SMILE.
IN THE FACE OF SUCH BEAUTY...
GRR
...EVEN WE LOSE.
SLUMP
OH, COME NOW. AN EMPEROR SHOULDN'T CRY OVER SUCH A THING.
EVEN AN EMPEROR WOULD CRY AFTER LOSING LIKE THAT!
WE FINISHED FOURTH! AND WE LOST BY LOTTERY, OF ALL THINGS!
HEE
AND ARE YOU GIVING YOUR HALF-OFF COUPON CONSOLATION PRIZE TO ME?
YOU WILL ACCEPT IT?
OF COURSE!
IT'S THE VERY FIRST THING YOU'VE EARNED THROUGH YOUR OWN EFFORT!

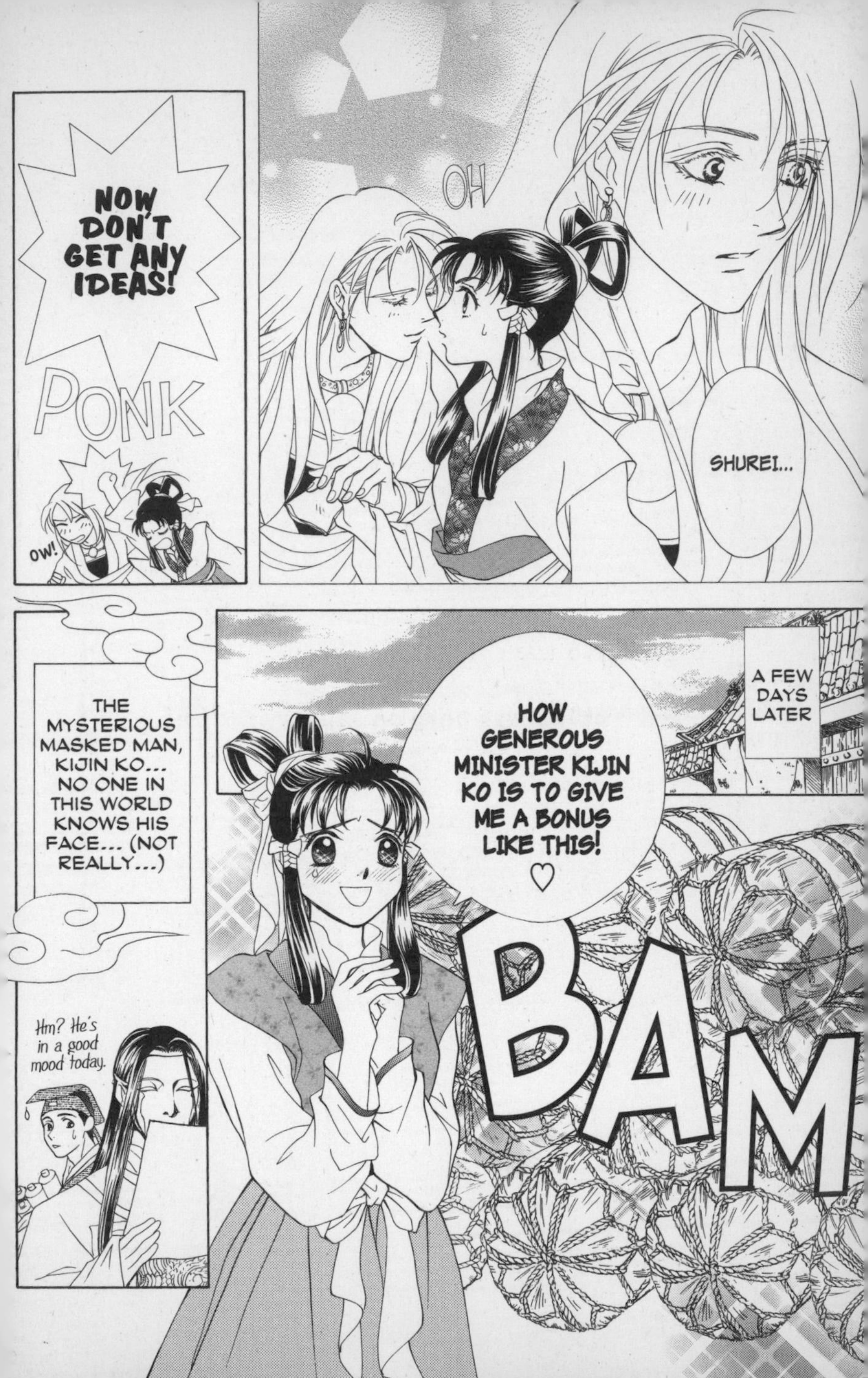
SHUREI...
OH
NOW DON'T GET ANY IDEAS!
PONK
OW!
A FEW DAYS LATER
HOW GENEROUS MINISTER KIJIN KO IS TO GIVE ME A BONUS LIKE THIS! ♡
BAM
THE MYSTERIOUS MASKED MAN, KIJIN KO... NO ONE IN THIS WORLD KNOWS HIS FACE... (NOT REALLY...)
Hm? He's in a good mood today.

Kairi Yura was born on January 16. She is the illustrator of both the manga and the YA novels for *The Story of Saiunkoku*. She is also the creator of the *Angelique* series. Yura's hobby is going to the theater.

Sai Yukino was born on January 26. She is author of both the manga and the YA novels for *The Story of Saiunkoku*. She received an honorable mention and the Readers' Award for Kadokawa's Beans Novel Taisho Awards. When she's not busy writing, Yukino enjoys massages.

THE STORY OF SAIUNKOKU
Volume 8

Shojo Beat Edition

ART
KAIRI YURA
STORY
SAI YUKINO

Translation & English Adaptation/Su Mon Han
Touch-up Art & Lettering/Deron Bennett
Design/Yukiko Whitley
Editor/Nancy Thistlethwaite

Saiunkoku Monogatari Volume 8

First published in Japan in 2011 by KADOKAWA SHOTEN Co., Ltd., Tokyo.
English translation rights arranged with KADOKAWA SHOTEN Co., Ltd., Tokyo.

Printed in Canada

Published by VIZ Media, LLC
P.O. Box 77010
San Francisco, CA 94107

10 9 8 7 6 5 4 3 2 1
First printing, October 2012

RATED T FOR TEEN

PARENTAL ADVISORY
THE STORY OF SAIUNKOKU is rated T for Teen and is recommended for ages 13 and up. This volume contains suggestive themes.
ratings.viz.com

www.viz.com

www.shojobeat.com

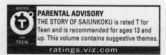

ᐯIᛅᛖᗩᑎᎶᗩ

Read manga anytime, anywhere!

From our newest hit series to the classics you know
and love, the best manga in the world is now available
digitally. Buy a volume* of digital manga for your:

- iOS device (**iPad®, iPhone®, iPod® touch**)
  through the **VIZ Manga app**

- Android-powered device (**phone or tablet**)
  with a browser by visiting VIZManga.com

- **Mac or PC computer** by visiting VIZManga.com

VIZ Digital has loads to offer:

- 500+ ready-to-read volumes
- New volumes each week
- FREE previews
- Access on multiple devices! Create a log-in through the app
  so you buy a book once, and read it on your device of choice!*

To learn more, visit www.viz.com/apps

* Some series may not be available for multiple devices.
  Check the app on your device to find out what's available.

Music To
Your Eyes

An original art collection personally selected by creator Arina Tanemura, this hardcover art book features:

- 214 original illustrations
- Beautiful *Full Moon* character designs
- Artist Commentary
- Additional images from *I.O.N*, *Kamikaze Kaito Jeanne* and *Short-Tempered Melancholic*

Plus, a bonus oversized poster of original art!

Complete your Arina Tanemura collection— get her manga and *The Art of Full Moon* today!

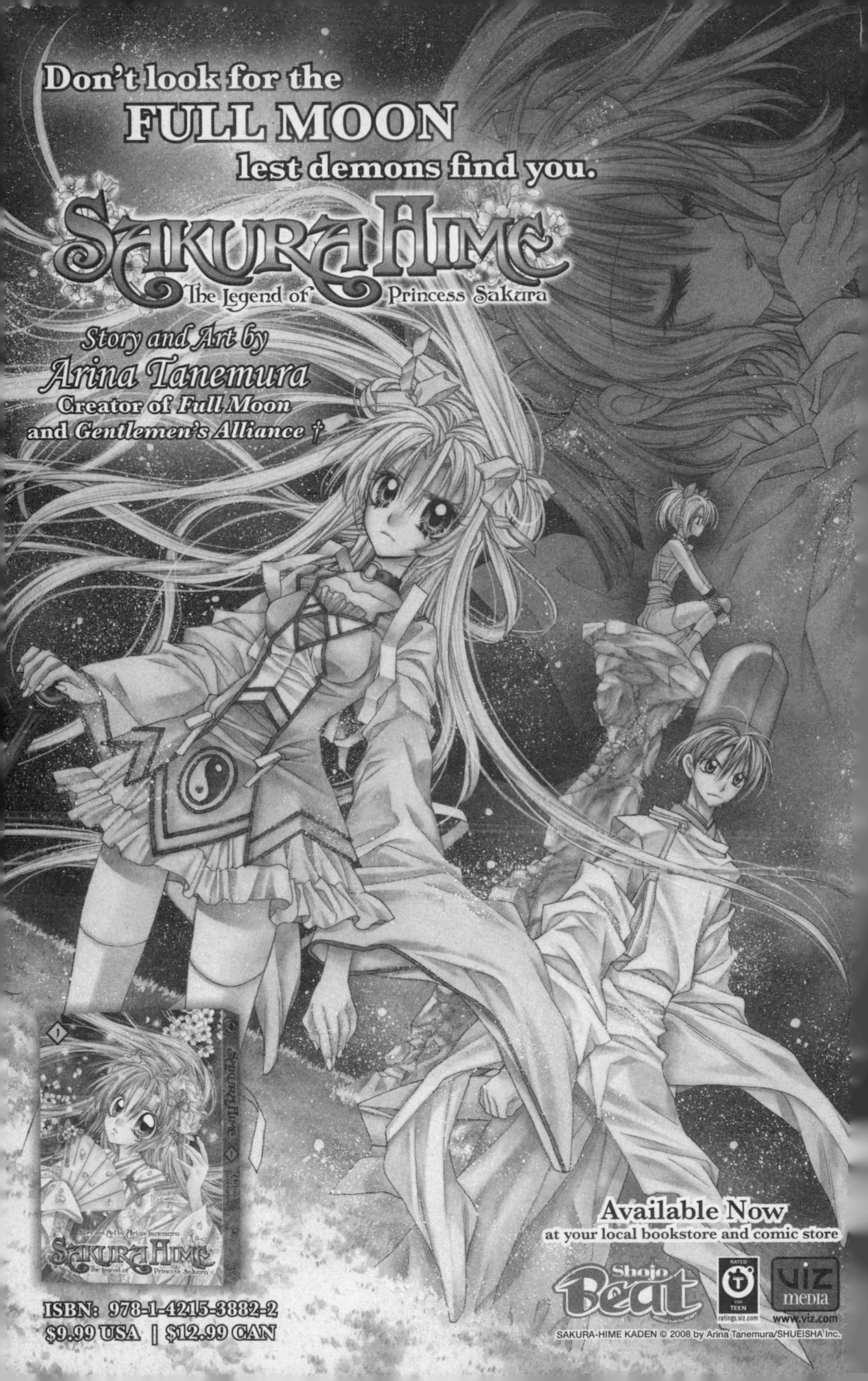
Don't look for the
FULL MOON
lest demons find you.
SAKURA HIME
The Legend of Princess Sakura
Story and Art by
Arina Tanemura
Creator of Full Moon
and Gentlemen's Alliance †
Available Now
at your local bookstore and comic store
ISBN: 978-1-4215-3882-2
$9.99 USA | $12.99 CAN
Shojo Beat
RATED T TEEN
ratings.viz.com
VIZ media
www.viz.com
SAKURA-HIME KADEN © 2008 by Arina Tanemura/SHUEISHA Inc.

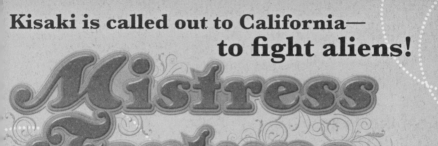
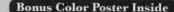

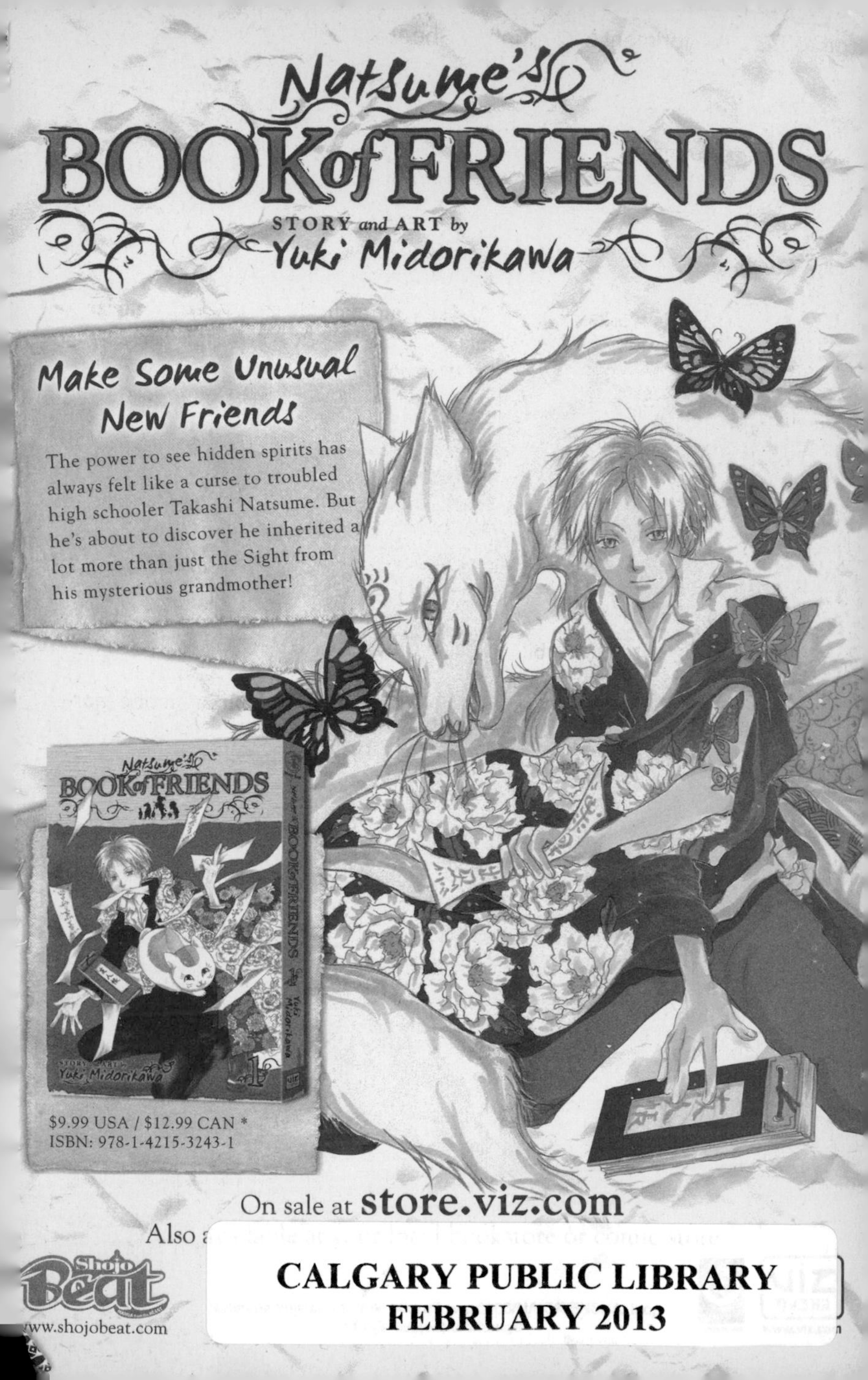
Natsume's
BOOK of FRIENDS
STORY and ART by
Yuki Midorikawa
Make Some Unusual New Friends
The power to see hidden spirits has always felt like a curse to troubled high schooler Takashi Natsume. But he's about to discover he inherited a lot more than just the Sight from his mysterious grandmother!
Natsume's BOOK of FRIENDS
Yuki Midorikawa
$9.99 USA / $12.99 CAN *
ISBN: 978-1-4215-3243-1
On sale at store.viz.com
Also a
Shojo Beat
www.shojobeat.com